MW00748069

A Rich and Fruitful Land

Main photo: An annual fishing party was a ritual of Salmon Arm's leading citizens. This 1932 photo was taken at Fish (Salmon) Lake on the Douglas Lake Ranch. BCARS B-01643
Inset photo: Workers at a fish trap on Shuswap Lake, date unknown. Vernon Museum
Previous page: Apple box label courtesy Denis Marshall.

A Rich and Fruitful Land
The History of the Valleys of the Okanagan, Similkameen and Shuswap

Jean Webber
for the Okanagan Historical Society

Harbour Publishing

Published by
HARBOUR PUBLISHING
P.O. Box 219
Madeira Park, BC Canada
V0N 2H0

Cover design by Roger Handling
Page design and composition by Roger Handling / Terra Firma Digital Arts

Photo notes: All photos not credited are courtesy Jean Webber Collection. The photo credit acronym ASMAS refers to the Armstrong–Spallumcheen Museum and Arts Society/Armstrong Museum. BCARS refers to British Columbia Archives and Records Service. Fruit box labels courtesy Denis Marshall.

Printed and bound in Canada

Harbour Publishing acknowledges the financial support of the Government of Canada through the Book Publishing Industry Development Program (BPIDP) and the Canada Council for the Arts, and the Province of British Columbia through the British Columbia Arts Council, for its publishing activities.

The BC Heritage Trust has provided financial assistance to this project to support conservation of our heritage resources, gain further knowledge and increase public understanding of the complete history of British Columbia.

THE CANADA COUNCIL | LE CONSEIL DES ARTS
FOR THE ARTS | DU CANADA
SINCE 1957 | DEPUIS 1957

Canadä

Canadian Cataloguing in Publication Data

A rich and fruitful land

Includes bibliographical references and index.
Includes material originally published in: Okanagan history.
ISBN 1-55017-197-6

1. Okanagan Valley (B.C.)—History. 2. Similkameen River Valley (Wash. and B.C.)—History. 3. Shuswap River Valley (B.C.)—History. I. Webber, Jean.

FC3845.O4R52 1999   971.1'5   C99-910902-2
F1089.O5R52 1999

For Margaret Anchoretta Ormsby BA, MA, PhD, LLD, OC, OBC

Who taught us that history is made through the lives of ordinary people

Contents

Preface 9

Acknowledgements 10

Chapter 1 • The Land 11
  The White Silt Cliffs 11
  Ancient Rocks 13
  Glaciation 16
  Recent Modifications to the Landscape 18
  Climate, Flora and Fauna 19

Chapter 2 • The First People 22
  An Okanagan Communication 22
  Where Did the First People Come From? 23
  The Culture 24
  Contact 29
  Efforts on Behalf of the First Nations 34
  The Native Renaissance 34

Chapter 3 • The Fur Trade 36
  The Brigade Trail 36
  Other Trails 40
  New Hudson's Bay Company Posts Established 42

Chapter 4 • The Colonial Era 45
  The International Boundary .45
  Gold, Gold Commissioners and Customs 46
  The Overlanders 51
  The Great Cattle Ranches 54
  Colonial Transportation and Communication 59

Chapter 5 • Missionaries and Churches 64
  The Roman Catholics 64
  Presbyterian and Methodist Missionaries 67
  The Anglican Church 71
  The Baptists 74
  Religious Institutions Today 75

Chapter 6 • From Colony to Province 77
  Confederation 77
  MPs and MLAs 78
  The Bennett Years 81
  The Civil Service 82

Chapter 7 • Stage Drivers and Mail Carriers 84
  Stagecoaches 84
  Mail Carriers and Post Offices 88

Chapter 8 • Community Life 91
  The Family 91
  Simple Pleasures 95

Chapter 9 • Schools 97
  Rural Schools 97
  Education: A Private Affair .98
  The First Public School 99
  Expansion of Public Schools 101
  Other Educational Institutions 104

Chapter 10 • Medical Services 107
  The Preprofessionals 107

Pioneer Doctors 109
Nurses, Hospitals and Pharmacists 112

Chapter 11 • A Developing Economy **115**
New Opportunities 115
Technological Changes in Agriculture and Milling 116
Sawmills 119
Brick Making 124

Chapter 12 • Hard-Rock Mining **126**
Fairview 126
The Great Gold Robbery 127
Feeding the Miners 131
Hedley and the Nickel Plate Mine 132
Other Mining Ventures 137

Chapter 13 • Boats and Trains **140**
Railways .140
Commercial Boats 145

Chapter 14 • A Growing Population **153**
Influx of Settlers 153
Incorporation 156
Lifestyle 158
Outdoor Sports 160
Telegrams, Telephones and Newspapers 162

Chapter 15 • Tree Fruits, Ground Crops, Vines and Agro-industries **167**
The First Orchards 167
Irrigation and Land Development 170
Fruit Growers 175
Growing Concerns 179
Changing Technology 181
Ground Crops 184
Grapes 188
Free Trade and Estate Wineries 190
Agro-industries 192

Chapter 16 • Military Matters **195**
Early Military Organizations 195
World War I 198
Depleted Manpower 199
World War II 200
Commando Bay 205
Other Services 206

Chapter 17 • Communication: Highways, Planes, Radio, TV **207**
Highways up to the Mid-twenties 207
The Kelowna Crossing 210
More About Highways 213
Air Travel 214
The Air Crash 217
Radio .218
Television 220

Afterword **224**

Bibliography **226**

Notes **229**

Index **235**

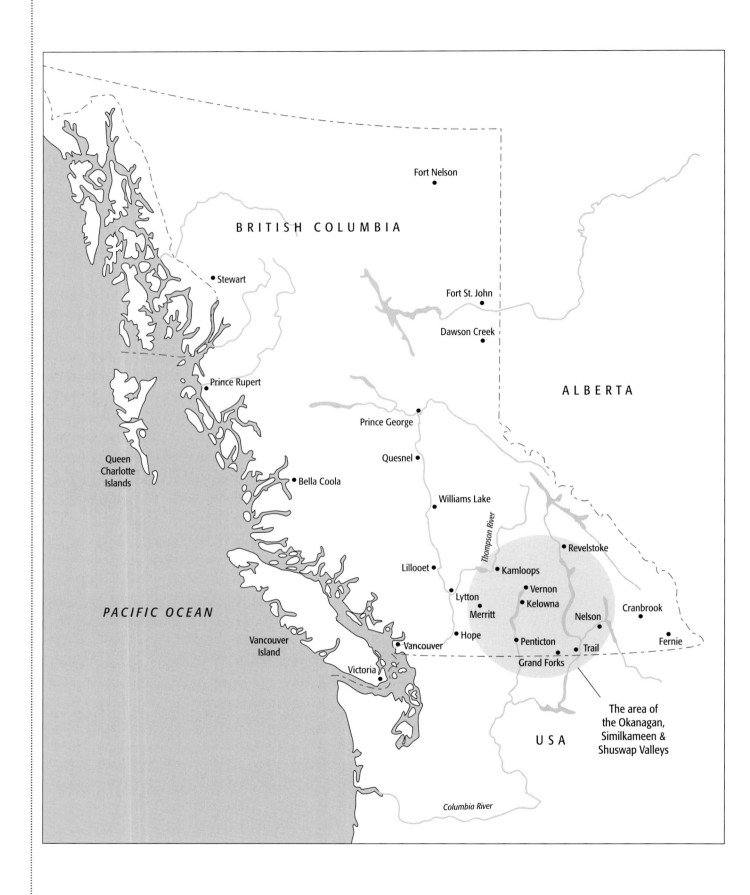

The area of the Okanagan, Similkameen & Shuswap Valleys

Preface

A Rich and Fruitful Land: The History of the Valleys of the Okanagan, Similkameen and Shuswap is a book with a dual parentage. First, there was the gift of $5,000 from Mr. Guy Bagnall for the writing of a history of the Okanagan and its related territories, the Similkameen and Shuswap. Secondly, as the publication of the *Sixtieth Annual Report of the Okanagan Historical Society* approached there was a desire to mark this anniversary in some special way. A proposal to combine these two objectives met with general approval. Hence *A Rich and Fruitful Land*.

Richard Guy Pearse Bagnall, born in Dublin October 8, 1882, left his homeland to serve in the Boer War, after which he travelled to Canada, reaching Vernon in 1906. There, with the exception of his World War I service, he lived for the rest of his life, participating in a number of business projects and always finding time to support any local initiative which would benefit the community. He was a Founding Member of the Okanagan Historical Society and a Life Member from 1979 until his death February 2, 1983. With regard to the writing of a history, the late Mr. Stuart Fleming of Vernon undertook this project but illness prevented him from bringing his work to fruition.

The Okanagan Historical Society was founded in September 1925. The Society has participated in a number of projects which commemorate the colourful history of our area, the principal one being the recording of significant events and the experiences of our pioneers in its *Reports*. For this work the Society has received national and international recognition.

In *A Rich and Fruitful Land* the editor has endeavoured to tell the story as far as possible from articles printed in *Okanagan History: The Annual Reports of the Okanagan Historical Society*, especially as many of these articles were written by people who had participated in the events recounted. However, where there are lacunae in the record other sources have been used. The objective has been to present not a history in exhaustive detail but a general picture to which a reader might relate details known to him. Those individuals named are by no means all who deserve to be remembered, but rather examples of the kind of men and women who have created the society which we inherit.

It is hoped that readers will be stimulated to read further on their areas of special interest. The *Reports* themselves are a treasure house of information to which our *Indexes* supply the key. Although many *Reports* are out of print, complete sets are available for public use in some libraries and museums throughout the area.

The publication of *Okanagan History: The Annual Reports of the Okanagan Historical Society* has been possible because of the loyal support of the members who, yearly, have purchased the current edition. We urge you to join us in support of this worthwhile activity. *Reports*, which come off the press each October, can be purchased from book stores and Okanagan Historical Society Branches.

Jean Webber

Acknowledgements

The editor of *A Rich and Fruitful Land: The History of the Valleys of the Okanagan, Similkameen and Shuswap* wishes to acknowledge the contribution to this project of the officers, past and present, of the Okanagan Historical Society. Without this strong organization there is no way this priceless history could have been collected, published, and thus preserved and made available to the public. The writers, who have contributed their work without remuneration throughout the years, are key players. But let us not forget those who have presided at meetings, recorded minutes and added columns of figures and, not to mention, driven miles at their own expense to see to the Society's business. Nor do past presidents rest on their laurels. For years Hume Powley has accepted the responsibility of seeing that the directors have a suitable place to meet when they gather in Kelowna for regular or special meetings. Our thanks also to successive editors and especially to David MacDonald and his committee who produced our *Index*, an essential tool in the preparation of the present text.

Finally, thanks are due the patient and conscientious reading committee without whose criticism of both style and substance this volume would have been less than it now is. Those who have served in this capacity are: David MacDonald, Jessie Ann Gamble, Peter Tassie, Denis Marshall, Hume Powley, Dorothy Zoellner, Michael Burn and, informally, Mae Browne and my husband Bernard Webber.

The pictures which appear in the book come mainly from the museums of the area and from the Archives of the Province of British Columbia, although a few are from private collections. I acknowledge the help of Archivists Linda Wells, Frances Surtees, Joan Cowan, Laura Klassen, Suzanne Haverkamp, members of the reading committee listed above, as well as Elaine Dickson and Joan and Victor Casorso.

The Land

The White Silt Cliffs

Okanagan Tidal Wave[1]
by Olive Evans

Saturday, July 21, 1951 will always stand out in the minds of Dr. and Mrs. Myles Plecash. They had recently moved to Penticton and were renting a comfortable lakeside cottage slightly south of Three Mile Beach on the east side of Okanagan Lake. They considered themselves fortunate to have found such idyllic rental accommodation.

About 6:45 p.m., while his wife prepared dinner, Dr. Plecash read a bedtime story to his three-year-old daughter Penny. Baby Gail, not quite a year old, lay sleeping in her crib in the children's bedroom.

An intense rumbling broke the silence. Glancing towards the window Dr. Plecash was horrified to see an immense wall of water rapidly bearing down on the cottage. Even as he shouted a warning to his wife it broke against the house, smashing in the window. Snatching up the terrified Penny who had been washed off her feet by the inrushing water, he fled through the rear door and scrambled up the steep incline close behind the cottage. Placing Penny as high on the bank as he possibly could, he admonished her to remain there until he returned for her.

The water receded as quickly as it had come. Racing back to the house, Dr. Plecash found his wife, dazed and badly shaken, wedged beneath a chaise longue on the veranda. Fortunately the railing had kept her from being swept away.

The door to Gail's room was jammed shut and Dr. Plecash scrambled through the broken bedroom window which also faced the lake. Inside he found by some miracle the mattress from an upper bunk bed had settled atop the crib, protecting Gail from chunks of wood and other debris which lay piled on top of the mattress and about the room. Gail's only injury was a quarter-inch cut on her forehead.

In the interior of the house a partitioning wall was broken. The bathtub, ripped from its proper place, sat wedged in the hallway, while the livingroom and master bedroom furniture lay smashed and splintered beyond repair.

When insurance adjustor Clement Battye conducted his investigation he found silt imbedded in linen on the top shelf of a floor-to-ceiling cupboard, indicating water had entirely filled the house when the wave crashed over it. As well, dead fish were found on the roof.

Outside, a half mile of beach lay ravaged. The doctor's car, parked on the driveway which led at an angle down the bank to the rear of the house, was picked up, tossed about and came to rest at the lake's edge.

A two-ton sailboat lay canted over on the beach a hundred feet from her mooring, while a four cylinder marine engine was found fifty feet from its stand. A boathouse and brick wall were demolished, and large cracks were plainly visible in a nine inch retaining wall close to the Plecash home.

The tidal wave was caused when an estimated acre of the Eric Bomford orchard slid into Okanagan Lake. The Penticton city engineer blamed the slide on continual irrigation, explaining, "Seepage of irrigation water down to an impervious layer of blue clay allows the overlying soil to slide en masse much as a ship slides down a greased way."

Extensive repairs to the cottage restored it for comfortable occupation. It still stands, staunch and serene on its secluded beach.

(*OHS*, 1986)

White silt cliffs on the west side of Okanagan Lake between Penticton and Summerland.

For the cause of the disastrous wave which Mrs. Evans describes so vividly we must go back ten thousand years to the period when the Okanagan Valley was filled with the great postglacial Penticton Lake, a lake that extended north from Vaseux Lake beyond present-day Armstrong and Enderby and even to the Thompson River Valley. It was from the relatively still water of Penticton Lake that the white silts were deposited that now form the cliffs that stretch from Penticton to Summerland on the west and to Naramata on the east. When saturated with water the silts are subject to piping, a phenomenon which can bring the cliffs down in slides that cover roads and even houses. In 1970 a slide in Lower Summerland engulfed one house, causing the death of one man, and dislodged two other houses from their foundations.

Not all the effects traceable to these ancient dispositions are tragic, however.

A Juicy Tale[2]
by Mary Gartrell Orr

There were and still are many deep, dangerous potholes which result in such news items as that from *The Summerland Review* of October 22, 1926. "Mark Scurrah's dog fell into a pothole while he was hunting pheasants and Mark's brother, Phil, went down a rope about sixty feet to rescue her."

Across the road from the Landry farm meadows at the north end of Trout Creek Point, steep clay cliffs rose to flatten out into the orchards of the W.A. Caldwell family.

During the 1930s codling moth had got out of control and as there was at that time no use for cull apples, Mr. Caldwell and his sons got the contract to dispose of the culls. In addition, in 1935 early heavy frosts froze between 20,000 and 30,000 boxes of apples so these, with the culls, were dumped into the potholes bordering the Caldwell property. In the spring they were covered with a foot of soil. Gradually the apples rotted and fermented. The weight of the soil forced the juice out and it seeped down through the potholes, under the road into the fields below.

Grazing on the Landry farm meadows was a herd of Jersey cows. The pungent odors from the fermented juice drew clouds of frantically buzzing bees and wasps and we natives remain convinced those Jerseys showed varying degrees of intoxication.

(*OHS*, 1983)

The geologist Dr. Arthur H. Lang explains the phenomenon of the pot-holes as follows:

Several so-called sink-holes occur about one mile south of Summerland...These holes occur in the White Silt Formation...In this silt there is a great deal of seepage water, travelling from the hills to the lake. The holes have been formed where water from the surface has seeped downward to join one of these underground streams. The fine particles of silt were naturally washed down with the water, resulting in "sink-holes" such as the one above mentioned.

True sink-holes are formed in soluble rock, like limestone, where underground water dissolves part of the rock and forms holes and caverns...This mode of formation is quite different from that of the holes under discussion which were simply formed by the mechanical transportation of fine silt particles.[3] (*OHS*, 1935)

Ancient Rocks

The geological history of the Okanagan goes back millions of years before the creation of Lake Penticton. The complexity of that history has fascinated geologists and laymen alike. In 1877 Dr. George Mercer Dawson, "the little giant of Canadian geology,"[4] visited the Okanagan and recorded his observations. He was followed by others from the Geological Survey of Canada and by civil servants in the employ of the Government of British Columbia.

In "The Origin of Okanagan Lake," first published in *The Transactions of the Royal Society of Canada (1943)*, S.J. Schofield FRSC describes the Okanagan region as follows:

Okanagan Valley is situated in southern British Columbia in West Longitude 119 degrees 30 minutes, where it crosses the international boundary at the 49th parallel of latitude. The drainage is southward and flows into the Columbia River at approximately 48 degrees latitude. The valley is occupied by several lakes, the largest being Okanagan Lake which is 65 miles long and 3 miles wide. The lakes are at an elevation of 1,130 feet above sea level. The valley is U-shaped.

Rising 900 feet above the lake is a series of terraces cut in the White Silts of the Pleistocene Age. The valley walls continue to rise to a height of 3,000 feet above the lake and are composed of rocks consisting of mica schists intruded by granitic sheets and tongues, limestones and interbedded volcanic rocks for the most part.

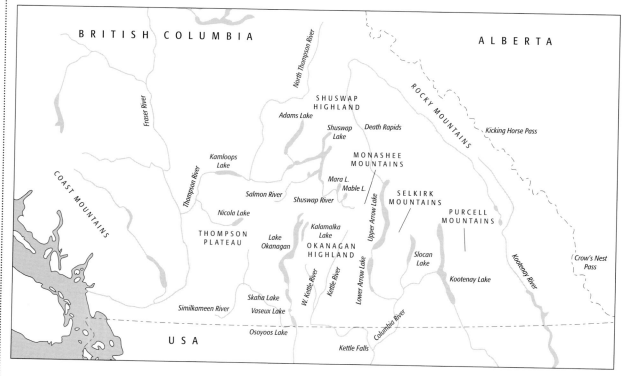

Physical Geography

At this elevation the plateau is reached which consists of a series of low rolling hills into which the Okanagan and other valleys have been cut. Some bluffs appear in the landscape where horizontal lava flows make their appearance. The plateau is part of the Interior Plateau of Dawson and is really an uplifted peneplain which has an elevation averaging 4,500 feet above sea level with monadnocks rising 1,000 to 2,000 feet above the plateau. The plateau is covered with trees of small size.

Rocks probably of late Precambrian age are exposed along the east side of Okanagan Lake…and can be examined in the rock cuts along the Kettle Valley Railway which ascends the eastern steep mountain side by a series of switch backs.[5]

In its book *The Geology of the Kelowna Area*, the Kelowna Geology Committee dates these ancient rocks of the Okanagan, Monashee Gneiss or Shuswap as being two billion years old or more. The committee describes their metamorphosis[6] and tells us where we can best view them today.[7] The rocks are part of the Precambrian Shield from which our continent developed and in fact probably once formed the western shore of our continent.

Oyama from the east. On the left: Wood Lake, the headwaters of the Okanagan chain. On the right: Kalamalka (Long) Lake. The strip of land between the lakes was called "The Railway." Just beyond the mountain in the middle ground lies Okanagan Lake.
BCARS B-01979

Since the 1960s the theories of plate tectonics have informed geological research. C.J. Yorath in his book *Where Terranes Collide* writes:

> Throughout the Paleozoic and early Mesozoic Eras, the edge of the continent was somewhere in the western Okanagan, Quesnel Lakes, Prince George regions. The pieces that form most of British Columbia and the western Yukon weren't there. They were somewhere else. Somewhere, in the vast Panthalassan ocean.[8]

Quesnellia is the name geologists give to the particular terrane or chunk of the earth's crust that borders the western shore of Okanagan Lake and underlies the lake to some degree. To the north is the Shuswap Terrane which, like Quesnellia, drifted in from somewhere else. These events happened approximately 160 million years ago.[9]

About sixty million years ago, during the Eocene Period, the Okanagan fault occurred. The fault is at least twenty kilometres deep and can be traced for two hundred kilometres. Geologist Murray A. Roed believes that "the influence of this fault on the geologic development of this part of the province has been profound."[10] Roed says that an east-west-trending fault near Okanagan Mission has caused the displacement of the primary north-south fault and created the bend or "knee" of Okanagan Lake.

During the millennia that have preceded our present time the Okanagan and adjacent territories have undergone immense geophysical and climatic changes. Mountains have been thrust up and later worn down by erosion. A warm period allowed lush subtropical growth, the record of which can be read in the fossil beds west of Princeton and those south of Penticton on the White Lake Road. Finally swamp vegetation of the period developed into the coal deposits found in Enderby, Westbank, White Lake and Princeton.

There were periods of volcanism, one 50 to 60 million years ago, another about 20 million years ago and one as late at 762,000 years ago. These were responsible for the caldera in which Vernon, Kelowna, Penticton and Summerland now sit and for the throwing up of mountains such as Knox, Dilworth and Boucherie. We find evidence of these times of volcanic activity in the basalt outcroppings that caught the attention of early European settlers and visitors because of their spectacular formations. Layer Cake Hill in Mission Creek Canyon, described by Dawson in 1877,[11] has proved one of the most interesting and most puzzling basaltic formations. In *The Geology of the Kelowna Area* John D. Greenough presents an interesting explanation of the hill, claiming that the formation is basically vertical columns, not horizontal layering as many have believed.[12]

Layer Cake Hill east of Kelowna. A basalt formation. Kelowna Museum

Reverend John Goodfellow, always interested in the physical features of the Similkameen and their origins, has written not only about the fossil beds and coal deposits of the Princeton area but also about the basalt of the Keremeos Columns, which he describes as follows: "The columns are estimated to be over a hundred feet in height, and together about three hundred feet across. In the centre they are upright, but tend to slope inward from both sides. They might well be described as a vast pipe organ in stone."[13] In 1939 Dorothy Hewlett Gellatly, when she learned that Public Works was hauling basaltic columns from the north side of Mount Boucherie (near Westbank) to be used for rock cribbing in the new ferry approach being built across from Kelowna, gathered some friends for an outing to view these interesting rocks. Members of the party were intrigued by the fact that the columns could be pried apart with the crowbar they had taken with them.[14]

One may well ask what significance geological information has for us today apart from satisfying our curiosity about our surroundings. The answer is *great* significance, for those ancient occurrences determine where we build our roads, what we plant and where, where we mine and for what treasure, where our cities develop and, very important, where we should or should not build our houses. So significant is earth science with respect to land use, development and water management that Roed and his Kelowna committee devote a chapter of their *Geology of the Kelowna Area* to the subject. "Geology," they write, "affects every aspect of modern life in the Okanagan."[15]

New orchards near Oliver, late 1920s. Notice terraces or "benches" in the upper left of the picture: a common feature of Okanagan landscapes. BCARS B-09699

Glaciation

The Okanagan which we see today has been greatly modified by the glaciation of the Pleistocene epoch, a period of about one million years during which temperature changes and variations in precipitation caused ice to advance and then retreat over the land several times. During the glaciation, ice lobes spread from the Monashee Mountains and wore the valley into the U-shape which we know today. The Similkameen Valley was subject to much the same process. At the height of glaciation the ice reached an altitude of about eight thousand feet, which meant that the mountains of the Okanagan were covered.

About ten thousand years ago the ice began its final retreat, exposing first the mountain tops and leaving the valleys filled with great ice lobes which were sometimes active and sometimes stagnant. As the glacial ice melted, copious meltwater streams found their way to lower elevations, carrying with them sands and gravel. Hence the great outwash terraces like those on the west side of the valley at Okanagan Falls, or the Salmon River outwash delta which became the Grandview Flats in the north. Before it began to debouch into the main Okanagan Valley, meltwater from the Marron Valley lobe found its way south into the Similkameen, creating the passage now used by vehicles travelling from Penticton to Keremeos.

An especially interesting feature of this late Pleistocene epoch was the formation of the huge glacial lakes. Lake Penticton has already been discussed above. South of McIntyre Bluff was Oliver Lake, extending from north of the town of Oliver to the 49th Parallel where it was halted by outwash material. Inevitably these lakes drained until they reached the water level we know today.

Hugh Nasmith in his study of the glacial history of the Okanagan has an interesting comment on the gradual lowering of glacial Lake Penticton:

> The drainage of the Shuswap River, Shuswap Lake, and possibly much of the lake system occupying the South Thompson Valley was probably to the south through Lake Penticton during much of the late glacial stage, but no well-defined channel existed until the level of Lake Penticton fell and the glacial-lake silts were exposed. A prominent channel was then cut south from near Enderby to the north end of Okanagan Lake in the glacial-lake sediments when the level of Lake Penticton stood only 50 feet or so above the present level of Okanagan Lake near Vernon.
>
> The abandonment of this meltwater channel and the diversion of the Shuswap drainage to the Thompson and Fraser Rivers may be regarded as marking the end of late glacial time in the Okanagan Valley. Near Armstrong, Fortune Creek built into this abandoned channel an alluvial fan which now forms the divide between Okanagan drainage to the Columbia

A very flat divide located one mile (1.6 km) east of the City of Armstrong. J.A. Gamble

River and Shuswap drainage to the Fraser River. The reduction in the flow of water through the Okanagan River channel south of Skaha Lake permitted tributary streams such as Shuttleworth and McIntyre Creeks to build alluvial fans across the channel along which the undersized Okanagan River meandered.[16]

The divide between the Fraser drainage system and the Columbia is just north of Armstrong. It is so flat that considerable interest has been shown over the years in the construction of a canal between the Shuswap and the Okanagan systems.

The Spallumcheen and Okanagan Canal[17]

by Judith N. Pope

Early settlers will remember the efforts that were made at one time to induce the Government to build a canal from the Spallumcheen (or Shuswap) River to Okanagan Lake. We applied to the authorities at Ottawa for information about this canal and the following letter was received in reply:

Department of Railways and Canals,
Ottawa, Ont.
August 23, 1926.

Dear Sir:
Your letter of the 3rd August to the Parliamentary Librarian has been handed by him to the writer for attention.

I find that in the latter part of 1882, an Engineer named L.B. Hamlin, who was in charge of one of the mountain sections of the Canadian Pacific Railway, was instructed, by order of the first minister of this department, the late Hon. Sir Charles Tupper, to conduct an exploratory survey of the valley lying between Spallumcheen River and Okanagan Lake with a view to connecting Lakes Okanagan and Shuswap by means of a canal.

The surveyor's report was forwarded to the Minister of Railways and Canals in January, 1883, by Joseph W. Trutch, agent of the Dominion Government at Victoria, B.C. In forwarding the report, Mr. Trutch stated that the survey had established that the construction of such a canal would be quite practical, but that it would cost far more than had been estimated by those who had been urging that it should be undertaken in the mistaken apprehension that it could be carried into execution with but little excavation and only one lock at each end of the proposed canal.

Mr. Hamlin reported that four or five locks would be necessary; that the canal would require to be 18 miles in length and would cost about $27,000 a mile, depending greatly on the style of work which might be approved by the Government.

A shallow-draft canal, with a navigable depth of four or five feet only, was proposed, with locks 150 feet in length and about 50 feet in width. Mr. Trutch, in forwarding the report, was of the opinion that the approximate estimate contained in Mr. Hamlin's report was altogether too low for the construction of a canal of any practical value. Mr. Hamlin, in his report, stressed the agricultural possibilities of the district which would have been served by the canal, which requirements have, no doubt, been largely supplied by the railway since constructed. In April 1883 the Lieut.-Governor of British Columbia forwarded a report adopted by the Executive Council of the province urging the immediate commencement of construction of the canal. The communication was referred to Privy Council and by Council to the Minister of Railways and Canals. An Order of the House of Commons was adopted on March 24th 1883 for a return of the correspondence and the surveyor's report, and this order was complied with in Return No. 22 of the same year.

Yours truly,
Geo. W. Yates,
Assistant Deputy Minister

While some believed the project too costly, others, especially the intrepid Captain T.D. Shorts, believed that it need not be. George H. Morkill tells us:

Captain Shorts' plan for utilizing the waterways was simple and inexpensive. He intended to dig a ditch about one and a half miles to connect Davis Creek with O'Keefe Creek. This would give a continuous waterway from the Lake to Enderby, and in the bed of this water he intended to lay a chain from end to end of it, and for motive power he intended to use a scow with a steam-driven drum in front and so arranged that the drum would pick up and drop the chain as it passed along. It is very questionable whether this was practicable, but Shorts often discussed its feasibility with his friends during the winter of 1889.[18]
(OHS, 1935)

Recent Modifications to the Landscape

Modern industrial construction and road building accomplished by the heavy equipment now in use are demolishing ancient deposits. At first the cuts into hillsides tend to reveal geological history as we read the nature of the stratification. Were the gravel, boulders, sand or silt delivered by ice, by fast-running water or by lake water? Generally speaking, the coarser the material the faster running was the water which deposited it. Eventually the process of removing the gravel or other depositions destroys the evidence of just how a land-form was created.

A minor modification in the Okanagan landscape occurred when the Federal Government, in 1909, dug a canal through the "The Railroad," the isthmus between Wood Lake and Kalamalka, and caused Wood Lake to be lowered six inches and the water in Kalamalka to rise eighteen inches.

Perhaps the most noticeable change in the landscape has been between Okanagan and Osoyoos Lakes, where the river which once meandered through wetlands has been forced into a rigid channel where flows have been regulated.

Water, Life Blood of the Okanagan[19]
by D.A. Dobson, P. Eng.

After the glaciers retreated following the last Ice Age a large lake remained, stretching from the present City of Kamloops to the north of McIntyre Bluff, a few kilometres south of the City of Penticton. Gradually, the barriers at either end of this huge lake were worn down and the water drained away leaving a number of smaller lakes connected by a meandering river along the valley floor. Remnants of the ancient lakeshore can still be seen in the form of terraced benches along the valley walls.

The lakes as we know them today start at Wood Lake–Kalamalka Lake in the north, Okanagan Lake, Skaha Lake, Vaseux Lake and ending with Osoyoos Lake in the south. Water to feed the lakes is supplied primarily from the melting of the winter snow in the surrounding hills. The change from winter temperatures of as low as -25 degrees C to a summer high of +30 degrees C can occur very quickly resulting in a rapid melt in the mountain snow packs. Under these circumstances the valley lakes would fill and flooding occur to adjacent lowlands...

The flooding in the spring was soon forgotten when replaced by the hot, arid days of July and August. These seasonal fluctuations are compounded by the annual variations. Too much water one year may be followed by too little water the next.

In 1942, as a result of agitation by the towns and municipalities throughout the valley, a joint Board of Engineers was formed by the governments of Canada and British Columbia. The task confronting this Board was to study and report on flood control measures for the Okanagan Valley. The Board determined that the natural river system was not able to handle the peak spring flows and therefore flooding was an annual occurrence. They also determined that, as a result of no storage capacity in the main stem lakes, there was a shortage of water for irrigation purposes during July and August when water was sorely needed.

[The board recommended that control dams be built on the Okanagan River at Penticton, Okanagan Falls and McIntyre Bluff in order to hold back waters from the spring runoff for use during the dry summer season and that the Okanagan River between Okanagan Lake and Osoyoos Lake be contained within a properly designed channel with adequate dykes to safely pass the high spring flows.]

The difference in elevation between Okanagan Lake and Osoyoos Lake is 64 meters. The new straight channel which replaced the old meandering river was found to be 23 kilometres shorter and therefore had too steep a gradient. To maintain the original water surface gradient over this shorter, steeper channel required the integration of seventeen smaller structures known as vertical drop structures, between Okanagan Falls and Osoyoos Lake.

It was also recognized that the Okanagan River is an important spawning stream for sockeye salmon that migrate up the Columbia River. To protect this salmon run a 2,700 meter section of river north of the Village of Oliver extending to the McIntyre Dam was left in its natural state to provide spawning and rearing habitat.

With all the facts collected the final report by the Board was submitted and accepted by the two governments in 1950. The first construction contract was called in September of 1952 and the final phase was completed in Osoyoos Lake in 1958...

Downstream of Osoyoos Lake, in Washington State, there is another small dam on the Okanagan River known as the Zosel Dam. This dam, constructed in 1927 to provide a log sorting pond for the Zosel Lumber Company, created an artificial level on Osoyoos Lake. In 1945 the International Joint Commission issued an order to affect control of Osoyoos Lake levels since the lake is an international water body. The control level is 277.66 meters at the dam foreby. However, this level is complicated by a backwater condition when the Similkameen River is in flood. The Similkameen River joins the Okanagan River 5 kilometres downstream of the Zosel dam, south of Oroville. When this backwater condition occurs water cannot drain from Osoyoos Lake and flooding may occur around the lake...

It should be noted that the old wooden Zosel Dam is being replaced by a new structure immediately upstream. Construction commenced in April and should be completed by early 1987. The new dam will not eliminate the problems associated with the Similkameen River but will help to minimize their effect. When the new dam is operational it will conclude the work on the flood control system for the Okanagan Valley that began 35 years ago. [The new Zosel Dam was dedicated in May 1988.]

Flood control is not flood elimination; it is a practical approach to minimize the undesirable effects of our climate. The quality of life in this valley as a result of the Okanagan Flood Control Project attests to its effectiveness.

(OHS, 1986)

In 1993 a slight modification to the river project was made. Realizing that water birds were suffering from the almost complete destruction of their wetlands habitat, a few oxbows to the east of the new river channel and just north of Road 22 were reflooded. Elsewhere along the course of the river one can see where swamp has been turned into productive pastureland. However, there are some who begin to wonder if Osoyoos Lake pollution is due in part to the destruction of the wetlands through which the Okanagan River once meandered and its waters were filtered.

Climate, Flora and Fauna

As storms sweep in from the Pacific Ocean and pass over the interior of British Columbia the moisture-laden air is forced to rise over the Coast Range and Cascades. This upward movement has a cooling effect and much of the moisture is dropped as rain or as snow. By the time the winds reach the lower mountains of the Okanagan they are descending and thus warming under compression. Hence the winds are drying and produce the arid and semi-arid conditions we find in the Okanagan region. Generally speaking, the farther south one goes the drier the climate.

Max H. Ruhmann, who served the provincial government in the Okanagan as plant pathologist and entomologist until he became provincial entomologist in 1935, writes:

> The greater part of Canada is covered by the Arctic, Hudsonian and Canadian Zones. The Transition Zone is only present in small areas north of the International Boundary, appearing in Nova Scotia, New Brunswick, Quebec, Ontario, Manitoba, a considerable portion of Saskatchewan and Alberta, the southern interior of B.C., the southernmost portion of Vancouver Island, and a small area around Vancouver.
>
> The Upper Austral Zone is entirely confined to the United States and does not approach the Canadian line at any point except in the southernmost portion of the Okanagan Valley in B.C. where the subdivision of this zone known as the Upper Sonoran Faunal area occurs. This area commences approximately west of the 100th Meridian, running south to northern Mexico and north to Dakota, Montana and Washington in continuous but irregular lines extending from central Washington by a very narrow arm into the Okanagan Valley, merging abruptly into the Transitional Zone at Okanagan Falls.
>
> This intrusion is unique in that in this small area can be found plants and animals which do not occur in any other part of Canada.

A hillside near Osoyoos. The dark-stemmed shrubs are antelope bush or greasewood, peculiar to the South Okanagan. Among them are sagebrush which blooms in the spring and rabbit bush which blooms in the fall. When the scant winter snows first melt, residents watch eagerly for the short-stemmed buttercups which shelter under the shrubs. In May balsam root (sunflowers) gladden these slopes. Webber

> Except in California the most conspicuous vegetation of the Upper Sonoran area is the true sagebrush (*Artemisia tridentata*) which, however, is equally abundant in the Transitional Zone. Several species of the so-called "grease woods" which are represented by the Antelope Bush (*Purshia tridentata*) in the Upper Sonoran area occur in B.C. This bush is most distinctive as it does not occur anywhere in B.C. outside of this area and does not appear in the Transitional Zone.
>
> Among the characteristic birds and mammals are the Burrowing Owl, Brewer's Sparrow, Nevada Sage Sparrow, Lazuli Finch, Sage Thrasher, Nuttall's Poor-will, Bullock's Oriole, Rough-winged Swallow, Five-toed Kangaroo Rats, Pocket Mice, Grasshopper Mice, Sage Chipmunk, Sage Cottontail, Idaho Rabbit, Black-tailed Jack Rabbit and the Oregon, Utah, and Townsend's Ground Squirrels.[20]
> (*OHS*, 1926)

Seventy years later (in 1996) the naturalists Richard and Sydney Cannings, writing about this unique region of Canada in their *British Columbia: A Natural History*, tell us:

Erosion pillar at Pillar Lake. Similar formations occur in other parts of the area. The large stone on top has protected the column from the effects of rain. BCARS C-06889

> ...The south end of the Okanagan and Similkameen Valleys is a special place. About a third of British Columbia's rare or endangered plants and animals make their home there. Birders come from all over the continent to see the special birds of the grasslands and the dry pine forests. And invertebrates are unusual too—a recent collection of wasps on the sand benches north of Osoyoos netted thirty-five species, thirteen of which were previously unknown to Canada.[21]

In Osoyoos the efforts of an energetic and persistent Osoyoos Desert Society, whose aim is to establish a desert interpretative centre, appear at last to be bearing fruit. The society has the support of Dr. Geoff Scudder and a team of dedicated biologists who see the project as preserving "an eco system full of rare species found nowhere else in Canada."[22]

As the Cannings brothers remark, "The south end of the Okanagan and Similkameen Valleys is a special place."

2

The First People

An Okanagan Communication

Letter from Jerry Eneas[1]

Okanagan Historical Society,

Narcisse Bone was born about the year 1890. Narcisse Bone is a descent from the Okanogan[2] Indian Tribe. Narcisse Bone is the son of Narcisse Bone Jim and Julie Isaac Sam.
Narcisse Bone and Margaret George were united in marriage about Oct. 24, 1924.
Narcisse Bone was working for Val Haynes during the early years of 1900. Val Haynes owned a cattle ranch south from Vaseaux [sic] Lake. The cattle ranch is on the west side of Highway 97.
There was a brush fire or forest fire on the hill or mountain somewhere west of Oliver, B.C. There were cattle on the hill or mountain and the cattle were close to the fire. Narcisse Bone was trying to save the cattle from the fire. Narcisse Bone try to bring the herd of cattle away from the fire. Narcisse Bone and his saddle horse got caught in the ring of fire. The saddle horse of Narcisse Bone die in the fire. Narcisse Bone was burned and needed medical attention. Narcisse Bone never die during this time. Narcisse Bone got burned from the fire sometime during the years of 1920 or early years of 1930.
Narcisse Bone die from cancer on the day February 11, 1956, at Spokane, Washington. Narcisse Bone and his sister Madeline Wells are buried in the Indian cemetery at Charlie Eders ranch about 3 or 4 miles north from Oroville, Washington.
Joe Bone was born on the day January 20, 1907. Joe Bone is a descent from the Okanogan Indian Tribe. Joe Bone is the younger brother to Narcisse Bone.
Joe Bone and another Indian and his name is Aberaham Alex were hunting in the hills or mountains on the Indian Reserve somewhere west of Penticton, B.C. Joe Bone was

attacked and mauled by a Grizzly bear. Aberaham Alex was carrying a big rifle, maybe 30-30 Winchester rifle. Aberaham Alex ran to the Grizzly bear from behind. Aberaham Alex aim at the head of the Grizzly bear, and Aberaham Alex shot the Grizzly bear. The Grizzly bear fell down and died from the gunshot of the big Winchester rifle. Joe Bone never die from the Grizzly bear attack during this time. Many thanks to a brave Indian of the Okanogan Indian Tribe, Aberaham Alex.

I wonder if the story of Narcisse Bone and the fire on the hill or mountain was ever printed in the newspaper.

I wonder if the story of Joe Bone and Aberaham Alex and the Grizzly bear was ever printed in the newpaper.

Can you help me? Thank you.

Send information to Sarah Bone McCraigie, Route 2, Box 65-P, Omak, Washington 98841. Sister to Narcisse Bone and Joe Bone.

Jerry Eneas

The above letter was received in 1986, neatly hand printed on a single sheet of paper. Brief as it is, it reveals some important characteristics of the First Nation people of the Okanagan. There is the pride in family and race based on respect for the brave and selfless behaviour of both Narcisse Bone and Aberaham Alex, each meeting an obligation deeply felt. The writer wishes to celebrate these deeds. In earlier times the stories would have been told and retold about the campfire. Now they should be committed to the printed page. The tentative manner in which the stories are offered for publication illustrates some of the "complex communication norms" of which the linguist Anthony Mattina writes in his essay "Okanagan Communication and Language."[3] We observe the importance of genealogy in Okanagan culture. The stories have a precise geographical setting and the characters a recognized place in their society. The letter, written from Washington State about events that took place in BC, suggests the irrelevance of the International Boundary for Okanagan speakers.

Where did the First People come from?

About ten thousand years ago the ice that had covered the Okanagan melted, revealing a landscape somewhat like that we know today. Gradually life returned to the mountains and lakes until at last the land was ready for human habitation. The archaeologist Mike Rousseau believes that the First People arrived "12,000 to 11,000 years B.P."–Before Present.[4]

Where did these people come from? James Baker believes that archaeological investigations indicate that the first inhabitants of the Okanagan probably arrived from the south, where occupation sites on the Columbia Plateau and in Oregon and Idaho date from as much as ten thousand to fifteen thousand years ago.[5] It is likely that these people were the ancestors of the Interior Salish who archaeologists say have enjoyed cultural continuity from about nine thousand years ago to the present.[6]

Over the centuries the speech of the Interior Salish has diversified into several distinct languages, the Okanagan tongue and the Shuswap being among them. Speakers of the Okanagan language occupied a large area in what is now southern BC and Washington State. Kinship ties established through marriages encouraged relations throughout the region. Families would go on extended visits sharing in their relatives' hunting and fishing rights. Christine Galler, who under the pseudonym of Mourning Dove wrote *A Salishan Autobiography*[7] could claim kin from as far away as Nicola on the west and, on the east, Tobacco Plains in the East Kootenay. Her family's home was Colville, Washington but each September the family visited relatives in the south Okanagan and participated in the fishing at the narrows on Osoyoos Lake.

Okanagan–Colville Language Group (as defined by Douglas R. Hudson and R. Bouchard[8])

Okanagan
1. Northern Okanagan–along upper Okanagan
2. Similkameen Okanagan–along the Similkameen River
3. Southern Okanagan–along the lower Okanagan River
4. Methow Okanagan–along the Methow River (Washington)

Colville
5. Sanpoil-Nespelem–along the Columbia River
6. Colville–along the Colville Valley
7. Lakes–Columbia River, Arrow Lakes, Slocan Lake

The Okanagan Indians and their neighbours

Cementing relationships through marriage sometimes had political significance. Pelkamulox II, who sought recognition by the whole of the Okanagan, married four wives, the first a Spokan, the second a Shuswap, the third a Sanpoil and the fourth an Okanagan and the grandmother of N'kwala.[9] Sometimes the reasons for a marriage were economic as well as political. After 1811 both Okanagan chiefs and fur-company officers often found marriages between daughters of local chieftains and the traders or factors mutually advantageous. A wise native wife bridged the cultural gap, acted as an interpreter and more than once played the role of peacemaker.

The Culture

The Okanagans were what Louis Binford would call "collectors," people who follow "a logistical strategy where specific resources are exploited at different times by organized groups operating from base camps."[10] Surplus

food was preserved for winter or used in trade. Roots collected in the spring included balsam (*balsamorchiza sagittata*), spring beauty (*claytonia lanceolata*) and bitterroot (*Lewisia rediviva*). This last was dried and ground into a flour. During the summer berries were collected as they ripened. Fishing depended on when the run occurred. At Kettle Falls early summer would see families gathered from a vast area. An August fishery of a few weeks' duration occurred near present-day Oroville and, later, the fish that escaped the Oroville weirs would reach Okanagan Falls and provide a fishery there. Fall was the season for hunting large mammals.

An Indian family, after contact, standing in front of the racks used for drying fish or game. Kelowna Museum File 21

The various activities were executed with both order and ceremony. A chief was chosen in each case to perform the introductory ceremony and oversee the harvest. For example, with regard to the salmon fishery Douglas R. Hudson tells us:

> Salmon fishing was controlled by a Salmon Chief, who directed the construction of the traps and weirs and performed a ceremony to mark the capture of the first salmon. This ceremony, called the First Salmon Ceremony, symbolized the dependence on the salmon and the need to maintain a proper relationship with this renewable resource. Under the

guidance of the Salmon Chief, the first salmon caught was cooked and distributed to members of the assembled community. The bones were returned to the river to maintain the cycle...A set of prohibitions underscored the practical and symbolic importance of salmon. Swimming was banned upriver from the weir, and menstruating women and recent widows and widowers could not come near the weir, nor partake in the consumption of salmon.[11]

Division of labour was observed. Men caught the fish and hunted the larger mammals. Women dug up roots, gathered berries, gutted and prepared fish for drying, dried venison, tanned animal skins and made them into clothes. Women snared small animals such as squirrels and hare. They cooked food for immediate consumption and preserved the surplus. Stored food was in the care of the women and hence they governed its use whether as family food or as an article of trade.

Louise Gabriel, an Elder of the Penticton Indian Band, has spent twelve years on her Band Council and has been a representative of her people on the National Council of Indian Elders of Canada. Many years ago Mrs. Gabriel prepared a dictionary of Okanagan words and their English equivalents for her friend Hester White. It is believed that the article "Food and Medicines of the Okanakanes" is derived from that dictionary.[12]

from **Food and Medicines of the Okanakanes**[13]

by Louise Gabriel
(As compiled by Hester E. White)

My people, the native Canadians of the Okanakane (Okanagan) Tribe, inhabited this lovely valley from north of the Okanagan Lake to south of the river of the same name, a distance of about two hundred miles.

This valley was ours, to roam at will its length and breadth. It was our privilege to enjoy its beauty and to partake of its bounty...

Long before *Sa-ma* (the white man) set foot on *Tee-khwhat* (Okanagan Lake) shore, there was plenty of game of all kinds. *Papa-lat-cha* (elk) was the most plentiful. Elk made their home on *Sa-ya* (Deep Creek) hill and were chased down into the lake by our trained dogs, long since extinct. They were much like the Alaskan huskies, yellow in colour, tails curled up. Because the elk were very fast in the water there would be five or six paddlers to a canoe and a hunter with bow and arrows. The elk lowest in the water would be the fattest, so it was the target.

We had a variety of animals, fish and birds to use for food as the seasons came. We made broth from meat and fish, and dried leaves from different plants were steeped for drinking. We ate berries both fresh and dried, mushrooms and nuts. There were many kinds of roots to eat, but most of them had to be cooked...

The first root to be dug is *speet-lum* (rock rose), which has many uses. It is dug with a *peecha*, a long stick made from *wa-wa-hilp* (syringa). All roots are dug in the same way.

Most kinds of roots have to be cooked before drying. These are *skwin-kwin-em* (wild potatoes), *stlo-kum* (wild carrots), *ha-leo-whah* and *ukee-ukups* (wild onions), *sta-cheen* (tiger lily), *speet-lum* and sunflower.

A cooking pit is dug and lined with hot rocks, then a layer of *skook-welp* (rosebush branches) to prevent roots from burning. The (peeled if *speet-lum*) washed roots are put in the pit and another layer of *skook-welp,* then *de-kwah-lep* (timber grass) and finally *lok-la* (earth) is added. A hole is made in the top and *see-colkh* (water) is poured in to make *s'hool* (from the hot rocks to cook the roots). Some roots were cooked overnight. When cooked the roots are put in the sun to dry out on *to-ook-tan* (tule) mats.

Sku-lep (Indian bread) is cooked the same way. This is made of the long hairlike moss which hangs from fir trees on *mook-way-ut* (high) mountains. The moss was cleaned and covered with *spe-a-kaluk* (dried berries) to sweeten and flavour it. When done the *sku-lep* was cut in pieces and dried...

Skul-kuklt-meo (men) get ready for the *pia-hem* (hunting) by making their *cho-kweek*

(bows) and *cha-kalen* (arrows) of *wa-wa-hilp* (syringa). The *tina* (bowstring) is sinew taken from the *kas-hum* (back) of the animal. The bows are tipped with *sta-hina* (flint) and the other end has feathers.

Then the men have their *kweel-sten* (sweat-house) to be clean so the *sla-cheenem* (deer) will not get their *ska-yowh* (scent) even if they are close to them. It is built beside water. The *kweel-sten* is made from a framework of bent sticks with their ends stuck firmly into the earth to make a round little house like an igloo. This is covered with bark and packed earth, except for a small opening. Inside it has *kwayl-chen* (fir boughs) on the ground and a little *skloo-eestan* (pit) is dug and hot rocks are put into it. The men bathe in the cold water, then go into the *kweel-sten* and pull a *chip-teen-tin* (covering) over the door. They pour water on the hot rocks to make steam, then they rub with clean grass to remove the *slo-weet* (soil) from their bodies. Any callouses are rubbed off with a smooth stone. After the sweat-house they bathe in the cold water again.

Then they go to hunt the *sla-cheenem* (deer), the *papa-lat-cha* (elk), the *st'chemell-cha* (mountain sheep), *ka-low-na* (grizzly bear), and *skem-heest* (black and brown bears). Sunflower leaves are used to wipe out the insides of the deer...

Framework for a sweat lodge. The framework is covered with evergreen bows and a flap of hide is hung in the doorway. Stones are heated in a fire outside the lodge then rolled into the lodge where water is sprinkled on them to create steam. The sweat bath is a time of cleansing both physically and spiritually. After the sweat the bather plunges into a nearby lake or stream.
Kelowna Museum File 21

Next comes the *h'wee-koom* (tanning) of the *s'e-pee* (hides). First they *ai-i-kam* (scrape) the *kap-ka-in-ten* (hair) off the skins with a *sk'rom-a-l'xt* (bone) taken from the *t'kem-aks-tin* (leg) of a deer. The hair is washed off in clean water and the skins are stretched and laced on poles like a loom. When a hide is dry it is taken off and *en'p'l-keecha* (smoked) over a

fire of dry *yah-kway* (rotten wood). Then it is soaked in warm water full of the *st'm-ken* (cooked brains) of the animal. Now it is laced back to the frame. Bear-skins are stretched and used for rugs.

The women have a *so-whey-whey-sten* (smooth rock) tied on the end of a stick, which they work and scrape all over the skin to soften it. When dry it is taken off and smoked again. It is soft and pliable now and ready to make into *si-see-pe-hen* (moc-casins) and clothing. A stone *nik-emen* (knife) is used to cut the skins. Thread was made of sinew. Needles were fine bones taken from a deer-leg. A special needle was made from the leg-bone of a swan...

An Indian weaver constructing a basket.
Kelowna Museum File 21

Okanakane Medicine

For every illness there was a cure nearby and we knew how to make tonics, salves, anti-septics, and hot drinks. We bathed often and our *kweel-sten* (sweat-house) was for health and spirit as well as cleanliness. *Kula-meen* (cottonwood ashes) was like soap for our buck-skin clothing. For hair-washing we went to Spotted Lake near Richter Mountain or White Lake nearer home. Baskets of this clay or mud were carried home to use for washing.

These are a few of our medicines:

(1) Baby Care—We picked the soft, white filling from *kwis-kwas-kin* (bullrushes, not tules), and used it for absorbent cotton. It was packed around the babies for clothing and diapers. After babies were weaned from the breast they were given *se-yah* (berry) juices and the long *sku-leep* moss from the trees was melted into a syrup, something like Karo syrup.

This was good for them. If a baby had *enow-k'cheen* (sore mouth), *tk-tk-l-emp* (wild strawberry leaves) were baked and crushed into a powder and dusted into the baby's mouth. This is soothing and healing.

(2) *Stik-tik-ch'welp* (red willow) is used for irritated skin, bruises, rashes, toothache, and for steaming sore throats. It is the best for infection and blood-poisoned cuts.

(3) Spring tonics were brewed from the evergreens, *ch'k-ialp* (fir), *mar-eelp* (spruce), *ch'kwelwh* (balsam), *poo-neelp* (juniper) and *sj-ar-sil-malwh* (Oregon grape). Roots of Oregon grape were cleaned and boiled with *ka-ka-leext* (sarsaparilla). This is the best blood tonic.

(4) For bad colds we used the different kinds of *papa-l'm'lkh* (sagebrush) steeped. Dried fish-heads were boiled and the broth taken for colds. *Too-wah-tee-wah* (mint) leaves are brewed like tea and this takes fever from the body.

(5) For a laxative we use *so-ho-sameelp* (soap *olallie* branches) boiled. This is a mild remedy. A strong laxative is *ha-hala-hoops* (rattlesnake weed) brewed like tea.

(6) There are two kinds of *ha-you* (wild parsnips). The one that grows on the side-hills is the one we used for medicine. It makes a good poultice on open wounds and for soreness in broken bones. The swamp-parsnip is poisonous.

(7) We have plants like onions. They are *ha-leo-whah* and *ukee-ukups*. The bulbs are mashed and put on poison ivy sores.

(8) For internal haemorrhage and diarrhoea we steeped the inner bark of *stik-stik-chu-welp* (thornbush) and drank the tea.

Nature has a cure for every illness and many of these medicines are still used today in the homes of our people.

(*OHS*, 1954)

For the Okanagans, work periods were also social occasions. At the annual fishery trading went on; sports such as foot races and horse races were enjoyed; men gambled as they played lahal or the stick game; marriages were arranged. As cousins were regarded more as siblings they were of the same kinship group and marriage between them was taboo. Spouses must be found beyond the kinship. Parents played an important part in keeping track of who was eligible and who was not a proper spouse for their son or daughter. Marriage was regarded as serving the society rather than gratifying the two individuals involved. The status of a family depended on observing tradition as well as performing its economic role. Those who through carelessness or neglect lost status were said to "have lost their history."

The summer home of a native family was the teepee, consisting of a framework of poles planted in a circle and brought together at the peak, then covered with tule mats. Such a structure could be easily dismantled and

Winter pit house or Kick Willie. The pole at the centre serves as a ladder for entering or leaving the house which is built over an excavation four or five feet deep. Kelowna Museum File 21

moved to a new place of harvesting. The winter home was a more permanent dwelling, a pit house in a setting where wood and water were readily available. A settlement consisted of the headman and his extended family.

Ties were maintained with other bands and sometimes a common chief acknowledged. However, such a chief ruled by consensus rather than through edicts. An Indian did not expect to be ordered about except in unusual circumstances such as a battle or a hunt, when he deliberately put himself under the authority of another. Robert W. Sterling writes of this sparseness of command among the Okanagans in both language and behaviour in *Okanagan Sources*.[14] Maria Houghton Brent has said, "The trait which the Salish Indian has in common with all other Indians is his hatred of domination, of anything which interferes with his personal freedom...Indians never made satisfactory slaves. In captivity they soon died."[15]

Winter was a time for the performance of dances and songs by means of which the cultural traditions, including spiritual values, were passed on. Native spirituality was also found in First Fruits, First Roots and First Salmon Ceremonies during which gratitude was expressed for the food provided by nature. The sweat bath also had religious significance. It was a time of spiritual cleansing as well as physical.

Young people, even girls, at the onset of puberty were often sent on vision quests. The young person went alone to some wild place where he or she fasted and waited for his or her power to appear. If the power came, which was usually in the form of an animal or bird, the young person was assured of a supernatural helper throughout life. People with power or *sumix* might become healers or shamen.

The spiritual and moral values of the Okanagans are illustrated in their myths, many of which are about a time when there were only the animal people from whom men and women later evolved. The myths express the close relationship maintained between the human and natural world. Coyote figures prominently. He is a maker or creator, a helper and a trickster. Perhaps the ambiguity of coyote's character tells us something of the world view of the Okanagans.

The Legend of Shuswap Falls[16]

by Maria Houghton Brent

A long, long time ago, when the world was young and fresh, before hatred, greed and strife entered, and all was peace and happiness, and all the animals lived harmoniously together, the Bear, Elk, Fox, Coyote and all animals and birds were ancestors of human beings.

Coyote lived in a lovely but very lonely place far away from everyone, where he had no one with whom to speak or play or feast. At last he became very lonesome and made up his mind ever afterwards to break the monotony and invite all his friends once a year to a great feast and jollification.

So he set himself to work and built a great rapid and gave it the name of Shuswap Falls. Then he made a big kettle out of stone with legs under it and hung it over the Falls. Over this he constructed a fish trap, also out of stone, where he could catch many salmon and boil them in the Big Kettle. Then Coyote made a seat for himself out of stone beside the Falls and also where he could talk with his old cronies and at the same time see the sports and watch the feasting.

When he got all this finished to his satisfaction, the buds on the fir trees were just bursting out. By this sign he knew the salmon run was due. So he called aloud for his friends to come and feast. His voice could be heard afar and near as it can even to this day; so it sounded in the long, long ago on every hill, in every vale and all Coyote's friends said, "Hark! There is Coyote calling. Let us go."

Coyote could distinguish who was coming as his friends called out to him on their way, accepting his invitation. He was overjoyed, running round and round to catch his tail, as he heard the bawl of the Grizzly, the howl of the Timber Wolf, the snort of the Elk, the hoot of the Horned Owl, the chatter of the Kingfisher and all the other voices he knew.

Soon they were all assembled and great was the astonishment and rejoicing when they beheld the wonder Coyote had wrought and the provisions he had made for their entertainment. It was a busy time, what with the feasting and the sports which lasted a fortnight with camp fires burning brightly by day and by night, until all were dead tired, and the time came to depart. Then all shook old Coyote by the hand with grateful hearts for his hospitality. They all promised to come again when next the fir trees were bursting out into bud. So all went home happy.

Now all this happened a very long, long time ago. To this day when the firs are in bud each Spring, the hills around Shuswap Falls still re-echo the invitation call of Coyote and the answering call of Coyote's friends, and the camp fire lights reappear.

Wise people say this is only fancy, but we know better.

Such is the Legend of Shuswap Falls as narrated by the old folk of the Okanagan tribe, and translated from the Okanagan dialect by Mrs. William Brent.

(*OHS*, 1948)

Maria Houghton Brent, born December 10, 1870, was the daughter of Captain (later Colonel) Charles Frederick Houghton and Sophie N'kwala, the daughter of the great Chief N'kwala. Sophie died while Maria was very young and the child was raised by her great-aunt Teresa, wife of Cyprienne Laurent. As a young woman Maria spent some years in Montreal with her father, who had become a widower for the second time. Later she returned to Vernon, marrying William Brent and settling down to farming on reserve lands. Maria wrote numerous articles for our early *Reports*. She spent her last years in a resthome near Republic, Washington on or near the Colville Indian Reserve. After visiting Maria Brent there in June 1958 Elsie G. Turnbull wrote in *British Columbia Historical News*: "A tiny gray-haired woman of 86 with a crippled hand, her eyes still bright yet dimming with age, she greeted us with courtesy and quiet pride...She was still striving to tell the story of the Indians and the white men of earlier times." [17]

Contact

Face-to-face contact between the Okanagans and Europeans began in 1811 when the first Europeans penetrated Okanagan country. In that year David Stuart and Alexander Ross of the Pacific Fur Company travelled up the Columbia from Fort Astoria on a fur-trading expedition. At the confluence of the Okanagan River and the Columbia they established Fort Okanagan and Ross remained there for the winter trading with the local bands. Stuart, accompanied by a French Canadian by the name of Montigne, pressed north to the Thompson River where he established a post at Kamloops.

The Indian Roman Catholic Church on the Reserve near Penticton. Penticton Museum 2-025

This was not the first time the Okanagans had felt the impact of the arrival of Europeans on the continent. Early in the sixteenth century Spaniards introduced the horse into Mexico. The animal found the climate and grasslands of the continent congenial and the herds multiplied. By the late eighteenth century the horse had reached what is now south-central BC where it revolutionized travel.

The second effect of the European presence was not so benign. Diseases including the dreaded smallpox were introduced and decimated populations. Often diseases passed from one Native group to another which, as yet, had had no contact with the newcomers. James Baker believes that the Okanagans were affected by the epidemics of 1775 and 1781 and may even have suffered from outbreaks of smallpox which began in the east in 1634 and 1639. [18]

During the era of the fur trade relationships between traders and the people of the First Nations were symbiotic. The latter wanted the newly available trade goods such as iron pots, blankets, knives, axes and guns. The fur companies needed the Natives to harvest the furs and prepare them for shipment. In the Okanagan, where fur-bearing animals were not plentiful, the Native contribution was generally horses for the brigades. Okanagans also served as wranglers. In spite of the mutual advantages there was the occasional ugly incident such as the murder of trader Sam Black at Kamloops in 1841. [19]

When the gold rush was followed by cattle ranching in the 1860s the Okanagan men could still find congenial employment in the dominant economy. Some Native families had their own herds. Having had horses, the Indians of the

Okanagan knew something of the value of land for pasturage and when James Douglas instructed W.G. Cox to mark off reserves in consultation with local band leaders the Natives had the foresight to ask for sizeable acreages. However these original reserves were never gazetted. When Douglas stepped down from office in 1864 one of the first acts of the new administration was to send out John Carmichael Haynes to cut back the reserve lands.

As white settlement increased, land became more valuable. Fences were erected and a hunting-gathering people were denied access to traditional food sources. While white homesteaders were allowed to pre-empt 160 acres Indians were allotted much less. Members of the Osoyoos Band at Inkameep believe that they were tricked out of land in 1875 when the crown granted approximately four thousand acres to J.C. Haynes at Osoyoos as a result of "a settler's bad faith and a clerk's error."[20] This decision returned to haunt governments in the 1990s. Finally, having refused two offers of compensation, on November 27, 1997 seventy-five percent of the Osoyoos Band voted to accept $11.7 million, one third to be paid by the provincial government and two thirds by the federal government.[21] Another example of First Nations land being alienated through questionable means is the transfer of land at the north end of Kalamalka Lake to John Kennedy in 1908.[22] Land was "cut off" from some reserves by the McKenna-McBride Commission (1913-1916) on the excuse that the land was not being used by the Native owners. Compensation for these cut-off lands was finally won in the 1980s.

Difficult as the land question was, the matter of water was even more vexing. From the 1890s, when fruit growing became a viable industry, great irrigation systems were required. Suddenly water resources that had been used without concern for centuries were granted by licence to orchard-development and irrigation companies or to individual white settlers. Duane Thomson writes that in 1911 Paul Terbasket, who had fifty acres under cultivation including an orchard in the Lower Similkameen, was denied a water record. The record was granted instead to the Similkameen Fruitlands Company. When Terbasket tried to save his crops with the water he had used all his life he was jailed.[23]

Robert L. de Pfyffer writes of an altercation over water at Westbank: "Not long after the inquiry (Ditchburn, 1917), the wife of Westbank's Chief Tomat, "High Tone" Mary, took an axe and chopped up David Gellatly's irrigation flume. For this action Gellatly had Mary jailed in Kelowna."[24]

The period during and following the influx of European settlers was a bitter one for the First Nations people. Not having the right to vote they could not influence decisions made by provincial and federal agents regarding their welfare. Dissatisfaction resulted in the gathering of Shuswap and Okanagan chiefs at the head of Okanagan Lake in June 1877. Many settlers feared an Indian uprising. Indeed there is evidence that the young Natives favoured war but were restrained by their Elders. The nascent confederacy was undermined and violence averted when several influential chiefs were persuaded to withdraw from any militant action.[25]

Even during difficult times, however, relationships between Natives and non-Natives were often amicable and a source of mutual enjoyment and economic advantage. Each year while hops were being grown on the Coldstream Ranch a colourful band of Nez Perce Indians, accompanied by their Roman Catholic priest, rode north from their Washington reserve to work on the harvest. Below we have a story about one of these annual visits.

Nez Perce Indians at the Coldstream Ranch.
Vernon Museum 911

The Nez Perce Indians[26]

by E.V. de Lautour

The history of the Nez Perce Indians travelling from Nespelem on the Columbia River in Washington to the Coldstream Ranch at Vernon for the seasonal work of "hop-picking" is interesting in itself to those who remember seeing them as they passed up and down the Valley...These fine, clean, well-dressed people certainly knew how to pick hops. For a number of years they had done this work in Southern Washington. We found all this out as the years went by.

At first they were very uncommunicative and pretended they could not talk English. You would ask a question in English and the Chief would say, "Halo Kumtuks Boston-man wau-wau hyas Kloshe mika wau-wau Chinook." They talked to the Shuswaps, Nicolas, Thompsons and the Coast Indians in the same jargon, though they used "the Moses" talk to the local Okanagans. Chinook was quite OK for us, as almost everyone used it more or less in those days, even the Chinamen [sic]...

[NOTE: hop picking generally started during the first week of September.]

About 1904 I made the trip down to the Columbia by saddle horse, via Omak Lake and thence to Nespelem. I made a deal with one of their important men—by name, Charlie Wilpoken (sounded softly)—to meet them at the Boundary and bond them through and to arrange an escort from Osoyoos to Vernon.

Before this was done we had made arrangements with Ottawa to allow these workers to come into Canada. Ottawa's main provision was that their horses were to be counted at the line and that we put up a bond to guarantee the same number would be returned on their leaving Canada. We saw to it that this was done. It may be said here that they showed a fine business streak re these horses. There would be a number of splendid saddle horses well broken and trained; these could be sold for what was then good money at around forty-five to one hundred dollars each according to their customers. Then enough five and ten dollar cayuses were picked up from the Blacktown Indians to keep their official and bonded number intact for their return to the South.

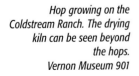

Hop growing on the Coldstream Ranch. The drying kiln can be seen beyond the hops.
Vernon Museum 901

The number of pickers varied in different years, but would average about one hundred. Wilpoken was always in charge of details and received one dollar per head for selecting them, besides an honorary bonus for his supervision of his flock. His wife and young daughter between them would also make about three dollars a day picking.

What might almost be called a cavalcade, particularly from Osoyoos north, was always well-organized. There were mostly saddle horses and a few hacks, as these people kept well together and allowed no stragglers in passing though the little settlements of Peachland, Kelowna or Penticton. If supplies were needed a few persons were selected to buy for the camp as a whole. When putting up camp the teepees were always lined up like army tents. When camped they had a regular guard in charge. They also brought a few young men as

hunters. For these last we were able to get a "visitors' permit" to shoot game in BC...

There were a few excellent pickers from the head of the Lake. However, though no local pickers were ever refused work, they were not encouraged to apply, mainly because they knew too many people locally and many liked to visit rather than work. Those from a distance, like Nicola or Lillooet, came to work and make a stake towards the forth-coming winter. Those from Nespelem definitely came for several reasons. They "Hyiu tikki King George illahie." They were "skookum tum-tum" about "King George men" whom they considered an honest people. The old leaders considered "Boston-man hyiu cultas" because he had not played the game after these unconquered people had made a treaty with some general who evidently had no power or ability and whose lies had never, even now, been forgiven...

Getting these people up to Vernon sometimes caused a funny situation. For instance, on one occasion it was necessary to send an inexperienced man to the Boundary to check them in. The young man knew little of trails, nor could he talk Chinook. I think the young braves had lots of fun at his expense. He was a very nice chap, but very, very helpless. At Penticton the Indians put most of their women and children on the boat and the men rode over the hills, taking with them the spare horses, riding to Kelowna on much the same trail that the West Kootenay Power and Light line covers now. Well! the young man slept in the Penticton Hotel and when morning came found he had NO Indians. The boat was gone. It had left about 6 or 6.30 a.m. The Indians had entirely disappeared. He was very distracted. Where

Kloochman's Canoe Race at Enderby, May 24, 1908. (Kloochman is Chinook jargon for wife or woman.) The women, from the Spallumcheen Band of the Shuswap Indians, are paddling traditional cottonwood dugout canoes. Enderby Museum #220

were they all? Someone told him that about daylight the Indians had taken off over the range east of the townsite. "Oh dear, oh dear! The poor fellows will be lost!" The young man got really wild about this time and lit out over the hills trying to track them. He then got lost in the timber around Chute Lake or thereabouts. However, he struggled on until he "found" himself. We could never get the full details of how he actually got back to Vernon. All I ever knew was that the Indians were in camp and settled down ready for work several days before their "escort" turned up!...

At the Fall Fair in Vernon these Nez Perce Indians put on quite a display. Men, women and children were all in regalia. Everything was done to entertain the whites, dancing, a pow-wow, etc. They picked up some money, too, with horses entered in some of the races. One year they brought up a race horse which was good, but they had no jockey whose weight would allow him to ride according to the Race Committee rules. They finally found a man who could almost make the weight, without the saddle. After a lot of wrangling, it was agreed that he should ride bareback. He just put a light cloth and surcingle on the horse. The race started—the horses were bunched at the half-way—then the Indian horse simply flew through them into the lead and was at the finish, lengths and lengths ahead of the field.

What amused me was the Indians and the bookies. Our friends took no chances on that score. They had plenty of money, so had bet quite heavily and had been given "long odds," as no bookie could imagine a horse winning with a bareback rider. So as soon as the horse got in front, a couple of big husky young braves were posted at each of the bookies' (two offices) front and back exits and all the other exits to the track and grandstand. These men stayed at their points of observation until all bets were fully paid. It was a day the bookies never forgot.

These Indians always had money, possibly some sort of Treaty money, as they always had a number of twenty-dollar gold pieces each, their own and those of their relatives and friends who had not come with them to BC. This money was brought up for the purpose of getting Hudson's Bay blankets and other woollen goods in Canada that, at that time, were too costly in their own country, even, perhaps, not procurable.

After picking-time and the "pay off," with their earnings and their gold, they spent several thousand dollars at the Vernon Hudson's Bay store, all on good materials. After their first year or two, Charlie Simms, the manager in Vernon, used to get blankets and stroud by the bale, ordered from Glasgow by boat via Victoria. He would take the order before the Indians went home, for delivery the next season. Charlie knew they wanted good material and that none could be too high class for these cash customers. And we must not forget that Charlie could also tell all kinds of stories in Chinook to keep his customers in a good humour, as he well knew that an Indian who was "skookum tum-tum" was a good spender.

I think hop-picking ceased in Vernon after 1912. That was the last year that I made the Nespelem trip...

(*OHS*, 1950)

A glossary of some of the Chinook terms used:

Kloochman—Female. Nothing to do with the term "Squawman."
Stroud—After the British manufacturing town of that name, and a trade name for heavy, strong woollen material.
Hyas Kloshe—*klosh* being good, *hyas* being big, combined could be better.
Hyiu—Much, great, many.
Tikki—Thing you like or want.
Skookum—Big, strong, good, etc.
Tum-tum—Think.
King George—British.

King George Man—Canadian or Englishman.
Boston Man—Yankee or American in general.
Illahie—Town, home or land.
Cultas—Bad. Generally no good.
Mika—You.
Nika—Me or I.
Yaka—They.
Kumtuks—Understand.
Wau-wau—Talk.

Efforts on behalf of the First Nations

Maria Brent in her article "The Indians of the Okanagan Valley" writes:

> The Indians never had a chance to come back. The invasion of their country by the whites not only disrupted their usual mode of living and crumpled up and destroyed their old-established customs and usages which had endured for centuries, but it deprived them of their country as well. They were soon exiled to the reservations. The Salish Indian of the Okanagan Valley today is an expatriate, a man without a country, although still dwelling in the land of his forefathers. It will be many years yet before these people fully recover from the shock of this double catastrophe.
>
> The immediate hope for them lies in the education of the children.[27]
> (*OHS*, 1935)

When the missionaries established schools many forward-looking whites hoped that, in them, the people of the First Nations would acquire access to the best that European culture had to offer as well as find a means for defending themselves against the worst effects of white greed and indifference. When the federal government took responsibility for Indian education it chose to administer it through the offices of the missionary church that was dominant in each region. In the Okanagan this was the Roman Catholic Church. This practice continued at least until 1951 when legislation was passed and financial arrangements made with the provincial government to assume responsibility for educating First Nations children who wished to attend local public schools.

The attitudes of nineteenth-century philanthropists were informed by the cultural Darwinism of their day. Missionaries of all denominations, in their anxiety to help their pupils adapt to the new reality, believed that the sooner they destroyed the old ways the quicker their aims would be accomplished. The ultimate expression of this view was the residential school system under which children of a tender age were taken from their parents, punished for speaking the only language they knew and trained to be little whites. Not only were the children cut off from their cultural roots but they were deprived of family life and the lessons they could have learned about parenting. Only now do First Nations people begin to recover from the deficiencies and even cruelties of this system.

During the period we are discussing there were a few non-Natives ready to assist a band to fight injustice, men such as James Halbold Christie, who arrived in Armstrong in 1907.[28] Christie advised Natives of the North Okanagan on making legal protests against outrageous decisions by bureaucrats. He sent telegrams and wrote letters and articles in the face of human greed, official indifference and political interference.

During the 1930s another individual was labouring on behalf of the Indians in the South Okanagan, Anthony Walsh, the teacher for ten years at the one-room school at Inkameep. Walsh believed fervently that if First Nations children were to develop self-respect they must learn to appreciate their own cultural heritage. This idea is taken for granted today, but during the 1930s it was radical indeed. Walsh taught through the visual and performing arts. His work was supported by the Society for the Revival of Indian Arts and Crafts of which Albert and Daisy Millar of Oliver were the local leaders.

In 1942 Anthony Walsh left Inkameep to join the Legion War Services. The society then turned its attention to preparing and circulating widely a brief to the prime minister of Canada entitled "Native Canadians—A Plan for the Rehabilitation of Indians." This action resulted eventually in the opening of the Indian Act.

In an editorial which appeared in *Saturday Night* September 23, 1944, it was stated:

> It seems odd that the most intelligent and understanding suggestions for the modernization of Canada's policy towards the Indians of the Dominion should have come from a little community in British Columbia [i.e. Oliver]. But such is the case.
>
> The Brief of the Okanagan Society shows how Canada has allowed her Indian policy to lag unchanged in a fast moving world, and how much ashamed of it we shall have to feel if we do not bring it up to date soon.[29]

The Native Renaissance

In the early 1930s the population of First Nations bands throughout BC began to increase. By the 1960s Natives were beginning to express a new confidence in themselves, an awareness of their needs and a determination to have a say in their own affairs. In 1979 the Okanagan Tribal Educational Committee launched its Okanagan Indian

Revival of Indian dancing at a pow-wow at Ashnola, 1995. Webber

Curriculum Project whereby social studies units were prepared which presented Okanagan history from the Native point of view. Resource guides, video tapes and a 16-millimetre film were prepared by band members. Two source books were published: for elementary use Jeannette Armstrong's *Enwhisteetkwa*, and for senior students *Okanagan Sources*, edited by J. Webber and the En'Owkin Centre.[30]

In 1990 a committee that included both First Nations people and non-Native educators produced for the Secwepemc Cultural Educational Society in Kamloops a book entitled *Shuswap History: The First 100 Years of Contact*. This book is used in high school social studies courses throughout the Shuswap area.

It is plain that the Okanagan, Shuswap and Similkameen bands of today are taking responsibility for their own welfare. The Central Interior Tribal Council's study "Major Steps Towards Self-sufficiency" is bearing fruit economically, socially and educationally.

Sixty years ago Maria Houghton Brent wrote, "The immediate hope for [the Indians] lies in the education of the children." Would Mrs. Brent not be delighted with the Okanagan Indian Curriculum Project and the En'Owkin Centre at Penticton which houses the native publishing company Theytus Books, conducts upgrading courses for First Nations people and runs a two-year creative-writing school in conjunction with the University of British Columbia? And wouldn't she be amazed to find the young people so at home with computers!

3

The Fur Trade

The Brigade Trail

"The background to the entire picture is the Hudson's Bay Company. They had, to the sufficiency of their purpose, surveyed and tapped the area long before its natural development began."–Susan B. Allison.[1]

from The Significance of the Hudson's Bay Brigade Trail[2]
by Margaret A. Ormsby

It was the Americans who first discovered the suitability of the rolling and well-covered hills of the Okanagan Valley for transport and the transmission of goods. In the autumn of 1811, David Stuart, Astorian[3] and former Nor'Wester, with a few companions accompanied Thompson to the junction of the Okanagan and Columbia Rivers. From that point the Astorians started northward to travel to the Thompson River country where they wintered. In May, 1812, another Astorian, Alexander Ross, undertook a trading expedition to the same vicinity, and later in the same year David Stuart chose a site at Kamloops as a post for his company. This marked the end of American operations in the interior, for shortly afterwards the Nor'West Company purchased the rights and property of the Pacific Fur Company.

Meanwhile, the Canadian company had also built a post at Kamloops, and had sent John Stuart from Fort St. James to try to find a waterway connecting the two great rivers. He found that he had to travel by land between Kamloops and Okanagan Lake, but he advised his Company to use the Okanagan Valley route...In 1816 it was decided that New Caledonia as well as Thompson River should be supplied from the Columbia. This practice continued for the next five years, supplies being brought out from England to the Columbia River, transported up it to Fort Okanagan by boat, packed overland by horse-train to Kamloops and to Alexandria, where a place of deposit and storage was built in 1821, and then taken by boat to Fort St. James for distribution to the northern posts.

After the amalgamation of the Hudson's Bay Company and the North-West Company in

1821, the same route was used for two years, since the North-West Company had previously sent out to the Columbia a large shipment of goods and provisions...Governor George Simpson came out to spend a winter in the Columbia Department and apparently became imbued with the idea of again making use of a Pacific outlet for the New Caledonia furs... sufficiently encouraged by the reports he received to adopt it when he reorganized the whole transport system of the Pacific slope...Minutes of Council [Hudson's Bay Council] July 1825 ordered William Connolly to take out the New Caledonia returns to Fort Vancouver in the spring of 1826, and to obtain there the outfit for 1826. This decision marked the real institution of what is now referred to as the Hudson's Bay Brigade Trail.

Forts and Travel Routes of the Hudson's Bay Company 1821–1846

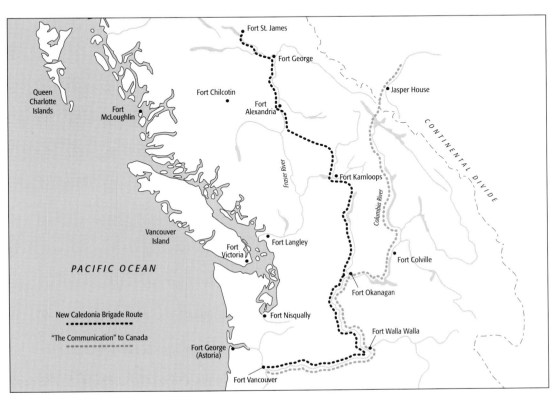

The depression through the trees left of centre was made by the brigades of some 300 pack animals that passed through this region twice a year between 1812 and 1847. Webber

After 1826, the overland trail through the Okanagan Valley was regularly and constantly used for a period of 20 years. Each winter the furs traded at the posts in the northern interior were brought to Fort St. James, the headquarters of New Caledonia, with dog sledges. As soon as the ice broke up, generally about April 20, boats loaded with cargoes of furs started from Stuart Lake to pick up the furs from Fort Fraser, Fort McLeod and Fort George. At Alexandria, the horse brigade started out for Fort Okanogan, sometimes accompanying and sometimes following the Thompson's River brigade, which was taking out the furs of the Kamloops district. There was a gen-

eral rendezvous of the Thompson, New Caledonia and Colvile traders at Fort Okanogan, and then a senior officer took charge of the united brigade for the boat run to Fort Vancouver. There were many dangers to be passed before that place was reached around

June 15. About a month was spent there collecting supplies, then the return trip to Fort Okanogan took 20 days. At Fort Okanogan the Colvile brigade branched off to the east, and the Thompson and New Caledonia outfits started overland. In all, it usually took two months to make the trip from Fort Vancouver to Fort St. James, the navigation of the upper Fraser from Alexandria to Fort St. James taking 20 days.

Some 200 to 300 horses comprised the brigades which travelled the long trail from Fort Okanogan to Fort Alexandria. "A beautiful sight was that horse brigade," a fur-trader once wrote. "With no broken hacks in the train, but every animal in his full beauty of form and color, and all so tractable!..." Most of the travel took place over the trail in summer, and the horses were turned out to winter at Alexandria or Kamloops. There was occasional travel in the winter, and in certain parts of the Valley traces can still be seen of both a winter and a summer trail.

David Douglas, the distinguished botanist, has left us a sketch book of maps of the trail as it was in 1833. Commencing at Fort Okanogan, it followed the eastern bank of Okanagan

River to the point where it crossed it just south of Osoyoos Lake. It then climbed the hills on the western side of Osoyoos Lake and proceeded northward through the hills until, after crossing Lambly (Trepanier) Creek, it came down close to the shore-line of Okanagan Lake. At the head of Okanagan Lake it turned west, crossed Salmon River, and reached the Thompson River where Monte Creek joins it. The trail then crossed the Thompson just above the junction with the North Thompson to Fort Kamloops, then recrossed the river to the southern side to climb the hills south of Kamloops Lake. At the foot of that lake it crossed to the northern side, then continued to Bonaparte River, travelling along it, Green Lake and Horse Lake to Lac La Hache. It next followed San Jose River, Williams Lake and Williams Lake Creek, and then went overland to reach the Fraser, following its eastern bank until Old Fort Alexandria was reached.

A sprinkling of snow helps to identify the fur-brigade trail through the Marron Valley west of Okanagan Lake. Webber

Over this long trail, each horse usually carried two "pieces" of 84 pounds each. With this heavy pack it could travel fairly comfortably 20 miles a day, but sometimes the stopping places were slightly further apart than that. One of the stopping places most frequented, and which we find marked on the fur-traders' maps, was that near the lone tree at Westbank.

The Valley was admirably adapted for travel by pack-train, since there was bunch-grass, water and soft ground. It was not, however, good fur-country, and most of the furs that were taken down it to Fort Okanogan came from the posts north of Alexandria...While the Okanagan brigade trail was still in use the Hudson's Bay Company permitted missionaries to travel with the outfits going to New Caledonia. In 1842, Father Demers, who had twice before visited the Valley, accompanied Chief Factor Peter Skene Ogden to the interior, and passed the winter in New Caledonia. The same year, Father DeSmet, the famous Jesuit missionary, travelled through the southern part of the Valley on his way from Fort Colvile to Fort Vancouver, and three years later, after he had been to Europe to obtain reinforcements, he accompanied Father Nobili over the brigade trail to New Caledonia. According to A.C. Anderson, with whom the priest spent the winter of 1845 at Alexandria, Father Nobili formed in 1846 "an establishment at the Taillis D'Epinettes on the Great Lake of Okinagan." Anderson says that while this house was located somewhere near the head of Okanagan Lake it was maintained only for three years. If it existed, and there is little reason to doubt Anderson's word, it was the first religious establishment in the southern interior of British Columbia. It was to be some 14 years before the Oblates made their appearance in the Valley, and when they planted a mission it was on the side of Okanagan Lake opposite the brigade trail, at the place called by the traders "L'Anse au Sable."

The drawing of the Oregon boundary line in 1846 caused the abandonment of the Okanagan brigade trail. A.C. Anderson had already undertaken exploratory missions to see if a trail could be located between Alexandria and Fort Langley on the lower Fraser. Finally in 1847, the last Hudson's Bay Company caravan passed through the Okanagan Valley, and the following year, the difficult Hope trail was opened through the Coquihalla Valley to Kamloops. The Fraser River route had at last been adopted...

Both the Nor'Westers and Hudson's Bay Company had failed to establish in the Okanagan a post around which settlement could develop. In fact, the very qualities which made the Valley suitable for a highway handicapped its settlement during the fur-trading days.

The Hudson's Bay Company was prepared when the Fraser River route had to be adopted. Had it never considered using it, and had it built posts between Fort Okanogan and Kamloops the Okanagan Valley might have been settled long before it was, and it is remotely possible that a different division of territory might have taken place in 1846.

(*OHS*, 1949)

Dr. Margaret Anchoretta Ormsby, author of the article printed above, is one of Canada's most outstanding historians. She was born near Quesnel but was brought at a tender age to the Okanagan where she grew up.

Her interest in history led to an academic career in that discipline. In 1964 she became head of the History Department at her alma mater, the University of British Columbia, a position she held until her retirement in 1974. Dr. Ormsby has won many honours including honorary doctorates from BC's first four universities, appointment to the Order of Canada, the Order of British Columbia and as Freeman of the City of Vernon and election as a Fellow of the Royal Society of Canada, president of the Canadian Historical Association and Life Member of the Okanagan Historical Society.

A number of the early *Annual Reports of the Okanagan Historical Society* were edited by Dr. Ormsby. She established the direction the *Reports* would take and she remained interested in each new edition until her death at her home in the Coldstream on November 2, 1996.

Among her numerous publications are the books *British Columbia: A History* (1958), *A Pioneer Gentlewoman in British Columbia: The Recollections of Susan Allison* (1976), and *Coldstream Nulli Secundus* (1990).

The Hudson's Bay Brigade Trail[4]

by F.M. Buckland

In the early morning, fires are lit and breakfast of dry salmon prepared and eaten. Next the horses are run in and roped. Then commences the tedious job of packing. They must be very careful and throw the diamond hitch just right, or the pack will become loosened and the horses will have sore backs. But these men are experts. They go through the same performance perhaps a hundred times in a season. When everything is loaded, merchandise or furs, camp-pots, blankets and all, they file away on the trail preceded by a couple of expert hunters, who go ahead to the next camping ground where there is good feed and water, to shoot, if possible, fresh meat for the next meal. First comes the Factor, or Chief Trader, dressed in his suit of broadcloth with white shirt and collar to his ears, wearing on his head the tall beaver hat of that day; for you see his position demands something a little different from the rest of the company. But he must have a hard time, poor fellow, riding under the trees with that stove-pipe hat. He carries with him his fire bag which contains his flint and steel, tinder box, touch-wood and tobacco. Our Hias Tyhee Trader must have a separate fire when in camp, and his tent must be the first to be erected. Salutes are fired upon his departure from, and on his return to the fort. All this ceremony is considered necessary as it has a good effect on the Indians and adds to his dignity in the eyes of those under him. But that hat! Father Morice says in his *History of Northern Interior of British Columbia*: "Proud indeed was the Indian who was fortunate enough to be presented with his cast-off hat. It would be worn on all occasions, and in warm weather he might be seen divested of everything but the hat."

Riding beside the Trader there might be a priest or missionary, and no doubt there were many arguments and debates to while away the hours of travel. Next comes the piper, for no H.B.C. Fur Brigade is complete without the bagpipes, and many a Strathspey has echoed back from the rocks and hills of the old Hudson's Bay Trail. After the piper comes a long line of pack horses with here and there a packer, while the rear is brought up by the families and their "iktis" of bedding and cooking utensils.

The day's journey usually started about 9:00 a.m. and lasted until 4:00 p.m., when all would make camp and the horses be turned out to grass...On the Westbank Reserve there stood a great fir tree, until a year or two ago, and under its sheltering boughs the old traders opened up their packs of trade goods to barter with the Indians who met them there, as they passed up and down the valley.

Kamloops was the great halfway house of the Interior. Here the horses that came up the Okanagan were turned out to rest and a fresh band was run in...When the brigade arrived back at Kamloops, loaded with the winter's catch of furs, the traders would turn those horses out and take a fresh band for the trip down the Okanagan Valley.

But the settlement of the boundary question changed the course of travel and from 1848 on the brigades from the north instead of descending to the Columbia took the route of the Fraser Valley to Fort Langley and for about ten years, until the influx of miners took place in 1858, the old Hudson's Bay Brigade Trail was in disuse.

(*OHS*, 1953)

Other Trails

Even before the Oregon Treaty was signed in 1846 the Hudson's Bay Company realized the importance of finding a new all-British route to the Pacific. Because the Fraser River was unsuitable for navigation between Alexandria and present-day Yale another route must be found through the formidable Coast Range. The original pathfinder through the morass of mountains was Alexander Caufield Anderson of the Hudson's Bay Company who, in 1846, made his way on foot from the Fraser up the Nicolum, Sumallo, Skagit, Snass and Tulameen Rivers to Kamloops.

In "The Proposed Cascade Wilderness," H.R. Hatfield writes of historic trails, remnants of which can be found in a very small area just north of Manning Park.[5] Excerpts from Hatfield's article, beginning with the explorations of A.C. Anderson, follow:

It was an epic trip, though for various reasons its results were not harvested for some fourteen years. It is worth noting here that Highway 3 follows [Anderson's] track from Hope to where it crosses the Snass at the top of the rhododendron flat. And from 1860 to 1949 when the highway was completed all the various trails between the Similkameen and Hope did the same. In discussing the Brigade Trail we will see how, if not why, it took a different way.

In the meantime let us join Anderson in his crossing. Third of June 1846:

"Set out at 3-1/4 A.M. and breakfasted at 6 among the rhododendrons. Set fire to the fallen timber to make a landmark and to improve horse pasture for possible future use. Set out again at 8:20 and reached summit at noon."

This was at the Punch Bowl where he estimated the snow as still ten feet deep:

"Our Indian assistants turn back here—We have no one who knows anything of the country beyond this point. The water must guide us..."

In 1848 the Kequeloos or Coldwater-Spuzzum Trail was tried but brigades made only three trips over this difficult route. Hatfield refers to the 1859 journal of Lieutenant H.S. Palmer, RE:

Palmer mentions that Manson Ridge is dangerous before the first of June or after the first of October due to its steepness and the heavy snowfall and then goes on:

"Mr. McLean of the Hudson's Bay Company, who crossed in 1857 or 1858, on the 16th of October had a very disastrous trip, and lost 60 or 70 horses in the snow. Traces of their deaths are still visible, and in riding over the mountain, and more particularly on its eastern slope, my horse frequently shied at the whitened bones of some of the poor animals, who had broken down in the sharp struggle with fatigue and hunger, and been left to perish where they lay..."

THE DEWDNEY TRAIL

In August 1860 Edgar Dewdney and Walter Moberly of C.P.R. location fame were given a contract to build a trail [from Hope] to Vermilion Forks (Princeton). It was built to the head of Snass Creek that year and on to Princeton the next. Several years later Dewdney completed it to Wild Horse Creek; the first trans-provincial highway...[It should be noted that Dewdney's contract was with the colonial government, not the Hudson's Bay Company.]

Dewdney was born in Devonshire in 1835. He came to what is now British Columbia in May 1859 and for the next ten years did engineering surveying and construction. After 1869 he held various important posts in the B.C. and Dominion Governments, retiring in 1897 as Lieutenant Governor of British Columbia. He died in Victoria in 1916...

THE HOPE TRAIL

The term "Hope Trail" came to be used to denote any of the various trails which spread out through the Interior settlements and by one way or another arrived at Hope, the point of arrival or departure for them all on the Coast side. However here we will use it more specifically to mean that diversion of the Dewdney which went by the Hope Pass and down the Skaist River to rejoin the Dewdney Trail at the Snass...

This diversion, located by Captain J.M. Grant, R.E. in 1861, was open for a longer season than the "Canyon Trail" section of the Dewdney by the Snass and eventually became the usual route of the Hope Trail. The writer rode over it in 1924 and it was still the common route for pedestrian or equestrian travel.

(*OHS*, 1980)

The Dewdney Trail Contract.

...Up the Snass and the canyon of its west fork was built in 1860 the Hope-to-Similkameen Mule Road, located by the Royal Engineers and built under contract for the Colony of British Columbia. This was certainly one of the first Public Works contracts made on behalf of the government. The price was seventy-six pounds sterling per mile to be paid partly in cash and partly in British Columbia bonds bearing interest at six per cent. The Mule Road was to commence at a point on the Hudson's Bay Company's Brigade Trail about four miles from Hope and terminate at a point on the Similkameen River...The road was to be not less than four feet wide with the centre foot and a half to be smooth and hard.[6]
(*OHS*, 1979)

Harley R. Hatfield came to the Shuswap in 1907 when his father, A. Seaman Hatfield, decided to leave Nova Scotia and seek his fortune in the west. In the spring of 1910 the family moved to Kaleden in the South Okanagan. There Harley grew up. He qualified as a civil engineer at UBC and spent most of his working life with the family firm Interior Contracting Company.

Harley devoted twenty years of his retirement to tracing historic trails such as the Fur Brigade Trail and those in the Cascade Wilderness. Not only did he research the trails in the Provincial, Federal and Hudson's Bay Company Archives, but also he has thoroughly explored the relevant areas on foot and horseback. For this work Mr. Hatfield was honoured with an award from the Heritage Canada Foundation February 16, 1981. In this work Mr. Hatfield has had the support of both the Okanagan Historical Society and the Okanagan Similkameen Park Society and of men like the late Victor Wilson. It has been a disappointment to those interested in our heritage that successive provincial governments have not seen fit to protect more rigorously this relatively small area from the development that will in time obliterate these historic trails.

The first Hudson's Bay Company post in the Similkameen stood near the clump of trees seen on the other side of the pond which is known today as "Gint's Pond." The spring that fed the pond assured that water was available for horses all winter. Webber

New Hudson's Bay Company Posts Established

Finding new routes to tidewater was not the only challenge faced by the Hudson's Bay Company. After the boundary settlement, trading posts had to be moved into British territory. However, this did not happen immediately as the company sought and finally obtained compensation from the American government for the surrender of its posts.[7]

In 1860, Francois Deschiquette was ordered to move the Fort Okanagan operation to the Similkameen. The trader chose a location beside the pond that is now in the centre of the Cawston community–"Gint's Pond."

The post was generally referred to as Similkameen although sometimes the local Indian name, Keremeos, was used. Deschiquette set about building a simple structure to serve as living quarters and storehouse and began to conduct the company's business. In September, Edward Huggins arrived with a band of horses and mules which he had driven from Fort Nisqually, the Hudson's Bay Company centre for animal husbandry, and delivered them to Deschiquette. Similkameen was to prove an ideal location for wintering and rearing stock...

Judge William C. Brown...quotes Robert Stevenson as writing:

"Franswa was a short, stout French half breed, and not any more than thirty years of age in 1860 when I first saw him at Old Fort Okanagan...Yes, he was educated some. Could read and write and was a pretty good bookkeeper..."[8]
(*OHS*, 1993)

Not everyone in the Company agreed with the location of the Similkameen post nor with the appointment of Francois Deschiquette to manage the affairs of the Company in an era of change. Chief Factor Alexander Grant Dallas thought that the new post should be at the Forks (Princeton). Dallas wondered, too, if Deschiquette would have the poise to deal with the white miners who were arriving. Before October 1862 the trader was dead, having been shot by Frank Peto in a quarrel.

Replacing Deschiquette was not an easy task. The dilapidated state of the buildings was given as one reason for the reluctance of a qualified man to take on the post. However, by June 20, 1863 a man had been found, Roderick McLean. McLean's experience as an axeman with the Boundary Commission surveyors must have stood him in good stead when it came to rebuilding the post...

Roderick McLean, in addition to seeing to lands, fences and buildings, was the supervisor of a ranch with herds of horned cattle and horses. When a post in the southern interior required a pack train, it was his responsibility to prepare and dispatch needed animals, charging expenses up to the post concerned. He was expected to get out into the surrounding country to buy furs from the Indians. He oversaw the trade with white settlers. If Company mail arrived, he was expected immediately to find a reliable messenger to carry packages destined for places other than Similkameen in the appropriate direction. [In addition, there were subposts to supervise. Bernard Lequime tells us that John McDougall ran such a post in 1861 at Okanagan Mission "under Chief Factor McLean who was then at Keremeos." Then, between 1867 and 1872, a Hudson's Bay Company trading post, managed by Theodore Kruger but under the supervision of Similkameen, operated in Osoyoos.]

Shrewdness in trading, energy and practical knowledge in farming and building, and the keeping of careful records were demands on the post manager. McLean did not always measure up with respect to record keeping.

In 1864 the Company decided to acquire good farming land nearer the Dewdney Trail and there to carry on its trading and agriculture while retaining the original property for a stock farm. Then, in October 1867 John Tait succeeded McLean as Post Manager. In spite of the improvements made by Tait, we find the Company preparing to close Similkameen during the outfit 1871–72.[9]

(*OHS*, 1993)

Similkameen was proving a poor place to do business. All the unsold livestock and other stock was transferred to Thompson's River and John Tait was appointed officer of that post. The 1,140 acres of land owned by the Company was rented to W.H. Lowe. Today a heritage park, which contains the grist mill built by Barrington Price, lies just to the west of that property.

Laurie Land in her article "A Hudson's Bay Post at Keremeos" outlines some of the activities at the Keremeos post:

Shimilkameen [sic] could not be supported by the fur trade alone...A major portion of the pre-empted land was used for raising livestock for the Company. The operations of the H.B.C., including the fur trade, were heavily dependent on good pack animals. Richter was put in charge of the breeding program. Horses were needed at all forts in order to transport furs and supplies along the trails. Cross-breeding horses and asses must have been practised since McLean used mules to travel to Fort Shepherd. (On one trip he used fifty mules.) These animals were hardy and able to endure considerable adversity, which meant they would be very useful on mountain trails and in bad weather conditions.

Cattle and oxen were also important assets to the H.B.C. The post supplied beef for barter with local Indians and meat and milk to travellers...Oxen were used for another of the Shimilkameen's main functions—horticulture. These animals would be used to plow the fields for the raising of ground crops. Potatoes and other vegetables were grown for trade with the Indians.[10]

(*OHS*, 1981)

The operations of the Hudson's Bay Company underwent a profound change in the 1850s and 1860s. Not only did the establishment of the 49th Parallel as the border affect the manner in which business was carried on, but also the discovery of gold at Rock Creek in 1860 and at Blackfoot, six miles north of Princeton, in 1861 brought an influx of miners into the region. These were soon followed by settlers. The posts, instead of being limited to bartering with First Nations people for furs, became important retail outlets selling hardware, food supplies and liquor to the growing European population. Settlers became customers for Hudson's Bay Company livestock. New skills were required in post managers to accommodate these changes.

Perhaps even more upsetting to Company management was the fact that, from 1858 on, the Company had to recognize a civil authority in the area of its activities. Gone forever were the days when the Company conducted its business, kept law and order and administered justice as it affected its servants without being answerable to anyone.

Looking back from a vantage point in the late twentieth century we tend to see the fur traders as the explorers of our land. They established and recorded paths of communication and commerce, following for the most part routes used by the First Nations people for centuries. The soundness of the fur traders' choices is confirmed when we see how often modern roads and railways follow the old trails.

It was not the policy of the fur companies to encourage settlers on the land, a policy which led to the loss of the Washington and Oregon territories. Too late the Hudson's Bay Company learned that land is held by settlers, not traders. Had the company encouraged Europeans to take up homesteads in the territories they controlled, the International Boundary might very well have been established south of the 49th Parallel.

4

The Colonial Era

The International Boundary

In 1845 the threat of an impending Anglo-American war hung over the Pacific North-west...Few or none would concede anything to the British when the latter argued that both present possession and past history entitled Britain to the lands to the north of the Columbia River, and that the long overdue boundary should leave the 49th parallel of latitude close to today's [City of] Trail, and follow the Columbia in its south-westerly course to the Pacific. The least that the Americans would settle for was the 49th parallel all the way to the sea. The more militant, seeking all the land up to Russian America, shouted "Fifty-four Forty or Fight."

When, early in 1846, the belligerent Polk became President of the United States, everybody knew that a showdown on the Oregon boundary was imminent...

But the anticipated war was never fought. The British government, at the urging of Lord Aberdeen, its pacifist Foreign Secretary, backed down and, on 15 June 1846, the Treaty of Washington was signed, conceding to the Americans the 49th parallel as their boundary all the way from the Rockies to the Pacific. True, the Americans had to agree that after the boundary line reached the sea it would dip southwards and pass through the Strait of Juan de Fuca, leaving Vancouver Island entirely British[1]...[The Lord Aberdeen mentioned here was the 4th Earl, grandfather of the 7th Earl who purchased the Coldstream Ranch.]

The above quotation is from *British Columbia Chronicle* by Dr. G.P.V. and Helen B. Akrigg. Leonard Norris, writing on the same subject in his article "The Boundary Line," says: "It is well also to bear in mind that when the old election cry of 'Fifty-four Forty or Fight' threw the people of the United States into a fever of excitement and war was imminent, it was BC (and the Okanagan Valley) that was at stake."[2]

In 1818 the 49th Parallel had been adopted as the boundary line between British and American territory from the Lake of the Woods to the Rocky Mountains. At that time the Americans were willing to adopt it as the boundary through to the Pacific, but the English refused. For twenty-eight years this disputed territory was subject

Leonard Norris, the founder of the Okanagan Historical Society, was born on a farm near Brampton, Ontario in 1865. He moved to Langley with his family as a boy of nine and first saw the Okanagan in 1882 when he was seventeen. He worked on ranches in the Lumby area and, in 1887, pre-empted land near Round Lake. Shortly afterwards he reluctantly accepted the position of provincial police constable at Lansdowne. In 1890 he became collector of the provincial revenue tax and in 1893 he began his thirty-three years of service as government agent at Vernon. In her tribute to Leonard Norris after his death in 1945, Margaret Ormsby writes: "The spirit that permeates all [Leonard Norris's] writings reflects something of the quality of the man himself—for he reveals his kindly feeling towards his fellow men, his high moral standards, his patience with and amusement at human foibles, and his great sincerity."[3]

In his articles, Norris always sought to place Okanagan history within the larger context of what was happening beyond the confines of the Valley. One wonders at the accomplishments of Norris, Buckland and other early recorders of Okanagan history when we stop to realize that they wrote before there were any public libraries in the area. Travel to places like the Provincial Archives was more difficult than today and long-distance telephone expensive and not always satisfactory.

to a treaty signed October 20, 1818 which allowed each of the contestants "occupancy without sovereignty." By 1843 the Hudson's Bay Company deemed it wise to establish Fort Victoria on Vancouver Island and in 1849 the Company headquarters were transferred from Fort Vancouver to Victoria and James Douglas was put in charge.

On January 13, 1849 Vancouver Island became a crown colony and by 1851 James Douglas became governor of the Colony of Vancouver Island in addition to his being chief factor for the Hudson's Bay Company. When the mainland became the Crown Colony of British Columbia in 1858 with New Westminster as capital, James Douglas became governor of both colonies on the condition he sever his ties with the Hudson's Bay Company. He held this double governorship until his retirement early in 1864. In 1866 the colonies united, taking the name of the mainland colony. New Westminster was the first capital after the union, but in 1868 the capital was moved to Victoria.

The most noticeable effect of the Treaty of Washington in the Interior of the province was the cessation of the annual fur brigades. The last year of the great cavalcade was 1847. Life in the South Okanagan came to a standstill until the British and American Boundary Commissions began their task of surveying and marking the 49th Parallel in the late 1850s, a time which coincides with news that gold was to be found in the streams of the southern Interior. Norris writes:

> It was while Cox was at Rock Creek that the International Boundary Line was marked on the ground along the 49th parallel by the two Commissions, one American and the other English. He reports: "I also perceive that the English Commissioners have built their monuments more than 200 yards south of those built by their American companions." And again on April 27th, 1861: "The American Boundary Commission passed through here (Rock Creek) yesterday en route to Osoyoos to rectify some error connected with the parallel by them committed, I presume. The English Commission has proceeded eastward." Instructions were sent to Cox and Haynes to see to it that the monuments erected along the Boundary Line were not interfered with. Haynes in his letters calls them "obelisks."[4]
>
> (*OHS*, 1935)

With the boundary marked everyone knew just where he was whether in British territory or American.

Gold, Gold Commissioners and Customs

The Hudson's Bay Company was quite aware of the placer gold to be found in the rivers of BC. Before the great rush they were buying gold discreetly from Indians who lived along the Fraser. However, by 1858 the secret was out and miners who had worked the California placer deposits were beginning to look for new fields. Faced with this influx of foreigners James Douglas realized that unless civil law under the Union Jack was established, the lands north of the 49th Parallel would be lost to the empire just as those to the south had been. Hence the formation of the Crown Colony of British Columbia with a police force and a civil government that insisted the miners buy licences.

Under the colonial government, policing was in the hands of the able Chartres Brew. Matthew Baillie Begbie was chief justice. However, government administration throughout the colony was in the hands of the gold commissioners who collected licence fees, served as magistrates, dealt with land pre-emptions and sent reports to the governor concerning the quality of land, the climate, condition of trails, etc. W.G. Cox was made assistant gold commissioner in 1860 and assigned to Rock Creek where a number of miners were already at work after the discovery of gold the previous October by the Canadian Adam Bream.

W.G. Cox and His Times[5]

by Leonard Norris

Governor Douglas visited Rock Creek in 1860. He was at Cayoosh (Lillooet) on the 7th September. From there he travelled by canoe to Lytton, which he reached on the 11th; Keremeos on the 21st, Osoyoos on the 24th, and Rock Creek on the 25th, where he addressed a meeting of the miners on the following day. On the return journey to Victoria he reached Hope on the 5th October...

From October 1860 on, Cox's letters give us a pretty good insight into what was going on in the Rock Creek camp, but before that date we have to depend on what can be picked up from old newspaper files...

A letter appeared in the *Portland Advertiser* on the 30th April, 1861, which reads in part as follows:

"Rock Creek, British Columbia,
April 8th, 1861.

Editor, *Advertiser*,

Rock Creek or Tenasket City for its age is quite a beautiful little place. It contains twenty houses. Some are occupied by merchants and some by saloons and saloon keepers. Also a Court House which was built last month for the Government. The expenses of it when the building is completely finished will not be less than $2,500..."

The following passage is taken from Cox's letter to the Colonial Secretary at New Westminster, W.A.G. Good, dated 7th October, 1860: "I have spoken to several parties respecting the practicability of navigating the Similkameen from Vermilion Forks to a certain point, but all consider it impossible except at high water. Two days after His Excellency left this place I witnessed the washing out of Mr. Bream's sluices (one day's work) when $65 was taken out. I am sure His Excellency will regret to learn that this man's savings are all

Osoyoos Customs House. In 1865 the 1861 customs house was moved from the head of Osoyoos Lake to a location near Osoyoos's present-day Sun Bowl Arena. There it was enlarged to serve as government office, living quarters and jail. In the picture: second from left Colonel Houghton, then J.C. Haynes, Emily Haynes, and an Indian who became Chief Francis. This building burned to the ground in April 1878. BCARS A-00626

swallowed up at the gambling table, the owner of which nuisance I have notified to quit in ten days. The inhabitants here are exceedingly peaceful and well ordered, and I trust this good feeling will not be interrupted."

It was thus the gambling element, the men who lived off the miners, were dealt with at Rock Creek...

In 1861 Cox staked out the Reserve at the head of Okanagan Lake...On the 10th August, 1865, J.C. Haynes, who succeeded Cox as Gold Commissioner, was given instructions to alter the boundaries as the Reserve was considered to be unnecessarily large. What alterations were then made we do not know, but they must have been considerable because in 1868 Thomas Greenhow, C. O'Keefe and W. Coulter were given pre-emptions of land which was formerly within the Reserve, staked as a Government Reserve but afterwards usually referred to as the Indian Reserve.

The sketch plan Cox made of the Reserve is dated June 30th, but his report is dated July 4th. He was then back at Rock Creek and, on the same day he reported the staking of the Reserve, he also reported the killing of a white man by an Indian. The Indian's name was Charley or Saul, and his victim's name was Pierre Cherbart. The crime was committed on June 13th. The inquest was held the 19th and the same afternoon a party of miners rode over to the "Traverse" [the ford at the south end of Osoyoos Lake in American territory] where the Indian was and the next morning he was lynched. In Cox's report he said that there had not been "an assault or outrage" committed by either white men or Indians in that part of the country from the previous September to that date, which speaks well for both the miners and the Indians—but he should have touched wood...

On August 14th he had to report that a young Englishman, a supposed deserter from the Navy, had been caught robbing sluice boxes. After the culprit was found guilty he was given five minutes to prepare and ten minutes within which to leave the camp, and Cox—the Gold Commissioner and Magistrate—adds: "We all assisted in the ceremony of drumming out." A truly patriarchal method of administering justice.

(*OHS*, 1935)

The house built on the east side of Osoyoos Lake for John Carmichael Haynes between 1878 and 1882 that served as residence and government office. Later owners covered the log walls with stucco. Recent owners were Doug and Dorothy Fraser.
Webber

The importations of livestock on which duty was paid during the years 1861 and 1862 while Cariboo [placer mining] was at its height are given below. The cattle for Cariboo were driven over the Hudson's Bay Company trail on the west side of Okanagan Lake.

	Horses	Cattle	Mules	Sheep
Jan.1 to Oct. 19, 1861	356	625	92	–
Oct. 19 to April 30, 1862	172	250	–	–
May	963	681	203	–
June	1,065	488	135	–
July	461	1,532	238	400
August	141	163	82	646
September	172	958	6	–
October	54	53	–	325
November	–	67	19	–
December	12	–	3	–
	3,396	4,817	778	1,371

Customs business was to prove more lasting than mining both at Rock Creek and farther east at Boundary Creek. However, during the less than two years when gold fever was at its height and W.G. Cox was gold commissioner in the Rock Creek office, Norris tells us:

> In November 1860, when the final clean-up was made, it was ascertained that $83,000 in gold had been taken out of the creek by twenty individual miners and small companies of miners...
>
> On November 20, 1860, Cox reported that "five sections of agricultural land have been pre-empted and partly plowed..." On April 14, 1861 he reported that five persons had recorded land with him, viz., Father Richards, J.C. Larimie, W.G. Cox, Gideon Pion and J.C. Haynes...
>
> The prices of provisions in the camp in 1860 were: Flour, 20c per pound; bacon, 50c; lard, 50c; sugar, 40c; coffee, 50c; beans, 50c; onions, 25c; potatoes, 22c; dried apricots, 40c; rice, 50c; tea, $1.25; candles, $1; and butter, none. Labourers were paid $4 a day without board.[6]
>
> (*OHS*, 1935)

Once the border had been surveyed and marked, customs houses were established in both Keremeos and Osoyoos. In fact Cox's first responsibility in the area had been as customs officer at Keremeos. When the gold rush made it necessary for him to be at Rock Creek, John Carmichael Haynes was appointed his assistant and stationed at Keremeos. Then in September 1861 Haynes was moved to the newly built customs house at the head of Osoyoos Lake.

The Colonial Government expected customs ports to pay their own way through their collections and it could be tough with its servants as the following story shows.

> On the 16th April, 1861, J.C. Haynes reported to the Government that he had seized sixteen horses and goods at Osoyoos. It appears this pack train came into BC following the route usually travelled from Osoyoos to the foot of Okanagan Lake where the seizure was made. They should have stopped and reported at Osoyoos, but this they failed to do. What excuse they had or what explanation they gave for failing to do so is not recorded...
>
> The goods consisted of liquors, tobaccos, cigars, candles, etc., and the total value must have amounted to several thousand dollars, and Haynes seized everything, including the horses and saddles, leaving the men without food and on foot. This was a pretty severe

Unveiling cairn placed to mark the site of the 1861 Osoyoos Customs House. Attending the ceremony July 7, 1957 were four of the offspring of J.C. Haynes and his wife Emily. From left to right they are: Val Haynes, Irene Parkinson, Hester White and Will Haynes. BCARS C-00488

measure to take. The infliction of twice or three times the ordinary duty would have been enough in the circumstances, at least one would think so.

When the matter was brought to the attention of W.G. Cox, who was Haynes' superior, he allowed each man to take a horse and saddle and he allowed them one pack horse with enough food to take them through to Cariboo, but kept the rest of the horses and goods. When the reports reached Governor Douglas he wrote highly complimenting Haynes for his vigorous enforcement of the law, and informed Cox that he (Cox) would have to pay for the food and horses he gave the men.[7]

(*OHS*, 1935)

John Carmichael Haynes, carrying a letter of introduction to Chartres Brew and testimonial letters from the mayor and chief magistrate of the city of Cork, arrived in Victoria from his native Ireland on Christmas Day 1858. By the fall of 1859 he was chief constable at Yale. Then he was made deputy customs officer at Keremeos and later at Osoyoos. Towards the end of 1861, when Cox was moved to Kamloops, Haynes became gold commissioner.

Haynes remained in Osoyoos for the rest of his life, leaving only to attend to official business as when he travelled to Wild Horse Creek in the East Kootenay to establish law and order and collect mining fees owed the government. Offices that he held included stipendiary magistrate, county court judge, and Member of the Legislative Assembly. His administrative responsibilities extended from the border to Spallumcheen and from the Coast Mountains to the East Kootenay.

In addition to his official duties Haynes became the owner of a large herd of cattle. He was in an ideal position to acquire and increase his herd, often buying cheaply animals that by the time they had reached the customs port appeared too weak to finish the long drive to the goldfields. There is evidence too that Haynes improved his herd by buying well-bred cattle from the Hudson's Bay Company.[8] As the herd increased so did Haynes's land holdings until the original pre-emption of 160 acres had become an estate of 20,756 acres.

J.C. Haynes of Osoyoos died July 6, 1888. His published obituary reads:

July 14, 1888—Mr. Haynes left Osoyoos for Victoria the middle of last month. He was returning home bringing with him his two sons who had been at school, two boys of Mr. Ellis's and a daughter of Captain Pittendrigh. The party left New Westminster for Hope and from there rode over the trail to Mr. Allison's, Princeton. On the way Mr. Haynes drank a large quantity of snow water. He complained of severe pain and was unable to go beyond Mr. Allison's. Dr. Chipp was immediately sent for to Nicola, but before he could arrive Mr. Haynes was dead, the immediate cause of death being inflammation of the bowels. A coffin was made at Princeton and the body taken to Osoyoos where the funeral took place.[9]

(*OHS*, 1943) Photo: BCARS A-01337

Placer mining gave an impetus to the development of the Okanagan but the mining itself was of short duration. By the fall of 1861 everyone had left Rock Creek, most moving first to Mission Creek and then on to Cherry Creek. Some took up land and remained in the Okanagan while others went on to the Cariboo. In the Similkameen in 1861 a tent town sprang up at Blackfoot, six miles up the Similkameen from Princeton. Today there is no trace of the town.

Placer mining at Granite Creek and Tulameen did not flourish until the late 1880s. Reverend John Goodfellow tells us:

From July 5 [1885] to October 31 gold to the value of $90,000 was reported. In December Henry Nicholson (mining recorder) estimated the population as 600 whites and 300 Chinese. Tents were soon replaced by log buildings. In January 1886, G.C. Tunstall (Gold Commissioner) reported forty homes, six saloons and hotels, and seven stores. The peak production was in 1886 when gold and platinum to the value of $193,000 was taken, chiefly from Granite Creek. By 1900 Granite Creek was another ghost town.[10]

(*OHS*, 1954)

Hard-rock mining had to wait until the 1890s when improved technology and transportation made it practicable. There was one exception, the Cherry Creek Silver Mine. A joint stock company operated there in 1866 exploiting what was believed to be a fabulously rich ore body. The company did manage to extract seven hundred pounds of good ore and ship it to San Francisco for smelting. Imagine the cost in time and money even at 1866 wages! However, the vein ran out. G.C. Tassie summed up this operation: "One more British Columbia mining company, starting out under favorable auspices, went to the bone-yard."[11]

The Overlanders

One of the most colourful parties of gold seekers to reach the interior of BC were the Overlanders of 1862, the first Europeans other than fur traders to cross the prairies and penetrate the Rockies from the east. Both the Schubert family and Enderby's first pre-emptor, Alexander Leslie Fortune, were in this party.

In 1923 James Schubert, who was being honoured with a life membership in the Native Sons of British Columbia, told his audience:

Augustus and Catherine Schubert. The Schubert family were part of the first group of Europeans—aside from fur traders—to cross the Rockies from the east.

"I was born at St. Paul...It was in 1860, when I was a few months old, that the incident took place that caused my parents to flee in mid-winter for the protection of Fort Garry, now the city of Winnipeg." [An Indian had broken into the bedroom of the baby and Augustus Schubert, fearing that the Indian was intent on kidnapping the child, had severely beaten the man with a poker. The local Indians were incensed.]

"At last we [the Schuberts and their three children] reached Fort Garry, and the stone walls of the old Hudson's Bay post were indeed a welcome sanctuary." [This trip was made between Christmas and New Year!]

The Schuberts remained at Fort Garry until the summer of 1862. Then it was that the Hudson's Bay Company's steamer, *International*, made her first trip from Georgetown down the Red River to Fort Garry.

The whole settlement turned out to welcome the boat, and were surprised when nearly 150 men came off the steamer. They were on their way to British Columbia, then practically unknown...Gold had been discovered in a section of that country called the Cariboo.

The tales told by the adventurers fired the imagination of Augustus Schubert and he determined to join the party. Mrs. Schubert declared that she would go with him...Great preparations were made...Red River carts, big, clumsy, wooden-wheeled affairs were purchased and to these spans of oxen were hitched, while horses were provided for the men and one woman.

In place of an ox, in one of the carts was a cow, which the Schuberts brought along to provide milk for their young family. Mrs. Schubert bestrode a big buckskin horse. Two basket cradles were fashioned and these were slung across the shoulders of the horse. In one rode little Mary Jane and in the other August, the older of the boys. Little Jimmie was carried either by his father, or when he was ahead as one of the advance guard, by Peter McIntyre.

The wagons were loaded with mining implements, tents and foodstuffs, mostly pemmican. There were 96 carts that drew away from Fort Garry on the afternoon of June 2nd, 1862... after being blessed by Bishop Tache.[12]

(*OHS*, 1961)

The Peter McIntyre mentioned above, after an adventurous life ranging from the Mackenzie River to the Gulf of Mexico, settled just south of Vaseux Lake at the foot of the great bluff that now bears his name. At the time of the Native Sons celebration Peter McIntyre, Augustus (Gus) Schubert and James Schubert were the only members left of that great company that came through the mountains in 1862. "When invited by the Native Sons to attend with Mr. Schubert the dinner in honour of the Overland Expedition Peter McIntyre wired his regrets saying, 'I am not as strong now as when I swam the Athabasca with little Jimmie Schubert on my back sixty-one years ago.' "[13] [Peter McIntyre died February 12, 1925 at the age of 91.]

The Overlanders reached Edmonton on July 21 and there they sold their Red River carts and oxen and bought horses. By August 13 they were in sight of the Rockies. The trip through the mountains was difficult. The trail was rough, food supplies were low, game was scarce and the decrease in daylight hours cut down their travel time. However, by August 27 the expedition had reached Tete Jaune Cache. Here they separated into two parties.

One party, which included A.L. Fortune, built a great raft eighty-five feet by twenty-two feet and started down the Fraser. The Schuberts threw in their lot with the second party, which worked its way through the mountains to the headwaters of the Thompson River. The horses were turned loose and the group began the perilous descent of the river on rafts. Fort Kamloops was reached October 14, 1862.

The article quoted above goes on to say:

> The rafts were run ashore above the fort and a tent was hastily run up by Mr. Schubert and in it a few hours later, was born the first white girl in the Interior of British Columbia, Rose Schubert, now Mrs. Henry Swanson of Armstrong. An Indian woman from the fort attended Mrs. Schubert when the baby was born...[Rose Schubert was the first white *girl* born in the interior of British Columbia while Gaston Lequime was the first white child, having been born at Okanagan Mission in December 1861.]
>
> (*OHS*, 1961)

The Schuberts remained at Fort Kamloops for the winter and then proceeded in the spring of 1863 to Lillooet which remained home for the next fourteen years. Two more children were born, Charles in 1870 and Catherine in 1872. Augustus Schubert Sr. followed the mines, without any great luck, until 1879 when A.L. Fortune persuaded him to take up farming at Round Prairie near present-day Armstrong. Meanwhile Mrs. Schubert, who may have been teaching school in Lillooet, accepted a position in 1877 as matron at the new government school at Cache Creek. The school had both girls and boys, some of whom were boarders and some day students.

Mrs. H.A. Fraser, nee Catherine Schubert, in writing about her mother's move to the farm at Round Prairie, gives us some idea of the transportation of the day.

> On June 28, 1883, mother gave up her position at the school and, with my brother and me, came to our new home. We left Cache Creek at 4 p.m. by stage, with Mr. Alex McDonald as driver. The first night we stayed at Savona, the second at Kamloops, and the third night at Grande Prairie, now called Westwold. Then on July 1 we arrived at O'Keefe's in time for dinner. At 3 p.m. we started for Round Prairie...[14]
>
> (*OHS*, 1950)

Rose Swanson, Catherine Fraser and Augustus Schubert were to remain in the Armstrong area for the rest of their lives.

Writing of Alexander Leslie Fortune, Margaret Ormsby says:

> It is quite impossible to think of the development of the northern end of the Valley without associating it with the name of Mr. Fortune. He was made Justice of the Peace in 1877, and worked to maintain law and order. He and Mrs. Fortune are remembered for their good works and for the fact that they exemplified in their lives all the best qualities of pioneer settlers....
>
> Mr. Fortune was born at Huntingdon, Quebec, on January 20, 1830, and died at Enderby on July 5, 1915. In 1862 he was married to Miss Bathia Ross of Lancaster, Ontario, who remained behind when her husband joined the Huntingdon group of Overlanders. Mrs. Fortune arrived at Spallumcheen in 1874 and resided there until her death on November 13, 1930. Both are buried in the old cemetery at Lansdowne.
>
> In his autobiography, Mr. Fortune describes his journey to the Cariboo gold-fields from the time he left his home in 1862...Late in the spring [1866] he returned to Seymour on Shuswap Lake, and then, traveling by canoe, proceeded to Sicamous, and, entering the Spallumcheen River, began to ascend it. Near Enderby four claims to land were staked in the names of Fortune,

Alexander Leslie Fortune, an 1862 Overlander and first settler in Enderby.
Vernon Museum 5092

Malcolm, Burns and Dunn...On June 18, 1887 Mr. Fortune obtained crown grant for two claims of 348 acres.[15]
(*OHS*, 1951)

In 1903 A.L. Fortune wrote an article entitled "The Overlanders" in which we find colourful passages such as the description of the 1862 journey by raft down the Fraser and, later in the Cariboo, the account of the effect of the camel train on his gentle ox. The author tells how the Lillooet Native Big Louis facilitated his settlement in the Spallumcheen and his relationship with the local Shuswaps. Mr. Fortune writes:

To carry on the work we got a promising boy to live with us in late harvest time. His example proved to be a good influence over a few other Indians, who saw a chance to benefit by the wages paid. We were always honest in our dealings with them, and treated the sick with such remedies as we knew to be safe.

The women and children worked with us at digging and pitting potatoes and so we became better known to them. On Christmas Eve, 1867, we invited all in Spallumcheen (22 all told) to a feast in our log house. We had cooked game and beef, with vegetables, dried fruit (2 kinds), good bread and tea with sugar but no milk. The bread was cooked in two "gold pans" buried under hot coals and ashes. The guests sat on the floor and had to do without knives and forks. In due time the fragments were gathered and the tin dishes put to one side. I called for order and sang a hymn. Then they sang one learned from the priest and also others, which pleased everyone. I tried to give them some impression of the importance of civilization and the benefits to be derived from cultivating the land. I measured some of the men and showed how little they differed in stature and natural ability from untrained white men, and also what education could do for both whites and Indians. I compared their custom of making drudges of their wives with the loving consideration of white men in their homes. Big Louis was my interpreter. When they left they all shook hands with me. The two babies put their right hands in ours and their mothers thanked us kindly for our advice.[16]
(*OHS*, 1956)

Bathia Fortune who travelled from eastern Canada in 1874 to join her husband at Fortune's Landing (Enderby). "The hospitality of her home was proverbial."
Vernon Museum 5092

Bathia Fortune, who was to prove a most appropriate helpmate, reached her husband's farm in 1874. Burt R. Campbell tells us of her coming:

The arrival of Mrs. Fortune in August 1874, as related by herself to Mable Durham, a *Vancouver Province* writer, in 1918 makes a real romantic story. She had awaited twelve years the return of her gold-seeking husband to escort her from Ontario to her new home in Spallumcheen. The journey was made by way of the United States to San Francisco by train, by boat to Victoria and again to Yale, then wagon to Savona. Here she was taken aboard a little flag-bedecked boat and on inquiry as to the reason of the decorations was told by the captain, "We have a person of note on board." Asked who, he replied, "The first white woman to go into Spallumcheen."[17]

In the same article Mr. Campbell lists the names of other Overlanders who remained to leave their mark on the North Okanagan and Thompson River area:

With the Schubert branch of the Overlander Party also came William Fortune who settled at Tranquille on the site now [1950] occupied by the sanatorium. There he built in 1868 the first flour mill in the vicinity, having as partner for a short time James McIntosh.

Another Overlander who took a prominent part in development of Kamloops was John Andrew Mara. He was associated with James McIntosh in Shuswap Milling Company (lumber

53

and flour mill built in 1878), the Mara and Wilson store, was a steamboat operator, and with the coming of the C.P.R., became a member of the townsite company then formed. He was a member of the Provincial Legislature 1871 to 1886, first representing Kootenay and Yale. He also served as MP from 1887 to 1896 when he was defeated by Hewitt Bostock in the Yale–Cariboo–Kootenay election. George C. (Judge) Tunstall, also of that party, served for years as government agent at Kamloops prior to his death in 1911.
(*OHS*, 1950)

Cattle round-up in the North Okanagan in the fall of 1888. *Vernon Museum 5021*

The Great Cattle Ranches

American cattlemen, already made aware through the California gold rush and its aftermath that hungry miners created a ready market for their beef, began driving their herds through the Okanagan north to the goldfields. Generally speaking they followed the old fur-brigade trails. Because of the abundance of bunch grass, which often grew so tall that it "bent over the saddle" as one writer put it, cattle were usually rested, fattened and even wintered in the Okanagan before being driven the final lap of their journey to the Cariboo. Men already farming in the Similkameen and Okanagan were quick to recognize the possibilities of this lucrative market. Thomas Ellis was one of these.

Tom Ellis had arrived in Victoria from Ireland on January 17, 1865. He spent his first summer in BC as the man in charge of stores for the construction of the Dewdney Trail east of Osoyoos. In 1866 he pre-empted land at what is now Penticton. This was the first step in building the great empire which earned for him the title "the Cattle King of the Okanagan Valley." When John Carmichael Haynes died suddenly in 1888, Ellis was able to acquire the mortgage on the Haynes estate and foreclose, thus bringing his own holdings to some thirty-one thousand acres.[18] Kathleen Ellis has written a short biography of her parents Tom and Mina Ellis in which she says:

Thomas Ellis built a cattle ranching empire on the land that would later become Penticton. *BCARS G-00394*

Tom Ellis it was who in 1874 planted the first orchard in the Okanagan Valley, who in 1890 built the first steamboat...It might have been added that Tom Ellis was one of the two first white settlers in Penticton in 1865–66, first store-keeper, and first postmaster officially appointed in 1889 and one of the first magistrates in the valley. He also built Penticton's first Protestant church, now known as the Memorial Chapel, and which is part of St. Saviour's church in Penticton—a lot of "firsts" for one man.

The old timers had much in common...They were...rugged individualists, possessed of vision and courage, the milk of human kindness and

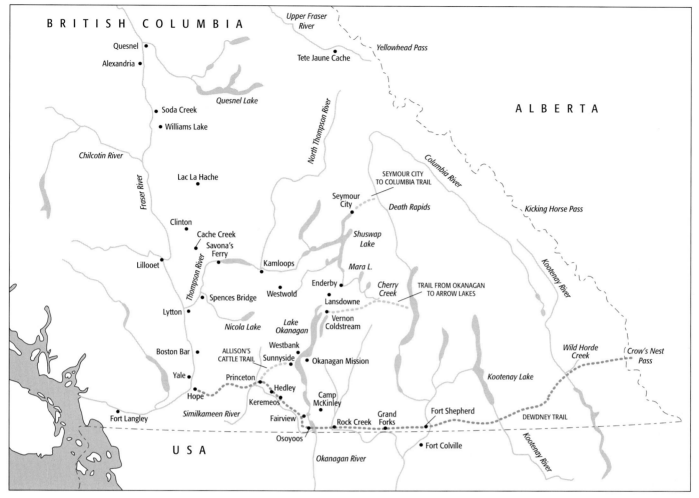

Some historic places mentioned in text

personal integrity...Agreements were made by word of mouth and were more binding than the most formidable legal documents of today...My father had all these qualifications together with a stern sense of justice, coloured of course, by his own judgment...He drove hard bargains and kept them, but lent and gave freely to those he felt were in real need...

Like most early settlers, Tom Ellis worked unremittingly. The ranch itself was a home for the family and left largely to the management of tried and trusted foremen. Large gangs of men were employed during the haying season. My father's attention was centred on the raising of cattle. His herd of seven heifers grew and multiplied, as did his early investment in land. Ranches at Osoyoos, Okanagan Falls and the Mission were added, with grazing rights covering vast areas. He was in the saddle at all hours and slept in the hills when necessary. However, he seldom failed to make home for the week-end and as far as possible Sunday was a day of rest with his family.

Exposure and hardships took their toll later in my father's life, when he walked only with the aid of crutches. He rode long after he was unable to mount a horse in the usual way and even then chose horses that less skilful riders avoided.

The concluding years of Tom Ellis's colourful life were spent in Victoria where he died February 1, 1918.[19]

(*OHS*, 1950)

The Similkameen too had its early cattlemen, one of the first being John Fall Allison after whom Allison Pass is named. J.C. Goodfellow in his "Outline History of Similkameen" writes:

John Fall Allison, pioneer settler, was born in England in 1825. His father was house surgeon in Leeds Infirmary. The family moved to Illinois, U.S.A., in 1837. As a young man John went overland to California in 1849, and in 1858 came to Victoria. On the advice of Governor Douglas, Mr. Allison explored the Similkameen Valley, prospecting for gold, and mapping trails. He was appointed Justice of the Peace in 1876, Assistant Gold Commissioner in 1885, and became one of the best-known cattlemen in the whole valley. He died in October, 1897, and was buried at the base of Castle Rock.

John Fall Allison, a pioneer rancher and the man after whom Allison Pass is named. BCARS A-01961

Mrs. Allison was born on August 18, 1845, in Colombo, Ceylon, where her father, Stratton Moir, was a tea planter. Susan Louisa, his youngest daughter, was sent to England for her education. Mr. Moir died, and later his widow married a Mr. Glennay. In 1860 the family came to British Columbia, arriving in Hope on Susan's birthday. Four years later, her sister was married to Edgar Dewdney, and for a time Susan was the only white girl in Hope. Here she met Mr. Allison to whom she was married in September, 1868. Soon after they crossed the Hope Trail, and made their home just below the forks of the Tulameen and Similkameen Rivers, a little east of Princeton. With the exception of some years in the Okanagan Valley [at Sunnyside (Westbank) where today the Allison log cabin has been restored by the Quails' Gate Vineyard Estate Winery and serves as its wine shop], Mrs. Allison remained in Similkameen till 1928, when she went to Vancouver to reside. She died on February 1, 1937, and was buried in the Allison cemetery at the base of Castle Rock, two miles east of Princeton. Her reminiscences appeared in Vancouver and Princeton newspapers. She had a keen insight into the native mind, and embodied local history and legend in fifty pages of verse, published under the title of *In cow-mas-ket* by the Scroll Publishing Company, Chicago, 1900. Stratton Moir was her pen name. [In 1976 Margaret Ormsby edited and published Susan Allison's recollections under the title *A Pioneer Gentlewoman in British Columbia*.]

The rolling, bunch grass hills made an ideal range. The Hudson's Bay Company servants were quick to see its possibilities. There was always a ready local market for packhorses, and a market for cattle at the coast. Lieutenant Wilson [of the Boundary Commission] writes in his diary, August 14, 1860: "We travelled up the much talked of valley of the Similkameen...the finest part of the valley was occupied this spring by the Hudson's Bay Company and we found a Canadian half-breed in charge; he had some cows and a large number of oxen so that we had

Osoyoos cowboys. From left to right: Ed Richter, Charlie Richter, Will Haynes, Jack Mackenzie, William Manery and William Richter. BCARS C-835

a good drink of milk, a thing not to be despised in this part of the world."

Frank Richter, after whom Richter Pass is named,...came to lower Similkameen in 1860...He sold out to Richard Lowe Cawston and Mrs. William H. (Ella) Lowe in 1884. Other well-known cattlemen in early days were Frank Suprement (better known as Surprise), Manuel Barcelo, Jack Knowles, Louis Marsel, J. Coulthard, W.J. Manery and Dan McCurdy...

Barcelo was a Mexican who arrived in the early sixties, and took up the first homestead near what is now Cawston. He brought from across the line many horses for packing. Mrs. Allison gives him credit for establishing the first flour mill in the valley—"a primitive affair, like a gigantic coffee mill."[20]

(*OHS*, 1954)

Kathleen Stuart Dewdney in her article entitled "Francis Xavier Richter" portrays the colourful life of Frank Richter. The future cattle rancher was born in Austria in 1837. He rejected an assured future in his father's textile mill for life in the New World. After a decade of adventures in the United States he, with a partner named King, arrived in the Similkameen in 1864 with forty-two head of cattle purchased in Oregon with all the resources the two had. To eke out a living he entered the employ of the Hudson's Bay Company, managing his herd on the side. Mrs. Dewdney writes: "In March, 1865, [Richter] and King dissolved partnership, and Richter filed a claim on a pre-emption of 320 acres. This homestead within three years became the nucleus of a prosperous venture known as the 'R' Ranch."[21]

Frank Richter acquired ranches in the Boundary Country and in Penticton as well as butcher shops, enough to leave his sons by his native wife, Lucy, well established in various enterprises by the time of his death in December 1910. The youngest son, Francis Xavier, made his own mark by being elected as MLA for Similkameen in 1953 and serving the province as minister of agriculture.[22]

In "Pre-emption Claims in Okanagan Valley"[23] Margaret A. Ormsby lists many of the early pre-emptors at l'Anse au Sable (Okanagan Mission). The information is taken from a book now in the Provincial Archives at Victoria which gives, in the handwriting of W.G. Cox, the dates and descriptions of the various pre-emptions, most of which are for 160 acres: November 30, 1960—Father Richard; December 15—Cyprian Laurence; then through 1961—John McDougall, Gideon Peon, Eli Lequime, William Peon, Bazel Peon, George Ford, Augustus Calmels, Charles Fizet, Peter Dougherty, Joseph Christian, John Moshoh. These Mission settlers were not interested in becoming cattle barons. Their mixed farms were their homes and if they were ambitious, as was Eli Lequime, they preferred to make their money in trade.

In 1863 Captain Charles Frederick Houghton arrived in the North Okanagan accompanied by the brothers Charles Albert Vernon and Forbes George Vernon. Margaret Ormsby writes of Houghton:

...Formerly an officer in the 20th Regiment of the Imperial Army, Houghton had been gazetted out on June 29, 1863, and had left England two weeks later. He had expected to qualify under the British Columbia Military Settlers ordinance of 1861, and acquire a military grant of 1,450 acres. In the spring of 1863, however, the ordinance had been repealed, and Houghton found that he was entitled only to 300 acres under the new ordinance of 1863. In February, 1864, he petitioned Sir James Douglas and the Legislative Council of British Columbia for special consideration. Douglas endorsed the letter containing his request, "acknowledge receipt of this letter—and inform the writer—that it is not in my power to grant his request."...

Captain Charles Frederick Houghton, an early settler at Coldstream.
BCARS F-06864

Houghton's claim to a military grant of 1,450 acres was not recognized until 1872. In the meantime, Forbes G. Vernon and Charles A. Vernon, who had accompanied him to the Okanagan in 1863, mined at Cherry Creek in 1864, and in 1866 pre-empted land between Priests' Valley and

O'Keefe homestead. In 1868 Cornelius O'Keefe acquired a homestead of 162 acres just north of the head of Okanagan Lake. Within 40 years his cattle were grazing 15,000 acres. In 1872 the ranch became the location of the first Canadian post office in the North Okanagan.
BCARS B-05677

Okanagan Landing. This land was later acquired by Houghton, and the management of the Coldstream Ranch, his military grant, was turned over to the Vernons.[24]
(*OHS*, 1949)

Like Haynes and Ellis, Houghton and the Vernons belonged to that group of Protestant Irishmen so prominent in early BC history. Margaret Ormsby has written of these well-educated, energetic, ambitious Anglo-Irish:

> Most of the men who served in official positions in the colonial period were Anglo-Irish, some of them men of the "Dublin Castle" class who had connections with the gentry...They were loyal subjects of the Crown, professing a desire to help in building British power in a new country...
>
> Most of them dearly loved social life and were punctilious in observing the niceties of the rules that prevailed at home. Peter O'Reilly carefully paid his respects to his Excellency whenever he was at the capital and thoroughly enjoyed the balls and dinners at the Governor's residence...[25]

In her book *British Columbia: a History* Dr. Ormsby writes of Governor Anthony Musgrave's first trip about the Colony of British Columbia. The following paragraph is included:

> At some of the road-houses, Musgrave found ranchers who had sufficient means to employ Indian and Chinese labour and enough leisure to enjoy sports. At Ashcroft Manor, Clement Francis Cornwall and his brother Henry, "a tall regular First-Trinity man," had introduced foxhounds for coyote-hunting. To participate in a meet, Gold Commissioners Peter O'Reilly and John Carmichael Haynes sometimes contrived to ride miles out of their way. For a similar purpose, Captain Charles Frederick Houghton, late of the 20th Regiment of Foot, and his two Irish friends, Charles and Forbes George Vernon, travelled several hundred miles from the Coldstream Ranch in the Okanagan Valley.[26]

There was another Irishman with a different background who was about to cut a swath in the North Okanagan along with his business associates Thomas Greenhow and Thomas Wood. Peter Carstens says of him:

Cornelius O'Keefe came to BC to explore the Cariboo goldfields and became one of the Okanagan's most prominent cattle ranchers. Vernon Museum

Cornelius O'Keefe was born in 1837 in the pioneer settlement of Fallowfield, now a suburb of Ottawa. His father, Michael O'Keefe, was a farmer of Irish stock, and his mother, Esther Demers, was a French Canadian. Cornelius is said to have been restless and ambitious as a young man, and he left home at the age of twenty-four to explore the West, especially the Cariboo goldfields. He travelled via New York by sea to Panama, crossed the isthmus by railway, and then by sea again to Victoria via San Francisco. He arrived at the Cariboo later in the year (1861). Like so many others, he was an unsuccessful miner, but he remained in the Cariboo for five years and managed to save $3,000...In the spring of 1866, while on his way to Oregon to buy cattle, he met another settler named Thomas Wood. Wood was the son of an Anglican clergyman and a Newfoundlander who had also failed to make his fortune in gold but had earned some money "hauling freight on the Cariboo Road between Lytton and the mouth of the Quesnel River." Wood travelled to California in 1865 with his savings to buy cattle to drive to the mines in British Columbia...

O'Keefe and Wood combined their efforts and their business skills to become successful cattlerunners. The following year they met Thomas Greenhow, another settler, who joined them in the cattle business.[27]

In June 1867 the three, on their return from Oregon with their cattle, stopped at the head of the lake to rest and fatten their stock. The Cariboo mines were petering out and the Kootenay mines beginning to show

Haying on the Hill ranch at Osoyoos in 1915. BCARS C-00851

promise. The three decided to remain in the Okanagan. O'Keefe and Greenhow registered their pre-emptions on July 25, 1868. Wood took up land near Irish Creek which he later sold to Greenhow, he himself pre-empting again near the lake which is named after him. O'Keefe and Greenhow continued to expand their holdings.

One should not leave the subject of North Okanagan pre-emptions without mentioning that of Luc Girouard, Lot 71, the land through which the western part of Barnard Avenue now runs. Girouard registered his pre-emption September 1, 1867 but did not secure his crown grant on the property until July 15, 1887.

A large holding which had its origin in the colonial period was the Stepney Ranch near Armstrong. The property finally included some 1,600 acres. The ranch was created by three men who had tried the goldfields of the Cariboo and found them disappointing. In 1869 Moses Lumby, Preston Bennett and Fred Bennett entered the Okanagan with the intention of farming. Years of back-breaking effort faced them.

During the colonial era cattle ranching was probably the dominant Okanagan industry.

Although the great cattle holdings were destined to be subdivided and much of the land used for fruit farming, animal husbandry remains a viable industry engaging a sizeable portion of the population. Even in a more scientific age many of the early practices are still recognizable in modern applications.

Colonial Transportation and Communication

The Cariboo Road, which was wide enough to accommodate a stage or wagons, was built through the Fraser Canyon in 1862. However, Okanagan transportation remained a matter of travelling by boat or, if overland, by horse or on foot over trails which followed old Indian routes. The opening of the Dewdney Trail in 1860 and its rerouting in 1862, made possible by the blasting of a ledge around the Skagit Bluffs, was a wonderful improvement to communication between the coast and the southern Interior. Missionaries, cattle drovers, miners, government officials, settlers, all manner of folk used the trail.

The old Brigade Trail continued to serve the north-south traffic. There were other trails: the Sky Line, south of the Dewdney Trail and so beautifully described by Florence Willis in her letter of about 1919[28]; the Indian Road or Allison Trail through the mountains between Princeton and Sunnyside, which was blazed and cleared by Allison in 1874 so that he could move his cattle more easily between their summer range near Princeton and their winter range at Okanagan Lake; the Pandosy Trail up the east side of Okanagan Lake between Penticton and the Mission; the Fire Valley Trail explored and established by Captain Houghton in 1866 as a shorter route from the Okanagan to the mines of the Big Bend on the Columbia, as well as the trail from Seymour Arm on the Shuswap through the mountains to the Columbia.

F.M. Buckland's story "Mr. and Mrs. Lequime" gives us some idea of transportation of both people and freight in the colonial era. Mr. Buckland writes:

> When the California boom ended and the Fraser excitement drew men north, the Lequimes followed and packed their stock of goods and supplies to Hope, the head of navigation on the Fraser...The summer of 1860 saw Mr. and Mrs. Lequime start out on a journey of over 175 miles over a newly made trail which at one place reached an altitude of 5,000 feet. The children were carried in panniers on the back of an ox...The nights in the higher altitudes were cool and the whole trip was roughing it. Eventually the party reached Rock Creek where Mr. Lequime at once opened a store and saloon, continuing at that place until the fall of 1861, when the camp petered out.
>
> Their next move was to Okanagan Mission. Here they prospered; the country was rich in mineral wealth, and the miners had ready money to spend for supplies. Lequime operated a cattle and horse ranch, a blacksmith shop, the post office, and a sawmill, and had the only trading post between Kamloops and Osoyoos. In those days the Hope Trail was the connecting link with the Coast. A pack train of forty mules, carrying Lequime's goods and equipment was a common sight on the Trail. In this way, the first piano and billiard table were brought into the Okanagan, as well as many other heavy articles, such as wagons, mowers and other machinery.
>
> Accomplished linguists, the Lequimes did business in French, English, Spanish, Chinook, or any of the Okanagan tongues as the need arose.[29]
> (*OHS*, 1953)

In an addendum to the Buckland article Bernard Lequime, son of Eli and Marie Louise, writes:

> Eli Lequime was born at Bordeaux, France, on December 2, 1811...in the spring of 1860 the Lequimes left Fort Hope. They travelled over the old Hudson's Bay Trail on Manson Mountain to Tulameen where they came to the Similkameen River. Everyone except the two small children, Bernard and Gaston, had to walk since the three horses were used for packing supplies...
>
> The Lequimes remained at Rock Creek until October, 1861. During their stay, they added a cow to their possessions...It was to serve as an additional beast of burden when they left on their next journey. This time their objective was Cariboo, some 300 miles away. The destination was not reached, however, since at Penticton Mountain they met the Oblate missionary, the Rev. Father Pandosy, a Frenchman from Marseilles. He advised Eli to locate in the Okanagan Valley at the Mission, about three miles southeast of where Kelowna now stands.
>
> The advice was taken, and at Okanagan Mission Lequime built a log cabin, fourteen by twenty feet, with floor and roof of dirt...As he had done at his trading post at Rock Creek, Eli now packed in supplies from Walla Walla, Washington.

Eli Lequime prospered in the Okanagan as the operator of a ranch, a smithy, a sawmill and a post office.
Kelowna Museum

The fur trade was good and my father's business grew...We were making four and five trips a year to Fort Hope. My father always took the first trip of the year and went on to Victoria to purchase articles over and above the usual supplies. After the first trip the pack train was entrusted to an Iroquois Indian.

Mail in those days was carried only once a month, and the only newspaper we took was *Le Courier* of San Francisco. It was one of the few contacts we had with the outside world. Our supply of reading material was purchased once a year when my father sent to Victoria. My father and mother were both great readers, and their favourite author was Balzac.

(*OHS*, 1935)

There was one outfit that refused to believe that wagons could not be driven north through the Okanagan. F.M. Buckland writes of them:

The First Wagons in Okanagan Valley[30]
by F.M. Buckland

...In the year 1858 an event of importance took place which is well remembered by some of the older Indians; the coming of the first wagon train, the Palmer and Miller expedition, as it came to be called. These adventurers outfitted a train of wagons filled with merchandise on the American side and, coming up the Columbia to Okanagan, travelled the old Hudson's Bay Brigade Trail through to Kamloops.

There were no wagon roads in those days. If a hill was too steep to climb the teams were doubled up, and to descend a steep hill ropes were attached to the wagon with a turn around a nearby tree to ease it down. Or, perhaps a Mormon brake, in the shape of a small tree, would be attached to the rear axle and allowed to drag along the ground. It is said that when a bit of country was encountered that was too difficult to take the wagons over the wagons were unloaded and taken apart and packed with the merchandise over the rough place on the backs of the horses and oxen until wheeling could be resumed. Then the wagons would be reassembled and loaded and with the oxen yoked up they would go creaking over the country, up hill and down.

Frank Morgan Buckland was born in Guelph, Ontario, in 1873. At the age of nine he moved with his father to Manitoba and as a young man engaged in farming till coming to Kelowna in 1904. Here he was for five years in partnership with the late D.W. Crowley in a butcher and cattle-dealing business, eventually selling out to the Burns organization. During World War I he operated a cattle ranch at Shingle Creek, west of Penticton, and later owned a large orchard in the Rutland district.

For some years he was president of Morrison Hardware Co., which also held the Ford agency for cars and tractors. He was the first to introduce the tractor into the Kelowna district. Later he managed Highland Fruits Ltd., which ultimately amalgamated with Okanagan Packers.

His social and civic activities included the following–charter member and president Kelowna Rotary Club, representing the district at the 1937 convention at Nice, France; city alderman (four years); school trustee; president of the Board of Trade; Kelowna Hospital Society; Kelowna Fire Brigade; United Church.

He married Maud Secord in 1898. She pre-deceased in 1942, as did a daughter, Frances, in 1917. Three sons, Jack, Doug and Charles live in Kelowna and district. [1959]

He was co-founder with L. Norris of Vernon, of the Okanagan Historical and Natural History Society in 1925. He was the major contributor to the Society's first *Report* in 1926, and throughout the remainder of his life it was rare to find his name missing from the list of contents in any report. His collection of Indian relics, stuffed animals and birds, coins, and other items of historical value formed the nucleus of the present Okanagan Museum on Mill Street.

The results of his painstaking research in Okanagan history were organized into book form as *Ogopogo's Vigil*, copyrighted in 1948. Only a few copies are extant...

He passed away on Tuesday, Sept. 15, 1953. An editorial in the *Kelowna Courier* at the time closed with these words–"His writings will be his memorial."[31]

(*OHS*, 1959) Photo: Kelowna Museum

When they arrived at Kamloops they were told that it would be impossible for them to continue their way any farther north owing to the roughness of the country. They consequently disbanded there. The provisions they brought with them were sold at a very high price. Potatoes were sold as high as eighty dollars per ton while sugar, beans, rice and tobacco brought correspondingly high prices. The oxen brought a very high price, and were slaughtered for beef by the miners, some of whom tasted the flesh of a domestic animal for the first time in years.

Among the manuscripts relating to the Palmer expedition there is, in the University of California at Berkeley, a document which is more or less in the form of an interview with Palmer. It was written at a pioneers' camp meeting at Salem, Oregon, held on the 14th June, 1878, at which Palmer was present. In part it reads:

"When I got to Okanagan Lake I went up on the hill and there I came into a district of country covered with timber and cut up into ravines so that it took too much labour to get along with ox teams. So I just went up on one of the mountains and cut timber and hauled it to the lake and made a raft. We put everything on the raft and towed it along the shore until we got past the bad ground. Then we hitched up to the wagons again and away we went. We had a party of men making a road and cutting timber all the way until we got to Cariboo."

(*OHS*, 1935)

Joseph Brent's account of the first stone grist mill in the Okanagan tells us how a primitive industry managed in spite of the lack of roads.

The First Stone Grist Mill[32]
by Joseph Brent

The first grist mill, equipped with a stone for grinding, was owned by my father, the late Frederick Brent, of Okanagan Mission. (Previous to the introduction of this mill, my father had a small steel mill which he packed over the trail from Hope.)

The stone grist mill was bought in San Francisco, and came by water to Fort Yale, thence by freight team to Savona's Ferry, and by water to Fortune's Landing, now Enderby. This was about the year 1871.

I was with my father when he went out to bring the stone in. We had a team and home-made wagon, the wheels of which were hewn from a solid block. We brought the mill in the wagon from Fortune's Landing by way of Round Prairie, Round Lake and O'Keefe's, to Okanagan Landing. There was no wagon road then to Okanagan Mission, so it was brought down the lake in a rowboat, by an Indian named Nitasket. The wagon and rowboat were both owned by the late Luc Girouard.

The mill was erected on my father's pre-emption claim and was driven by water from Mill Creek. Three grades of flour were produced, one-third of the grist being the toll usually taken by my father for grinding the grain. Most of the wheat was brought to the mill on pack horses by Indians, who usually paid in horses, buckskin and other things for the grinding of their wheat.

Wheat was brought to the mill from as far south as Keremeos and Osoyoos, and as far north as the head of Okanagan Lake. When there was sufficient supply the mill would run from the time the ice was out of Mill Creek in the spring until it formed again in November, grinding about one ton of wheat in a run of 24 hours. Once a year the mill picks for dressing the stones were sent to San Francisco for sharpening and tempering. This continued to be done until about the year 1885, when a blacksmith's shop was built in Vernon.

(*OHS*, 1935)

Considering the evidence which we have at hand, what can we say in general of the colonial period?

The land, except for a relatively few pre-emptions such as those at L'Anse au Sable (Okanagan Mission), was in its natural state. The great cattle ranches made use of the natural ranges and hay lands.

The indigenous people could still hunt and gather, but progressively they were finding that fences barred them from land they had used for generations. As for the settlers, they resented what they regarded as the underuse of reserve lands. When the Indians did try to adapt to an agricultural and ranching economy they soon found their land base of less than twenty acres per man inadequate. White pre-emptors started with 160 acres.

Transportation was primitive. There were no wagon roads. Travel was either by horse or on foot with some use of small boats which could be rowed or paddled.

The stories of some of the first settlers recounted above may be misleading in that the biographies are continued into the postconfederation period. Actually the only white women dwelling in the area before confederation, apart from Charlotte Haynes and Annie Christien whose lives were tragically brief, and Mrs. Christien's niece Ellen Mackin, were Susan Allison, who arrived in Princeton in 1867, and Marie Louise Lequime, who had walked over the Manson Mountain Trail in 1860. Frequently white men took Indian women as country wives.

Administration was in the hands of able, well-educated immigrants from the British Isles, many of them Anglo-Irish. They were equal to the rigours of travel and living in this new land but were often subject to loneliness. They could foresee that the land about them would increase in value and some built up fortunes based on the acquisition of property at very low prices. Such men were poised to profit from confederation.

5

Missionaries and Churches

The Roman Catholics

Last night we reached the site we have chosen for a mission. It is a large valley situated on the left side and is about the middle of Lake Okanagan. This sandy cove is the largest valley around here and highly spoken of. The tillable land is immense.[1] —Father Pandosy, October 9, 1859

(*OHS*, 1949)

After a trip fraught with difficulties Father Pandosy, Father Richard and Brother Surel had accomplished their journey from New Westminster to the Valley of the Okanagan. (The Dewdney Trail was yet to be pushed through the mountains.) They spent a miserable winter in quite inadequate shelter somewhere near Duck Lake

Father Pandosy Mission established in 1859 and restored by volunteers who began their work in 1958. The three buildings we see here date from 1860. In the distance: the brothers' residence; the higher building on the right was the chapel and school, as well as living quarters; on the right edge of the picture, the food storage building made with double log walls with soil between for insulation. A fourth building was beyond repair and its materials were used in the restoration of the three above. H. Powley

(north of Kelowna). Then in the spring of 1860 they drove in stakes to mark the boundaries of their pre-emption on the banks of Mission Creek (near present-day Kelowna). Next came the task of erecting a chapel, a school and a mission house as well as planting a garden—all this in addition to their pastoral duties of baptizing, marrying and attending to the dying and the dead and in general encouraging their charges to live Christian lives.

In November of 1863 J.C. Haynes, collector of customs at Osoyoos, sent Constable W.C. Young to report on the mines at Cherry Creek. Young's way led past the Mission and this is what he had to say:

Father Charles Pandosy had a significant impact on the Okanagan not just as a missionary and educator but as an agriculturalist.
Oblate Archives

Arrived at the Mission on the 28th—weather warm and pleasant and the country free from snow. The cabins, barns, fences, hay stacks in every direction give the country a pleasant appearance after travelling the dreary mountain trails.

The Catholic Mission buildings are new and very neat. The settlers' houses are generally of the smallest and poorest description. W. Pion's and J. McDougall's are good, well-built houses, and the best in the settlement. The land, though not of the best quality, appears to produce abundantly; all crops have been very good this past season and that without any aid from irrigation. I saw some very good tobacco of their own growing.

I was informed by the Rev. Father Richard of the Mission that the total produce this year is not less than: Wheat, 1000 bushels; barley, 200 bushels; potatoes, 2000 bushels.

The priests have a school for the children of the settlers. On my return I found the Rev. Father Richard in a neat school room teaching five or six children to read and write. All instruction is given in this school in the French language.[2]

(*OHS*, 1935)

In three years the missionaries had established a community with a church, a school and a productive farm.

Father Pandosy and his fellow Oblates were not the first missionaries to visit the Okanagan. In 1838 the bishop of Quebec, in response to a request made by French Canadians in the employ of the Hudson's Bay Company, had sent two missionary priests of the Diocese of Quebec, Father Norman Blanchet and Father Modeste Demers, out to the Oregon territory. Both were Oblates, members of the Order of the Immaculate Conception or Oblate of Mary Immaculate (OMI). The priests travelled west with an express brigade of the Hudson's Bay Company.[3]

Father Pierre Richard was known for his vigorous health—a helpful attribute for a frontier missionary.
Oblate Archives

In his article entitled "Roman Catholic Missionaries in the Northwest" Bishop W. Emmett Doyle says:

[In] 1842...Father Demers...came back up the Columbia River, turned north along the Okanagan, and came through the valley. He met a number of French Canadians and their Indian wives and their families, marrying and baptizing many of them. He asked them to build a church at the place where he met them, at the head of Okanagan Lake, the mission of St. Joseph's which was just a little west and north of the city of Vernon. He went further...through New Caledonia to Fort St. James...[4]

A Jesuit presence was established in the territory in 1842 when Father Peter John De Smet was sent west from St. Louis in response to a request from Nez Perce and Flatheads who had been evangelized by an Iroquois named Kah-put (or perhaps Ignace) about 1816. In 1845 Father Nobili, a Jesuit, travelled from Fort Colvile through the Okanagan north to Fort St. James, visiting on the way the little churches the natives had built at the request of Father Demers. Father Nobili returned and with a German Jesuit spent the winter of 1845-46

Saint James Roman Catholic
Church, Vernon, built in
1908–1909.
Vernon Museum 7348

somewhere near Wood Lake…In 1846, when the boundary between the American territory and British territory was established, it was agreed that the Jesuits would work south of the boundary and the Oblates north.

Father Pandosy had arrived in the Oregon territory in October 1847, one of a party of five Oblates who had come from France to serve in the Mission to evangelize the Natives. Denys Nelson in his article "Father Pandosy, O.M.I."[5] tells us, "Charles John Felix Adolph, known in religion as Charles Marie and throughout the Okanagan Valley as Father Pandosy, was born on November 21st, 1824 near Marseilles, France…His was a land owning family…During his classical studies the boy won distinction, carrying away prizes in Latin composition and French literature."

Primrose Upton in her article "Father Pandosy, O.M.I."[6] gives us a thumbnail sketch of this priest. She says:

What makes this man so outstanding? He was intelligent and well-educated. He was a huge, powerfully built man with a booming voice and ready wit. He had large deep-set eyes, well-marked eyebrows, long straight nose, high scholarly forehead, curly black hair and a full beard. He had a very hot temper and was capable of amazing feats of strength, yet was gentle. He served his flock as teacher, doctor, lawyer, orator, botanist, agriculturist, musician, singing teacher and sports coach. A member of the Boundary Commission wrote: "Father Pandosy is a very pleasant, well-informed man and has not forgotten the pureness of his native tongue. He would pour forth the fondly remembered songs of La Belle France."
(*OHS*, 1962)

In January 1891, Father Pandosy received a call to perform a marriage in Keremeos. In inclement weather he caught a cold and became ill. In spite of the protests of his friends he tried to travel home. At Penticton he was so ill that he had to seek refuge in the home of his old friend Chief Francois. He died in the arms of the Chief. Tom Ellis arranged for the transportation of the father's body up the lake to the Mission.

Speaking of Father Pandosy and Father Richard, Georgina Maisonville writes:

No greater contrast in types would seem to be possible than is seen in these two men. Father Pandosy, musical and intellectual, taught the Indians how to sing and to play on hand instruments and Father Richard, practical and helpful, tramped through mud and bush to recover horses, taught the Indians to make fences and showed them how to raise crops after the manner of the white men. The record of his life closes with these words— "Father Richard made use of his vigorous health not only to procure souls but also the best for the bodily welfare of his brothers and the savages [sic] by application to work in the garden. He had a pronounced taste for gardening and rendered service of this sort most useful to the mission. To the last he was the Good Gardener (*le Bon Jardinier*) in every sense of the word, cultivating the most beautiful virtues in his soul, notably a great love for the congregation and perfect regularity which was for his brothers always an edifying example.[7]
(*OHS*, 1949)

In the cavalcade of characters who left their mark on the Okanagan, the Oblate fathers along with A.L. Fortune of Enderby stand out as men whose aim was to build a community in which all were worthy regardless of race or wealth. The Oblates recruited Giovanni Casorso to work at the Mission with the prospect of acquiring land of his own and persuaded the Lequimes to settle in the Okanagan rather than travelling on to the Cariboo. How shrewd the fathers were in their judgment as to who would contribute to the settlement.

The Mission work was the primary concern of the priests but in performing their duties these very practical, educated men have left us important demographic information. In the Maisonville article we read: "Later in 1860 Bishop d'Herbomez wrote from Lake Okanagan: 'About 2,000 Indians—of these 3 or 4 hundred have been baptized. There are 5 to 600 whites—from 2 to 300 are Catholics. In each centre there is a residence with a chapel as fitting as means permit.' "

Later we read of 22 schools or chapels being blessed in the area which extended from Kamloops south to the border and into the Similkameen. Perhaps the earliest Inkameep church that Katie Lacey writes about in her article "The Churches of Inkameep" would be one of these. The author describes the early churches: "The early Indian-built churches were of log construction, windowless, pole and sod roof or shakes, dirt floors and tulle mats, no seats." [8]

Presbyterian and Methodist Missionaries

from **The Presbyterian Church in North and Central Okanagan**[9]
by Rev. William Scott

(This article was written in 1927 when Rev. Scott was in the ninth year of his pastorate in Armstrong.)

The first settler in the North Okanagan was also the grand old man of Presbyterianism in the Valley. Alexander Leslie Fortune, in his early manhood, had studied theology in Knox College, Toronto, with the ministry in view. Impaired health, however, compelled the abandonment of his high hopes...

[In July, 1886, just twenty years after he had arrived in Spallumcheen, A.L. Fortune welcomed the first resident Presbyterian minister to the area, Reverend J.A. Jaffray.]

In 1875, The Church of Scotland had sent the Reverend George Murray into the Nicola Valley, one hundred miles westward. Here, in 1876, the first Presbyterian Church in the interior of British Columbia was built...

The church in Nicola became the parent church of all the churches in the interior. It was used by other denominations. The Reverend James Turner of the Methodist Church, whose name is a household word among old-timers both in the Cariboo and the Okanagan, also made his headquarters in Nicola. But the missionaries of those days travelled far and wide and had many a weary trip...

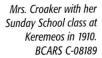

Mrs. Croaker with her Sunday School class at Keremeos in 1910.
BCARS C-08189

These men were very welcome guests at Mr. Fortune's home. His home was noted for its hospitality...Situated at the head of navigation he had ample opportunity for the exercise of this virtue. Mrs. Fortune arrived in 1874 to fill the long vacant position of hostess.

Among the other clerical guests who shared the bounty of their home were the Oblate Fathers, who had taken over the care of the Indians as early as 1860. Mr. Fortune carried on missionary work among the Indians of the neighbouring Reserve with the full concurrence of the priests.

In the eighties, other missionaries began to arrive. Reverend Robert Jamieson, of St. Andrew's Church, New Westminster, visited Mr. Fortune. In 1884, Reverend John Chisholm, successor to Reverend George Murray, at Nicola, made a memorable trip in fulfilling a commission of his church to explore the territory between Nicola and the Rocky Mountains. In the course of this tour, he conducted public worship "up the Spallumcheen Valley from Sicamous to Vernon in seven centres; along the Okanagan Valley from Vernon to the international boundary line, including Granite Creek, in six centres." It was on Mr. Chisholm's recommendation, followed by a petition from settlers themselves, that Reverend Mr. Jaffray had now, in 1886, been appointed to the new field of Spallumcheen.

[Because the Protestant clergymen were often married their wives played an important role in supporting and extending their work and influence as the following stories show.] Since Mr. Fortune was associated with all ministers, we must also tell of Reverend John W. Patterson of the Methodist Church, who preceded Mr. Jaffray. He lived in one of the houses on the Schubert Ranch, at Round Prairie (about a mile from where Armstrong is now). Mrs. Patterson was a very clever woman. In addition to her scholarly abilities she was a good judge of cattle. That was no mean accomplishment in the Spallumcheen in those days, for the whole valley was a cattle country. When the Pattersons came, Mr. Fortune offered them a cow and allowed Mrs. Patterson to choose her animal. Mrs. Patterson looked over the herd with practised eye, then stepping up to her choice to verify the quality by inspecting the skin, she promptly made her choice. Mr. Fortune was greatly pleased, for it was the best cow he had. On a similar occasion, in later years, when another minister's wife made a very poor choice, he would not let her take the cow she had chosen, but chose a better one for her.

The only house available for Mr. and Mrs. Jaffray at first was one known as "Leduc Stop," the Indians adding the "stop" to the owner's name of each place. It was very inconvenient, being some distance in the bush from Lansdowne and added many weary miles of riding. But before the year was out, another house was secured in Lansdowne, "The Village." Here also dwelt Dr. Offerhaus, Spallumcheen's doctor, who later married Miss Choquette, Mr. Fortune's niece. Here also were Furstineau's Hotel, Wood and Rabbitt's store, and Schneider's blacksmith shop. So now there was companionship for Mrs. Jaffray, when her husband was off on his periodical trips to Grand Prairie, or Priests' Valley, or the Mission.

Mrs. Jaffray is described by old-timers as being an ideal pioneer minister's wife. "She never complained but took everything as it was and made the best of it." She was also a very beautiful woman and general favorite. One of the choice articles in her home, which was also used for public worship, was an organ sent out from the east by her father, for the Canadian Pacific Railway was now operating...On Sunday evenings the people of the village, especially the young bachelors, used to gather round the organ and sing the old hymns over and over again.

Rev. Mr. Jaffray's pastorate lasted for three years...The man chosen to continue this missionary work was Rev. Paul F. Langill...

In Vernon...the services of worship were held in the school at first and the entire population, consisting of about three dozen men and three white women, would crowd the little building to capacity—how they would sing and listen to the reading of the gospel! Gradually a change came over the town; the popular Saturday night ball and Sunday carousing ceased; the stores and, finally, the bars were closed on Sundays...In this transformation, Mrs. Langill had no small part. For two years her home was but a shack,

Benvoulin Church, Kelowna.
Kelowna Museum

and the furniture home-made, but the latch was always on the string and old-timers dropping in were sometimes deeply moved at the sight of little children. Thus a real home softened the hardness of life...

The Benvoulin church is now practically the only outstanding landmark of the early period. It was built in 1892—in Rev. Mr. Langill's day—by W.H. Raymer, the Presbyterians of Guelph, Ontario, contributing to its support as part of their missionary work. Its name, "Bethel," was bestowed by Lady Aberdeen...

There is one minister of the Okanagan Centre field who cannot be passed over—

REID HALL
DEDICATED 1957

BENVOULIN CHURCH
DEDICATED 1892

Rev. C. Campbell-Brown, who was a missionary of the English Presbyterian Church in Amoy, China, for some twenty years. His health failing, he sought the climate of the Okanagan, and purchased a small ranch at Rattlesnake Point [Amory Point], on Kalamalka Lake, settling down to as quiet a life as his eager spirit would allow. When his health had improved somewhat he was asked to take charge of the Okanagan Centre field and accepted. Usually he walked between his preaching points of Okanagan Centre, Winfield, Commonage and Okanagan Landing. His literary gifts and his other scholarly attainments made him a prime favorite, especially at Okanagan Centre, where his fortnightly Saturday night lectures at the Rainbow Ranch were a feature of the community's life; but it was his other great gift of spirituality that drew men to him everywhere. While outwardly he seemed to find little response, the real facts were much in evidence when, after six years among them and a brief absence, he passed away in Vancouver. Men who had never even attended any of his services felt his death very deeply and on every hand men still say "Mr. Brown was a good man."

(*OHS*, 1935)

Writing of visiting missionaries in the Similkameen Verna B. Cawston says:

Informal church services were held whenever a minister of any cloth called at a ranch-house. The well-loved "Father Pat" (Henry Irwin) and Archdeacon Green are mentioned as the earliest visitors. From the *Penticton Herald* files comes this item: "The first public Protestant service in the lower Similkameen was held at the McCurdy ranch by Rev. Allan K. Sharpe in August, 1891."[10]

(*OHS*, 1949)

It was not until after the turn of the century that the Similkameen Valley had permanent Protestant church structures. The first church in Keremeos was built "on the hill" in 1906 and dedicated by the Presbyterians in 1908.[11] The first Anglican church was built "down town" in 1921.[12]

In Hedley, because of the larger centralized community due to mining, church building came somewhat earlier. In "Early History of Hedley Camp" Harry D. Barnes writes:

In the summer of 1903 Grace Methodist Church was built. This was the first, and for many years the only, permanent church building in the town. It was built mostly by volunteer labour under the enthusiastic direction of Rev. J.W. Hedley and, for many years, played a prominent role in the life of the community, serving as headquarters for the school, the Twentieth Century Club, and the library.[13]...

The Presbyterian church soon began to conduct services, at first with Rev. G.L. Mason in charge...Presbyterian services were usually held in Fraser's Hall (or Fraternity Hall, as it came to be called), which after 1905 was shared on alternate Sundays with the Anglican Church.

In May, 1905, the Archdeacon of Columbia, Ven. Edwyn S.W. Pentreath, visited Hedley, and as a result the congregation of St. Mary's was organized, complete with Ladies' Guild. Rev. E.P. Flewelling became the first resident Anglican clergyman. Rev. Henry Irwin ("Father Pat") so well known in Rossland in the early days of the camp and remembered for his many kindly acts, was an occasional visitor to Hedley...and when here would conduct services in one or other of the hotel dining-rooms. An Anglican church, however, was not built until the early years of World War I...From the early days of Hedley, Roman Catholic services had been conducted at frequent intervals by visiting priests.

(*OHS*, 1948)

Reverend J.C. Goodfellow tells us of a Methodist church in the vicinity of Princeton, "built in 1912 and designed as the religious centre of a town which was to grow around a cement factory. A huge plant was actually built. It brought nothing but grief to speculators."[14] John Goodfellow, in addition to serving the people of Princeton for more than thirty years as minister at St. Paul's Church, was active in many local organizations and during the years of World War II he was editor of the *Similkameen Star* when the owner/publisher, Dave Taylor, was absent on a war assignment.

Margaret Mitchell in her "Reminiscences of Early Princeton"[16] gives us a vivid sketch of the celebrated Dr. H.E.D. Ashford, Rev. John Goodfellow's predecessor at St. Paul's. Rev. Ashford seems to have been something of

Princeton, looking along Bridge Street c. 1900. BCARS C-08181

Reverend John Christie Goodfellow (1890-1968) came to Canada as a student missionary in 1908 from his home in Scotland. Of him Eric M. Goodfellow writes:[15]

A man of independent mind, though linked with the church for most of his life, he had a varied career...sailing before the mast, serving at Gallipoli, spreading the gospel to and studying the culture of Coast Indians. He was, however, specializing in the history of the United Church in British Columbia, for which service he was awarded an honorary Doctorate of Divinity in 1950.

He was secretary of the B.C. Synod (Presbyterian) Historical Committee from 1923 to 1925, and the B.C. Conference (United) Historical Committee from 1925 to 1950, and its convener from 1946 to 1950.

He was Council Member of the B.C. Historical Association, its President 1941-42, and a frequent contributor to its Quarterly magazine. A life member of the Okanagan Historical Society, he held various offices, among them editor of its Annual Report 1954-56, to which he was a prominent contributor.
(*OHS*, 1969) Photo: Princeton Museum

Vernon Methodist picnic. Vernon Museum 829

a latter-day Father Pat. He began his ministry by offering to referee hockey games, much to the consternation of the more conservative members of his congregation. However, Dr. Ashford's methods proved productive in both church and community.

In 1926 Methodists, Congregationalists and some Presbyterians throughout Canada joined to form the United Church. Not all Presbyterian congregations were willing to submerge their identity in the larger organization. Hence we still have Presbyterian congregations in our area.

The Anglican Church

When the Anglican Diocese of New Westminster was founded in 1879 the Right Reverend Acton Windeyer Sillitoe was named bishop. In 1880 and again in 1883 the bishop and Mrs. Sillitoe visited both Penticton and Osoyoos, having travelled over the Hope Trail. The second visit coincided with the visit of General Sherman to Osoyoos. Mrs. Sillitoe recalls the occasion in her *Memoirs*:

On Tuesday, Aug. 21, 1883, with an Indian guide, we set off on the last stage of our journey southward (from Penticton) and reached Osoyoos thirty-five miles distant, in ten hours and a half. Osoyoos on the Canadian side of the line consists of two families, the Haynes and Krugers, and it was arranged therefore that service should be held on the United States side of the line, where a considerable number of people reside, and where was also the encampment of the troop of United States cavalry, that had formed the escort of General Sherman. About ten o'clock we [the bishop, Mrs. Sillitoe and Mr. Haynes] started in a row-boat for the foot of the lake, and proceeding to the camp, found arrangements made for the accommodation of quite a large congregation.

...The sacrament of baptism was first administered to four children (August and Theodore Kruger and Harry Grainger were three of the children).[17]

(*OHS*, 1951)

Chrestenza Kruger in her article "Early Days on Osoyoos" recalls the same incident but with somewhat inflated figures. The US Army report quoted by Mrs. Hester White numbers the company at 81 persons, 66 horses and 79 mules. But here is Mrs. Kruger's colourful account of the evening:

In 1883 there was trouble on the American side with the Nez Perce Indians and General Sherman was sent in with a troop of cavalry to quell any disturbance which might arise and also to report on conditions in the country. The U.S. Government had in mind, at one time, the erection of a fort at Oroville. The army headquarters were at, or near, Okanagan Smith's ranch, south of the boundary line...Bishop Sillitoe of New Westminster also visited Osoyoos about this time and one Sunday evening he held service at the General's headquarters. There was no building in which to hold the service so the soldiers constructed with branches of trees a sort of booth (and an altar), the entrance to which was an arch, and for seats they had long rows of sacks of oats. I shall never forget that service. It was a calm, clear evening in August. While the bishop read the Church of England service, about 250 soldiers stood reverently grouped around the booth. They joined in the singing; some of them sang very well and at the offertory one of them sang a solo...Advantage was taken of the presence of the Bishop to have a number of the children baptized—twelve in all, and among them my two boys, Theodore and August.[18]

(*OHS*, 1935)

The original St. Saviour's Anglican Church in Penticton. In 1934 this church was moved and attached as a chapel to the newer structure on Winnipeg Street.
Penticton Museum 2-030A

The Historical Committee of St. Saviour's Parish in Penticton writes:

...Every Sunday religious services were held in the home [of Tom and Mina Ellis] and, except on the rare occasions when a pastor of some denomination happened in the area, the services were taken by Mr. Ellis, or a member of the family. Besides the ranch workers, any persons in the neighbourhood at the time were invited.

Such was the local situation when the first Bishop of New Westminster, Right Reverend Acton W. Sillitoe, visited the Okanagan with his wife on September 23rd, 1880. Full Church services were conducted in the Ellis home...The Bishop and Mrs. Sillitoe again visited the Ellis home in August, 1883...

In 1891 the Ellis family while en route to Kamloops, became involved in a very serious accident by the team of horses taking fright and bolting. As a thanksgiving that all were spared from death, Mr. Ellis caused to be erected on his property, the first Protestant church in Okanagan and so named it St. Saviour's... [Actually, St. James at Lansdowne had been built in 1885.]

Sunday, November 6th, 1892, Bishop Sillitoe, assisted by Rev. W. Outerbridge, conducted full services in the church to capacity congregations and the Bishop preached an eloquent sermon on "Consistent Christianity." His Lordship expressed surprise in finding a complete church with nave and chancel, oak lectern and reading desk, an organ and carpet and drapes in the Sanctuary. Seating for fifty. The Bishop at this time consecrated the Sanctuary only, as it was thought wise to allow remainder of the building to be available for use by pastors of other denominations.[19]

(*OHS*, 1964)

After considerable discussion, in 1934 the surviving members of the Ellis family gave permission to move the original St. Saviour's from Fairview Road and attach it to the south wall of the new church [on Winnipeg Street]...And so the little church, restored to its original design was re-erected and dedicated on September 23, 1934 as the Ellis Memorial Chapel to the memory of Thomas Ellis, his wife, Wilhelmina, and her brother, Alfred Wade.[20]
(*OHS*, 1986)

The name "Father Pat" has occurred above. Even during his lifetime the Reverend Henry Irwin (his real name) was a legend:

from **An Anglican Sky Pilot**[21]

by Rt. Rev. A.H. Sovreign

Henry "Father Pat" Irwin at times had to rely on his own two fists for survival when serving as a missionary in rough-and-tumble mining camps.
Anglican Archives

...On August 2nd, 1859, Rev. Henry Irwin, affectionately known as "Father Pat," was born in Ireland, where the Wicklow Mountains roll down to the Irish Sea. His father, his grandfather and his great grandfather had been priests of the Anglican Church in Ireland. This bright, happy Irish boy said frequently as a child—"I am going to be a missionary." He was educated at St. Columba's School near Dublin and at Keble College, Oxford, where he distinguished himself as an athlete, especially in rowing and in boxing. He was ordained to the ministry and accepted a curacy at Rugby. Then a call came to him from the Rt. Rev. A.W. Sillitoe, Bishop of New Westminster in British Columbia and, in 1885, he embarked for Kamloops through which the C.P.R. was being built...

His field of work reached from Kamloops to Osoyoos and from Princeton to the Nicola. His letters to England are most revealing. "Thanks for the clothes which arrived safely and are a great blessing to me. You cannot think how nice it is to feel respectable out here, where one has to put up with almost anything in the way of clothes...Last week I started with those riding pants you sent me, but after about 300 miles they went to pieces, and I had to get into a vile kind of garment they call "overalls," striped like a zebra and cut like a sailor's pantaloons. You would open your eyes wide to see a parson at work out here...I am now as hard as a cake and a brown one at that. I finished in June a trip of 570 miles in the saddle, and by the end of that time I was a dirty brown."

During the year of 1886, he gave much of his time to the Nicola and Princeton area where several mines had been opened and were in operation. "Nothing but mines and gold is heard here. The mines are just 12 miles away, but the men register here (Princeton), so we see hundreds. There are all sorts and conditions of men—lawyers, farmers, cowboys from the United States and Manitoba, a jolly lot of rough cards, but rare, good, fine-looking fellows and very hearty; and then more than a thousand Chinamen. Such is the pack there on the mines at Granite Creek. I had a nice time in the mining camp; lots of friends there, and I had quite a number of visits for meals. I shall have a service there tomorrow morning."
(*OHS*, 1959)

While stationed at Kamloops Father Pat met his future wife. The story is told by Mrs. Jerome Mercier in her little book *Father Pat: A Hero of the Far West*.[22] Frances Stuart Innes was the youngest daughter of a public servant in Victoria. She met Henry Irwin at the Horlock home in Kamloops while on the way to spend a holiday with her sister Mrs. Shildrick in Spallumcheen. Henry Irwin visited Frances in Spallumcheen. The courtship resulted in an engagement which lasted four years before their marriage could be arranged.

Bishop Sovreign continues:

And now there came into [Father Pat's] life the greatest happiness and his greatest sorrow...

On January 8th, 1890, Henry Irwin and Frances Innes were married at St. Paul's Church, Esquimalt, on Vancouver Island. They were very happy! Perfect love and perfect sympathy were manifested in his chivalrous devotion and her tender grace. But then, sadly, quickly came the end. In the autumn days of November a little child was born who never drew breath in this world—and then, three days later, the gentle mother was called to the Paradise of God. The loving mother and her babe were laid to rest in that beautiful cemetery overlooking the ever-rolling stream, the mighty Fraser, at Sapperton...

Once again Father Pat was given a new sphere of labour, and this time, it was in the Kootenays with its headquarters at Rossland. Here he laboured with deep devotion among the miners and railroad men who had come hither from many lands. He opened a free library and a reading room to care for the ebb and flow of restless men. He built churches and called to one and all to come and worship their God. His journeys over the mountains were phenomenal; he seemed to be tireless. He loved the wilderness where he was alone with his Heavenly Father...

His final "Parish" was that of Fairview, a mining camp in the mountains near Oliver. Many anecdotes are told of his life and labours in this area...[Once] among a group of miners was one coarser than the rest and he ventured to insult the Padre, but Pat paid no attention to him until the miner added other epithets which were an insult to religion and to our Lord Himself. Father Pat turned to him sternly, saying—"I don't mind your insulting me, but you shall not insult my Master." The miner drew nearer to Pat in a threatening manner, thinking to overawe him with his superior bulk, but without further warning Pat turned on the man and with his scientific skill as a boxer, he punished the man severely, and in the end, the miner went down like a log, unconscious and bleeding. Down on his knees went Father Pat, anxiously examining the injuries. Then and there, in a fit of remorse, he cried—"O Lord, forgive me for not telling the man that I was a champion boxer."

On January 13, 1902, while on his way home to Ireland for a rest, Henry Irwin died in Montreal. He was 43 years of age. His body was buried beside those of his wife and child in the Sapperton cemetery.

The first Anglican church in the North Okanagan was St. James Church, built at Lansdowne in 1885. The church was relocated in Armstrong in 1891, when people moved from the original centre of population at Lansdowne to a location near the newly constructed railway. In the same year, 1891, St. George's was built in Enderby.

An interesting result of the work of the Anglican missionary Rev. Canon William Cooper, assistant to Rev. D.H.W. Horlock at Kamloops, was the establishment in 1888 of the first Masonic Lodge in the Okanagan, Spallumcheen Lodge No. 13. The lodge met at E.M. Furstineau's Lansdowne Hotel until it followed the village population to the new location at Armstrong. So keen was Mr. Cooper's interest in Freemasonry that he was willing to serve as worshipful master for the first year, a duty which entailed a monthly trip from Kamloops, a two-day ride away.[23]

St. Michael's and All Angels Anglican Cathedral, Kelowna. Kelowna Centennial Museum 10528

The Baptists

In 1888 John Moore Robinson arrived in the Okanagan from Brandon, Manitoba to form a mining company...J.M., as he was usually called was president of the company...On Trepanier Creek, adjacent to the site of the mining, was a ranch owned by the Lambly brothers. This ranch was primarily given to raising cattle and horses, but they had planted a few peach trees...One day J.M. had a meal at this ranch and ate some of the peaches then at the peak of their maturity, and their excellence gave him an inspiration that changed the lives of thousands of people.[24]

(*OHS*, 1973)

J.M. Robinson decided that his gold was to be found in buying up land and subdividing it into ten-acre orchard lots which sold at $100 per acre. Thus began a process of subdivision which was to affect the development of Peachland, West Summerland, Naramata and Kaleden. In 1903 James Ritchie came to the Okanagan from Pilot Mound, Manitoba and he participated in these developments. Because Mr. Robinson and Mr. Ritchie were from the prairie it was there they sought buyers for their orchard plots and, because they were Baptists, many of their associates were of that denomination. Hence the new communities had a strong Baptist element.

These were the communities which were ready in 1905 to support the creation and operation of an Okanagan Baptist College. A free building site was found in Summerland and construction of the college building begun. In the fall of 1906 classes were begun in rented premises. Douglas Scott writes:

> For a new and small College, Okanagan had an extensive and varied curriculum. Instruction in high school subjects was always a "staple" item. Many young people in the area had missed the chance to get a high school education, and the College provided a good opportunity for this. With the formal opening in 1907 a Commercial course, including Stenography and Typewriting, was provided, as was a course in Music—instrumental and vocal. In the 1909–10 session, university work to the end of the second year was included, with the expectation that the College would soon be able to give a B.A. degree through affiliation with McMaster University.[25]
> (*OHS*, 1982)

Frank Haskins in his article "Okanagan Baptist College at Summerland"[26] quotes Professor Aaron J. Perry's description of the buildings:

> "The College residence is a handsome frame building, eighty by forty, with an L, forty by thirty, three and one-half storeys, with concrete basement. The building is heated throughout with hot water, and lighted by electricity. Every flat is supplied with hot and cold water...The students' rooms are large and commodious...There is ample accommodation for between forty and fifty resident students, besides teachers and household staff. The class rooms number seven, all large, airy and bright and furnished with special classroom chairs, having armrests attached. In addition to these are: a large chapel, music rooms, reception room, principal's office, and in the basement the dining room, seating 100 students..."
> By the autumn of 1910 a gymnasium and a women's residence had been added to the buildings. During the time the College functioned, the members of the Summerland Baptist Church donated 22 acres of land and paid over $40,000 to the College...
> Heavy indebtedness and declining enrolment contributed to the decision of the Board of Education of the Baptist Union of Western Canada, in the autumn of 1915, not to reopen the College. The venture had been poorly timed, but during the short period of about seven years it functioned it permitted a number of students to receive the benefit of higher education at a nearby institution.
> The college building was totally destroyed by fire in 1941.
> (*OHS*, 1949)

Today none of the buildings remain. The last, after undergoing several transformations, was transported in its entirety to Penticton on July 7, 1988. Unfortunately the new owner's plans for the building were not realized and on February 11, 1991 the structure was gutted by fire.

Religious Institutions Today

That local churches were important to the early settlers is shown by the number of stories about individual churches to be found in the *Annual Reports of the Okanagan Historical Society*. In our more urbanized culture, churches still remain important in the Okanagan. Denominations have proliferated. Then there are the non-Christian groups who encourage their adherents to find dignity and self-worth as part of some greater whole—the Buddhists, the Sikhs, the Baha'i, for example.

Besides their purely devotional activities congregations reach out in very practical ways to those in need.

They participate in food banks, in thrift shops, in building affordable housing for the poor or elderly, in the preparation of Christmas hampers–this latter activity often achieved by co-operation of various denominations under the chairmanship of the Salvation Army. The Dorcas groups of the Seventh Day Adventists have come to the immediate aid of families overcome by disasters such as fire. During the turbulent 1960s St. Saviour's Anglican Church in Vernon turned their smaller parish hall into a hostel for wandering youth. The list is endless.

Then there are the individuals who find their inspiration in the religious ethic but who often work outside any denominational institution. One extraordinary example of such a person was Dr. Hugh Campbell-Brown, son of the Reverend Colin Campbell-Brown mentioned earlier. Dr. Campbell-Brown practised medicine for many years in Vernon. His daughter Elizabeth Hieronymi writes of him:

> Religion was a life-long quest in his life. He spent years searching for what was "right" for him...Finally in 1953 he joined the religious Society of Friends (Quakers) and he remained actively involved with Friends until his death [in 1982]...
>
> His interest in humanity never ceased. He served on the Vernon Social Planning Committee, was on the Boards of both the Venture Training Centre [a sheltered workshop] and the United Nations Friendship Centre during their formative years. He was always interested in the welfare of the members of the Okanagan Reserve, as patients and as friends. He was deeply committed to and served as a Board member and President of the North Okanagan Branch of the John Howard Society and of Howard House. He also supported Amnesty International.[27]
>
> (*OHS*, 1985)

6

From Colony to Province

Confederation

Canada, which consisted in 1867 of Ontario, Quebec, Nova Scotia and New Brunswick, saw that the inclusion of British Columbia in its domain would assure access to the Pacific Ocean. At first the fact that the intervening territory, which was finally to become Alberta, Saskatchewan and Manitoba, was still held by the Hudson's Bay Company made confederation impracticable. However, in 1869 the company surrendered its Rupert's Land territories to the government of Canada and the lands between the Rockies and Ontario became the Northwest Territories. In 1870 Manitoba became a province, to be followed by British Columbia in 1871.

Pioneer justices of the peace in 1891. From left to right standing: Cornelius O'Keefe, Moses Lumby, Luc Girouard, James Crozier. From left to right sitting: E.J. Tronson, Bernard Lequime, F. Brent, I. Boucherie, Tom Ellis. Vernon Museum

Under the colonial government the colonial Legislative Assembly, consisting of elected members, had played an advisory role but power had remained with the governor and his appointed Executive Council. From 1864 to 1866 John Carmichael Haynes, as magistrate for Osoyoos and Kootenay, sat on the Legislative Council.[1] Once the 1866 Act of Union had been passed, creating a single colony of the former crown colonies of Vancouver Island and British Columbia, Haynes's name no longer appeared in the list of council members. In 1867, 1868 and 1870 Francis Jones Barnard is named as the representative for Yale.[2] The centre of power in the Okanagan was shifting to the north.

In honour of the contribution made to Vernon's development by Frank Barnard and his son Francis Stillman Barnard, the town's main street was once named after the family. In his article entitled "Vernon's Street Names" Stuart J. Martin writes:

> Barnard Avenue.—Francis Jones Barnard, who arrived in Victoria in 1859, started a pony express from the Cariboo to the Coast, B.C. Express Company. Barnard purchased the B.X. Ranch at Vernon in 1864. He served in the Legislative Council of British Columbia as member from Yale in the pre-Confederation period, and was later Member of Parliament representing Yale. After his death in 1889, his business was carried on by his son Francis Stillman (later Sir Francis) Barnard and Stephen Tingley. F.S. Barnard was one of the members of the syndicate, Okanagan Land and Development Company, which laid out the townsite of Vernon, constructed the Coldstream Hotel and Kalamalka Hotel, installed a waterworks system, and started the *Vernon News*. Later he was Lieutenant-Governor of the Province.[3]
> (*OHS*, 1949)

MPs and MLAs

Confederation made it possible for a citizen of British Columbia to vote for a Member of Parliament to represent British Columbia's interests in Ottawa and for a Member of the Legislative Assembly to represent the interests of the constituency in Victoria. Of course it was one thing to pass a bill making British Columbia a province but quite another to establish the electoral paraphernalia necessary for democratic government. Thus the election of Captain C.F. Houghton as first MP for Yale was certainly irregular by modern standards.

The First Federal Election in Yale[4]

by B.R. Atkins

The most unique election in Canada since Confederation was probably that held at Yale, B.C. in December 1871, when two votes, and two only, sent to Ottawa the first MP for all of British Columbia's great southern hinterland. He represented the country of the Kootenays, East and West, the Boundary, the Kamloops and Thompson Rivers, the Okanagan, the Nicola–Similkameen...indeed all the territory from the Rockies to the Cascades—then known as Yale.

The returning officer, Hon. Arthur T. Bushby, was a conspicuous figure in colonial administration.

And this is the story (much condensed) as told a few days after the death of the honourable and gallant member then elected.

"The morning was, naturally, regarding the season and locality, cold, which the tin stove was doing its best to alleviate. Suddenly Mr. Bushby said, 'This is nomination day, and, by the way, about the hour for the receipt of nominations. While I send the constable to rouse up the voters, I'll read you the writ.'

"He was a quick reader, but he hardly got through before the constable reappeared with two puzzled-looking voters. He explained that the others had refused to leave their fires, their game of pool or cards, saying there was 'nothing in it.'

"However, the two escorted voters were there, and one asked, 'What's it all about?' Told, he asked, being inquisitively intelligent, 'Has the writ been read?'

" 'Just finished as you came in,' said the returning officer, 'we are all ready to receive nominations.'

"Hurriedly they talked between themselves, canvassing several names of men who might not object. Then the inquisitive one voiced his view, seconded with relief by the other, 'I nominate Captain Houghton.'

" 'Good,' said the returning officer, 'are there any other nominations?' There were none, and after a reasonable pause, Captain Houghton with all the proper solemnity was declared duly elected by acclamation as federal member for Yale.

"About a half an hour afterwards, the latch lifted, and a lone, cold elector strolled in to enquire if this wasn't election day. 'Sure is,' said the returning officer. 'You're late. It's all over. Captain Houghton was elected by acclamation.' 'Captain Houghton, who is he?' 'A rancher in the Okanagan, I think. He—' 'Oh, it's all right; I don't know him, but I s'pose he'll do.'

"And the lone voluntary of the large constituency, in its choice of a representative in that young nation's council, left quite satisfied that everything had been done for the best."

After one or two sessions at Ottawa, Houghton resigned his seat, and in March 1873 was appointed district adjutant of British Columbia and he organized its militia. He served in the North-West Rebellion, being present at Fish Creek and Batoche. In 1888 he was given a military district command with Montreal as headquarters, but he resigned in 1897 to come back to British Columbia. He died in Victoria on August 13, 1898.

In the words of this eye-witness of his election: "He was well and favorably known as a genial gentleman of conspicuous ability and scholarly attainments, a soldier and a desirable citizen."

(*OHS*, 1951)

Hence Captain Charles Frederick Houghton went off to Ottawa as one of six MPs from British Columbia, all of them Conservatives. Houghton's constituency was huge, embracing the Kootenay as well as the land west to the Fraser River. However, Houghton was not a happy MP, preferring military life to that of a politician. In an 1872 byelection following Houghton's resignation, Edgar Dewdney, the civil engineer and trail builder, was elected and served until 1879.[5] Francis Jones Barnard appears to have followed Dewdney as Member of Parliament and then in 1887 the Overlander John Andrew Mara was elected and served until 1896. Mara had already served as a member of the Legislative Assembly of British Columbia from 1871 to 1886, being speaker for the last three of those years. As the population of the Interior increased, constituency boundaries were redefined and the number of MPs and MLAs increased.

In 1875 Forbes George Vernon, the younger of the two brothers who had accompanied Charles Houghton to the North Okanagan and who by 1875 was the sole owner of the Coldstream Ranch, was elected by Yale East to a seat in the Legislative Assembly of British Columbia.[6]

*Left to right: Colonel Baker (MLA Cranbrook), Lord Aberdeen, his daughter Lady Marjorie, his son Archie with Lady Aberdeen, Lt. Gov. Edgar Dewdney, Mrs. Baker, Mrs. Dewdney, Miss Allison, Dewdney's aide-de-camp, Forbes George Vernon (MLA East Yale). The picture was taken in Victoria just before the 1894 election.
Vernon Museum 809*

Susan Steinke writes:

Forbes George Vernon's appointment a year later to the post of CCLW [Chief Commissioner of Lands and Works] made him, next to the premier, the most powerful cabinet minister in the government and the senior mainland representative. Robert Cail writes:

He found himself responsible for such diverse matters as roads, bridges, government buildings, water rights, drainage and irrigation works, maps and surveys and government lands—agricultural, timber, mineral and coal.

The CCLW, in control of land sales and grants for the entire province, was considered by colleagues and settlers alike to be a "high and mighty individual."[7]
(OHS, 1987)

When Vernon was defeated in the election of 1894 by Donald Graham, a politically inexperienced Spallumcheen farmer, it became evident that a profound change was taking place in the social landscape of the Okanagan.

In 1898 Price Ellison, a young Englishman who had arrived in the Okanagan via the Hope Trail in 1876 and had amassed large holdings of agricultural land in the North Okanagan, was elected as a Conservative to the Legislative Assembly and served as party whip. Ellison had married Sophia Johnson, Vernon's first school teacher, and their home became a social centre in the Vernon area.[8] Among the portfolios that Ellison held were commissioner of lands, minister of finance and minister of agriculture. Ellison's accomplishments included the building of the courthouse in Vernon,[9] the preservation for the public of Strathcona Park on Vancouver Island and the establishment of a public ferry at Kelowna.

L.A. Hayman, in his history of that lake crossing, writes:

By 1905 the community of Westbank was becoming important. As an election was on, Price Ellison was a candidate. His meeting was held in Shannon Marshall's house. We asked for a ferry. Later it fell to my lot to row the candidate across the lake to Kelowna. Alexander McLennan, a Socialist, was on the beach when we were getting started. When we were a short distance off shore Ellison turned to me and said, "Wait a minute, Len," and turning to McLennan he said: "What about your vote, Alec?" "Well, give us a ferry and put it in this bay and it's yours," was the reply. Ellison then turned to me and said, "Row on, Len." So that is how we got the ferry.[10]
(OHS, 1943)

Vernon Courthouse built 1911–1914 while Price Ellison was MLA and minister of agriculture.
Vernon Museum 5014

Inkster Quarry on the east shore of Okanagan Lake a few miles south of Okanagan Landing, c. 1911. Granite for the Vernon Courthouse came from this quarry.
Vernon Museum 1057

In 1916 J.W. Jones (Conservative), a partner in the Central Okanagan Land Company and a former mayor of Kelowna, was elected MLA for South Okanagan. He served as minister of finance and industry from 1930 to 1933. He is credited with originating payroll deductions for income tax.[11]

Dr. K.C. Macdonald (Liberal), a Vernon dentist, served as MLA 1916–1924. The 1924 election in North Okanagan was a four-way race which Macdonald won. However, when he was appointed to the cabinet he was required by law to resign as MLA and submit his name to the electorate once more before taking any government position in which there was remuneration. In the byelection Macdonald was opposed by one candidate, A.O. Cochrane, a Conservative. Cochrane won. This rather awkward procedure, called "confirmation,"

Conservative MLA Price Ellison helped establish the public ferry at Kelowna.
Vernon Museum

was ended by law in 1929.[12] K.C. Macdonald served as MLA again from 1933 to 1945. He held the portfolio of minister of agriculture. In 1941 he, with his fellow Liberals, entered into a coalition with the Conservatives.

In 1924, Grote Stirling of Kelowna was elected Member of Parliament for Yale and continued to be re-elected until his resignation due to ill health in 1947. Grote Stirling served as minister of defence as well as acting minister of fisheries in the R.B. Bennett government during the 1930s.

A list of others who have served as cabinet ministers includes: R.W. Bruhn (Conservative and Coalition) of Salmon Arm; from Similkameen W.A. McKenzie (Conservative); from North Okanagan C.W. Morrow (Coalition), Patricia Jordan and Lyall Hanson (both Social Credit); from Similkameen and South Okanagan Francis S. Richter (Social Credit); and Bill Barlee (New Democratic Party). L.H. Shantz from North Okanagan served as speaker of the House.

The Government Agent's office in Vernon.
Vernon Museum 443

The Bennett Years

The Okanagan reached the zenith of its importance in the legislative life of British Columbia when a Social Credit government was elected in 1952 and William Andrew Cecil Bennett, MLA for South Okanagan (Kelowna), was sworn in as premier. M. Anita Tozer, daughter of W.A.C. Bennett, has given us a biographical sketch of her father:

> Cecil Bennett came to Kelowna in 1930 in search of a hardware store in which to invest. [He bought out David Leckie]...
>
> Cecil Bennett was an active citizen of Kelowna and the Okanagan Valley from the beginning. He joined the Board of Trade, the fore-runner of the Chamber of Commerce, and was its president at one time. He joined the Gyro Club, the Masons, the Kelowna Club. He was active in the United Church...the Red Cross, the Salvation Army and Community Chest campaigns...
>
> In 1941, when he gained the Conservative nomination, W.A.C. Bennett was elected MLA for South Okanagan....The Conservatives and the Liberals formed an uneasy Coalition government to fight the C.C.F. party which was gaining strength and they remained locked together in an uneasy truce until 1952.

Finding himself unable to reform either the Conservatives or the Coalition from within...in 1951, in a bold and dramatic gesture, Cecil Bennett crossed the floor of the House and sat as an Independent. When he decided to join the Social Credit Party he again reported directly to the Okanagan electorate and when the Provincial Election of 1952 was called his new party...won the most seats—one more than the C.C.F....

William Andrew Cecil Bennett became the longest serving Premier of the Province of British Columbia long before his government was defeated in 1972. He gave British Columbia twenty years of dynamic leadership and over thirty years of political involvement before he retired in 1973. He died in February 1979.[13]

(*OHS*, 1995)

W.A.C. Bennett's years as premier coincided with those years following World War II when a growing population and industrial development produced a buoyant economy. Bennett had the vision to take advantage of this circumstance and the astuteness to attract and challenge, both within the cabinet and outside, men who were intelligent, imaginative and energetic.

One of Bennett's major projects was the development of the network of roads and bridges throughout the province. The Kelowna bridge was built in spite of nay-sayers who believed the structure would never be used sufficiently to justify the expense. He built the ferry fleet serving the coast. Trade schools and community colleges were established. Dams were built to expand the potential of BC Hydro which had taken over BC Electric. However, no megaproject caused the premier to forget the interests of his home community.

In 1972 Cecil Bennett's younger son, William, was elected as MLA in the constituency which his father had held for so many years. When the Social Credit Party won the election of 1975 Bill Bennett became premier. Under his premiership the Coquihalla Highway, which had been planned under the previous administration, was completed and the connector linking Kelowna more directly to the coast was begun.

W.A.C. Bennett., the twenty-fifth premier of BC (1957–72), began his political career in Kelowna.
Kelowna Museum

The Civil Service

In the transfer from colonial to provincial status many of the administrative officials in the field maintained their positions. John Carmichael Haynes of Osoyoos, for example, continued his duties, reporting on provincial matters to Victoria and on federal to Ottawa. It was not until his sudden death in 1888 that his tasks were divided between two officials. In 1889 Theodore Kruger assumed the federal duties of customs officer and postmaster and C.A.R. Lambly served as government agent at Rock Creek, Camp McKinney, Osoyoos and Fairview.

After confederation, while the term "gold commissioner" was retained as it is to this day, the more comprehensive term of "government agent" came into usage. The following excerpt from Kathleen Dewdney's article "Walter Robert Dewdney" gives us some idea of the duties of the office.

Walter Dewdney Senior was appointed Government Agent at Yale in 1881 and remained there until he was transferred to Enderby in 1884. When the Provincial Government Agency was moved from Enderby to Priests' Valley in 1885 he became the first Government Agent at what was to become Vernon and he held this position until his death in 1892. He was the brother of the Honourable Edgar Dewdney, pioneer civil engineer, land surveyor and trail-blazer...

Walter Robert [son of Walter Sr.]...was a member of the government office staff in Grand Forks from 1901 until 1912 when he was transferred to Greenwood as Government Agent. On April 1, 1922, he opened the first government office in Penticton and remained there as Government Agent until his official retirement on January 1, 1947.

At that time he held the following fifteen appointments: Government Agent, Water Recorder, Registrar of Voters, District Registrar of Births, Deaths and Marriages, Marriage Commissioner, Gold Commissioner, Commissioner of Lands, Mining Recorder, Registrar of the County Court, District Registrar of the Supreme Court, Clerk of the Peace, Provincial

Collector, Stipendiary Magistrate, Magistrate of the Small Debts Court, and member of the Board of Management of the Penticton Hospital.[14]
(*OHS*, 1956)

In 1913 Walter Dewdney married Kathleen Stuart Ferguson in Greenwood, a booming mining town at the time. When the couple moved to Penticton in 1922 Mrs. Dewdney was able to pursue her interest in Okanagan history.

Mrs. Dewdney...was born in Calgary, Alberta. She spent her school days in Trail, Midway, Grand Forks and Vancouver. She graduated as a teacher from the Provincial Normal School in Vancouver, and taught in a well-built, comfortable log school house—grades 1 to 8 inclusive—on Ingram Mountain near Midway.

In 1922 the growing City of Penticton became the centre of government administration and Mr. Dewdney was transferred here as a Government Agent...

Kathleen became actively committed to the preservation of Okanagan–Similkameen history. For two years from 1968 to 1970 she served as president of the Okanagan Historical Society (Parent Body).

Dr. Margaret Ormsby of Vernon, an active member of the O.H.S. since 1935 and now [1979] B.C.'s senior historian,...congratulated Mrs. Dewdney not only on the authenticity of each article, but in particular on the structure and realistic feeling of each... "Her qualities," said Dr. Ormsby, "are best exemplified in an article which she did in our first Centennial Year, 1958. This article on the Dewdney Trail stands out as surely one of the most important articles in any or all of the *Okanagan History Reports*."[15]

(*OHS*, 1980)

Kathleen Dewdney died in her Penticton home in 1985 at the age of ninety-five.

Photo: Penticton Museum

Voters' List for the Rock Creek Polling Division 1875[16]

Armstrong, Hugh, Penticton, Labourer, Resident.
Barcelo, Manuel, Similkameen, Stock Raiser.
Cawston, Richard Lowe, Osoyoos Lake, Stock Raiser, Resident.
Cole, Thomas, Similkameen Valley, Farmer, Pre-emptor.
Ellis, Thomas, Penticton, Stock Raiser, Freeholder.
Kruger, Theodore, Osoyoos Lake, Trader, Pre-emptor.
McCauley, Joseph, Grand Prairie, Kettle River, Stock Raiser.
McConnell, James, Grand Prairie, Kettle River, Stock Raiser.
Mendoza, Francisco, Similkameen Valley, Stock Raiser, Resident.
Nicholson, Henry, Similkameen Valley, Stock Raiser, Resident.
Price, Barrington, Similkameen Valley, Stock Raiser, Resident.
Shuttleworth, Henry, Similkameen Valley, Farmer, Pre-emptor.
Suprennant, Francois, Similkameen Valley, Stock Raiser, Resident.
Richter, Frank, Similkameen Valley, Stock Raiser, Resident.

Barrington Price, Collector
Sept. 15th, 1875.
(*OHS*, 1931)

Missing from this list are the names of women, Natives and Chinese who lived in the area. Women did not receive the BC franchise until 1916 and the federal until 1918. East Indians were granted the right to vote in 1947 and by 1949 Natives, Chinese and Japanese had the right to vote in federal and provincial elections.

7
Stage Drivers and Mail Carriers

Stagecoaches

The completion of the Cariboo Road in 1862 meant that travel by stagecoach or wagon in the Interior of British Columbia was now feasible. The construction of the road through the Fraser Canyon and along the lower reaches of the Thompson had been difficult and expensive. However, a branch line into the Kamloops area and on to the Okanagan was a much easier matter. Most of the grass-covered prairie and benchlands could be crossed with no road building.

In "Stagecoaches in the North Okanagan—1872–1892"[1] Ken Mather tells us: "Mail service began very soon after Confederation when the British Columbia Legislature, in 1872, petitioned the Federal Government for such a service." According to Mr. Mather the *Victoria Colonist* of August 6, 1872 reported that temporary arrangements had been made with "Mr. Barnard for a weekly mail service to Kamloops and the Okanagan."

Francis Jones Barnard was no stranger to mail delivery. Once the Cariboo Road was constructed he was in business.

Francis Jones Barnard, founder of the BX Express Co. mail delivery service.
Vernon Museum

[F.J. Barnard] started out by carrying mail from Yale to Barkerville, 300 miles on his back at $3 per letter. It must have been a profitable business, because it developed into a pony express, and finally into a stagecoach line. In order to keep the stage running he developed a ranch in the Okanagan, known as the Barnard Express Ranch, or BX Ranch. To assure an adequate supply of good horses for his BX Express Co., F.J. Barnard, in association with Stephen Tingley, developed the BX Ranch about five miles northeast of Vernon's city centre. In 1868 Tingley, who had been a "crack" driver on the Cariboo Road, went to New Mexico where he procured some 400 horses of the Morgan breed to stock the 6,300-acre ranch.[2]

(*OHS*, 1963)

Barnard Express stagecoach.
Vernon Museum 37

Ken Mather writes:

The stagecoaches that ran on the Cache Creek to Kamloops to Okanagan run were smaller "two-horse specials" also known as "jerkies" or two-horse thorobraces and they usually had two or three seats. They were painted in the same standard colour scheme as the regular B.X. stages with the body of the stage red and the running gear yellow...Like the Concord stagecoaches, they were built with thorobraces (or thoroughbraces), layers of leather which extended the length of the stage. The body of the stage had rockers on each side which fitted on these thorobraces so that the entire body of the stage was supported on them. The result was to give the stage body a rocking, swaying motion not unlike a ship at sea...

The Concord type stage coaches, with their high wheels, were able to travel through the most difficult mud holes and moderate depths of snow. But, during the worst winter months, when heavy snows made travel by coach impractical, sleighs were used to carry the mail, freight and passengers over the road to Okanagan.[3]

(*OHS*, 1988)

Benjamin Franklin (B.F.) Young was one of the first Okanagan settlers to drive stagecoaches. Young had fought in the American Civil War, participated in the honour guard when the body of the murdered President Abraham Lincoln had lain in state in Philadelphia, and had later made his way to British Columbia in search of a living, finally settling in Spallumcheen. Young reminisces:

It was some time in 1872 that I commenced to drive stage...My regular route was from Barkerville to Yale, but once a week I was detailed to take the stage from Cache Creek to O'Keefe's...

Driving stage in those days was hard work, but I liked it...The horses we had were small, mean to handle, and tough. A horse in those days which weighed 900 or 1000 pounds was considered to be a good-sized horse. We were supposed to get through on time. The weather might be bad and the roads full of holes or blocked up, or harness might break, or the stage coach itself might break down; but that made no difference. A driver was supposed to overcome small difficulties of that sort and finish the trip on time.

For some years the mail was taken from Cache Creek to O'Keefe's, and from O'Keefe's to the Mission on horse back. The contract for carrying the mail in this way was in Alex Vance's name, although it was generally understood that he held it for the BX Company.[4]

(*OHS*, 1935)

When Robert S. Hall came to the North Okanagan in 1887 he noted that a road was being constructed along Mara Lake. Late in 1890 Price Ellison offered Hall the job of driving the mail stage from Sicamous, which was on the CPR mainline, to Vernon and then from Vernon to the Mission. Hall writes:

> This made a drive of about 280 miles a week, sometimes over roads so bad that it taxed the strength and courage of the best horses, tugging long hours through mud and slush in the winter months; in the summer there was the heat and dust. Passengers were charged ten cents per mile and extra for excess baggage. Express ranged from 25 cents up.
>
> About this time Captain Shorts was building a steamboat on Okanagan Lake. One of Price Ellison's instructions was to assist this venture by picking up Captain Shorts and giving him a free ride...This order I tried to carry out, but on one occasion, when he was waiting for me on the side of the road around eight o'clock at night in the dark and the mud, with a bundle of old iron he had gathered in the Spallumcheen Valley, I was forced to refuse to take on this load of iron. The four horses were loaded to the limit and it was two o'clock in the morning before I finally arrived with the mail at the Vernon P.O. where L. Girouard was postmaster. This P.O. was a bare room without desk, table or shelf. Instead of letter boxes, Girouard had a system of using the cracks between the floorboards to hold the letters and papers. When a citizen called for his mail, he was asked to go and pick it out for himself from the crack in the floor that was assigned to him.[5]
>
> (OHS, 1955)

Riding in a stagecoach was often uncomfortable, even dangerous.
BCARS A-09775

After driving the stage for a year and a half, Robert Hall took up farming. However, in 1897 he returned to the road, this time in the South Okanagan and Boundary Country where a mining boom created a good deal of business for freight carriers. Hall would pick up his freight which had been brought down the lake by SS *Aberdeen* under Captain Estabrooks and then set off for the Boundary mines via Okanagan Falls, Camp McKinney and Rock Creek. Greenwood was then in its heyday...A freighter received two and a half cents a pound for his load—it was a one-way haul. After two seasons Hall won the mail contract between Penticton and Oroville, Washington and hired Sam McCurdy of Cawston to assist him. Sam's route was north from Oroville, through Osoyoos, over the Richter Pass to Keremeos.[6]

As the mines prospered in the Similkameen the need for stagecoach service increased. Jessie Ewart Bird writes of that period:

> In 1898 work was begun on the now famous Nickel Plate Mine. At this time Princeton was connected with the outside world by a stagecoach line from Spences Bridge via Nicola and Granite Creek. The southern part of the [Similkameen] Valley was reached by a trail which was used by pack trains and ranchers...The definite discovery of gold and the consequent influx of people made a connecting road between Penticton, Keremeos, Hedley and Princeton a necessity. During 1899 and early 1900 a road was built from Penticton through Keremeos and to Hedley, and after much delay, was finally completed to Princeton in the fall of 1901...
>
> It was not until 1903 that tenders for a bi-weekly mail contract were called for. The contract from Princeton to Hedley was awarded to Mr. Fred Revely...and from Hedley to Penticton to Mr. W.E. Welby...
>
> [Welby's Concord coach] was a well known sight on the road between Penticton and Hedley from 1905 to 1913. Here is a day's schedule, the rate being $7.00 Penticton to Hedley one way. Leaving Penticton at 7 a.m. it arrived at Clark's on the Green Mountain Road for lunch and change of horses, in Keremeos from 4 to 5 p.m., and again changing horses and it reached Hedley between 8 and 9 p.m.
>
> Mr. Welby's advertisement of 1907 reads: "A beautiful drive over the best of roads. Fast stock and the best of drivers."[7]
>
> (OHS, 1937)

The "best of roads" could be hard on coaches. One Monday a rear wheel came off the Princeton coach, allowing the axle to plow through a mud-hole. *The Hedley Gazette* reported:

> When the passengers had scrambled out they resolved themselves into a committee of ways and means. The axle was cleaned, the wheel put on again, but on a dry axle—what was to be done?... A lady passenger came to the rescue and produced the thing necessary—a lubricant—this she fished out of her travelling bag in the shape of a bottle of castor oil.[8]
> (*OHS*, 1937)

Riding in or on a stage could be quite uncomfortable and sometimes dangerous. Hester White tells of a trip she made in late October 1899 from Midway to Penticton. She writes:

> I left the Lancashire [Hotel] at Midway at eight o'clock in the morning on the stage which had arrived from Greenwood. I was to sit on the high seat next to driver Curtis, so I climbed up with one foot on the hub of the wheel, and the other on a small metal step on the stage box. Curtis piled the mail bags under my feet for support, and then my year-old child was lifted up to me. A passenger sat on the outside of the seat on my left, and there were eight passengers in the back of the open stage, one a dear little prim lady, with a dolman wrapped closely around her, and a small black bonnet tied with a bow at the side of her face. With a crack of the whip, the four horses were off....
> With patient, steady steps the horses pulled the heavy load up the steep road with its many switch-backs towards Camp McKinney...Occasionally the fellow passenger on my left would relieve me of my small son, for there was no support at the back of the high seat and the strain was continual. In the late afternoon the stage pulled up in front of C.W. Hozier's stopping place. Curtis handed me the reins and all the passengers walked into the saloon,

Constructed in 1862, the Cariboo Road made stagecoach travel to the Interior possible. BCARS A-09777

leaving only the little lady, Mrs. Croyell, in the back of the stage. While we were waiting the bartender approached the stage carrying a very small tray with two glasses of port wine, which he presented with Mr. James' compliments. The kindly thought and the wine lifted our spirits, and the steady up-hill haul of twelve miles still to come did not seem so impossible to endure....

Eventually we arrived at Hughie Cameron's. In his kindly way, Hughie helped Mrs. Croyell and myself down from the stage. Supper was ready for us, and out in the main room, men were sitting and smoking around a large iron box stove. We were to leave on the Fairview-Penticton stage at eight o'clock in the morning, so I was up early the next morning. Since there was about four inches of fresh snow on the ground I wrapped my small son papoose fashion in a gray flannelet blanket I had bought in Greenwood. Outside I found the "Thro'Brace," our Concord coach, with its four horses and Billy Armstrong, the driver....[9]

(*OHS*, 1949)

Mail Carriers and Post Offices

One of the most intriguing stories of mail delivery anywhere must be that told by Daniel William Harmon in his journal for the years 1800 to 1816.[10] Harmon was stationed at Stuart's Lake (Fort St. James) in New Caledonia. On April 6, 1812 six Indians arrived from Fraser Lake with a letter for Harmon which had been written by David Thompson on August 28, 1811 while the latter was at Kettle Falls on the Columbia. Thompson told of his trip to the mouth of the Columbia. The letter was given to a Native with instructions to see that it reached Harmon. When we consider that the letter began its journey among Okanagan-speakers and crossed several major language boundaries before reaching a trader in distant New Caledonia we are amazed. Not only was a letter delivered, but also it would seem a postal route was being established, for in 1813 Harmon writes again from Stuart's Lake: "September 25, Saturday. An Indian arrived from below and delivered me three Letters from Mr. Stuart, the last of which was wrote but a short distance from the Columbia River."[11]

It was essential for the personnel of fur-trading companies to keep in touch with each other. Hence they established the first lines of communication. Letters would arrive at one post with instruction to the post manager to find a carrier to take certain letters on to a more distant post. Reliable carriers such as Hiram F. Smith were employed time and time again. ("Okanagan Smith" settled on Osoyoos Lake south of the 49th Parallel in the early 1850s after being a carrier for the Hudson's Bay Company from Fort Hope east.) Often the mail carriers were Indian. How reliable were they? A story told by Susan Allison in her diary informs us on that question.

Mrs. Allison, who was living at the home ranch near Princeton at the time, tells us about a night in February 1870 when the temperature dropped suddenly to forty below zero. The next morning the mail carrier Poo-la-lee, whose feet were frozen, was carried to the Allison home by a Native friend. In Susan's kitchen, the friend doctored the frozen feet by holding red-hot coals to the soles. Susan writes: "The faithful old man insisted on going into Keremeos the next day with his mail. He had agreed to make Osoyoos at a certain time. When he left I went into the kitchen to clean it up after the doctoring and I found in the fireplace two leather soles—yes, soles of human flesh—that after the burning were cut from Poo-la-lee's feet!!"[12]

As settlers began to trickle into the country they may have been accommodated to a degree by the Hudson's Bay Company in the matter of sending and receiving mail. After 1858 the Colonial Government began to establish post offices. Among these were: Hope 1858; Similkameen 1859-1863; Rock Creek 1859-1863; Lillooet 1859; Ashcroft 1865; Savona's Ferry 1866-1870; Seymour 1866-1870; Duck & Pringles (later Monte Creek) 1870; Kamloops 1870.

Burt R. Campbell tells us that Savona and Seymour were operated by arrangement with HBC officials[13] and it is likely that this was the custom with other colonial post offices. We are told that Moses Lumby, who was later to become prominent in Vernon's development, once had a contract to carry mails into the Big Bend mines on the Columbia River. Burt Campbell writes: "Mr. Leighton credited Moses Lumby...with carrying mail in a rowboat from Savona to Seymour, 1867-1871, making his own charges. (J.B. Leighton was a stage owner who held a mail contract between Kamloops and the North Okanagan 1881-1885.) Certainly rowing from Savona, up through Kamloops Lake, up the South Thompson to Shuswap Lake, then through the lake up to the end of Seymour Arm was a daunting feat. Alleyne Tull, in her story about the town of Lumby, describes Moses Lumby at a much later date as "a rotund little man with a jolly outlook on life and a mania for fishing."[14]

The establishment or closure of post offices reflected the economic activity of the region. Of the twenty-eight Colonial Postmasters in 1871, only six remained into the era of confederation, one of these being J. Duck at Duck & Pringles.

George H. Melvin, in his book *The Post Offices of British Columbia: 1858-1970*, gives us this note about the first Okanagan post office. It was called "Okanagon" until 1905, when the spelling was changed to "Okanagan," and was located at the O'Keefe Ranch, five miles northwest of Vernon. The post office opened August 14, 1872 and closed January 31, 1924. Cornelius O'Keefe was the first postmaster and served until 1911.[15]

Other Government of Canada post offices established between 1871 and 1889.

Post Office	Date	First Postmaster	Post Office	Date	First Postmaster
Okanagan Mission	1872	E. Lequime	Okanagan Landing	1898	Mrs. M. Grant
Nicola Lake	1872	J. Clapperton	Peachland	1898	D.H. Watson
Spallumcheen	1881	G.J. Wallace	Okanagan Falls	1899	J. McLellan
Priests' Valley			Olalla	1900	W.C. McDougall
(renamed Vernon 1887)	1884	Luke Girouard	Adelphi		
Douglas Lake	1884	R. McRae	(renamed Westwold 1926)	1900	W.H. Homfray
Osoyoos	1884	T. Kruger	Westbank	1902	N.S. Marshall
Shuswap	1885	A. McBryan	Carmi	1902	J. Kerr
Grande Prairie			Green Mountain		
(near Westwold)	1885	A.J. Kirkpatrick	(renamed Allen Grove 1908)	1902	L.A. Clark
Revelstoke	1886	T.A.W. Gordon	Malakwa	1902	E.R.B. Baynes
Sicamous	1887	E. Forester	Summerland	1902	F.S. Moule
Enderby	1887	O. Harvey	Hedley	1903	F.M. Gillespie
Keremeos	1887	T. Daly	Gellatly	1903	C.D. Osborne
White Valley			Mable Lake	1904	W.G. Proctor
(renamed Lumby 1894)	1889	P. Bissett	Maud		
Penticton	1889	T. Ellis	(renamed Bridesville 1907)	1905	H.S. Edwards
Salmon Arm	1890	C.A. McGuire	Oyama	1906	H.H. Irvine
Tappen Siding	1892	F. McCulla	Deep Creek	1907	R. Davison
Armstrong	1892	D. Rabbitt	Myncaster	1907	A.B. Sowter
Fairview	1892	T. Elliott	Okanagan Centre	1907	J.D. Kearns
Kelowna	1893	T. Spence	Naramata	1907	J.S. Gillespie
Notch Hill	1893	C. Castle	Whiteman Creek	1908	V. Willet
Mara	1893	S. Appleby	Celista	1908	J. Riley
Lumby			Wilson Landing	1908	Mrs. M.V.H. Goodacre
(formerly White Valley)	1894	A.M. Seed	Rutland	1908	P.E. McDonald
Hullcar	1894	D. Crane	Marron Lake	1909	A.J. Sweeten
Midway			East Kelowna	1909	E.C. Paynter
(formerly Boundary Creek)	1894	T. McAuley	Meyers Flat	1909	Mrs. Keller
Kualt (near Salmon Arm)	1895	A. Genelle	Trinity Valley	1909	A.J. Conn
Sidley (near Osoyoos)	1895	J.L.S. Hughes	Kaleden	1910	A.S. Hatfield
Creighton Valley	1897	W.H. Phillips	Hupel	1910	H. Hupel
Falkland	1898	W. Bell			

During the next decade post offices were established at the following places: Tappen, Grindrod, Lavington, Glenrosa, Eagle Bay, Sorrento, Adams Lake and Allenby. Oliver Post Office was opened in 1921 with D.P. Simpson as postmaster.[16]

The establishment dates for post offices at Revelstoke, Sicamous and Enderby are associated with the completion of the Canadian Pacific Railway in 1885. The opening of the Shuswap and Okanagan Railway in 1892 also influenced the pattern of mail delivery. Generally speaking the railway replaced stagecoaches as carriers on trunk routes. Mail to settlements not on the railway was carried by stage or horseback. Robert S. Hall tells us, "Mails were re-sorted at the Mission P.O. Those for the south were carried by Joseph Brent on pack-horse or on snowshoes, according to the season of the year."[17]

R.F. Marriage, who for ten years served as secretary to the Okanagan Historical Society and is at present its historian, writes on the subject of Railway Post Offices with specific reference to the Okanagan.

For 60 years the Okanagan Valley was dependent on the railways for the transport of mail to and from the rest of the country....

The railways held two types of contract to carry mail on their passenger or mixed trains: (a) "RPO" (Railway Post Office), using cars equipped for sorting in transit by clerks employed by the Post Office Department; (b) "BCS" (Baggage Car Service) carrying closed mails in postal bags handled by the train baggageman. A "closed" mail shipment is one that is not opened until it reaches the depot named on the label...

The S&O [Shuswap and Okanagan Railway] carried closed mail as soon as it opened in 1892. A similar service commenced in 1893 on Okanagan Lake when the steamer *Aberdeen* was launched. However, the growth of settlement and business in the Valley obviously warranted use of a postal car to make up mails for local exchange on the line, together with a closed bag to go south on the boat...

Early in the century it became obvious that the closed mails on the lake steamers were inadequate and Ottawa was urged to supply an RPO. After much pressure was applied by municipal councils and other bodies, the *Aberdeen* and *Okanagan* were fitted with mail rooms on their freight decks in 1911...Plans of the *Sicamous* (launched in 1914) included a mail room. The trains and boats with clerks sorting mails en route offered a quality of service never since equalled.

This arrangement lasted until 5 January 1935, when the still crude highways of the day forced the CPR to withdraw the *Sicamous* from service. The vessel was reported to be losing $14,000 a month, a sizeable sum at that time...

The writer was employed on trains 708 and 707 the last day the Railway Post Office car operated, 30 September 1954.

From 1915 to 1957 BCS on the Kettle Valley line carried mails to and from the RPOs terminating westbound at Midway from Nelson, and at Ruby Creek or Hope eastbound from Vancouver. Penticton was a busy forwarding office serving that large area. Over-night service to and from Vancouver was an accepted routine for 40 years.

It's hard to realize now (1995) another 40 years have gone by. Truck service has been extended and improved, but a substitute for sorting in transit has never been developed. And in combination with other factors, this has resulted in a decline in quality of service. Modern methods of communication have rendered the mails relatively unimportant to the great majority of people.[18]

(*OHS*, 1996)

Other changes have taken place in our mail service since 1970, the cut-off date Mr. Melvin chose for his study. Household delivery is becoming a thing of the past. Recent closures of post offices in cities like Penticton, Kelowna and Vernon signal the passing of an institution. We no longer meet our friends and acquaintances on a regular basis on the post office steps, exchange our news and discuss matters of local concern.

8

Community Life

The Family

In the immediate postconfederation years European women began to arrive in the Interior of British Columbia in increasing numbers. Before 1871 only five white women had moved to the Okanagan. The first was Mrs. Eli Lequime, who was born Marie Louise Atabagoeth. Marie had walked with her husband from Hope over Manson Mountain to Rock Creek in 1859. Father Pandosy persuaded the Lequimes to settle at the Mission where they established the only trading post between Kamloops and the border. The business prospered. In 1893, when Mrs. Lequime visited Vernon for the very first time, the *Vernon News* said of her:

> Thirty-three years ago Mrs. Lequime landed at Okanagan Mission with but little money to start on, but by patient industry and careful economy she has since seen her possessions grow until now she has the satisfaction of knowing, not only that old age has been provided for, but to each of her family may be left a rich patrimony; and while she had thus done well for herself, she has also aided a great many other settlers and helped them along...[1]

Building a haystack. Kelowna Museum

The second white woman to arrive in the area was Susan Allison, who had married John Fall Allison in 1867, ridden the Hope Trail and settled in Princeton (Vermilion Forks). Later Mrs. Allison was to spend much time at Sunnyside (now Westbank) where her husband wintered his large cattle herds. Mrs. Allison and Mrs. Lequime became friends. Both women were intelligent, energetic, courageous and physically tough, bearing their children and caring for them in conditions very different from those in which they themselves had been

Susan Allison, the second white woman to move to the Okanagan.
Princeton Museum

nurtured. (Susan had fourteen children.) Both women experienced disasters. One Lequime toddler was drowned at Rock Creek in a miner's ditch. Once, when John Fall Allison was away from home, the house burned to the ground, leaving Susan to fend for her children and herself. But both Marie Louise Lequime and Susan Allison survived and each made a remarkable contribution to the life of her community.

In 1862 Catherine Schubert had arrived in Kamloops with the Overlanders. However, it was 1883 before she settled in the Armstrong area, having spent the intervening years at Lillooet and Cache Creek.

Two women who made a tragically fleeting appearance in colonial history were Charlotte Moresby Haynes and Annie Curran Christien. Charlotte Moresby married John Carmichael Haynes on September 26, 1868 and arrived in Osoyoos as a bride of eighteen years, "the only white woman within a radius of one hundred miles."

In 1871, when official business took Haynes to Wild Horse Creek in the East Kootenay, Charlotte accompanied him. At the end of the season they rode through to the coast. Haynes purchased a cottage at New Westminster and there Charlotte awaited the birth of their son Fairfax Moresby Haynes, who was born February 10, 1872. Charlotte did not recover from the difficulties of the birth and died May 5. Haynes, back on duty in the Kootenay, was to learn of her death from a newspaper handed him by a miner at Wild Horse Creek.[2]

Joseph Christien (or "Christian"—some family members preferred the anglicized spelling) settled at Okanagan Mission in 1861. In 1869 Joseph returned to his home in St. Anicet, Quebec, married Annie Curran and took her back to the Okanagan. Fortunately the couple were accompanied by Mrs. Christien's niece, Annie Ellen Mackin, for on April 25, 1870 a baby girl, Annie Christien, was born but the mother did not survive. Miss Mackin, then eighteen years of age, cared for the infant until the child was old enough to be put in the care of the Sisters of St. Ann in Victoria. Miss Mackin, after spending some time in Clinton and Cache Creek, on New Year's Day 1876 was married to B.F. Young in Kamloops at the home of John Tait, Hudson's Bay Company factor. Rev. James Turner, a well-known Methodist missionary, performed the ceremony. Mrs. Young came to live at Armstrong on the farm her husband had pre-empted.

Annie and B.F. Young, early settlers in Armstrong.
Armstrong Museum

Seven months before setting out in 1862 with the Overlanders for the goldfields of BC, A.L. Fortune had married Miss Bathia Ross of Lancaster, Ontario. It was not until 1874 that Mr. Fortune returned to eastern Canada in order to conduct his patient wife to her new home in Spallumcheen, just two years before Mrs. B.F. Young went to live there. The two women became close friends. Margaret Ormsby writes of them:

> Mrs. Young was a remarkable woman, and a splendid type of the womanhood of Eastern Canada of the past generation. Her whole life was devoted to her home and family. She was endowed with a graciousness and tact which made her an ideal hostess, and the hospitality of her home was proverbial.
>
> She and the late Mrs. A.L. Fortune, who died on the 13th of November, had much in common. They, for a number of years, were the only white women in Spallumcheen, and being of the type of women they were, their influence for good was marked. Their presence, especially within the circle of their friends and acquaintances, tended to soften and ameliorate the rather crude life which prevailed in the valley in early days.[3]
>
> (*OHS*, 1935)

These were the two women who welcomed Magdalene Ehmke to the district when she arrived with her husband

*Three-horse teams
harvesting grain.
Kelowna Museum*

Henry Jergen Ehmke from Germany in August 1877. Mrs. Ehmke, who had been born Magdalen Haack, was a niece of Herman Wichers, the first man to pre-empt land under the new provincial government. The Ehmkes had ten children, many of the descendants of whom still reside in the Okanagan.

In 1875 John Carmichael Haynes married again, this time to Emily Josephine Pittendrigh. Emily bore John seven children, the sixth of whom died at birth. The eldest was Valentine Haynes and the second Hester Emily, to whom we are indebted for her many articles about the early days in the South Okanagan. Here is what she has to say about some of the women she knew during her childhood in the Okanagan and Similkameen:

> Among the pioneer women I knew and at whose homes I visited were the following: Mrs. Allison, the first white woman to settle at Princeton, who as a young and delicate bride had experienced the rigors of travelling the [Dewdney] trail; Mrs. Daly, whose music, played on the piano that came over the trail, charmed her family and many visitors; Mrs. Cawston, who left her home at Sebringville, Ontario, and travelled from Colville, Washington to Osoyoos on horseback over "the little mountain trail"; Mrs. Coulthard who lived at the old Hudson's Bay Company's post at Keremeos; Mrs. Manery and Mrs. McCurdy of the lower Similkameen; Mrs. Kruger, Bavarian by birth, who at the age of sixteen came to live at the Hudson's Bay Company's store at Osoyoos; Mrs. Ellis who came out from Ireland in 1872 to grace the first home at Penticton; and Mrs. Frank Richter (now Mrs. Tweddle), who came from the United States to Boundary Valley when she was a young woman.[4]
>
> (*OHS*, 1952)

Verna Cawston has described Mary Ann Cawston (nee Pearson), the wife of R.L. Cawston from 1885, as "a true gentlewoman with all those attributes of courage, sympathy and generosity associated with the term, 'pioneer'."[5]

Arduous as their housekeeping tasks were many pioneer women participated in activities quite beyond the domestic sphere. Mrs. Allison and Mrs. Lequime would have kept shop while their husbands were away attending to some aspect of their business. The Krugers at Osoyoos ran not only a store but also a small hotel. Chrestenza Kruger would certainly have been involved. Henry Nicholson wrote of Mrs. Daly: "Mrs. Daly has for many years successfully managed her valuable stock ranch." Mrs. Daly was also Keremeos's first postmaster. Ellen Lowe upon the death of her husband managed to retrieve his investment in the partnership with Haynes and to invest her money, in partnership with her husband's nephew R.L. Cawston, in a Similkameen ranch.

Two families which played an important role in the early provincial period and whose descendants still participate in the economic and social life of the Okanagan are the Postills, who arrived in 1872, and the Casorsos, who came in the next decade.

Edward Postill and his wife, who was born Mary Dickenson, arrived in BC from Yorkshire, England via Ontario in 1872. While they were still at the coast they made arrangements to purchase land south of Duck Lake. Unfortunately Edward, having become ill as the family travelled to their new home, died at Priests' Valley (later Vernon). His widow and family had Edward's body interred on the ranch that he had never seen. Then

Mary and her young people—Alfred, William, Edward and Lucy (later to become Mrs. Robert Lambly)—set about managing the newly acquired ranch. They worked hard and their holdings grew to five thousand acres plus another two thousand acres of range. Primrose Upton writes: "Mrs. Edward Postill must have been a wonderful organizer and manager—the family prospered, new buildings were put up, and the Ranch grew." Mrs. Postill was known to have used a pair of field glasses to oversee her extensive ranch operations—living was hard and tough in those days, and "slackers" were not welcome on the Postill Ranch.[6]

Giovanni (John) Casorso in 1872 married Rosa Bevi Lacqua in their native Italy. In 1882, encouraged by his wife, Giovanni left his homeland for the new world. By the next summer he was at Okanagan Mission having agreed to work for the Oblate fathers for six years at $15 a month plus board, in return for the fathers' help in pre-empting land. Victor Casorso, Giovanni's grandson, in a book called *The Casorso Story*, has given us a vivid account of his grandmother's trip by ship around the Horn to San Francisco with her three small children. That proved only the beginning of her odyssey. No one in San Francisco seemed to know where "Okanagan Mission, British Columbia" was until someone noticed that the church bell purchased by Joseph Christien was on the dock and destined for the same place. Rosa was told to keep the bell in sight and go where it went, which she did, finally reaching the Mission in October 1884. Rosa was as quick as her husband in learning the skills which would enable her family to get ahead in this new land. Often the lessons came from Native women who knew so much about harvesting and preserving what the land had to offer.

One cannot leave the subject of women in the 1870s and 1880s without speaking of the Native women who entered into country marriages with European men. Some of these unions were regularized when the missionaries arrived. We read, for example, of the first marriage performed at the Mission, that "between Francois Ourtoland, of French origin, domiciled at this Mission...and Catherine, Indian woman of Wallamet, of lawful age, widow of Pierre Patirvan, also of this Mission." Father P. Durien was the celebrant. The date was November 18, 1861.[7] In many cases the country marriage proved lasting even without the ceremonial and legal blessing, the alliance maintained by "many tender ties."[8]

As white women became more numerous, however, Indian wives were sometimes put aside. The Native wife and her children were provided for if the husband was a responsible man, but there was no law obliging him to do so. No doubt there were scoundrels. Even when the husband showed some consideration there must have been many a heartbreak. It is reported that when one of the set-aside wives, who had been decently provided for, was asked how she felt, she replied, "It hurts here," and she put her hand upon her heart.[9]

Jean Barman has made an extensive study of country marriages in the Okanagan and Similkameen.[10] Her findings appear in an article entitled "Lost Okanagan: In Search of the First Settler Families." Barman points out that although the half-Native offspring of these alliances and their descendants were a part of every Okanagan community, a later generation of local historians tended to ignore their presence, making no reference to them in Okanagan history. They have been "lost."[11] Mel Rothenburger, a descendant of a Native woman and Donald McLean, who was Hudson's Bay Company servant and founder of the Hat Creek Ranch, also writes of this group. He says:

> It was common at the time [the late 1870s] to assign the problems of breeds [sic] to their mixed parentage, as though they were homeless, unable to connect. But the truth of the matter was that in the 1870s there were more breeds than "pure" whites in Kamloops or anywhere else in the Upper Country. Their generation was the majority, they were the baby boomers of their time, for their fathers were the Hudson's Bay men who had pioneered the country and their mothers were the Indian women taken as wives. As the children grew up, they were faced with a choice between white society and Indian society and, in general, the daughters married white men and so "went white" while the sons "went Indian."[12]

Many of the children of these mixed marriages did very well as they lived in a period when their knowledge of the environment and their practical skills were valuable assets. Charlie Richter, for example, was sought after as a guide by surveying and hunting parties. He was an expert at building Russell and "A" fences. "In running the line, it is said that his eye was as true as an engineer's instrument."[13] Charlie operated meat markets in both Princeton and Hedley and for a time ran Kruger's Hotel in Osoyoos.

Charlie and the other Native sons of Francis Xavier Richter—Will, Joe, Ed, and Hans—and John Haynes, the Native son of John Carmichael Haynes, whose fathers saw them educated and established on substantial land holdings, prospered. Self-respect, as in any culture, appears to depend on having the care of industrious and responsible parents. John McDougall, who had travelled through the Okanagan in the 1840s as a servant of the Hudson's Bay Company, registered his ownership of land at the Mission on July 29, 1861. When one of his

The sons of Francis Xavier Richter and his Native wife Lucy. Left to right, back row: Karl (Charlie), Hans (John), William; front row: Edward, Joseph. The picture was taken on the Richter ranch on the road between Osoyoos and Keremeos.
Doug Cox

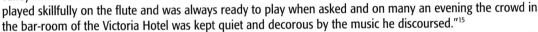

sons was asked if he was a "half-breed" the reply was, "No, Sir, I'm a McDougall."[14]

Simple Pleasures

No doubt, in the Okanagan as elsewhere, the principal amusement from earliest times was story telling. Good story tellers were definitely appreciated. Occasionally someone recorded his or her experiences in a diary. Susan Allison has left us her journal which Margaret Ormsby has edited and published under the title *A Pioneer Gentlewoman in British Columbia: The Recollections of Susan Allison*. In spite of her many duties Susan Allison wrote poetry, essays and articles. Her long poem *Naitaka*, published under the pen-name of Stratton Moir, was about the monster in Okanagan Lake.

Music was a joy. Many remarked on the splendid singing of the Oblate school children at the Mission. Pianos and organs that had been packed in through the mountain trails became the focus for musical evenings. Dances were another pleasure. If there was no fiddle or piano then a mouth organ would do. Joseph Christien might at times be persuaded to put on an exhibition of step dancing. John Creighton, a veteran of the Crimean War and the Indian Mutiny, came into the North Okanagan in 1884 and pre-empted land in the valley which was named after him. Leonard Norris writes of him: "He played skillfully on the flute and was always ready to play when asked and on many an evening the crowd in the bar-room of the Victoria Hotel was kept quiet and decorous by the music he discoursed."[15]

Game and fish were probably more plentiful than in any period since, plentiful enough to attract aristocratic hunters like the Archduke Ferdinand of Austria, who came with his retinue to hunt in the Similkameen,[16] or the Marquis of Lorne, who found time during a 1882 vice-regal visit to BC to hunt with Cornelius O'Keefe.[17]

Then there was horse racing! We are told that Charlie Richter's race horse Dandy was almost as well known as its master. In the early days races were run in the Native fashion. A blanket was spread on the ground and the bets in money or kind placed on it. At the finish of the race the winner and his supporters picked up the blanket and all its contents. The following story presents us with a variation on this theme of "winner take all."

Horse racing in Penticton in 1908. Judges' stand and bandstand shown.
Penticton Museum

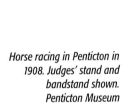

An Old Timers' Celebration[18]

by Thomas Stevenson

This old-timers' celebration, which was held at Priest's Valley (now Vernon), was the outcome of a matched horse race between Alfred Postill, of the Postill Ranch, and Louis Bercier, of Priest's Valley. The race was to be run at Priest's Valley on the 24th of May, 1887. At that time I was riding the range for the Postill Ranch, and helped to train Roney, their race horse. In a mile race we felt we had a sure winner. On the 24th of May, Alf, Ted, and Bill Postill and I, leading our race horse, Roney, rode into Priest's Valley, stopping at the Victoria Hotel. Bercier, with his race horse, Mountain Chief, had arrived before us with a good following of Indians from the Reserve. Then, like the gathering of the clans, from the valleys and the hills the old-timers came riding in to see the race. There were Bob Lambly, Frank Young, Tom Clinton, Connie O'Keefe, Alex McDonell, Pete Basset, the Connels, the Christiens, Dick Neill, Ned Woods, Robert Goldie, Leon Lequime, Tom Wood, Captain Shorts, Fred Barnes, Leonard Norris, Tronson, Price Ellison, W.F. Cameron, and many others. They were still milling around the race horses, shaking hands and chatting, and selecting and betting on the outcome of the race. Excitement ran high as the betting proceeded, and to show my confidence in Roney I had bet most of my winter's wages on him before I realized it. Hurrying out of the ring, I ran into an Indian wanting to bet his nice little appalouse stock horse on Mountain Chief. I took a fancy to the appalouse, and tried to swap my saddle horse for him. No go. But eyeing my new double rigged cheyenne saddle, he said: "Bet horse against saddle." Off came the saddle, and slapping it on the appalouse, we tied him to a tree—"winner take all."

Rodeos afforded cowboys the opportunity to show off the skills needed in cattle ranching. Even today rodeos range from informal get-togethers on some ranch to the highly organized circuit events such as those at Falkland and Keremeos.
Vernon Museum 1909

We then rode down the old road to the Landing, where Tronson, Chief Paul, and Price Ellison as judges, and Fred Barnes and Connie O'Keefe who had stepped off the mile, were ready to start the horses. After the usual jockeying before the start, they were off head and head. At the quarter, Mountain Chief led by four lengths. Bercier, laying on the quirt; Postill lying low on Roney, making no move. At the half; Bercier in the lead by six lengths, still whipping. Postill hand-riding Roney now. At the three-quarters, Bercier in the lead by three lengths; Postill riding hard and gaining. In the stretch, Bercier leading by a length, both riding hard, and Indians closing in from behind and from the sides, shooting in the air. On they came, both riders now laying on the quirt, as over the finishing line they went, Roney in the lead by half a length. Swinging up on my horse, I went back to the hotel to admire my new appalouse stock horse. What a thrill!

There were more matched races, as the afternoon passed away, for side bets, starting from Price Ellison's corral on the White Valley Road, and finishing at the Hotel. After supper we moved the furniture out of the dining room, and the dance was on. Then in the grey dawn of another day, with the sound of the hoarse "caller," and fast dancing feet, and laughter of the fast-swinging, high-stepping old-timer still doing his stuff, we swung up on our broncs, and with a farewell "Whoopee," headed over the Old Mission Road for the Ranch. Riding along, I was very proud that morning of my pretty appalouse horse, an aristocrat among horses, whose ancestors had roamed the plains of Arabia, and had made the long voyage from Spain to Peru.

(*OHS*, 1941)

9
Schools

Rural Schools

In 1872, one year after the formation of a provincial government, the legislature passed the British Columbia Public Schools Act. The objectives of the act were "to give every child in the Province such knowledge as will fit him to become a useful and intelligent citizen in after years." Writing in 1982 Lucy McCormick says, "This Act sets out the basic structure of education policy that exists today."[1]

Mrs. McCormick's article "Early Rural Schools of Vernon and White Valley" presents the history of one-room

The Commonage one-room school near Vernon, 1914. Vernon Museum 5017

schools built between 1898 and 1920 in the Lumby, Vernon and Commonage areas. However, the conditions she depicts were for the most part those existing elsewhere in the Okanagan, Shuswap and Similkameen as schools were established.

The duties of the school board were to provide a suitable building if the Provincial Department of Education granted permission to open a school. Often the requirement of 8 pupils had to be rounded up by hook or by crook and I mean that literally. In several instances we found that 4-year-olds were conscripted, and older pupils, who might be working or married, were sometimes added to the register so the school would have its quota. The teacher was hired by the board, which usually was made up of three members, one of whom acted as secretary. The building was usually of logs...

Equipment and supplies were minimal: desks were often homemade; benches, some-times logs split in half, and very uncomfortable, caused much shuffling of pupils...

On the bench at the back of the room, usually attached to the wall, stood the water pail with floating dipper used by everyone. A tin or enamel basin and a roller towel completed the indoor sanitary arrangements, while outside the two-holer stood at some distance from the school—this has helped to make us such a hardy race.

Originally blackboards were black painted panels...A photo of the King, a Union Jack, a globe and a school handbell seemed to be compulsory items of equipment.

The pupils walked, or came by horse and buggy or on horseback. There was usually a woodshed, and children with horses brought a bag of hay. They brought their lunch in the inevitable red lard pail, and in winter this was often frozen solid so had to sit by the stove to thaw.

(*OHS*, 1982)

Mrs. McCormick tells us about one district between Vernon and Lumby, Creighton Valley, in which the community chose to raise money for school equipment by holding a series of dances. Music was supplied by the Denison piano which, upon each occasion, was hauled to the school and back home on a stoneboat!

Education: A Private Affair

In colonial times there had been no public schools in the Interior of the province. The missionary denominations tried to fill this need. The Mission, for example, had a school almost from its inception in 1860 which was attended by both Natives and non-Natives. Instruction was in French, the tongue of the Oblate fathers and very acceptable to the French-speaking community that had pre-empted land at L'Anse au Sable. Instruction included religious teaching and music. John Carmichael Haynes sent his half-Native son, John, to this school and then on to the Oblate school in New Westminster.

English-speaking families who cared about the education of their children and who could afford it hired governesses, a practice which reached into the postconfederation era. Hester White tells us about these young women so important to her childhood.

Governesses[2]

by Hester White

In the very early days of the valley, there were no schools. To educate their children, Judge Haynes and Tom Ellis brought in governesses, young women who braved the dangers of mountain trails to enter upon a life so different to that they had left.

The first to come was Miss Fry, who arrived at the Ellis home in 1879 and went out the next year with the cattle drive. She would ride ahead of the cattle and then dismount and read, till they caught up with her. She married a Mr. Mainguy and was the mother of Admiral Harold Mainguy.

The first governess to come to Osoyoos to teach the Haynes children was Miss Deasy from Victoria. She stayed a year. Then came Miss Phipps, an Irish girl. She joined the family in Victoria in 1883 and journeyed with them to Portland, through Sprague and Coulee City, in a covered wagon, past Wild Goose Bill's place (now Wilbur), crossed the Columbia in an Indian canoe and finally arrived at Osoyoos. She also stayed a year, later married Mr. Charles Leggett, Registrar-General, and lived in Midway. In 1886 came Miss Sylvia Jenns, daughter of Rev. Percival Jenns, rector of St. John's Anglican Church in Victoria, sometimes called "The Iron Church." She had never been on a horse, but she rode the 150 miles from Hope to Osoyoos. She also stayed a year and afterwards married R.B. Punnett.

The last governess at Osoyoos was Miss Jennie Hunter, who was brought out from England by Canon Cooper of St. James Church, Vancouver. She came to Penticton by boat and rode from there to Osoyoos.

Others who should be mentioned were Miss Newton, who taught the Ellis family in 1888 and Miss Somner, who was with the Ellises for a time and then went to the Richters in Keremeos. She married Ed Richter.

In 1900 Miss Aramson arrived in Penticton and taught two little girls of the Atherton and Hood families at the Penticton Hotel. She married Jim Schubert and went to live at Tulameen.

(*OHS*, 1959)

When children grew beyond the governess stage they might be sent to New Westminster or Victoria to boarding school. When John Carmichael Haynes died July 6, 1888, on his way back to Osoyoos from Victoria, he was escorting home from school "his own two sons [Fairfax and Valentine], two boys of Mr. Ellis's and a daughter of Captain Pittendrigh."[3] Kathleen Ellis writes of the Ellis children "who eventually one by one went to schools in England."[4]

The R.L. Cawstons in Similkameen solved the problem of their family's schooling by returning to Ontario for six years. The boys had attended the public school established in Similkameen in 1892 but in 1903 the family moved back to Stratford, Ontario while still maintaining their ranching interests. By the time R.L. Cawston returned west in 1909 his three older sons were established in the world of commerce. Alfred (Gint) returned with his mother in 1910. Dick and Beauchamp returned to the Similkameen before the outbreak of World War I.[5]

The First Public School

Okanagan School[6]
by F.M. Buckland

The two Gazette notices establishing the Okanagan and Nicola School Districts are both dated July 31, 1874....

For a school [at Okanagan Mission] the government had paid $750 for William Smithson's dwelling house, and Smithson himself donated one acre for the site. It would appear, however, that the building was purchased and the School District decided upon some time before the services of a teacher could be secured, for the Superintendent of Education remarked in his report for the year ending June 30, 1875, that this commodious schoolroom and teacher's residence was waiting an occupant. He added further that a teacher from California was expected to take charge.

The expected teacher from California appeared later, in the person of Angus McKenzie of Pictou county, Nova Scotia, who came walking into the valley with his blankets and a bundle of school books on his back. His credentials, which entitled him to a temporary certificate, issued by the State of Kansas, enabled him to commence teaching at once. It was not until the 20th December, 1875, that he was engaged at a salary of $60 per month. Besides his salary his meat, milk, butter and eggs, and his fire wood were supplied free by the settlers. Boys and girls from Similkameen, Okanagan Falls and the upper end of the valley attended the school, living with the different ranchers and returning home during the holidays. Shy and backward children, we are told, were often treated to a big slice of bread and syrup to gain their confidence....

Mr. McKenzie continued to teach until 1878 when, in October, Miss M. Coughlan (a sister of Mrs. Greenhow's) was engaged. She taught until 1882. In 1881 W. Smithson's name was

dropped from the list of trustees and Alphonse Lefevre took his place. In October of 1882 R.S. Hanna, later a well-known dentist in Vancouver, was appointed at a salary of $60 per month...he missed the stage at Yale and he too walked in, carrying, if not his blankets, at least a fairly large valise. (When Mrs. Ellison resigned the Priest Valley School in 1885, she was succeeded by Mr. Hanna.)

Mr. McKenzie appears to have been a successful teacher, and his work is highly spoken of in the reports of the Superintendent of Education. In his report for 1877, the Superintendent says in part: "The school in this district (Okanagan) was visited on May 21, when all the children on the register, 21, were in attendance. The results achieved since the opening of the school have been so remarkably satisfactory in all respects that it is difficult to speak too highly of the work accomplished. Children who, eighteen months before, were utterly ignorant of the simplest rudiments and unable to speak a word of English, have advanced so rapidly as to be able, when the school was revisited, to read fluently and clearly in the fourth reader. The examination in grammar, geography and arithmetic was eminently creditable to teacher and pupils and must have still further increased the confidence and esteem which the parents entertain for their conscientious and hard-working teacher. The discipline was excellent and the scholars evidently took a hearty interest in their work. The settlers in the Mission Valley have every reason to congratulate themselves on their good fortune in securing so successful an educator as the gentleman in charge of this school."

Those who knew McKenzie intimately say he was a big man standing well over six feet and that he wore his whiskers like Abraham Lincoln, and had one wall-eye which he always partly closed when looking at anything intently. He was a gentle kindly man, but withal one not to be trifled with if his temper was up. He afterwards taught school at Hope and Langley Prairie, and elsewhere on the Lower Fraser and he was well liked wherever he went. He was just the kind of a man who, being appointed to a remote country school, with no thought of his own advancement and with no ulterior object in view, would turn to the work he had in hand with diligence and understanding, and give to the task of educating the children entrusted to his charge the best that was in him.

(*OHS*, 1935)

Parents of children growing up in a community where there was no school sometimes made arrangements for their children to board and attend an existing school. This was the situation with the Richters in Similkameen. Kathleen Dewdney writes:

With their brothers, Charlie and Will, Joe and Ed Richter attended the Government School at the Mission (later Okanagan Mission), near present-day Kelowna, then the only school serving the Okanagan and Similkameen. They made the long trip on horseback using the trail over the mountains to Penticton, then along the east side of Okanagan Lake. They boarded with Frederick Brent and returned home during the summer holidays.

Although Mr. Richter paid for their board they eagerly helped Mr. Brent's own boys with the chores. In addition to routine tasks such as cutting wood, feeding chickens, tending sheep, stacking hay and rounding up cattle, there were sacks to fill with flour at Mr. Brent's mill—the first stone mill in the Okanagan and Similkameen...

They also attended Father Pandosy's historic Mission Church School where they received their religious and musical instruction...

Father Pandosy had a school band. It included: Joe Richter, B-flat cornet; John Brent, E-flat cornet; Bill Brent, trombone; Joe Brent, alto horn; and John Haynes, B-flat cornet. Later Joe Richter and Joe Brent played the violin.[7]

(*OHS*, 1961)

Kelowna's first school jitney was once a wild horse. After school hours the patient Casorso animal was used in the delivery of meats and vegetables. The picture was taken in 1894 by the school teacher Harvey Watson. The children are from head to...: Felix Casorso, Fred Berard, Leo Casorso, Joe Casorso, George Small, Joe Berard, Henry Berard, Harold Small and Pete Casorso. Kelowna Museum Information: Victor Casorso

Expansion of Public Schools

In "Story of the Vernon Schools" H.D. Pritchard and Clarence Fulton give a detailed account of the building of schools in Vernon to accommodate the ever increasing numbers of pupils. Actually the Vernon experience was, in general, very much like that of other Okanagan communities.

Story of the Vernon Schools[8]

by H.D. Pritchard and Clarence Fulton

On October 22, 1884, the first school in Vernon, then Priests' Valley, was opened. It was located south of Long Lake Creek and east of the Old Mission Road (now 34th Street), and was built by Angus McDonald at a cost of $625. The first trustees were E.J. Tronson, Alfred McNeil and Price Ellison. The first teacher, Miss Sophia Johnson, later Mrs. Price Ellison, remained until she resigned in June 1885.

The following pupils appeared on the roll: Helen, George and Edward Tronson; Susan, William and Rebecca McNeil; Christine, Albert and Oscar Anderson; Christine and George Brewer; and Edward and Maria Houghton....

The second school was constructed by E.L. Morand for $500....Just as schools in remote parts of the province still do, this building served as schoolhouse, church and social centre combined. It was in this building that the late Percy French, who was later to give many valuable years of service as school trustee, received his first instruction. Here, too, Stuart Martin, Morrice S. Middleton, Mary MacKinnon, Oscar, Anna and Thekla Reinhard commenced their school careers...

The school population grew steadily and the present Park School was built in 1893 for $5,087...By 1908 the Park School was no longer capable of housing the fast-growing school population. The large brick building, now known as Central School, was built in 1909....

In the meantime, a high school had been opened in 1902 in a room twenty by sixteen feet in the rear of the building later used as Cossitt, Beattie and Spyer's real estate office. This was the second high school in the interior of the province (the first having been set up at Nelson). [The principal and only teacher, Clarence Fulton, taught all classes in every subject.]...

The junior high school was organized in September 1937, and grades seven and eight ceased to be part of the elementary school....The savage deadline of the old "Entrance" examination is now avoided by the junior high school system. In the "log cabin" days, the stern test of scholarship was: "Can they pass the Entrance?" When one principal was asked by an anxious parent if his son could pass the examination to enter Grade Nine, the reply was "Of course he can." "Why," said the parent, "do you say 'Of course?'" "Because," said the principal, "We have on our staff Miss Edith DeBou who can put anyone through the Entrance."

(*OHS*, 1951)

To the west of Okanagan Mission the new settlement of Kelowna was developing. J. Percy Clement tells us:

By December 1892, children of school age in Kelowna numbered thirty-three and under instructions from the Minister of Education, a meeting to elect trustees for a new school was held. A large number of residents attended and Messrs. C. Mair, Thos. Spence and H.W. Raymer were elected, with Mr. Spence as secretary. The superintendent agreed to send a teacher, and it was decided to use Lequime's Hall as a temporary school room. It was promised that at the coming session of the legislature an appropriation for a new school building would be made.[9]

(*OHS*, 1959)

In 1910, A.R. Lord, who was about to begin his eminent career in education in British Columbia, arrived in Kelowna to fill the post of principal. In a memoir he describes the town as he saw it.

from **Kelowna 1910**[10]

by A.R. Lord

Kelowna, in 1910, had a population of 1650, as we proved later in the year when the pupils of the Entrance class and High School conducted a census. There were, perhaps, two hundred Chinese, of whom two or three were wives and half-a-dozen were children who would soon attend school....

The Kelowna district, as distinct from the town, was predominantly of old-country birth.....Few children of English-born parents attended Kelowna Elementary School, which, from the viewpoint of their fathers, was the equivalent of the English "Board School" and socially undesirable. Some went away to boarding schools, but the majority were taught in small local private schools or occasionally by a governess....

I opened school on that August morning in 1910 with only 235 youngsters divided among five rooms. Four of these rooms were in a wooden building...at the corner of Glen Avenue and Richter Street. Built in 1904, it was Kelowna's second school; the first, a one-room building, was on Bernard Ave....It was there that D.W. Sutherland taught for a good many years...

The fifth room was just across the street in the, as yet unfinished, new school, a six-room brick building...The high school was also there, occupying one room which was fully adequate for its one teacher and 21 pupils. It had been established in 1907 with Elizabeth McNaughton in charge, a teacher whose record of consistent success has seldom been excelled in the province's history.

Mr. Lord writes of several teachers who went on to interesting careers, among them Clarence Fulton.

Clarence Fulton came from Nova Scotia with a Dalhousie University degree in 1902 to be principal and sole teacher of the Vernon High School. Ten years later, he was dismissed after considerable school board debate which was fully reported in both the local and coast papers. With the quick decision which was characteristic of him, he retired to his fruit ranch. Six months later he came to Kelowna to apply for a vacant position on our staff. I told him, "It is a Junior Third Class and the salary is $65 a month." His reply, "I don't care what it is. I want to show them I can make good." He was with us for a year and a half to our interest, satisfaction and occasional amazement....

Clarence Fulton, a Vernon High School teacher, was known for his individualistic teaching methods.
Vernon Museum

He had satisfied himself and "them" that he had made good, and at the end of June, he returned to his ranch. But his yen for teaching was strong. In September, he was appointed to the Vernon Elementary School. A few years later, he was made principal and finally rejoined the high school staff....

Clarence Fulton was never a conformist. His methods of teaching were his own and if they were in accord with the pedagogical theory of the moment it was accidental. Time tables to him were a convenient reminder, but nothing more. His pupils' examination results were fair enough but never startling. Yet, for me, he was one of the half-dozen best teachers I have known....Today, the faces of Clarence Fulton's old time pupils light up when they hear his name. He made men.

(*OHS*, 1993)

Establishing schools in Penticton and in Salmon Arm came a little later, at the turn of the century. In both districts the early schools moved from one location to another until numbers justified a school-building program. For Salmon Arm this came in 1900. By 1909 school trustees were planning the opening of a high school, fees to be the same as those charged in Vernon and Armstrong.[11]

According to A. David MacDonald in the 1983 publication *Penticton: Years to Remember*,[12] the self-appointed trustees Messrs. Wade, White and Nesbitt opened a school in a primitive cabin above the Penticton waterfront in 1902. The teacher was Miss Chisholm and the pupils Roscoe, Christine and Leslie Roadhouse; Annie, Maggie, Willie and Alfie Nesbitt; Flossie and Ethel White; and Florence Hood. For the first year or two it was a struggle to enrol the number of pupils required by the Department of Education. However, by the end of the decade Penticton like the towns to the north was trying desperately to build classrooms to accommodate a growing population. The result was the cluster of schools on Main Street south of Eckhardt Avenue, built with local brick.

Enderby in 1904 had a two-room school on Cliff Street. That year Miss Mabel Beattie arrived to teach the primary grades in which one hundred pupils were enrolled.[13] Miss Beattie was one of an Irish family of six girls and one boy who had arrived with their parents in Kamloops in 1893. All the young people became teachers. In 1912 the A.L. Fortune School was built and served the community until destroyed by fire in 1975. This building had been the pride of the community, built of local brick, each room having a hot-water register heated by a wood furnace until a conversion to coal in the 1940s.[14]

The first school north of Vernon was that built at Round Prairie in 1885 on an acre of land donated by Augustus Schubert. Farmers in the community laid the log foundation. Schubert and his son completed the structure using rough lumber from Patten's mill at Deep Creek and finished lumber brought from Kamloops. Thomas LeDuc taught for three years and was followed by Miss Martha J. Norris, sister of Leonard Norris.

Armstrong's first teacher was Osbourne McPherson, who had arrived in Lansdowne in 1891, sat for his teacher's exams that summer in Kamloops and, when Lansdowne moved to the Armstrong location, became teacher. A second teacher was not appointed until Mr. McPherson's class numbered 76 pupils.

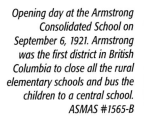
Opening day at the Armstrong Consolidated School on September 6, 1921. Armstrong was the first district in British Columbia to close all the rural elementary schools and bus the children to a central school. ASMAS #1565-B

As with so many rural schools Round Prairie closed when population centres changed. In the Armstrong area school consolidation put an end to most small country schools. Edgar Docksteader, writing about the Knob Hill community, tells us: "In 1922, consolidated schools were introduced in Armstrong. Pupils were bussed into town in Model T Ford trucks with home-built bus tops."[15] Armstrong was setting an example that other school districts would eventually follow. Today each school board operates a fleet of school buses and the one-room ungraded classroom with all its deficiencies and its advantages is a thing of the past.

The administration of schools has grown not only in complexity but also in standardization. Because education is a responsibility of the provincial government initiatives for policy changes tend to come from the ministry. Three Royal Commission Reports authorized by the provincial government had a profound influence on schools in the Okanagan, Similkameen and Shuswap: the Putnam–Weir Report of 1925, the Cameron Report of 1946 and the Chant Commission Report of 1960.

A significant change in schooling which originated outside the Ministry of Education and the school boards is the service to children with physical or mental disabilities. That these children were entitled to education originated with parents and people engaged in Provincial Health Services. Al Hiebert and Dorothy Alexander,

in their essay "Assisting the Mentally Handicapped in the Vernon Area: the First 25 Years," detail the struggle of a dedicated group to have the needs of such children recognized by educational authorities. They write:

[In 1955] no government funding was available....In May of 1956 it was announced that a government grant per student per month would be paid for children 6 to 18 years of age in schools such as My School [the Vernon facility]....The government grant would cover about half of the $4,000 needed to operate My School for one year....In 1959 the provincial government made it possible for schools for the mentally handicapped to operate from a solid and permanent financial base. The per student grant was considerably increased and policy changes made it possible for school boards to take over schools such as My School and to provide the necessary buildings and facilities.[16]

There were people in Kelowna and Penticton who, like the Vernon group, were pioneering a change of attitude in the public and its institutions with respect to those who had not previously found a place in the educational system. Since the 1950s opportunities have become increasingly available and universal.

Armstrong/Spallumcheen had the first fleet of school buses in British Columbia. In 1921 Joe Glaicar proudly shows off the bus that he has built on a truck chassis. In the 1920s and 1930s the vehicles were called school trucks.
ASMAS #5101

Joe Glaicar in 1922 with his load of school children.
ASMAS #5100

Other Educational Institutions

Private Schools
Private schools have also played a part in Okanagan education. Writing about the Vernon Preparatory School that he and his brother, Rev. A.C. Mackie, started in the Coldstream in 1914, Hugh F. Mackie says in part:

When we came to the Valley, there was no private school for boys between Vancouver and the Rockies. There had been a very small private school run by Rev. St. John Mildmay in the Coldstream, but this had disappeared some years before we arrived. Chesterfield School at Kelowna was not yet in existence. St. Michael's School for Girls in Vernon was in those days a healthy young institution about two years old under the guidance of Miss M. LeGallais. For many years it continued to expand until it became one of the best known girls' schools in Western Canada with an enrolment of about 100 pupils. Then, as schools will, it fell on evil days and was finally closed in 1937.[17]

St. Michael's School for Girls in Vernon.

The Vernon Preparatory School opened with five pupils, among them J.B. and J.R. Kidston (day boys). Establishing the school demanded all the strength of not only the Mackie brothers, but also of Mrs. Hugh Mackie to whom Mr. Mackie pays the following tribute:

> At first we all had a desperately hard struggle, especially Mrs. Mackie, who with two little children to look after, one of them chronically ill, somehow managed to cook for and feed the boys and us, keep the place spotless, and then lend a hand, often until after dark, with the Ranch. Much of the success of the School resulted from her never-ceasing energy and care for the boys.
> (*OHS*, 1948)

By the time the school closed in 1946 upon the retirement of the Mackies they had educated a total of 456 boys, and this without the financial assistance paid by the government today to private schools which meet ministry criteria.

Okanagan Summer School of the Arts and Other Artistic Activities

Outside school board responsibility but meeting with the support of the Penticton board was the Okanagan Summer School of the Arts (OSSA), which opened its doors to the public July 8, 1960.[18] Today it continues to present courses each summer in music, in the visual arts, in dance and in crafts. Through its auspices young people and adults—some valley residents, others visitors—have had the opportunity to meet and study under some outstanding teachers. Penticton citizens have given hours of volunteer time to serve on its board and to support its hired administrators. In this service no one has been more assiduous than Mr. George Gay and Mrs. Eva Cleland.

In one article on the OSSA we find an assessment of George Gay's contribution:

> George is essentially a "people" person. The individual matters. The arts are important because they enlarge the individual and enrich him. Therefore the arts don't belong in some remote ivory tower, but right here where people are. When articles about the school talk of "the friendly and informal atmosphere" in which people paint, play, or study they are speaking of an environment which is the direct outcome of George's philosophy regarding the arts.[19]
> (*OHS*, 1982)

Eva Cleland came to Penticton in 1928 as a Chatauqua organizer and returned in 1936 as the wife of Hugh Cleland. Once she was permanently settled in the Valley she was tireless in her support of any artistic activity—the Okanagan Music Festival, the Okanagan Symphony first formed in 1959 under the baton of Willem Bertsch and brought to maturity under Leonard Camplin, Community Music Schools, the Penticton Arts Council and the Okanagan–Mainline Regional Arts Council. Eva's gentle diplomacy worked wonders in winning financial and artistic support and in developing audiences.

Practitioners of the visual arts have always found the Okanagan with its strong uncluttered landscapes a congenial home. Artists have come here from other places, bringing their talent and training to the community. Increasingly, young people who have grown up here are developing their talents and making a name for themselves in a wider world. This vibrant arts community has contributed to the success of OSSA, the Okanagan Symphony and other arts activities.

In 1976 the Okanagan–Mainline Regional Arts Council (OMRAC), one of the pioneer regional arts councils in the province, presented a festival which it called "Okanagan Image." Paintings and sculptures were commissioned and mounted in a mobile gallery designed by Robert Dow Reid, an internationally known sculptor whose home and studio are in Kelowna. Playwright George Ryga, whose *The Ecstacy of Rita Joe* has been translated into many languages, accepted a commission to write a new drama for the occasion, *Ploughmen of the Glacier*. Music was commissioned from Art Lewis and Ernst Schneider. Jean Coulthard, as guest composer, created her *Kalamalka*. Gweneth Lloyd and Betty Farrally, both formerly of the Royal Winnipeg Ballet, created a ballet to be danced by students in their Kelowna school of dance to a composition by Michael Baker. All this music was performed by the Okanagan Symphony Orchestra.

A moving spirit in support of Okanagan Image was OMRAC president Ruth Schiller. Later Mrs. Schiller served on the Arts Board of British Columbia, on the executive of the Canadian Conference of the Arts and as a member of the Canada Council.

In 1985 the film *My American Cousin*, written and directed by Sandy Wilson, won the accolade of "Critics' Choice" at the Toronto International Film Festival. Six Genie awards were to follow.[20] The story is based on the author's girlhood at Paradise Ranch in Naramata near Penticton. Residents of the South Okanagan were thrilled to see Okanagan scenery and Okanagan events celebrated on film.

Herbert Business School

A private educational institution that played an important part in the development of the Okanagan was the Herbert Business School, which opened in Kelowna in September 1931 with five students enrolled. Both Gladys and Gordon Herbert taught and won the respect of a growing body of students for their commitment.

Okanagan University College

One of the more exciting educational developments in recent years has been the establishment of the Okanagan University College. The following is quoted from that institution's 1995–96 calendar:

> Okanagan University College is a public, comprehensive post-secondary educational institution offering a wide variety of career, continuing education, degree, developmental, trades, university transfer and vocational programs.
>
> The region served...extends from Osoyoos and Princeton in the south and west to Mica Creek and Revelstoke in the north and east. Established in 1965, Okanagan University College enrolled its first university transfer and career transfer students in 1968. During the period of 1970–1974 the College was melded with the B.C. Vocational School, assumed responsibility for Adult Education programs, and saw the Penticton School District join the College region.
>
> In 1988, the College created the K'noowenchoot Adult Education Resource Centre in Salmon Arm.
>
> In co-operation with the University of British Columbia and the University of Victoria, the College began to offer third and fourth year courses in 1989. With this new mandate, the name was changed from Okanagan College to Okanagan University College in 1992.

Classes were taught during the early years in temporary quarters. However, since then permanent campuses have been developed as follows: KLO Campus in Kelowna, North Kelowna Campus (January 1993), Penticton Campus (1988), Vernon Kalamalka Campus (1982), and Salmon Arm Ruth Park Complex (1991). The total enrolment in the 1994 fall semester in regular programs was approximately 6,500 full- and part-time students. In addition over thirty thousand students were expected to enrol in continuing-education programs during the year.

10
Medical Services

The Preprofessionals

An Amputation[1]
by Robert Lambly from "Early Days at Enderby"

A very distressing accident happened on Herman Witcher's ranch near Lansdowne on Monday, October 9, 1880. While threshing wheat Herman Witcher got his arm caught in the gearing of the threshing machine and torn off above the elbow. The arm was terribly lacerated and torn, and to save his life it was necessary to amputate the arm above the elbow. As a lad I had travelled around considerably with a cousin of mine, a practising surgeon in the east, assisting him with his surgical cases. Consequently, I had something of a reputation as an amateur surgeon and bone-setter, and I was sent for and begged to undertake the operation as there was no doctor nearer than the coast. It was a desperate case and I had no tools but a pocket knife and a meat saw, and even the meat saw had to be sharpened before it could be used. By dint of tying up everything I found that was not muscle or flesh I succeeded in catching up the arteries and stopping the flow of blood. The agony which Mr. Witcher endured must have been terrible, but he bore it all with a stoical courage and endurance

Herman Witcher lost his arm to a threshing machine.
Armstrong Museum

beyond praise. The operation was performed without an anaesthetic and the only ligature I had was cotton thread and a small quantity of carbolic acid for an antiseptic. Despite these disadvantages the operation was successful and Mr. Witcher made a good recovery.

(*OHS*, 1935)

In colonial times and well into the confederation era professional medical services were non-existent in the Interior of British Columbia. Faced with a crisis people had to do what they could for either themselves or their neighbours. Those like Robert Lambly and R.L. Cawston who had a smattering of medical knowledge were often called upon. Women like Mrs. Lequime had a wonderful fund of folk knowledge which they were ready to share. Regarding Herman Witcher's ordeal David Lloyd-Jones adds the following information:

> When Herman Witcher had his arm taken off in the threshing machine the doctor who came out from Kamloops some days afterwards pronounced the case hopeless. The neighbours then appealed to Mrs. Eli Lequime, who was very skilful in dressing a wound, and she sent them the ingredients and directions for making a certain poultice which they made and kept constantly applied to the arm, and he recovered. It is my recollection of the matter that the neighbours believed Herman Witcher would have died had it not been for Mrs. Lequime. Mrs. Lequime was a splendid woman; she never spared herself when she could be of assistance to her neighbours in a time of sickness or when an accident happened.[2]
> (*OHS*, 1935)

Kathleen Ellis remembers: "My mother prescribed for the illnesses of the Indians and others, being guided by a large volume known as 'The Doctor's Book.' When my father broke his leg, my mother diagnosed and set it according to directions in The Doctor's Book. Physicians reported later that a perfect union resulted."[3]

Many pioneer women had large families, most of whom arrived in this world without professional medical help. Mary Ann Cawston had the assistance of an Indian midwife, Agnes Kwalokin, during the birth of three of her sons. When Valentine Haynes was born December 21, 1875 Emily Haynes had the help of Mrs. McDougall. Katie Lacey writes: "It was necessary to bring in a mid-wife from Ft. Colvile, a good three days' ride away, the woman being a Mrs. McDougall, a French halfbreed [sic] who was 75 years of age at the time. The weather turned very cold and lots of snow came before she was able to return home and she was forced to return to Ft. Colvile on snowshoes."[4]

In all, six children were born to John Carmichael Haynes and his wife Emily. Susan Allison had fourteen children born in her wilderness home. Magdalene Ehmke, in Spallumcheen, had ten children, eight of whom were born after her arrival in Spallumcheen. Mrs. C.J. Patten (nee Sophia Ehmke), who was the first of the Ehmkes born in the North Okanagan, tells us that her mother was fortunate enough to have the assistance of a trained nurse who happened to be living in Kamloops in 1878, a Mrs. Todd. The same nurse attended the birth of Vance Young ten days later on October 25. However, in most cases, Mrs. Patten tells us that women in those days had to depend on the help of their neighbours.[5] Of the birth of the nine Ellis children Kathleen Ellis has this to say:

> The babies came in regular succession at two year intervals, with the exception of my two brothers who were separated by one year only. The rest were girls—seven of them....In the earlier days the family vacation took the form of a trip over the Hope mountains on horseback to provide for the safe arrival of the new baby. This usually took place in New Westminster, although three of us were born in Penticton, my father officiating as doctor, nurse, and mid-wife, with the help of an Indian woman.[6]
> (*OHS*, 1950)

Of course bearing children without the assistance of a doctor was not limited to the 1800s. Primitive roads into areas where people took up homesteads, even in the 1920s, forced women to make what arrangements they could. Katie Lacey writes of two women from the Richter Mountain settlement who in 1916 had babies:

> Mrs. Parrish gave birth to a son. One room of the old log courthouse at Osoyoos was fixed as a temporary maternity ward and the baby was born there. A few weeks later, Mrs. Harry Walker, also from Richter Mountain, came here to have her baby. Dr. Effner of Oroville (Washington) was the attending physician and Mrs. Germyn, wife of the Osoyoos Customs Officer was the nurse for both cases. The courthouse later became the first Osoyoos school.[7]
> (*OHS*, 1955)

A premature baby born to Edna Dignan in the Richter Pass settlement was cared for by grandmother Elene Vardier, who kept the baby in a cotton-lined shoe box in the warming oven of the kitchen range. This ailing infant grew to be a healthy little girl.[8]

Pioneer Doctors

from **Early Medical Services in the Okanagan Valley**
by F.W. Andrew, M.D.

An epidemic of smallpox raged throughout British Columbia in 1883 and the terrified Indians became ready victims. The Government sent some vaccine to R.L. Cawston and engaged him to vaccinate the Indians of the Similkameen and South Okanagan Valleys. The amount was quite inadequate. At that time there were no regulations to prevent the taking of the virus from a person whose vaccination was at its height and using it to inoculate another. Cawston, being conscientious, had recourse to this method. The usual technique was to scarify the skin of the arm with the point of a needle or sharp knife, and then rub in the vaccine. This was too slow for Cawston, so he drove a number of pins through a section of a whisky bottle cork, jabbed this contrivance on a vesicle that was ripe, gave it a twist, and repeated the movements on any healthy arm that was presented. Naturally, most of the arms were infected but this was overlooked for the mass vaccination soon ended the epidemic. Cawston considered he had done a good job for as he remarked, "They all took and had arms as big as their legs."

The first professional calls were made by a Dr. Webb of the Colvile Reservation in Washington. He attended some of the early settlers of Osoyoos and the Similkameen as early as 1885. In 1888, Dr. Chipps rode over from Nicola to Allison (Princeton) to make a professional call. [This was on behalf of J.C. Haynes at the time of his fatal illness.]...

It was not until 1893 that the first resident doctor appeared in the South Okanagan Valley. Mining prospects were good in the Fairview District and Dr. B. de F. Boyce was engaged by one of the first mining companies. As his practice was not confined to the miners, he saw much of the new country "from the hurricane deck of a cayuse" as he made his professional calls. He moved to Kelowna in 1895. Dr. Boyce was not registered until 1894. It frequently happened in the early days that a doctor with proper credentials was allowed to practise on a permit until a qualifying examination was held.

Dr. R.B. White came to Fairview in 1897 and attended the employees of the mines, as well as settlers on pre-emptions. When mining in Fairview began to wane, he moved to Camp McKinney where prospects were brighter. He, too, travelled about on horseback, carrying his supply of drugs and dressings in the old-fashioned saddle bags. When Camp McKinney closed down he moved to Penticton, then a small dusty hamlet. He was appointed Coroner in 1900....In 1908 he was joined by Dr. H. McGregor for a little over three years when they separated and carried on in different offices....

(*OHS*, 1948)

F.W. Andrew, M.D.
A Tribute by Grace Whitaker[9]

The Okanagan Historical Society lost one of its first, most valuable and enthusiastic members with the passing of Dr. Frederick William Andrew in the Summerland Hospital on November 24, 1957...

Dr. Andrew came to Summerland in 1908 and practised medicine here until his retirement in 1944...Dr. Andrew and his dog Klinker were familiar figures on the steep and dusty roads of Summerland in the horse and buggy days. Klinker's faithfulness inspired his master's book, "A Country Doctor's Dog."

Dr. Andrew's rewards and recognition in so many fields of his endeavours bear witness to his qualifications in his profession, his scholarship and civic affairs.
(*OHS*, 1958) Photo: Summerland Musuem

Many of the doctors mentioned in Dr. Andrew's article came for only a few years but there were those who stayed, administering to the sick and injured, often travelling, as Ed.W. Aldredge has said, "hour after weary hour in the saddle in snow and pouring rain, or later, driving unreliable cars over even more unreliable roads."[10] These men were a force in the establishment of hospitals but in addition participated in the general life of the communities in which they served. Dr. Andrew talks of Dr. W.J. Knox, who arrived in Kelowna in 1903, as being "an exceptionally bright personality and, for several years, President of the Provincial Liberal Association."

Dr. Andrew writes: "Probably the first medical man to practise in the Okanagan Valley was Dr. E.J. Offerhaus, a native of Holland, who registered in 1883. He lived at Lansdowne and after the completion of the Shuswap and Okanagan Railway, covered the Armstrong and Enderby areas." Dr. Offerhaus in 1891 married Miss Choquette, the niece of A.L. Fortune. They had two sons. After Mrs. Offerhaus's death from TB, Dr. Offerhaus retired to Holland where he died in 1915. An interesting side note is that the doctor served as postmaster at the Spallumcheen (Lansdowne) post office from April 1, 1896 until its closure July 20, 1908. Mrs. George Murray who was at the Offerhaus wedding remembers, "Dr. Offerhaus was the family doctor with Mrs. Frane acting as nurse....The doctor had the first buggy [in Lansdowne], a two-wheeled gig."[11]

Dr. Andrew tells us that the first medical practitioners in Vernon were Dr. D.L. Beckingsale who arrived prior to 1890 and Dr. W. Reinhard, a graduate of Leipzig, who began to practise in 1892. Dr. Osborne Morris, "a large, good-natured man, a colorful character," opened his office in 1893 and besides attending to his Vernon practice cared for the medical needs in Kelowna until 1895. In 1894 Dr. Gerald Williams arrived in Vernon. In 1896 Dr. Morris was appointed coroner and it was in that capacity that he sometimes went as far south as Osoyoos. Dr. Morris is remembered also for having one of the first automobiles in the Okanagan. One feels that he needed it! With transportation as difficult as it was in earlier times patients and doctors had to be resourceful when it came to exchanging medical information, as we see in the following article, which is based on a set of telegrams now in the archives of the Enderby Museum.

Hazel's Illness[12]

by Robert Cowan

At the end of the 19th Century, it was not uncommon for doctors in England to recommend a change in climate for their patients. While they generally had only second-hand knowledge of the Okanagan Valley, they nevertheless endorsed its climatic medical virtues.

In 1894 Graham Rosoman took the advice of his physician and moved to the Okanagan Valley, settling initially near the community of Mara. There a daughter, Hazel, was born in 1896. A few years later, he moved to Enderby where he was employed by the Columbia Flour Mill as a bookkeeper.

A paragon of Victorian virtues, he was noted for his faultless preparation of the Flour Mill business and his punctuality. His great hobby and pre-occupation was health. He sent for numerous pamphlets and paraphernalia that would improve his health or prolong his life. So when his daughter took ill in the spring of 1898, he was concerned. When her condition worsened, he became distraught.

As Enderby had no physician, Graham Rosoman wired to Dr. Morris in Vernon for assistance: "Baby grippe twelve hours now. Dangerously prostrated. Fever high. Half unconscious. Wire directions first."

On April 13th, Dr. Morris had just returned to Vernon and was unable to attend Hazel immediately. He wired Mr. Rosoman to give his child a hot bath, one grain of quinine every three hours and put a cold cloth to her head.

Graham Rosoman, who ironically settled in the Okanagan for his health, got a scare when his infant daughter became dangerously ill.
Enderby & District Museum

Dr. Osborne Morris saw the Rosoman child back to good health.
Vernon Museum

At that point Graham had not slept in thirty-six hours, keeping an almost constant vigil at his daughter's side. She had been experiencing a fever, convulsions, and a slight cough. He wondered in his reply to Dr. Morris if her nervous system was strong enough for bromide potassium, and if so how much should he give her?

Dr. Morris wired back: "Give five grains potassium bromide every two hours if convulsions continue. Every three hours if no convulsions. Wire later."

The next day Hazel's condition became worse. She scarcely moved, and her breathing was rough. She was perspiring and her temperature had reached 102 degrees. Graham wired Dr. Morris: "Cheeks purple. Flush. Greenish around mouth. Is there danger. Wire." He had already decided he needed to change poultices.

Dr. Morris wired back to Graham requesting he send a man to George Hutchinson's residence in Armstrong and pick up the medicine he was sending.

On April 15th, Hazel's temperature reached 105 degrees. Dr. Morris responded to Graham's queries with: "Yes. Give five drops brandy every two hours. Continue hot application every half hour. Give two grains quinine every three hours and wire in about three hours her condition."

Clearly, after three hours Hazel's condition had deteriorated. Dr. Morris now recommended: "Give ten drops of brandy every hour and use hot water bottles instead of poultices."

Whether it was increasing the brandy intake, changing the poultices, or having the disease run its course, Hazel began to slowly improve. Graham wired to Dr. Morris that she had some fever, but she was breathing rather better. Her strength was starting to return.

Dr. Morris responded with: "Give Beef Tea cold and milk every few minutes also brandy as directed. Child will be cross and peevish. Wire this afternoon."

By April 18th, Hazel's temperature was 99 degrees. Her strength continued to improve, but she was experiencing occasional pain in her lower abdomen. She slept only with discomfort. Dr. Morris responded to these improvements with: "Give tea. Spoonful of Castor Oil. Continue stimulant. Do not give powders or use poultices if temperature remains at 99 degrees."

With the danger over and Hazel's health improving, Dr. Morris recommended: "Continue stimulant. Give milk and Beef Tea every half hour. Do not remove from bed. Avoid drafts and do not have more than one person around the bed."

His last wire to Graham was on April 22nd and advised: "Give child custard, bread and milk. Gradually give solid food. Stop stimulant gradually."

Graham Rosoman was greatly relieved.

(*OHS*, 1987)

Dental services had a rather humble beginning:

...[In 1898 and 1899 Dr. Averille] drove a democrat in which he carried his equipment and covered the territory from Grand Forks to Princeton, and from Penticton to Osoyoos. Some of his living patients say his extractions were not exactly painless. Dr. C.A. Jackson was the first resident dentist in Penticton. When he retired, he was followed by Dr. T.B. Turner, a good dentist, but given to speculation in mines.

Dr. Andrew has omitted mention of another colourful pioneer dentist of whom David Lloyd-Jones writes: "Once at Okanagan Mission we had a visit from Dr. Jones, the negro dentist of Cariboo, who travelled the country with a horse and buggy, and had with him a machine for drilling teeth which looked like an old fashioned spinning wheel and was worked with a foot treadle."[13]

Dr. J.W.N. Shepherd was the first resident dentist in Kelowna. He opened an office in 1904. Dr. R. Mathison opened a second office in 1908. Vernon's first dentist was a Dr. Corrigan who came in 1902. In 1905 Dr. K.C. MacDonald began his dental practice, which included regular trips as far north as Enderby until 1911. (We have spoken of Dr. MacDonald's political career elsewhere.) As the population grew it became practical for dentists to set up practices in smaller towns of the valley.

Vernon Jubilee Hospital opened in 1897, the year of Queen Victoria's Diamond Jubilee. Vernon Museum 33

Nurses, Hospitals and Pharmacists

Cottage hospitals were often established before a community was ready for a full-fledged hospital. Miss Edith Hancock had such a cottage hospital in 1912 in Penticton. Mrs. Robert Sinclair had five beds for patient care in her home in Summerland. A nursing home was opened in Armstrong in 1913 and was granted government support the following year.

The Vernon Jubilee Hospital, so named to celebrate Queen Victoria's Diamond Jubilee, was opened in 1897. In 1921 this hospital had 70 beds. Between 1904 and 1931 a nurses' training school was conducted, even during those years for which Mrs. Beryl Wamboldt could find no records.[14] Those who had not completed their course before the closure of the school were encouraged to finish their training either at the Kamloops Hospital or at the Royal Columbian in New Westminster.

The Kelowna General Hospital opened in 1908 with 19 beds. By 1975 this hospital had grown until it had 255 acute-care beds and 109 extended-care beds. Between 1921 and 1944 the hospital offered a nurses' training school under the supervision of Mrs. Mary E. Wilmot, who had been named superintendent of the hospital in 1920. Hospitals were opened in Penticton (20 beds) in 1913; in Summerland (9 beds) in 1914; and in Enderby (7 beds) in 1917.

Lucy Hack (nee Crafter) reminisces about her training in the Kelowna General Hospital in the late 1920s.

> In 1925 typhoid was still common in Kelowna, so much so, that it was considered necessary to have a Public Health Doctor, with the hope that he could bring this disease under control. Dr. Ootmar, who had retired from his practice in Holland, was asked to undertake this task, and he also set up the first Kelowna laboratory in the Kelowna Hospital. Within a few years he had improved matters so much that typhoid became rare, and the last case I saw in the valley was in 1936. Typhoid cases entailed a lot of work; all their dishes had to be boiled and all their bed linen etc. soaked in disinfectant before being wrung out and sent to the laundry. As a probationer I seemed to be forever wringing out bathtubs full of linen, and I was heartily glad when winter finished off the typhoid season for the year....
>
> Later I became a Victorian Order Nurse in a scattered country district with no hospital. The depression of the thirties was just lifting and many of the patients were struggling to live with a minimum of equipment (apple boxes for chairs, etc.). When they fell ill or had a baby, one had to improvise. Then my training in a small country hospital stood me in good stead, as I had learned to make the best use of whatever was available.[15]
>
> (*OHS*, 1976)

In 1895 S.A. Muir arrived in Vernon to take over the business of R.N. Taylor, whom Muir calls the "first real druggist in the Okanagan—honest, fair-dealing and competent." Mr. Muir has left a colourful account of his experiences as druggist. He writes:

The territory served by Vernon was large. The nearest drugstores to the North were Kamloops and Revelstoke and to the South there were none to the Boundary....The doctors had a wide area to cover and there were no automobiles and few telephones. As I was secretary and manager of the Okanagan Telephone Company, the exchange was in the back of my store. It was frequently necessary for the druggist to wait late at night to fill the prescriptions. Also after a busy morning they would come in with a batch of prescriptions to be sent by train. It was the usual thing for me to rush to the station and throw a parcel into the express car as it moved out. The conductor used to say, "Has Muir been here yet?" and if I had he'd say, "I guess we can go now." On one occasion I started on my bike for the station but the train pulled out before I got there, so I headed for the Landing and caught the boat before it pulled out.

Mr. Carruthers of Kelowna was very ill with pneumonia and required oxygen. I happened to have a tank which the hospital had ordered and then gone back on. We routed out the only auto in town and they stripped it down to the chassis and loaded on the tank. (Not the nice small ones you have nowadays). Cars being what they were, a team of horses followed the auto in case it broke down. However, all went well and it arrived in time.

(*OHS*, 1988)

Henry Main had a drug store in Fairview until the settlement became almost a ghost town, when Main moved to Penticton, buying out the store which J.W.S. Logie had established there the previous year. Kelowna's first druggists were Wallace (1899) and P.B. Willits, who opened his store in 1903.

Ivan E. Phillips gives us a vivid picture of the life of a public health nurse in his account of Miss Kathleen Snowden's work at Keremeos, that included the creation of an improvised ambulance: "At first Kae managed to make her rounds on foot or on horseback but she soon realized that she must have a car and with a loan of $300 from the Department she bought a two-door Ford sedan. With one front seat folded forward and an apple box between the seats plus a single mattress it served in an emergency as an ambulance."[16]

This "ambulance" was run at the nurse's expense. On one occasion the vehicle was used to transport a badly wounded man, who had been engaged in a knife fight with a cousin, to Penticton over hazardous winter roads.

Mr. Phillips tells of another event which earned the nurse a young man's gratitude:

Early one morning someone was pushed against Kae's door with a crash. She recognized the man as the little Chinese laundry-man, beaten and bleeding profusely. He was scared and embarrassed finding himself with the young nurse clad only in a dressing gown. It seemed that three or four of his customers had forcibly expressed their displeasure with his

The new Vernon Jubilee Hospital, built in 1911. Vernon Museum 3176

service. Although his wounds were superficial the doctor had to be called. The cost was $35 for the doctor's service and 50 cents for the dressings provided by Kae. The Chinese's gratitude took practical and, at times, embarrassing forms. He insisted that he alone would do Kae's laundry and became quite angry if by chance he saw her taking her uniforms elsewhere. From time to time roasted chickens garnished with fresh, scrubbed vegetables would be on the table when Kae returned.

The establishment of health units in the early 1940s was a trend towards regionalization of services which was to grow. Improved roads which enabled an ambulance service to transport quickly and safely patients from one centre to another, along with the growing complexity of medical practice, made it practical to have some services offered in particular centres where medical specialists would have the support of properly furnished hospital units and trained nursing staff. Today major surgery is performed in one of the three largest hospitals and even among the hospitals at Vernon, Kelowna and Penticton there is specialization.

During the 1960s an important change in the delivery of health services was made with the introduction of medicare. Hospital charges were covered by a government-administered hospital insurance. The result of these changes has been that health care is universal and no one need go without a necessary operation because of lack of funds. Currently the idea of regional planning has been extended to all health services. Long-term care, intermediate care, home care, hospital care, out-patient care etc. have been discussed by local committees and plans prepared for submission to the provincial government. In some cases this process has been completed and the new boards are in place and active.

By 1994, 864 acute-care beds were in use throughout the area, including 355 in Kelowna, 161 in Vernon, 181 in Penticton, 46 in Salmon Arm and 20 in Princeton. One hundred and sixty more beds had been approved by the Provincial Government. These figures do not include either extended-care or intermediate-care beds.[17]

Okanagan, Similkameen and Shuswap society has come a long way from operations performed with a pocket knife and a meat saw and even from cottage hospitals in less than 120 years.

11

A Developing
Economy

New Opportunities

James Armstrong Schubert saw economic opportunities in the Okanagan. He opened general stores in various sections throughout the valley, including Penticton, Hedley and Tulameen.
BCARS A-02450

James Armstrong Schubert was a very small child when his family reached Kamloops in 1862 with the great Overland Expedition from Red River. By 1883 his parents were settled permanently at Round Prairie,[1] having spent some years in the Cariboo and at Lillooet. In this story of James Schubert we see how quickly, within a lifetime, the economy was changing. New career opportunities were opening up for those with the vision to see and grasp them.

James Armstrong Schubert, Okanagan Pioneer[2]
by M.E. Hunter

As a young man [James Schubert] was apprenticed to a building firm in Victoria and he spent a year there learning to glaze windows. He then returned to the upper country, and took up land where the town of Armstrong now stands. He drove the stage from Kamloops to the Mission, and had many adventures. On one occasion, while the stage was descending a steep hill, a keg of nails fell off and broke open. Since nails were precious, the passengers had to alight to assist in retrieving as many as possible...The exposure to cold weather and the dust of summer brought on an attack of tuberculosis, and Mr. Schubert departed to Santa Barbara to recover his health. When he returned to the valley, he went to Vernon where he built the first house on the street named after him. He was instrumental in having a post office opened in Vernon [and in having the name changed from Priests' Valley]...

Mr. Schubert was later made Road Superintendent and, with David Lloyd-Jones, he built the first road on the west side of Okanagan Lake from Penticton to Trout Creek. Only a few

hundred dollars had been appropriated for the work, so all they could do was to widen and improve the old Indian trail far above the lake…He also built a bridge over Okanagan River, the first swing bridge, and with a gang of men constructed a road along Dog (Skaha) and Vaseux Lakes to the mining town of Fairview…Mr. Schubert's health again broke down at this time, and he had to be transported most carefully to the hospital at Kamloops.

After he had recovered some of his strength…he decided to open the second store in the little settlement of Penticton. [Schubert's store] later contained the post office and a baker's shop. Then the building became, in succession, the first high school, the home of the *Penticton Herald*, a fruit packing house, and eventually a flour and feed store.

There was still no connection by rail between Penticton and the Coast cities or the American cities to the south. Supplies were all brought down Okanagan Lake, and four or six-horse freight wagons were loaded at the wharf or at the two stores to carry goods along the single winding road to Keremeos, Hedley, Fairview, Princeton and the other settlements.

The mining development at Hedley attracted Schubert's attention and he left Charlie Reveley to manage his new store at Penticton. At Hedley he built a large department store and post office which was to be destroyed by fire in 1914…Mr. Schubert spent ten years in Hedley. He then acquired a store in Tulameen and began placer mining…Later Mr. Schubert became interested in the breeding of Jersey cattle and he brought in pure-bred sires from the Fraser Valley to improve the strain of milk cows in the district…He died at Tulameen on March 17, 1938.

(*OHS*, 1949)

J.A. Schubert's store at the corner of Ellis Street and Vancouver Avenue in Penticton in 1905. Is that a wedding party on the veranda?
Penticton Museum

Vernon's first Hudson's Bay Company store built in 1887.
Vernon Museum 69

Technological Changes in Agriculture and Milling

Joe Richter, in 1970 when he was 96 years old, described the farming practices when his father settled in the Similkameen in the mid-1860s. He said:

> At first the hay was mowed with a scythe, grain crops with a scythe and cradle—a forked device attached to the snaith, that gathered the falling stalks holding them until dumped at the end of the swath. Grain was threshed on the barn floor—sheaves were laid crossways and horses driven round and round for about half an hour or until the grain was trodden from the straw. After straw was forked away the grain was winnowed by a hand-cranked machine that blew the chaff and alien seeds away.[3]
>
> (*OHS*, 1970)

When machinery became available it had to be shipped to Hope, where it was dismantled and loaded on pack horses or mules for the trip over the Dewdney Trail, then reassembled when it reached its destination. This lasted until railway construction and connecting boats and wagon roads made the transportation of heavy equipment easier.

By 1903 we find a considerable degree of mechanization in the North Okanagan. Lyda M. Bell writes of her father's threshing activities:[4]

Charlie Hoover's harvesting outfit that did custom work in the North Okanagan.
Vernon Museum

Threshing
by Lyda M. Bell

Charles Hoover got his first threshing machine in 1903. It was powered by horses. Later he had two threshing machines powered by Case steam engines. Each summer, when the grain was ripe, his crews went threshing on farms from Westwold through the valley to the Coldstream Ranch. Charles usually ran one of these machines and his brother Edgar the other. Sometimes Floyd Hunter would be the engineer. A picture was taken of the one machine threshing on the Coldstream Ranch in 1910. They had threshed 2,300 sacks of oats. An inscription on the back of the picture says that his engine was used in plowing up the L.&A. Ranch in 1908.

On the farms, threshing was one of the major operations. Other farmers would come to the farm where the threshing was to be done and help. Sometimes the grain was ready in big stooks near the farm buildings and the bundles would be thrown into the machine. On other farms the grain was brought in from the fields with the bundle wagons and teams. The wives always had a very busy time preparing big meals for the hungry men.

There was a water tank along with the engine. Besides water, cord wood was needed to convert the water to steam and to drive the machinery. Very often there would be a crew of about a dozen men. The grain in those days was put into sacks which had to be sewn and tied. Threshing carried on in this fashion until the combines became prevalent. One of Charles's old engines was stripped down and the boiler was installed in the Cheese Factory in Armstrong.

(*OHS*, 1984)

It was not enough to grow the grain and thresh it. The sacks of wheat had to be ground into flour. Cuyler Page, curator and administrator of the grist mill at Keremeos, has not only documented the reconstruction of the Keremeos mill, but has also given us an authoritative outline of the history of milling in the Okanagan region.

Similarities of Several Okanagan/ Similkameen Pioneer Flour Mills[5]
by Cuyler Page

Barrington Price, founder of the Grist Mill at Keremeos, first came to the Similkameen in 1872 as a rancher and trader, having leased the former Hudson's Bay Company stock

Keremeos Grist Mill built by Barrington Price in 1877. Although the mill stood unused for many years most of the original machinery was preserved in the lower floor, thus making restoration possible. In 1979 British Columbia's Heritage Trust purchased the property and began a careful restoration. Notice the overshot water wheel.
Keremeos Grist Mill

ranch. His friend, Henry Nicholson, credits him with stimulating agriculture in the valley by building a grist mill in 1877. Gold miners in the Similkameen provided the market for its flour along with local settlers, natives and travellers on the Dewdney Trail which passed by the mill.

Several North Okanagan ranches of the 1870s had similar flour and feed mills. Even their markets were similar, with the Cherry Creek gold miners and local farmers all in need of basic flour. Historic photos from Keremeos, Coldstream Ranch, and O'Keefe Ranch each show mill buildings identical in size, shape and proportion. A log building reputed to be the Brewer–Tronson mill in South Vernon had the same appearance. The similarity is quite striking, especially when they are compared with other B.C. grist mills of the same period, all of which are noticeably different. These Okanagan buildings were all about 18 feet by 30 feet, two stories, walls about 14 feet tall with the upper floor wall portion only 5 feet high, and entered by a door in the gable end of the upper floor. Just from their appearance one might conclude that the same plan had been used for these four.

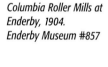

The notion that these mills may have all been built by the same millwright is supported by the historical sequence in which they began operation. From 1876 to 1879 a new mill was added at yearly intervals, and the first, at Keremeos, required about a year to build…It is interesting to consider the sequence in which these mills appear to have been built and the progression of efficiency in design of their power systems…

Columbia Roller Mills at Enderby, 1904.
Enderby Museum #857

The O'Keefe Ranch mill, built after the others, had a much improved system using a turbine installed beneath the floor of the building. All the driving machinery was protected from the weather, and, in addition, O'Keefe could grind flour in the winter when the other mills were frozen. A further benefit of the turbine was that it could operate efficiently with a low head of water, making possible the use of the quiet waters of Deep Creek as it flowed through the farmyard meadow.

Although the layout of the flour-making machinery appears to have been identical, the power supply to each mill was a definite improvement over its predecessor.

In 1887, a large modern steam-powered flour mill was built by Rashdale and Lawes beside the Shuswap River at Enderby. It used the newly developed roller milling system which allowed production of fashionable white flour. A few years later, when the S&O Railway was constructed into the North Okanagan, two more steam-powered mills were built beside the tracks in Vernon (1894) and Armstrong (1895).

The small ranch mills may have continued to grind feed for a while, but there was really no longer a need for their service and they appear to have been quickly abandoned in favour of the fine white flour available from the new mills...

Brent's Mill, built in 1871, has been well documented in several articles. It significantly predated the North Okanagan mills and utilized a traditional type of grinder with flat, round mill stones. In the building, which still remains near the Rutland turn-off from Highway 97, there is nothing to suggest a mechanical kinship with the other mills.

Nelson Duteau also had a mill in Coldstream...but little is known about it, and there are only brief mentions in historic letters and articles...

The Postill & Patton mill on Deep Creek was built on a pattern more like that of the mill at Tranquille on Kamloops Lake. It doubled as both a flour mill and a sawmill using the same source of water power. It was a common practice at these multi-service mills to saw lumber in the daytime and grind flour at night...

Price's mill at Keremeos is the only mill remaining with its building and machinery intact. Restored and managed by the British Columbia Heritage Trust, it is once again grinding flour and playing a significant role in the economy of the region by becoming an important part of the province's growing tourism industry...

(*OHS*, 1991)

Sawmills

Falling trees with spring boards, Mable Lake area in 1898. Enderby Museum #460

The first trees felled for use were probably those cut for the purpose of building houses. Skilled axemen trimmed the logs and fitted them into buildings such as those at Rock Creek in 1860, at Fort Shepherd, or those built for the Boundary Commission, all of which attest to the skill of the builders. No doubt one of Roderick McLeod's qualifications for being chief trader at the Similkameen Hudson's Bay Company post was that as a skilled axeman for the Boundary Commission he had the ability to restore the dilapidated buildings of the post.

Eric Sismey writes that Frederick Brent in 1871 built his grist mill in what is now Rutland of hand-hewn logs and whip-saw lumber.[6] David Lloyd-Jones gives us a vivid picture of whip sawing in his autobiographical piece, "Over the Hope Trail":

In 1879 my brother had the contract for building A.L. Fortune's house, not the present one but its predecessor, and he sent for me to come out from Ontario...My brother and I were carpenters and we followed contracting and building and took any work of the kind that came our way. I do not remember how much of the lumber in the Fortune house came from the sawmill at Kamloops, if any, but some of it was whip-sawed. A log was rolled onto two skids over a pit, and one man descended into the pit while the other stood on the log, and then up and down all day the saw went. It was considered to be a good day's work for two men to turn out 100 feet board measure in a day which made dear lumber, from $60 to $70 per 1000 feet. There was no planing mill and all doors, windows and dressed lumber for the Postill house was cut in their own sawmill. The first lot for the house was sold to J.C. Haynes for the erection of his house which is still standing on the east side of Osoyoos Lake. The lumber was hauled to the shore of the lake at Okanagan Centre and there made into a raft which had a

mast and a sail and two sweeps. In this manner it was taken to Penticton.[7]
(*OHS*, 1935)

Most of the Haynes house was constructed of hand-hewn logs which today are covered with stucco, but lumber for floors, windows and doors came from the Postill mill. According to Mrs. E.J. Lacey the raft of lumber was floated as far as Okanagan Falls where it was dismantled and the lumber carried around the falls and reassembled for the remainder of its journey to Osoyoos Lake.[8]

The Postill mill was powered by Peon Creek, later called Mill Creek,[9] the same creek that Frederick Brent had used for his grist mill. In 1883 the Postills extended their operations by erecting the first sawmill in the North Okanagan. James E. Jamieson writes:

> In the year 1883 Alfred Postill, with his two brothers,...preempted 640 acres of land on Deep Creek...On this land Alfred Postill erected a sawmill with a capacity of some 12,000 feet per day—the first sawmill in the North Okanagan. From this mill came most of the lumber used in the construction of bridges, stations and other uses in the building of the Shuswap and Okanagan Railway and a little later most of the lumber and heavy timber was supplied for the building of the SS *Aberdeen* on Okanagan Lake...The power was supplied by water from Deep Creek through a flume about one and one-half miles in length with a small dam near the old George Paton farm, now owned by Fred Mitchell.
>
> Mr. Postill, having other interests in the South Okanagan, and needing a manager for this sawmill sent for an old friend Levi W. Patten, to come out from Ontario. Mr. Patten with his wife and family arrived in the late fall of 1883 and managed the sawmill for the next five years when he purchased the property and almost immediately erected a custom grist mill using the same water power. Mostly on account of shortage of water the sawmill was run during the day and grist mill at night.
>
> Mr. Patten operated the sawmill for the next twenty-two years, the grist mill being discontinued when an up-to-date flour mill was erected at Enderby.[10]
> (*OHS*, 1962)

It was from the Postill/Patten mill that Augustus Schubert got the rough lumber for the Round Prairie School in 1885, the finished lumber coming from Kamloops. The symbiotic relationship between the sawmill owners and the settlers is illustrated in the experience of the Bowell family, originally from Newfoundland, who bought land in 1886 at Lansdowne. S.R. Bowell tells us:

> Lansdowne was the hub of the North Valley in those days...Our farm was lightly timbered, the north quarter with a fine stand of ponderosa pine, and the south quarter dotted with mountain fir. The pine was a godsend for Dad, who at that time had no logging equipment, because he sold it on the stump to Patten's mill. He also worked at the mill, and thus got a start in the new country.[11]
> (*OHS*, 1955)

In the next decade logs cleared from ranches at Okanagan Mission were skidded to the lake, boomed and towed around to the mill at Kelowna owned by Bernard Lequime and David Lloyd-Jones. However, throughout the whole area from Salmon Arm to the International Border there must have been great piles of good timber go up in smoke as settlers rushed to clear their land for farming.

The smaller mills were usually set up near the timber resource, a custom followed well into the new century. Joe Kass who logged in the Enderby area wrote of his experience in the late 1940s or early 1950s:

> My health being fairly good I went to Vernon and bought a small sawmill. I set the mill up in Trinity Valley on Harry Danforth's timber limit. It was a failure. The next spring I moved the mill to Albert Price's and bought logs from farmers. Later I moved the mill to our place (Bill Burris' homestead). When the cut was finished I sold the mill to Harry Danforth, and the homestead to Mr. McFarland. That was the end of my logging days. In my lifetime I had logged with oxen, horses, steam, gas, and diesel.[12]
> (*OHS*, 1970)

Hugh Charles Musgrave Leir's sawmilling business prospered at the turn of the century when Penticton experienced a development boom. Penticton Museum

When Hugh Leir decided to build his mill in 1904 three miles up Ellis Creek he was no doubt following this principle of taking the saws to the timber, in this case prime western yellow pine.

In 1902, Hugh Charles Musgrave Leir arrived in Keremeos with very little money. He had come from England. Seeing that the Similkameen was unbridged Leir initiated a ferry service, but when the freshet took his barge down the river and left it irretrievable on a sandbar he gave up the project. However, during the two years in Keremeos Leir learned the fundamentals of sawmilling.

Foreseeing the boom in real estate about to occur in Penticton because of the regular service of the SS *Aberdeen* on its lake run and also the expected subdivision of the Ellis lands, Hugh Leir moved to the Okanagan community. Upon obtaining a contract from the South Okanagan Land Company to supply three million board feet of flume lumber, the first million to be delivered in 1906 and the remainder by 1908, Leir set up his mill. He brought over from Keremeos a circular saw and edger, a cut-off and a steam engine. In Vancouver he acquired a boiler which had been used during the pile driving for the Granville Street Bridge. The boiler had to be shipped to Sicamous and south to Okanagan Landing by train, then by boat to Penticton from whence a team of horses dragged it up the road which had just been scraped into the hillside. Eight-horse teams were available but only four horses could manage the sharp curves on the road. Leir was his own millwright.

Logs were hauled in by contract. Leir soon realized that if production was going to be economically sound he would need a new location where logs could arrive by water. He, along with three other Englishmen—Francis C. Bird, Frank Richardson, and Edward Bullock-Webster—formed the Penticton Lumber Company and chose a mill site two miles down the river from Okanagan Lake where a bed of compacted gravel, the outwash of the area creeks and a backwater for log storage met the company's needs. Some time after 1910 the company fell on hard times and was finally taken over by Hugh Leir and renamed Penticton Sawmills. The new company was managed by Hugh Leir and later by his sons until it was sold in 1966 to Northwood Mills. By that time the mill was contributing over $1,000,000 in annual wages to the Penticton economy.

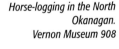

Horse-logging in the North Okanagan. Vernon Museum 908

We are indebted to Eric Sismey for the above information which was obtained in an interview with Hugh Leir. Mr. Sismey also includes the reminiscences of a man who could look back on sixty years' experience in the industry:

It was a never to be forgotten sight, Leir declared, to watch fallers, working in pairs, one on each side of the tree, stripped to their Stanfield undershirts, swinging razor sharp, double-bitted axes, first one then the other. Shunk-shink! Shunk-shink! as chunks of bark, white slabs of sapwood and then the heartwood flew from the undercut.

Then to the other side with the long saw. One man in the pull and the ride of the hands of the other on the saw handles; in the turns of the teeth and the rakers from one position to another in the kerf; and in the feel of just when to stop and slush coal oil on the sticky pitch in time to wedge against the bind.

On the steep downhill hauls logs were bolstered over a pair of wheels and often the dragging tail was not brake enough. Standing on his load the teamster braced himself with the help of the lines to his four horses while his team raced to keep the whiffletrees away from their flying heels.[13]

(*OHS*, 1966)

Jim Kehoe was a timber cruiser for the Penticton sawmill. He had come from Ontario and taken up land on Anarchist Mountain just east of Osoyoos. Of him Eric Sismey writes:

> From around 1905 [when he was about twenty-eight] until he quit work...Jim Kehoe spent his life in logging, usually in a foreman's capacity. At first he logged prime tamarack for the Porter Brothers Mill at Sidley taking much of the timber from his own land. This was followed by logging in many parts of the Okanagan and Kettle River valley. He was logging foreman at Peachland for the Bullock-Webster mill on the Carmi Road at Penticton. Jim Kehoe searched for and cruised timber for Hugh Leir's Penticton Sawmills all along the east side mountains from Squally Point on Okanagan Lake to Camp McKinney.
>
> Jim remembers the great stands of Ponderosa pine he found. Magnificent trees, some three feet through at the butt. These groves are gone. Jim remarked somewhat wistfully, and never again will trees of this size and grandeur be allowed to grow in the Okanagan.[14]
> (*OHS*, 1971)

Each of the hundreds of sawmills that have existed had its own character, but the Porter Brothers mill at Sidley was unique.

> Porter Brothers Sawmill at Sidley was served by a half-mile Great Northern spur. Railroad ties were an important product but it also milled rough and finished lumber. Logs were teamed from Sidley property, from Kehoe's and several others. The mill, perhaps a customs officer's headache, straddled the international boundary with the sawing machinery on one side of the line and the planers on the other. Lumber was shipped and sold on the side of the boundary where the best price could be obtained.[15]
> (*OHS*, 1971)

Sawmilling in Enderby began in 1894 when S.C. Smith of Vernon moved his milling operation from Okanagan Landing to a site on the Spallumcheen River. Norman McLeod of Armstrong was a partner in the enterprise. G.L. Ormsby writes:

> The opening up by Mr. Smith of the vast hinterland running back almost 100 miles through the Mabel Lake and Sugar Lake countries and drained by Shuswap and Spallumcheen Rivers was the prelude to intensive lumbering activity. Logs were cut as far back as Cherry Creek and even beyond to Sugar Lake, floated down the Shuswap River, over Shuswap Falls, where they joined Bessette Creek logs, and on to Mabel Lake, where they were rounded up into rafts and towed 14 miles to the mouth of the Spallumcheen River, and down to Enderby, 30 miles distant.[16]
> (*OHS*, 1948)

A.R. Rogers Lumber Co. logging in a backwater of the Shuswap River, 1908.
Enderby Museum #871

The Enderby enterprise changed hands several times and finally reached the zenith of its activity between 1905 and 1921 when under the management of A.R. Rogers. In 1912 the name was changed from A.R. Rogers Lumber Company to Okanagan Sawmills Limited. Joe Kass found a thriving community when he arrived in Enderby in April 1910. He describes the scene:

> When I got off the train I thought there was some sort of celebration going on. The platform and streets were crowded, but I came to understand that Enderby was booming.
> They had a big sawmill that had a two-way bandsaw which cut 100,000 feet of lumber in a double shift. There was a shingle mill and a lathe mill, both incorporated into one big mill, running double shifts. They also had a big planing mill. The company had lumber

yards in different towns across the prairies…

From daylight to dark the green lumber was piled in the Enderby yards…They shipped out a lot of ties and fence posts…South of the mill on the river bank there was a Hindu [sic] shacktown, a large Chinese community and also a big Japanese district. These people worked mostly in the mills. The Chinese ran a restaurant, where meals were served until midnight, and did all the local laundry…[17]

(*OHS*, 1970)

An interesting forest-products specialty of the Shuswap area was the production and sale of poles. Joan Cowan, curator of the Enderby Museum, has recorded the history of this industry.

B.J. Carney & Co.[18]
by Joan N. Cowan

B.J. Carney & Company was a major producer of western red cedar and lodgepole pine utility poles, with its primary market the government and utility companies of the eastern provinces and states…The head office was moved to Spokane, Washington in 1927…Carney Pole Company initiated operations in western Canada in 1908 in Chase, and established a pole yard in Sicamous. Attracted by the straight cedar in the Kingfisher and Shuswap areas, the company opened an office in the former office of Okanagan Sawmills on Old Vernon Road in Enderby. The Enderby office became the head office for the Canadian operations of B.J. Carney & Company in 1926.

Loading cedar poles on railway cars at the B.J. Carney Pole Company yard. (Photo taken by George Meeres in 1931.) Enderby Museum #592

Percy Farmer who at first was office manager became general manager in 1928 and remained with the company until 1965. Pole yards were established in Grindrod and Enderby. In April 1925, H.M. Walker reported in his paper that the pole industry had replaced sawmilling as the main industry of the area. Joan Cowan continues:

The Carney Company pays to Clark & Elliott, who handle the poles and run the camps, in the neighborhood of $4000 a month…about twenty per cent of the poles handled by this company come from farmers in the course of land clearing…400 carloads of poles are shipped annually.

The company still operates in the Shuswap area, although Sicamous rather than Enderby has become the centre of its operation as now most of its poles come from Revelstoke, Nakusp and Sicamous. The Enderby office closed in 1990. Mrs. Cowan writes of the memories of two former employees, Marion Baird and Harold Palmer:

> They could both remember pole camps when the trees were peeled and sized in the bush; now they are shipped to a peeling machine in Sicamous. They could remember when pole drives covered the length of the Shuswap River; now the poles are easily transported by truck. They could remember loading the railroad cars and paying the freight charges; now the poles are shipped by truck. They could remember when poles were partially treated; now they are usually full-length treated. They could remember when Carney's yards held strictly cedar poles; now three quarters of the poles are fir, pine or larch.
> (*OHS*, 1995)

Once orchards were planted and came into production a number of sawmills in the area produced "shook," as the components for apple boxes and crates for other agricultural products were called. Box factories sprang up in the various Valley towns. One in Kelowna was that of S.M. Simpson Limited.

S.M. Simpson came to Kelowna in 1913 and opened a mill-work shop in which he was at first the only worker. In 1924 the business expanded into box making and the manufacture of veneer. He made tin-tops, box lids, grape baskets and berry baskets. A revolutionary change in the handling of fruit came when the 25-bushel bins were designed by industry officials and Simpson management, along with pallets and shipping containers. In 1965 Crown Zellerbach bought out the Simpson interest. The previous year the payroll for the well over 700 people employed in the Kelowna area, not counting contract loggers, in the sawmill, box factory and plywood plant was over $2,250,000.

Other sawmills include: Vernon's first sawmill, owned by Tronson and Brewer and operated on Long Lake Creek, later to be relocated north of town; the first Grande Prairie or Westwold mill, which was of the upright variety and affectionately known as "Old Muley"; the first Salmon Arm mill at Tappen Siding, which was later relocated at Kault; and the Columbia River Lumber Company, with one of its timber limits east of Salmon Arm.

The industry which became the mainstay of Lumby's economy had its beginning when Paul Bessette built a water-powered mill on the Pierre Bessette property. Then when the Rogers Lumber Company closed its Lumby operation in the early 1920s Henry Sigalet, who had been born in Vernon, stepped in with his Lumby Timber Company and created a business which depended on hauling logs overland rather than running them down the river. Alleyne Tull says of the Sigalets: "Henry worked hard with his men and his wife, Margaret, was camp cook."[19] Their son Harold carried on the business.

Today the lumber business remains important to the Okanagan and Shuswap economy. Much of it is in the hands of multinationals. It would be very difficult now for an individual to start up a logging or sawmilling operation. Not only would he be up against enormous capital costs and strong competition, but timber sources also are no longer easy to acquire. Even established companies find that new environmental standards no longer allow the laissez-faire practices of the past.

Johnston and Carswell sawmill at Long (Kalamalka) Lake c. 1905. Vernon Museum 3183

Loggers' Sports on the Shuswap River at May 24 celebration c. 1950. Log rolling champions: Adrian Alexander and Casimir Felix. Enderby Museum #1222

Brick Making

Anciently, the fine clay settled out of the glacial Lake Penticton created deposits of the raw material needed for brick making. By the 1890s there were residents in the Valley who had the knowledge necessary to turn this clay into building material and, fortunately, there was a large enough population to create a market.

Beryl E. Gorman tells us that the Jacques house, which once stood on Vernon's 30th Avenue, was built in 1891 of bricks that came from "Vernon's Brick Yard which existed near the present Pottery Road on Highway 6. Bricks from this source were used and were called slop-bricks. They were wet and soft in composition. Despite the fact that they crumbled easily, they withstood deterioration for eighty-two years."[20]

David MacDonald writes that the Ellis School, which is now part of the Penticton Secondary School complex, was built in 1913 using bricks which were made in Penticton at Jacob Winger's brickyard on Norton Street. In Kelowna a brickyard was opened at the foot of Knox Mountain in 1905 by Messrs. Harvey and Jackman, the clay being dug from a deposit on the mountain. Ettie Adam, whose father Charles Clement, along with Herman Riggs, bought the business some time after 1910, tells us that business boomed because of all the construction going on in Kelowna. Her father's bricks were used in homes, schools and business blocks. There was also a market for bricks among settlers along the lake.[21]

It was in Enderby, however, that brick making became an important local industry that lasted for over fifty years. Dorothy Wanderer, who has written a history of the enterprise,[22] tells us that Marwood and Perry were established by 1891, making bricks with their Chinese crew. By 1894 they could produce twelve thousand bricks a day using their new brick-pressing machine. Mrs. Wanderer not only tells us of the various owners and those who set up competing businesses, but she gives us a very good idea of how the wood-fired manufacturing process worked. In 1909 a Mr. Gibbs assumed full ownership of the Enderby Brick and Tile Company. By May 1912 the company had all the orders it could fill. Enderby bricks were used in buildings from Revelstoke to Vancouver. The business continued to thrive until World War II broke out in 1939 and all the crew enlisted. After the war P.A. Gorse, who had taken over the business in 1924, and his two sons, just discharged from the air force, explored ways and means of reviving the brickyard but found that impractical.

One should not leave this consideration of the manufacture of building materials without mention of the Peachland Glazed Cement Pipe Company, which operated from 1910 to 1921. The company's history is documented by Sheila Paynter, who tells us the company's reason for choosing its location: "There is a piece of property on the lakeshore half a mile north of the mouth of Trepanier Creek…There is a sandy hillside backing it with suitable material for making cement. The lake frontage is ideal for a slip for shipping by barge and boat."[23]

Paynter's article includes a quotation from a 1912 edition of *The Vernon News*:

> There is also located here (Peachland) a cement pipe factory which is turning out a large amount of pipe with an ever increasing demand. It is probable that the capacity of the plant will be doubled next year. This cement pipe is doubtless to be used for drainage purposes, as drainage becomes necessary through this irrigated country.

This enterprise, however, became the victim of several disasters, the most spectacular of which was the collision of the *Skookum* with the SS *Castlegar* that sent the pipe loaded on the two barges towed by the former to the bottom of the lake off Squally Point.

The Paynter Family

The Paynter family, founded by Edwin C. Paynter, a veteran of the Boer War and World War I, settled in East Kelowna in 1910 and at Westbank after World War I. In both locations they cleared land, established orchards, participated in community affairs (especially the creation of irrigation works) and ran post offices. Six of the children of Edwin and Margaret Paynter have remained in the Valley. A member of the third generation creates and sells pottery decorated with Okanagan themes. Sheila Paynter has written several authoritative articles for *Okanagan History* as well as celebrating the Okanagan landscape in two books about her own unique adventures.

12
Hard-Rock Mining

Fairview

Thirty years after the gold rushes of the 1860s British Columbia was again in the throes of gold fever. However, this time the precious metal was to be won by lode mining rather than placer mining. Between 1885 and 1900 the Camp Hewitt Mining and Development Company along with others was searching for gold deposits in the area between Trepanier and Deep Creeks (between modern Peachland and Westbank). In 1893 J.M. Robinson of Portage la Prairie, Manitoba responded to the publicity the area was being given. Being already in Rossland, looking for gold properties, he decided to ride by horseback from Rossland to what is now Peachland, where he acquired ownership of several claims. However, the Kathleen Mine established by Robinson and his associates was disappointing and the Manitoban decided that the subdivision of land into orchard properties offered a more secure investment.

In the South Okanagan mining prospects proved much more profitable. In her article "Further Fairview Osoyoos Chronicles" Katie Lacey quotes from the first edition of a paper which started publication August 27, 1892 in Oro (now Oroville), Washington:

> Another promising camp in the Okanagan country is Fairview Camp, in British Columbia, eighteen miles north of Oro, close to the Okanagan River. Gold was discovered there first about four years ago but little was done towards development.
>
> The first mine to bring the Camp into prominence was the Rattler, discovered by Hank Mankin, and for a long time the only means of support he had was to take the quartz and grind it to pulp between two large stones, and then wash the gold out in a pan.

Was Mankin using the horse-powered *arrastre* to mill his ore? The paper goes on to state that some Spokane investors put in a stamp mill but a dispute among the partners put an end to the operation. Fortunately some English capitalists arrived from London looking for likely mining property and bought the Rattler, and were examining other properties. The paper says of them:

> They left London May 4th, and have been all through the Slocan and Kootenai districts

before coming here and are very favorably impressed with this country.

They have unlimited means at their command for legitimate mining investments and intend to make further purchases.[1]

Lode mining was expensive. Machinery had to be purchased–stamp mills, compressors, pipes, flumes, concentrators, etc. Wages had to be paid and the product, whether in the form of gold bars or concentrate, had to be transported. Capital was essential and in the South Okanagan this came from either the United States or from England. Until train and boat service were established through the Okanagan in 1892 all equipment and supplies had to be brought in from south of the boundary.

Other claims that had been recorded by the summer of 1892 included the Wide West, Brown Bear, Silver Crown, Joe Dandy, Wynn M., Ontario, and Stem Winder. Later claims that developed into mines were: Morning Star, Evening Star, August, Tin Horn, Smuggler, Black Diamond, and Wild Horse. In some mines, silver as well as gold was recovered.

Soon a thriving town grew up on the bench high above the valley floor, about three miles west of the present town of Oliver. Estimates of its population vary. Some think that at its peak three thousand people lived there and that Fairview was, for a time, the largest settlement in the Interior of British Columbia. As transportation improved, access became easier. Dorothy Amor tells us that her father, Arthur D. Hardie, in November 1902 brought her mother as a bride to Fairview. Having come down Okanagan Lake to Penticton on a sternwheeler, they travelled in an open freight wagon south to Fairview, a trip of twelve hours.[2]

Fairview's grand hotel called "The Big Teepee." The hotel burned down with the loss of one life.
Oliver & District Heritage Society

Two of the valley's pioneer doctors, Dr. B.de F. Boyce and Dr. R.B. White, founded their first practices at Fairview having been encouraged to settle there by mining companies. Because this was where the action was, in 1898 the government agent C.A.R. Lambly was instructed to move his government office from Osoyoos to Fairview. One can imagine the throbbing life of the town which had sprung up so suddenly–the hotels, the bars, the livery stables, stores, offices, a school, churches. Rev. William Irwin, known to the miners as Father Pat, had his Anglican congregation. But the town was not without its tragedies. The grandest hotel, known as the Big Teepee, burned to the ground with the loss of at least one life. A diphtheria outbreak took the lives of the children of another family.

But veins of ore run out and miners turn to better prospects. By 1910 Fairview was a ghost town. Today only one house from the great mining era remains and the passerby would not recognize the townsite were it not for the two lots which once belonged to the Presbyterian Church and are now the property of the Okanagan Historical Society. The church building was moved to Okanagan Falls, where it serves the United Church congregation. Its dismantling before its removal from Fairview bears testimony to the skilled use of explosives developed by mining men. A charge of dynamite was hung from the ceiling of the church. When the dynamite was exploded the walls were blown out momentarily and then returned to their original position but with all the nails loosened. The boards could then be removed without damaging them.

The Great Gold Robbery

While some prospectors were staking claims in the mountains to the west of Fairview others were searching for promising properties in the mountains across the Okanagan Valley. The Victoria claim was located in 1884 by A. Goericke, possibly acting for J.C. Haynes. But it was not until 1887 when Al McKinney and his associates, Rice, Burnam and Le Fevre, staked the Cariboo Amelia that any great interest was shown in the area. Robert Iverson in his booklet *Camp McKinney* tells us:

The rich ore exposed on the Cariboo Amelia claims over a distance of some seventy feet with a width of some forty to fifty inches brought about another gold rush of sorts...Mickey

Afternoon tea at Camp McKinney 1893. The three Cosens brothers arrived in the South Okanagan where they opened stores in Camp Fairview and Camp McKinney during the mining boom. They built the house shown for their parents who came out from England. Driving the team is Sydney Cosens. Sitting beside him, his father Cornelius. Next is Judge Matthew Begbie. Behind Mrs. Cosens is the maid she brought from England. Finally, on the right is Arthur Cosens. Connie Cumine

Monahan and a group from Spokane, hearing of the rich strike were soon on the scene. Organized as a private company, they bought out Al McKinney and his associates. The Cariboo Amelia first organized as Cariboo Mining and Milling in 1888 and it was shortly after to become a public company known as Cariboo Mining, Milling and Smelting. Capitalization was at 800,000 shares with a par value of one dollar.[3]

When Camp McKinney first came into being the only access to it was through Sidley. However, in 1893 the Government of British Columbia undertook to build a road from Okanagan Falls up past McCuddy and through Camp McKinney to Midway and on to Grand Forks. This was the only Canadian route from the Okanagan into the Boundary Country until 1911 when a road was built up Anarchist Mountain east of Osoyoos.

The camp, with a population of about 250 at its height, had six hotels, stores and other businesses, but no bank. The nearest bank in British Columbia was at Vernon. The Cariboo was Camp McKinney's major mine. When it ran out of high-grade ore it closed down in 1903 and Camp McKinney with it. However, the company had the distinction of being the first mining company in British Columbia to pay dividends which, by 1900, had amounted to $459,000.

For most people looking back to the turn of the century Camp McKinney's most exciting event was the great gold robbery. We are fortunate in having an account of the event from a man who was a storekeeper in the camp at the time.

The Gold Brick Robbery at Camp McKinney[4]
by Arthur K.W. Cosens

The Cariboo Mine at Camp McKinney of which Robert Jaffray was president, George B. McAulay, managing director, and Joseph P. Keane, superintendent, was a paying proposition from the grass roots down. James Monahan of Spokane was also a director of the Company and very instrumental in getting it under way after purchasing the property from the first owners, McKinney and Rice.

Monahan brought in the first unit of the stamp mill from the State of Washington, hauling it in with teams, and passing the customs at Osoyoos…In the year 1896 the Camp was running very smoothly. The stamp mill was pounding away incessantly day and night with only a cessation of the noise from the falling stamps for a short time twice a month during the time the "clean up" was in progress. After the amalgam had been retorted, the quicksilver being retained, the gold bricks of an approximate value of $30,000 per month were ready for shipment to the mint at San Francisco by express from the nearest railway which was at Marcus at one time, and later at Midway, after the advent of the railway to that point.

A certain amount of caution was usually taken when the bricks left Camp. Sometimes I have known them thrown into the jockey box of one of the wagons hauling concentrates or tailing to the railhead for shipment to the smelter at Tacoma. In this case the wagon would be met at its destination by one of the officials or trusted employees of the Company, the brick extracted and shipped, sometimes without the driver of the wagon knowing that he had been its custodian at all.

At other times it would be hidden in a sack of concentrates and the same procedure followed.

Then again it would be taken by the Superintendent on horseback, or driving a buckboard and followed by an armed employee a hundred yards or so behind.

The morning of the robbery, in August 1896, Geo. B. McAulay, who had been spending a few days in Camp and was returning to Spokane, left Camp at 7 a.m., driving a buckboard and had the proceeds of the last clean-up with him, some $14,000 in the form of three bricks, the value of the smallest brick being $1,600. About two miles from Camp on the road to Rock Creek he was ordered by a masked man who stepped from the woods with levelled rifle to throw out the bullion and "keep going." McAulay obeyed until he reached the ranch of C.W. Hozier some eight or ten miles farther on. Here he enlisted the services of Hozier's son, Leonard, a boy of some twelve years of age, to ride to McKinney and notify us of the happening. Leonard reached the Camp store which was in charge of the writer about ten o'clock—no time was lost in informing Superintendent J.P. Keane of the occurrence.

There was one person in the store besides the writer when Leonard arrived with the news—standing with his back to the stove—one Matt Roderick. It seemed to the writer that a slight smile passed over Roderick's face when Leonard imparted his message.

Camp McKinney at that time was what was known as a "One Man Camp," that is to say that the Cariboo McKinney Mining and Milling Co., Ltd. was the only company operating and the only employer of labour—therefore a miner who worked for wages, or a labourer had really no chance there unless he was acceptable to the management of the Company. The rest of the population was composed of claim owners and old time prospectors with interests or a stake in the country.

There was, besides the boarding house and store which was quite a popular place for the men to hang around when not on shift—especially those who did not drink—a saloon run by Hughie Cameron. The Camp later boasted no less than five saloons.

On being informed of the hold-up the Superintendent called out a number of the men and a thorough search of the woods in the vicinity was made, however, without result, nor was at that time the slightest suspicion attached to anyone. Local amateur Pinkertons were entirely at a loss and that the robbery had been committed by one of their own men was certainly farthest from their thoughts.

Matt Roderick, who hailed from Tacoma, Wash., had been employed by the Company as a miner for some time. He was a very reticent, quiet man, very well built, of medium height, and neither drank nor smoked, but he was an inveterate gambler. Every pay day he would get his cheque cashed, pay his bills at the store and immediately get into a poker game where he would usually stay until broke—sometimes over a period of two or three days—ignoring the time he was due to go on shift. He lived in a cabin on the outskirts of the Camp and at the time of the robbery was laid off—ostensibly being sick. The writer remembers that he was looking extremely pale, and owing to his indisposition there was nothing unusual for him to be in the store at 10 a.m. on the morning of the robbery. Some days later he stated that he had better go home to Tacoma and would return when he felt better—he had had the usual gambling reverses and I believe was assisted financially by some of the boys to enable him to go home.

The stage left at 7 a.m. Roderick climbed aboard sitting next to the driver in the front seat. He had with him a roll of blankets (it was customary, and I might say a sign of respectability, for a man to travel with his own blankets in those days). Just as the stage was leaving Keane appeared, and Roderick said to him, "Will it be alright for me to come back to work when I feel better, Joe?" Keane replied, "You needn't bother coming back, Matt." Hearing this conversation I took it that Roderick's work had not been satisfactory and that Keane did not want him again for that reason. Being a "One Man Camp" this prevented Roderick returning in the ordinary way, and accounts for the way in which he eventually did return. But there was not the slightest suspicion attached to Roderick at that time.

The management enlisted the services of a detective agency in the State of Washington. First thing they did was to check up on the movements of the few individuals who had left Camp since the robbery—among them Matt Roderick. They found that shortly after his return home he was paying up taxes on some property which had been considerably in arrears, and generally spending money freely. This naturally threw suspicion upon him and his movements were continually watched.

Soon it became apparent that he was preparing for a journey. The supposition was that he had brought out the small $1,600 brick with him, concealed in his blankets, and disposed of it and intended to return for the two larger bricks which he would probably have cached in the vicinity of his cabin. The Camp was notified that Roderick was headed north and instructed to keep a close lookout for him. It was also ascertained that he had purchased a fine iron grey saddle horse from the Sheriff in Conconelly, Wash., and that it would be his means of transportation.

There were two roads leading into Camp McKinney from the south and southwest, one from Anarchist Mountain, known as the Sidley Road, the other, from the Okanagan known as the Fairview Road. These roads converged about two miles from Camp. At this point of vantage an Indian, one Alexine from Inkanip [sic], selected for his intelligence and wood-craft, was stationed with instructions to notify the Superintendent of the approach of anyone unknown to him coming toward the Camp after dark.

On the evening of October 26, 1896, at about ten o'clock, the writer had just closed the store and adjourned to Hughie Cameron's saloon, and was watching the various card games. Two provincial constables, Louis V. Cuppage and Deane were present, also J.P. Keane, when a knock came at the door. It was Alexine with a request to speak to J.P. Keane. The message was, "He is coming." We left the saloon hurriedly for the store where the writer at their request provided the constables with six-shooters. The store always had quite an arsenal as many of the miners from the States often carried guns and in Canada left them with the storekeepers for safe keeping. It was an absolutely pitch black, dark night. Keane, who was a very alert man of very quick action was on his way, followed by Thomas Graham, before the constables had finished selecting their weapons.

Less than a mile from Camp, Keane overtook Roderick walking in the same direction leading his horse. As he was upon him almost before he realized it owing to the darkness, he accosted him, "Is that you, Matt?" Roderick whirled around. Involuntarily the muzzle of the rifle which Roderick was carrying in the crook of his arm was raised. Keane thought he intended to shoot and quick as a flash discharged his own gun. Roderick fell dead, shot through the heart. Upon examination Roderick's rifle was found to have a piece of rag in the muzzle and the six-shooter found in his pocket was quite rusty. He had evidently just taken them from their hiding place and was proceeding towards the place where the bricks were hidden. The body was removed to the Company office. The following day Dr. Jakes from Greenwood, coroner for the district, arrived and held an inquest, the following jury being empaneled: Henry Nicholson, foreman; A. Alwood, W.H. Blick, George Bennett, V.R. Swanson, and A. Cosens.

The bullet from Keane's gun had entered Roderick's body just below the left nipple and was just under the unbroken skin in the back. Dr. Jakes removed the bullet with a hair pin.

Roderick had left the Camp broke, but on the body about $100 in cash was found, and under his coat a canvas harness with two pockets, one under each armpit, of just the right size to accommodate the two larger gold bricks. The Jury's verdict was "justifiable homicide." There was not the slightest doubt as to the guilt of Roderick. It was most unfortunate that

Keane's precipitate action prevented the capture of Roderick as he might easily have been trailed to the hiding place of the bricks and been taken together with the swag. As it is the bricks were never found—they still await someone to stumble upon them in the jackpines at Camp McKinney.

Keane was tried for manslaughter at the Spring Assizes the following year in Vernon, Monday, June 14, 1897, with Chief Justice McCall presiding. A.G. Smith, Deputy Attorney-General prosecuted. The defense was conducted by Mr. Cassidy and J.P. McLeod of Greenwood. The sentence was one day's imprisonment, which had already been served.

(*OHS*, 1937)

From Hester White we have an addendum to the above account. At the time of the robbery Hester (nee Haynes) was married to C.A.R. Lambly, government agent and registrar of mining claims. The couple had moved from Camp McKinney down to Osoyoos. Mrs. White writes:

I can add to Mr. Cosens' story the information supplied by Tom Graham who was at Camp Fairview not long after the event. He had brought the gold brick there to ship by stage, and was about to leave for Camp McKinney, when an unknown woman, who had posed as a clairvoyant and water diviner during her short stay in Fairview, asked him if he would give her a lift. He took her there, and she remained a few days. Only after she had left Camp McKinney did suspicion grow that she was Mrs. Matt Roderick. It is supposed that she found the bricks and took them to Spokane. It is known that she had money and that she went to the Yukon later.[5]

Feeding the Miners

Mining at the turn of the century benefitted those engaged in agriculture whether in the Similkameen or in the Okanagan. Markets reached into the Kootenays where mining was an even more extensive activity. Eric Sismey interviewed Joseph Richter in 1970 when the old rancher was ninety-six years of age. Sismey writes:

During the mining boom along the Boundary in the '90s, fat cattle drives from the "R" Ranch were frequent. One drive in the fall of 1892 Joe remembers particularly. Two hundred and fifty head were driven from Keremeos to West Kootenay where Pat Burns waited to receive them. The drive followed the Dewdney Trail from Keremeos over Richter Pass to Osoyoos, up over Anarchist Mountain to Rock Creek, through Midway, Greenwood and Grand Forks over the hill to Rossland where fifty head were left at the slaughterhouse. Joe and his brother Ed, together with the drovers spent the night where the city of Trail now stands and in the morning the rest of the herd was driven to the Columbia River (Castlegar) where two Indians were hired to help take the cattle across. By prodding and pushing about twenty head at a time were forced into the river and with a canoe on either side the cattle swam to the opposite bank (Robson) where they were corralled.[6]

Victor Casorso in his *Casorso Story* writes about his grandfather Giovanni's trips to the mining towns with fresh beef and pork, fresh because it was still on the hoof until a buyer was found. Here is one of Casorso's tales.

On a hog drive to Camp McKinney, some of the Casorso pigs were bunched up not far from the embryo business section, with a drover in attendance. Then, four large boars decided to go for a stroll, wandering casually down the ruts that passed for the Camp's main street. At a house where some "painted ladies" did business, the door was open and the boars walked in, grunting. Four ladies ran screaming out the back door, into the gully below and the pigs had the place to themselves. They upset shelves full of supplies and a bed, ate food that was on a table and interested an oldtimer. "You should of heard those painted ladies squeal," he commented afterwards.[7]

It was not just meat that was sold to the miners. F.M. Buckland tells us of the efforts of a group of Mission farmers to get their produce to Kootenay markets.

Early in the 1890s times were hard in Mission Valley, since there was only a limited market for farm produce...In the mining country around Slocan Lake, however, there was a boom. The Kootenay imported its entire food supply. Here was a prospective market for Okanagan farmers. In the autumn of 1893, Alfred Postill called a meeting at Benvoulin school house to discuss the means by which this market might be developed. It was decided that four delegates should visit Sandon and arrange, if possible, to do business. The delegates chosen were Howard Dell, Mark Howard, John Casorso and R.S. Hall. The meeting collected $160 to defray their expenses. This marked the beginning of co-operative action by Okanagan farmers...

At the time, the Canadian Pacific Railway was building into Sandon...Between the railroad siding and the road to the mines, the Okanagan Mission farmers dug a cellar 20 feet by 60 feet. They traded vegetables and horse feed for lumber, and when they collected sufficient lumber, erected a feed house over the cellar and started business. R.S. Hall was left in charge of the Sandon warehouse. E.R. Bailey attended to the shipping of fruit, vegetables and hay from Kelowna...[8]

Hedley and the Nickel Plate Mine

By 1910, mining at Fairview and Camp McKinney had all but ceased. However there was at least one mine, the Nickel Plate, that was rich enough to sustain production for a longer period. Harry D. Barnes, who emigrated from England in 1890, arrived in Vernon during the spring of 1891, worked on the Postill ranch as well as on other Okanagan ranches and in 1901 arrived in the Similkameen. There he remained at Hedley and Nickel Plate for the major part of his working life. He has given us a full account of Hedley's mining history, part of which is printed below.

Early History of Hedley Camp[9]
by Harry D. Barnes

The little gold-mining town of Hedley, in the Similkameen Valley of British Columbia, lies at an elevation of about 1,700 feet above sea-level and is situated at a point where Twenty

The road to Nickel Plate Mine. Hedley is hidden by the treed mountain slope. In the valley bottom the Similkameen River snakes its way towards its junction with the Okanagan River.
Penticton Museum #028

The town of Hedley.
To the right of the town is the
reduction mill.
BCARS #08664

Mile Creek, after swinging around the western base of Nickel Plate Mountain, emerges from its canyon and has cut a boulder-strewn channel through the river-benches to flow into the Similkameen River a short distance below the town...

The first record of mineral claims having been staked on what is now known as Nickel Plate Mountain was in 1894 when James Riordan and C. Allison located three claims for the Hon. Edgar Dewdney; J.O. Coulthard of Keremeos had a claim on what was later to be known as the Kingston Mineral Claim. These four claims were recorded at Granite Creek, but were not considered worth doing the annual assessment work and were allowed to lapse. In 1897 Peter Scott located the Rollo and about the same time C. Johnson and Albert Jacobson, grub-staked by W.Y. Williams, then manager of the Granby mines at Phoenix, staked the Mound and Copper Cleft claims. In 1898 Peter Scott returned to do the assessment work on the Rollo and afterwards staked the Princeton, Warhorse, Kingston and other claims. In August of that year C.H. Arundel and F. Wollaston staked the Horsefly, Sunnyside, Nickel Plate and others. It was the Nickel Plate which was to prove the bonanza claim and to become the first producing lode mine of the Similkameen as well as one of the major gold mines of British Columbia.

It was about this time that Peter Scott and others agreed on "Camp Hedley" as a fitting name for the new camp, in honour of Robert R. Hedley, then manager of the Hall mines smelter at Nelson, B.C...The prospectors of the new camp had to travel to record their claims and assessment work to Fairview, where C.A.R. Lambly was the mining recorder and gold commissioner for the Osoyoos Mining Division. As news of the then recent strike began to circulate around the Fairview Camp, quite a number of the prospectors came over to the new camp in the early fall of 1898...Duncan Woods, for whom George Cahill staked the Mascot Fraction, did not come in until the spring of 1899. Later in the Camp's history it was the Mascot Fraction which was to become famous, for although it contains only 8 or 9 acres at depth it was to prove one of the Camp's richest spots. Seldom in the history of lode mining in British Columbia has so small an area produced so much wealth in gold. During the spring of 1899 many more prospectors came into Camp Hedley, and by the end of the year the surface of Nickel Plate Mountain was almost entirely covered with mineral claims.

The red, rusty ore outcrop of Nickel Plate occupied a small clearing on a fairly steep hillside…The ground both to the right and left, as well as below the outcrop was covered by an overburden and thickly strewn with jack-pine windfalls, amongst which a second growth of young pines had already made a good start. On the upper side of the ore outcrop a light-colored hard igneous rock stood out boldly several feet higher than the ore, with the contact between the ore and igneous rock being sharply defined. As the development proceeded, the igneous rock was found to be a sill which formed the hanging wall of the orebody. The igneous rock was later classified by Dr. Charles Cansell as gabbro. The red dirt from the outcrop panned gold very freely, and a gold pan of the material would often give twenty to thirty coarse colours about the size of a pinhead and also a long thick stream of fine gold…

In the fall of 1898 Wollaston and Arundel took out some samples of the surface ore of the Nickel Plate to the New Westminster Fair and exhibited them there. M.K. Rodgers, who was more directly connected with the early history and development of the Camp than any other person was so impressed by the appearance of the ore samples that he immediately started on a trip to the Nickel Plate to make a close examination and obtain samples. The examination proved so satisfactory that in November Rodgers took a bond on the Nickel Plate, Bulldog, Sunnyside, and Copperfield mineral claims.

In the early years of the Nickel Plate mine M.K. Rodgers obtained a British Columbia charter for the Yale Mining Company. Later on, when it was decided to build a mill, it was found that the original company's charter was not sufficiently broad to provide for the building of tramways, power flumes and the like, or for the expropriation of land for rights-of-way. Consequently a second company, the Daly Reduction Company Ltd., was formed and a charter obtained for it early in 1903, and from then on it became the operating company for both the mine and the mill.

Gomer P. Jones, who was to be connected with the Nickel Plate for so many years, was engaged by Rodgers as mine superintendent in August 1900. In the summer and early fall of 1900 a road about 15 miles in length was built over the mountains to the east of the mine to connect up with the Penticton–Keremeos road, and from then on supplies were hauled direct from Penticton to the Nickel Plate. In the fall of 1900 work was also commenced on the building of a road between Keremeos and Princeton, and it was completed by mid-summer of 1901. Before the building of this road only the old Dewdney Trail had connected these two points.

In the fall of 1899 Thomas Bradshaw came over from Greenwood and bought the newly built log hotel located near the mouth of Fifteen Mile Creek from a man by the name of Johnson. Shortly afterwards Mrs. Bradshaw and family came over to make their home on Fifteen Mile Creek. Bradshaw's stopping-place soon became well known to prospectors and others of Camp Hedley as a place where they could always be assured of a warm welcome, a good meal, and a comfortable bed. In course of time the establishment was expanded and, in addition, the Bradshaws had a thriving young orchard and alfalfa growing on their place. They had also acquired a small herd of dairy and range cattle…

The land where the town of Hedley now stands was acquired by the Hedley City Townsite Company, and in the summer and fall of 1900 R.H. Parkinson, P.L.S. surveyed the townsite, and almost immediately building was commenced…

In the fall of 1902 W.E. Welby commenced running a stage line between Penticton and Hedley. The trip usually took about twelve hours, which included a stop at the old town of Keremeos for dinner and a change of horses. Open stages were used, which carried six to

eight passengers, and the mail and travellers had to take the weather as it came. Later Welby acquired a Concord covered-in stage coach, but this was reserved for special trips and occasions. Fred Revely, who had bought out Deardorf's livery-barn, ran a daily stage to Princeton in conjunction with the Welby stages, but travellers from or to upper points had to stop over the night in Hedley…

In September 1903 Hedley held its first Labour Day celebration, which was rather a modest affair even although some two or three coach loads of merrymakers came from Loomis, Washington to join in the festivities and fraternize with the good people of Hedley. The main event was a baseball game between the Hedley team and one from Nighthawk and, although the visiting team was the better, due mainly to Wesley Rodger's pitching Hedley won the game, on which a good deal of money had been bet by the backers of the respective teams. In addition, there were two days of horse-racing and a grand ball marked the climax to the event, with music furnished by "that famous knight of the bow," Joseph Brent of Okanagan Falls. From a thousand to twelve hundred dollars would be given in prize money for rock-drilling contests, baseball, and horse racing. Rock-drilling teams would quite often come from places as far away as Rossland to compete in these contests…

By the late fall of 1903 the mill building was about completed, and a good start had been made on the installation of the machinery. The tramways were all graded and most of the track laid. Also good progress had been made in the building of the Twenty Mile flume. The ore-crushers and stamp-batteries were made in Eastern Canada, as was also the large air compressor for the new power-house. But the ore-conveyors, Frue vanners, water wheels, pumps for the cyanide plant, electric locomotives for the tramway, and most of the electrical equipment came from the United States, as did also the twenty large tanks for the cyanide plant. Twelve of these tanks were 34 feet in diameter by 6 feet in depth. All were made from California redwood, knocked down and shipped from San Francisco by boat to Vancouver, thence by Canadian Pacific Railway to Okanagan Landing. From there they were transferred to the lake steamer and delivered at Penticton and hauled by freight teams the 50 miles to Hedley.

The first stamps of the new mill were dropped on May 4, 1904 and the muffled roar of the stamps became a familiar sound in the town. For the first few years of the mill's operation a considerable proportion of the values recovered was in the form of free gold caught on the plates. Each month two gold bricks, one from the free gold off the plates and the other from the gold recovered in the cyanide plant, were taken out under special escort to Penticton, and from there shipped by Dominion Express to the United States assay office in

Seattle. The concentrates from the twenty-four Frue vanners, rich in gold, were pulled daily and dumped into the bin below, and after a period allowed for drying, the concentrates were then put into double sacks—a heavy cotton sack on the inside and a strong jute one on the outside—and the sacks well sewn. The sacked concentrates, weighing around a hundred pounds or better a sack, were hauled to Penticton, and from there were shipped to the Tacoma smelter. The four-horse teams which hauled in supplies also hauled out the sacked concentrates on their return trip to Penticton. Dougal Gillespie of Okanagan Falls, who then held the contract for hauling the company's freight, was paid $20 per ton on incoming freight and $9 per ton for the back-haul of concentrates. The round trip usually took about a week to complete.

During the years 1903–1905 the town grew rapidly and many new buildings were erected...In the summer of 1903 Grace Methodist Church was built...mostly by volunteer labour under the enthusiastic direction of Rev. J.W. Hedley. For many years it played a prominent role in the life of the community, serving as headquarters for the school, the Twentieth Century Club, and the library...In February 1906 the plan to build a two-room school was announced...Miss H.J. Blake was the first teacher in the new school. In passing it should also be noted that a school was started at the Nickel Plate mine early in 1905 under Miss K. Johnson...

In the summer of 1904 C.A.R. Lambly, Government Agent at Fairview, held an auction sale of the lots held at Hedley by the Government, and many of the lots were sold at good prices. About that time, too, M.K. Rodgers was successful in his negotiations with the Department of Indian Affairs at Ottawa for the purchase of the flat on Indian Reserve No. 2, which adjoined the company's millsite. With the acquisition of this land the company had ample room for buildings for its staff and also for sites for tailings-dam, lime kiln, and lumber and wood yards.

During 1904, too, electrical power became available. As early as December 1903 it was reported that "Electric light was used at Hedley on Saturday night (December 5) last, the dynamo being driven by steam power." Its use became more general the following spring, for in April the poles were in place ready to receive the wire, and that month electric lights were used for the first time in the Methodist church. By the fall the houses were being wired for electric light...

In September 1905, a change was made in the arrangement of the Daly Reduction Company. M.K. Rodgers was succeeded as manager by R.B. Lamb, A.H. Brown was succeeded as mill superintendent by W.H. Brule, and Arthur Clare ceased to be mill foreman. However, Gomer P. Jones continued on as mine superintendent...

As early as 1903 the possibility of telephone connection with other parts of the province had been discussed. However, two years were to pass before the dominion government built a line from Kamloops to Penticton, by way of Merritt, Princeton, Hedley and Keremeos. By February 1905 the valley had direct wire connection with the outside world, for a telephone had been installed in John Love's drugstore. Later an exchange was installed at the rear of this store and Love received the appointment as agent. Originally the wires had been strung on trees, but by July 1907 it was announced that they had been put on poles from Hedley to Vernon...

The Daly Estate in 1909 gave an option on all its holdings in the Hedley Camp to a New York syndicate headed by I.L. Merrill...A new company, the Hedley Gold Mining Company, Limited, now came into being and took over the former company. In the reorganization which followed Gomer P. Jones became general superintendent...

For years one of the great needs of the valley had been proper railroad connection with the outside. The agitation for such a line was prolonged and, with the advent of rival proposals, at times, heated. Principal contenders were the Vancouver, Victoria and Eastern Railway and the Great Northern Railway. In 1908 the latter company, having acquired the charter of its rival, commenced the grading of their line from Keremeos to Brookmere, and steel was laid during the following summer and fall. Regular train service was commenced on December 23, 1909, and the first train from Oroville to Princeton arrived at Hedley Station at 11 a.m.

The tram line which carried ore from the Nickel Plate Mine down to the mill at Hedley, 1909.
BCARS 01207

With the coming of the railroad the four-horse freight teams and stages disappeared from the roads, and a new era was entered upon.
(*OHS*, 1948)

The new era that Mr. Barnes wrote about in 1948 was not without its challenges. Mining has always had its unpredictable aspects. First mine owners are at the mercy of nature's vagaries in the way in which deposits of valuable minerals are laid down. A fault might interrupt the vein of profitable ore. Then fluctuating prices of metals on the world market determine whether or not a particular mine is economically feasible. Finally, changing technologies affect the demand for particular metals as well as the cost of recovering the metals from the earth.

Hedley's mining days were over when the Nickel Plate ceased operation in 1954, although several decades later an attempt was made to mine by the open-pit method. Recently the Candorado Company has been reworking old tailings to recover gold left in them. The Mascot Mine had been forced to close after about a decade of activity because its ore body, though rich, was limited in size. As for Nickel Plate's mill, now nothing is left but a scar on the mountainside.

Other Mining Ventures

Copper Mountain, ten miles south of Princeton, where copper was found in 1888 according to J. Goodfellow,[10] has operated when world copper prices justified investment in the mine. Between 1923 and 1944 the Allenby Copper Company was actively engaged at Allenby. Some gold and silver was recovered as well as copper. In 1971 the Newmont Mining Company initiated an open-pit operation which was taken over in 1988 by the Princeton Mining Corporation which operated its Similko Mine for almost ten years. Ore was mined on both

sides of the Similkameen River, a suspension bridge eight hundred feet above the river canyon being used to transport the Copper Mountain ore to the mill and to take the tailings back across the river to a tailings pond. Currently the company has suspended mining due to the low price of copper.

During the 1930s there was a flurry of gold mining which Robert Iverson explains: "On January 31, 1934 by executive order of President Roosevelt, the price of gold was increased from $20.67 per ounce to $35. It was a tremendous boon to all operating gold mines in the United States and abroad. Now properties that were considered low grade began to re-open."[11]

Mr. Iverson goes on to tell how the Dividend property at Osoyoos operated for six years under the name of Osoyoos Mines Ltd., managed by Professor J.O. Howells. Old Fairview mines also reopened, beginning with the Morning Star...The various amalgamations, the high grading and the stock manipulations will strike a familiar chord for any reader who has indulged in buying gold stocks. Finally, in 1939, World War II put an end to these activities.[12]

During the Depression wages even at $4 a day were not to be despised and many a young orchardist managed to care for his family by working as a miner until his orchard came into production. But there was a downside to working in the gold mines of Similkameen and South Okanagan, especially for those for whom mining was their sole occupation. The dust created in the mine contained sharp-edged particles which, when breathed in, cut the lungs. Iverson says:

Silicosis did not come under the compensation act until 1937. However, no claims were accepted until 1939. Of all the men that I had met and worked with at the mine, these stick in my memory: Bill Jones, Fred Haddock, Walter McKay, Jerry Cochrane, Burl Patton, and Wilfred Gervais. All these young men were to die of silicosis, some in a comparatively short time, some after a few years. Bob McNeil was to be a later victim when C.M.S. was operating the mine.[13]

(*OHS*, 1984)

Bernard Webber, who was CCF MLA for Similkameen from 1941 to 1945, remembers frequently being a miners' advocate both in the Legislature and before the Workmen's Compensation Board when silicosis was making it

Miners' Sports at Princeton, July 1, 1907. Rock-drilling contest. BCARS A-03566

Princeton's steam power plant which operated 1937–1957. BCARS F-04132

impossible for some men to work. Even when it was demonstrated that mine conditions were responsible for a man's illness only a fraction of the small pension allowed was paid if a portion of the miner's working days had been spent in a jurisdiction other than British Columbia. In one pitiful case a man who had worked in Ontario mines was paid a pension of just $14 a month. Finally the aluminum-dust treatment was installed in mine shower rooms to lessen the impact of the disease.

A mining operation that proved profitable for over twenty years was the Brenda Mines to the southwest of Kelowna. Molybdenum and copper were produced by open pit mining until a disastrous slide in April 1990 made further exploitation of the property impossible.[14]

Coal was being mined in 1904 in Logan's and Weir's Gulches in Enderby.[15] It was mined near White Lake, south of Penticton, during World War I. But the largest field of coal deposits was in the Princeton area, where the fields extended over an area of at least twenty-four square miles with the seam being as much as twenty-four feet in thickness. John Fall Allison found the deposit on the Similkameen just west of the forks in 1858 and local settlers hauled coal home for their own use, taking advantage of the frozen river in winter. At first commercial development was limited to a local market but as transportation improved it was possible to mine and sell coal at the rate of two hundred tons per day. Finally, in the 1950s, markets fell off and mining ceased. To the north-west of Princeton, Coalmont and Blakeburn carried on a viable operation from 1917 until August 13, 1930 when an explosion at Blakeburn Mine No. 4 killed forty-five miners, thus putting an end to a happy and vibrant community.

13

Boats and Trains

Railways

Canadian Pacific Railway and Shuswap & Okanagan Railway

A blast of dynamite at Yale, BC in May 1880 signalled the start of construction of the BC section of the Canadian Pacific Railway, the railway that had been promised in 1871 when British Columbia agreed to enter confederation. It had taken years to determine which route would be followed from the Rockies to tidewater through intervening mountain ranges and finally the Coast Range. Various engineers had examined possible passes but it was Walter Moberly's plan that was accepted in the end.

Moberly was no stranger to southern British Columbia, having been assistant to Edgar Dewdney in the construction of the Dewdney Trail in 1860. Then in 1862 he was in charge of the building of the Cariboo Road from Lytton to Cook's Ferry (today's Spences Bridge) and north to Lac La Hache. Besides being a very able engineer with an intimate knowledge of BC terrain, Moberly was a man of terrific strength and stamina as the following incident recorded by Ernest Doe illustrates.

In 1871, Walter Moberly, returning from exploration in the Rockies to Kamloops, chose to make his way along the south shore of the Salmon Arm.

"I was anxious to examine a gap in the low range of hills between the Salmon Arm and the main or easterly arm of the Shuswap Lake that I had noticed when first exploring through the lake in the year 1865. This gap, now known as Notch Hill, would, if practicable for railway construction, much lessen the distance that a line for a railway would otherwise have to take to reach Shuswap Lake.

Directing the members of my party to remain on the shore while I tried to cross Salmon Arm on the rather rotten ice to see if it was strong enough for them with their packs, which contained all the plans, profiles, field books, etc., connected with the exploratory survey so far made by me, and the loss of which would have been a serious calamity, I started on my adventurous trip.

When about half way across the arm, I fell through the ice and, being encumbered with rather heavy clothing, I had a long and hard struggle to save my life. When nearly exhausted and benumbed by the ice-cold water, by spreading my snow-shoes under my body in order to cover as large an area of the rotten ice as possible, and thus prevent its breaking under the weight of my body, I managed at last to scramble out and reach the shore where my Indians were.

We pursued our way along the south shore and when we were at a point opposite Notch Hill we found the arm clear of ice and made a raft and crossed to the southerly end of the Notch...”[1]

(*OHS*, 1950)

The crossing was probably made from a spot between Canoe and Engineer's Point. At the time there was no settlement, Native or non-Native, where the city of Salmon Arm is now situated.

The transcontinental railway was completed November 7, 1885 when construction crews from the west met the crews building from the east at Craigellachie, a point between Sicamous and Revelstoke. The last rail was put in place and Donald A. Smith, president of the Canadian Pacific Railway, drove the final spike. Railway construction had proved a boon to farmers in the northern part of the Valley. The great crews of workers had needed vast quantities of meat, flour and vegetables as well as feed for horses used on the project.

It is not surprising that in that era of railway building some of the more forward-looking citizens of Vernon wanted a rail link with the main line of the CPR. George H. Morkill writes:

The Canadian Pacific Railway was completed in 1885 and on the 2nd of June, 1886, the Shuswap and Okanagan Railway was incorporated by an Act of the Dominion Government. The share holders of the company were J.A. Mara, James Reid, Frank S. Barnard, R.P. Rithet, Thomas Earle, J.H. Turner, D.M. Eberts, F.G. Vernon, Moses Lumby and Dr. E.B. Hannington.

On the 7th April, 1887, the Shuswap and Okanagan Railway Subsidy Act was passed by the Legislative Assembly of British Columbia, whereby the company was granted a subsidy of $4000 per mile—not to exceed $200,000 in all—on condition that the company would build a railway from Sicamous to some point on Okanagan Lake...

On the second of May 1889, the Dominion Government passed an Act granting a subsidy to each of thirty-five railways in Canada...The Shuswap and Okanagan Railway is included in the list and is down for $3200 per mile, not to exceed in all $163,000, the mileage being computed at 51 miles...

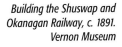

Building the Shuswap and Okanagan Railway, c. 1891. Vernon Museum

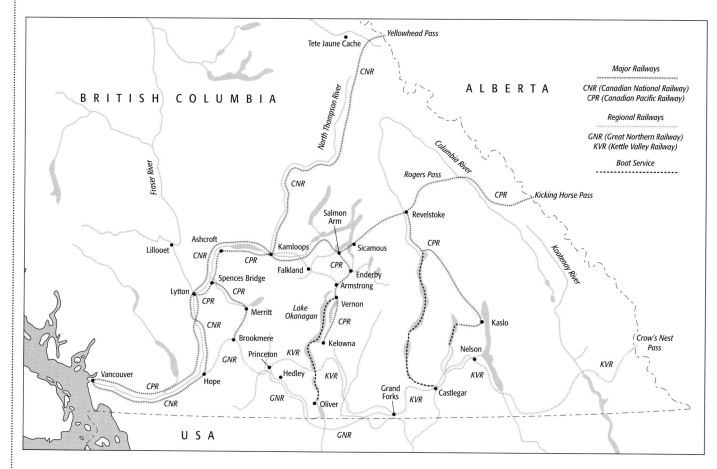

Railways, including some branch lines, and boat service

The work of construction was commenced some time in August 1890, and by the 12th of May, 1892, the rails were laid through to Okanagan Landing…During the construction of the road this valley was a busy place…There was a lot of freight to be hauled in from Sicamous in winter and from Enderby in summer. Consequently, hay and oats were in demand and everyone had work and everyone had money.

Although the C.P.R. did not take over the road until 1893 their first lease for 25 years is dated from 1890. They secured a second lease of the road dated 1st July 1925 for 199 years.[2]

(*OHS*, 1935)

Even before the track was finished it was being used to transport people. A steam-powered speeder, the *Kalamazoo*, could carry six to eight passengers. Then on October 13, 1891, when Lord and Lady Aberdeen were at Sicamous on their way to see the McDougall property at Kelowna that they had purchased through the agent G.G. Mackay, the marquis was able to hire an engine to pull his private car down the new track to Okanagan Landing. Lady Aberdeen tells us, "The train consisted of the engine, our car, two luggage trucks covered with a miscellaneous assemblage of men, dogs, packages, trunks, agricultural machinery and so forth, and a "caboose." And so to the Landing and then by boat to the new estate which they named Guisachan, "the place of the firs."[3]

There was another trip made before the official opening which cast a long shadow. Susan Steinke in her article "Forbes George Vernon Loses the Provincial Election of 1894" writes:

Just before the railway was officially operational, three flat cars loaded with grain shipments from the Coldstream Ranch were shipped to Sicamous without any freight charges being levied. This infuriated the other grain farmers who felt such favoritism was not only morally wrong, but also provided unfair economic advantage to the Coldstream Ranch. When the alleged impropriety was brought before the public during the campaign of 1894, Vernon claimed that it was the work of his manager, E.H. Wood, and that he knew nothing about it.[4]

(*OHS*, 1987)

Railway Avenue, Armstrong, looking west at the business section and Rose Swanson Mt. c. 1905. The S&O Railway, from Sicamous to Okanagan Landing was built between 1900 and 1902. Because the railway bypassed the pioneer settlement of Lansdowne, business people moved to the newly established town of Armstrong. ASMAS #1505

Lansdowne Hotel in the 1890s. ASMAS #3879

The completion of the track to Okanagan Landing was the signal for the CPR to initiate regular boat service on Okanagan Lake, thus enabling communities in the south to take advantage of CPR mainline freight and passenger service. The development of the North Okanagan and Spallumcheen was also affected by this new rail line, the most dramatic change being the withering of Lansdowne, which had for many years been the centre of North Okanagan services. Because the Shuswap and Okanagan Railway bypassed the settlement, businessmen moved nearer the railway and created the new town of Armstrong.

Great Northern Railroad

Railway service to the Similkameen began when an American company, the Great Northern Railroad, built its line from Oroville, Washington, to Keremeos. When Earl Grey, governor general of Canada, wished to visit the southern Interior of BC in September 1908, he arrived in Keremeos by the Great Northern Railroad. There he attended a reception at the Richter home, "Inglewood." The Richters were invited to afternoon tea in the vice-regal private car. Mrs. Tweddle (formerly Mrs. Richter) has said that the visit of the Governor General was one of the highlights of her life. "On the

The first passenger train into Hedley December 23, 1909. The line is the Great Northern built by Jim Hill, hence the nickname "Jimhillkameen" for the Oroville to Princeton section. BCARS A-08679

following day Earl Grey and his party, equipped with saddle horses at the Richter ranch and with Charlie Richter as their guide, rode over the Green Mountain trail to Penticton."[5]

Regular train service between Oroville and Princeton began December 23, 1909. John Goodfellow tells us that this railroad was dubbed the "Jimhillkameen," an indication of the importance the great railroad builder, James J. Hill, attached to it in his effort to capture all southern BC business. The struggle between the Great Northern and the CPR's Kettle Valley ended when Jim Hill died May 29, 1916, just two months before the rail line through the Coquihalla Pass was to open.

Between 1915 and 1925 the Great Northern carried out an unusual commercial operation, the cutting of ice on Otter Lake at Tulameen. In 1919, a record three thousand cars of ice were cut and loaded, the work being accomplished by man and horse power. Every Great Northern icehouse west of Spokane was supplied from this source. We are talking of a period when each boxcar carrying perishable produce had to be iced and it was impossible to make artificial ice in commercial quantities.

The Great Northern began to sell off its assets and by 1945 had divested itself of all its interests in this Canadian line. Today Highway 3 has been built on the Great Northern right-of-way along the Similkameen River.

Kettle Valley Railway

In June 1910 James J. Warren and Andrew McCulloch arrived in Grand Forks. The first was president and the second chief engineer of the newly formed Kettle Valley Railway, a subsidiary of the Canadian Pacific Railway. Actually there was track laid as far west as Midway. McCulloch's assignment was to find a way to build track between Midway and Hope, through mountain passes that Walter Moberly had rejected in 1874 as unsuitable for railway construction. By 1916 the task was completed with its enormous trestles, numerous tunnels cut by men using explosives and the simplest of tools. McCulloch had to use every engineering trick he knew to conquer the wild terrain.

Trout Creek bridge at Summerland, the highest railway bridge in Canada when it was built c. 1911. Penticton Museum

By 1912 the track had been laid from Midway to Penticton where a six-stall roundhouse was constructed. E.W. Aldredge, a well-known Penticton journalist and historian, worked in that roundhouse as an apprentice. In an article about the building he has written, "Completed in 1913, the roundhouse was a key item in Lord Shaughnessy's dream of having a Canadian railway in the southern area of B.C. that would out-do one-eyed Jim Hill's Great Northern Rwy. in providing service to that area." By January 17, 1964 the Kettle Valley had ceased to be a viable operation due to a fall-off in traffic during the 1950s and disastrous floods in the early 1960s.

Eddie Aldredge had the dubious distinction of being run over by a locomotive and surviving to tell the tale.

Run Over by Engine...and Lived[6]

by E.W. Aldredge

One of the great trestles on the Kettle Valley Railway east of Penticton. *Kelowna Museum*

A cloud of steam; the exhaust from the coal chute engine...something black looming through the fog that I hit with my head—and then passed out. I came to amid a blur of wheels. I was under the engine between the rails. I let myself go limp—all five feet and one hundred pounds of me. I dimly remembered I had been sent for chewing tobacco for Locomotive Foreman Ernie Mitchell, and had been running up the track; then all of that was lost in the pound of those big drivers on either side of me.

Next, the engine backed off of me—and I was still alive. I sat up between the rails shouting, "What did you run over ME for?" and then men came running, with my father in the rear. All I had to show for it was one tiny scratch over my left eyebrow—and countless bruises which didn't show. I got up limping, not from these, but because the whole heel-piece of one shoe was missing. My father found it moments later—outside the rails! He tacked it on. I hung around until quitting time for my mother mustn't learn of what happened to me. She did, but that was later. Meanwhile the exhaust of that coal chute engine was altered so it wouldn't blow across the tracks and the watchman, who should have been riding the rear of that reversing engine No. 3233, was severely reprimanded. Tommy

Instone, who had been at the throttle of the locomotive, gradually recovered from the fright of his life, as I recuperated from my bruises. Yet the memory of that experience lingers even now.

(*OHS*, 1987)

In May 1972 the CPR discontinued barge service on Okanagan Lake. Then in May of the next year train service between Penticton and Beaverdell ceased.

Commercial Boats

from **Commercial Boats of the Okanagan**[7]

by Harley R. Hatfield

Engines, boilers, names, even deck houses moved around from boat to boat in an amazing way in the early days of water traffic in the Okanagan Valley. Even boats themselves moved from rivers to lakes and from lake to lake. Stability seems to have been in the registration of the vessels at Victoria, which apparently remained the same even when one boat was lengthened by as much as twenty feet. For instance, when the SS *Jubilee* was ruined by being frozen in at Okanagan Landing during the winter of 1889–90, [the pioneer steamboat captain T.D.] Shorts put her machinery in a barge which he named *City of Vernon* in 1890. When he and Thomas Ellis put the SS *Penticton* into service in September 1890, he sold the *City of Vernon*, after which her new owners called her the *Mudhen* because of her propensity to go to the bottom and sold her again in 1896. These new owners built a new boat, the SS *Wanderer* and put the same machinery into it. The *Wanderer*...ultimately went to Long (Kalamalka) Lake. For a time in 1901, when she belonged to W.L. D'Aethe, she acted as a Kelowna ferry.

The north end of the west arm of Okanagan Lake was the launching site for one or two of the earliest boats, and for a short time was the terminus of their trips. The first Okanagan post office was at nearby O'Keefe Ranch, and Lansdowne was the closest settlement to the north end of the lake. However, as commercial boating got under way, Vernon soon become the more prominent settlement, and Okanagan Landing, a much more suitable site, soon became the centre for water borne commerce.

Captain T.D. Shorts, the colourful steamboat operator, ran boats up and down Okanagan Lake. Photo by Geo. A. Meeres Vernon Museum

Okanagan Lake

Much has been written about Capt. T.D. Shorts, his rowboat the *Ruth Shorts*, with which he started his freighting on Okanagan Lake in 1883, and its successor the *Mary Victoria Greenhow*, which he and partner Thomas Greenhow launched in April 1886. The first steamboat on the lake, the *Mary Victoria Greenhow*...was registered to carry five passengers and five tons of freight. She had a 2 h.p. engine and a kerosene burning boiler. Badly damaged by fire on the beach near Okanagan Mission while the skipper went to borrow more kerosene, she was quickly changed to a wood burner; but that did not prove satisfactory and she was replaced by the SS *Jubilee*. The second steamer, using the engine but not the boiler from the *M.V.G.*, was launched at Okanagan Landing in September 1887.[8]

The high point of Capt. T.D. Shorts' career as a steamboat operator came with the launching of the SS *Penticton* in 1890, a twin screw freight and passenger boat licensed to carry 25 passengers. Capt. Shorts and Thomas Ellis were joint owners...Sold in 1892, the *Penticton* ended her career as a passenger ship in 1895 and from then until 1902, served as the towboat for the Kelowna Sawmill and was then dismantled.

In 1888, the first serious competitor to Capt. Shorts' boats had made its appearance on Okanagan Lake in the form of the SS *Okanagan(1)*, formerly the *Red Star(1)* on the Spallumcheen (Shuswap) River, where it was found she had too much draught for that small stream...Two enterprising chaps had the abandoned hull hauled from the Spallumcheen to the head of the Okanagan in 1888. From there they floated it to Okanagan Landing, lengthened it by 20 feet, installed new machinery and named their vessel the SS *Okanagan*.

Boxcars being loaded onto a train barge at Kelowna, 1912. Kelowna Museum Neg. #1626.

The SS *Okanagan(1)* was sold to Lequime Bros. in 1891 and used as a log tower. It was sold again in 1894, and used in general service by Capt. Angus Campbell and partner until 1895, when she was moved to Kootenay Lake and used as a towboat until 1913...

A good deal of the freight handled by the early boats was destined for the mining camp of Fairview, so it was natural there should be an SS *Fairview*. The *Fairview* was not a Canadian Pacific Railway boat, but built to run on the Okanagan River between Penticton and Dogtown (Okanagan Falls). However, with a length of 55 feet, the *Fairview* proved too big for the river and was subsequently used in various passenger and freight work on Okanagan Lake. A wood-burning sternwheeler, the *Fairview*, caught fire at the Okanagan Landing dock in 1897. With the exception of the *Mary Victoria Greenhow* on her first trip, all of the early steamboats seem to have been wood burners. This was certainly using the materials at hand, but at a considerable risk to the passengers as well as the boats. [And inconvenience: passengers were expected to help load fuel as required.]

Skaha Lake

The earliest boat on Skaha Lake seems to have been the SS *Miramichi*, about which the early accounts do not agree as to either the spelling of the name or the owner of the boat. The captain, and at least nominal owner, is given as L. Holman, a member of the Snodgrass Syndicate promoting Okanagan Falls...Her career on Skaha Lake lasted from the spring of 1893 to the fall of 1894, when she was sold at auction in Vernon to be used for some time as a private steam launch at Kelowna.

The next ship to appear on Skaha Lake was the SS *Jessie*, which went into service early in 1894 and appears to have burned in 1898. She was reputed to be the first to navigate the river from Penticton to Okanagan Falls, but with what success we are not told...The SS *Greenwood* was the next boat on the lake, and unlike some of the others, spent her life on Skaha once she arrived there. She was built at Okanagan Landing in 1897 and burned at the Falls in 1903...

In 1899, Mr. Snodgrass had the SS *Maud Moore* shipped out from Ontario. She ran on Skaha Lake from then until 1905, when she was moved to Okanagan Lake and owned by J.M. Robinson, whereupon she became the unofficial Naramata to Summerland ferry and then the official one from 1908 to 1911. Apparently a screw steamer, the *Maud Moore* was a wood burner and carried about twenty passengers. There seems to be no note on her demise.

From 1905 to 1910, there appear to have been no commercial boats on Skaha Lake. The mines of Fairview, Camp McKinney and other places were petering out. More and better roads were coming into the picture and the importance of Okanagan Falls as a trans-shipment point was vanishing. However, movement by road was still slow and hazardous, so that when James Ritchie promoted the establishment of Kaleden, there was again need of water transport. After 1905, there was no steamboat seen on Skaha Lake until 1922, with the exception of one return trip from Penticton to Okanagan Falls, made by the C.P.R. stern-wheeler *Kaleden(2)* in 1910.

C. Noel Higgins secured the contract in 1908 for a ferry between Summerland and Naramata. He had a gasoline 30 foot launch built and named her the *Mallard(1)*. In 1910 Mr. Ritchie bought the *Mallard* for service on Skaha Lake and renamed her *Kaleden(1)*. She was then bought by Hatfield & Campbell (soon to be the South Okanagan Transportation Company).

Skippered by my grandfather, Capt. Charles Hatfield, a master mariner from Nova Scotia, the *Kaleden(1)* was used mainly for towing scows of woodstave pipe, cement and so forth from the head of Skaha Lake down to Kaleden. After two years, she was replaced by the motor launch *Cygnet* of 40 foot length, a 10 foot beam, with a heavy duty Fairbanks marine engine which was started by turning the heavy flywheel with a steel bar which fitted into sockets in the wheel. I can still see a hole in the cabin roof where the end of the bar went through one day when the engine backfired! During the early 1920s the *Cygnet* was moved to Okanagan Lake, and, after carrying express fruit to Kelowna at night for one summer,

was sold in the Kelowna area.

The sternwheeler *Kaleden(2)* was the only C.P.R. venture on Skaha Lake until the SS *York* made its appearance in 1922. The SS *Kaleden(2)* was built at Okanagan Landing in 1910...She was meant to run the Okanagan River between the two lakes, but was far too long. After the one trip, she was used on Okanagan Lake only and was dismantled in 1920. During the construction of the Kettle Valley Railway, she was busy hauling dynamite and other construction items.

In 1914, the South Okanagan Transportation Company put the motor launch *Mallard(2)* in commission to run between Penticton, Kaleden and Okanagan Falls. She was the only boat that could successfully navigate the river between the lakes. Her length was just 32 feet, and with a tunnel stern and propeller above the bottom of the boat, the *Mallard* was as well suited to the river as a boat of that time could be; even so, the down-river trip around the sharp bends could be quite exciting in times of high water.

The first control dam was built at the outlet of Okanagan Lake despite the fact that the river was rated as navigable water and the two road bridges and the railway bridge had all been fitted with swing spans. For some time the *Mallard(2)* managed to climb over the dam, but one day was forced against the side of the opening and had a large hole knocked in the hull so that she promptly sank with a ton of apricots on board...That was the end of navigation on the Okanagan River.

The last commercial boat on Skaha Lake was again a steamer, but this time a screw-driven one, the Canadian Pacific's SS *York*, launched in 1902. On Okanagan Lake she acted as relief passenger boat, freighter and tug, and sometimes as ice breaker...Between 1922 and 1931 the *York* worked on Skaha Lake pushing a barge loaded with locomotive and freight cars between the head of the lake and Okanagan Falls. When railroad tracking was completed along the west side of Skaha Lake, she was no longer needed as a railway link and was moved to the Arrow Lakes...

Shuswap Lake

The first steamer on the Shuswap was the SS *Marten*, built by the Hudson's Bay Company in 1866 to serve the village of Seymour en route to the short-lived gold mines on the Columbia River. She seems not to have ventured up river into the Okanagan country.

In 1872, a small, but interesting steamer was launched and put on the Savona to Fortune's Landing (now Enderby) run. One account says that she had a one-man crew and the owner-captain had lines rigged to the steering wheel so that he could control direction while busy at the boiler and engine. She was named the *Kamloops(1)*, and may well have been the flag-bedecked boat that brought Mrs. A.L. Fortune to Fortune's Landing in 1874...

The *Spallumcheen*, because of her light draught, was one of the more successful in the Spallumcheen River. Built by J.A. Mara & Associates, the *Spallumcheen* was followed by William Fortune's *Lady Dufferin* in December 1878. Unlike the *Spallumcheen*, the *Lady Dufferin* was a sidewheeler, and it is unlikely that she ventured up the Spallumcheen River often.

There were some twenty-two steamers that ran on Shuswap Lake at various times between 1866 and the 1930s. It is hard to tell which of them may have ventured up river into the Okanagan. The *Red Star(1)* was one of them, built it seems, in Victoria in 1887 for the Sicamous to Enderby run, but not suiting the river, was hauled to Okanagan Lake the next year and made into the first *Okanagan*. The *Red Star(2)* with machinery from *Red Star(1)* went into service in 1888 and continued into the 1890s, even for a time after the railway was built to Vernon. The *Red Star(2)* was an important link with the Valley in her day, and many pioneers entered the Okanagan on her. A sternwheeler, neither very large nor elegant, she managed to dodge the sandbars...

I suppose, because railway connections came earlier, none of the Shuswap boats approached the size or sophistication that the Okanagan and Kootenay boats eventually reached...In 1885 the *Peerless*, the largest steamboat on the Shuswap, was on a schedule between Savona, Kamloops and Eagle Pass, connecting with the SS *Spallumcheen* at the last point...There is still a motor boat with barge (*Phoebe Ann*) operating from Sicamous up Seymour Arm (1990)...

SS Ethel Ross *on the Shuswap River c. 1900. Enderby Museum #2280*

Shuswap Boats

Roland A. Jamieson in an article entitled "Early Shuswap Lake Boats and People"[9] supplies details regarding some of the Shuswap boats. The SS *Thompson*, soon after 1894, and the SS *Florence Carlin*, from 1906, served the lumber industry, the latter furnished with the overhauled machinery and boiler from the former. Captain G.B. Ward, a sailor and shipbuilder from New Brunswick in the late 1890s set up a shipyard in Kamloops where he built the SS *Ethel Ross* (1897), the SS *C.R. Lamb* (1907) and the SS *Andover* (1908). Of the *Ethel Ross*, Jamieson writes: "This boat became well known along the 300 miles of navigable water as it carried any

cargo available and towed log-booms, scows, piledrivers and dredges to the various points of lakeside development."

Wharfs became a necessity as commerce grew and as supplying them was a federal responsibility politics sometimes determined the where and the when. Salmon Arm got its wharf in 1907 but Canoe and Gleneden had to wait another seven years.

Tugs

The first diesel-driven steel-hulled boat on Okanagan Lake was the MV *Pentowna*... Who built the *Pentowna* seems unclear, but one would guess that the Canadian National Railway was involved. She was, indeed, run by the C.N.R. as a passenger and freight boat between Kelowna, Penticton and way points. Later, as water-borne passenger travel faded, the *Pentowna* was altered and became a tug in the C.N. car barge service. Her active career was between 1914 and 1972. At this time [1989] she is still afloat, tied to a dock at Peachland.

Most of the early boats were jacks-of-all-trades, carrying passengers, off or on schedule, on excursions of all kinds and hauling freight of every sort. They also provided tugboat service, towing or pushing scows and barges of every size and shape. The lumber companies soon felt the need for tugboats. The SS *Penticton* was used as the first tugboat for the Kelowna Sawmill Co., and she was followed by the SS *Kelowna(1)*. The *Kelowna(1)* was sold in 1911 to the Smith Lumber Co., that had a mill near Naramata. I remember when she was abandoned at the old Government Wharf in Penticton and partly sunk. The pilot house was still above water and we boys could ring the bell for full speed, much to our satisfaction. The Kelowna Sawmill Co. then built the SS *Orchard City*, and succeeding her, the SS *Orchard City II*, all wooden tugs of comparable size.

A rather unusual job for Okanagan tugs came up in connection with moving building stone from the granite quarry on the lakeshore south of Vernon. A small steam vessel did the job from 1903 to 1910. Then the C.P.R. did it until 1919, when the *Grace Darling(1)*, an early internal combustion driven boat, took over. She was followed by the 8 h.p. *Tum Tum*, and one has to wonder if by some chance she was the *Skookum(1)*, alias *Tut Tut* with a slight change in name. The horse power given for the two was about the same.

The last on the quarry scene came on the lake in 1923, this time, the *Grace Darling II*. She was a durable little ship, outlasting the quarry operation itself by four years, and then only being wrecked by a storm in 1960 when torn from her moorings. There were several small tugs, or boats acting as tugs, on Kalamalka and Mabel Lakes, mostly in the timber hauling business.

This brings us to the larger tugs operated by the Canadian Pacific and Canadian National Railways. Their barges carried almost exclusively railway cars on double-tracked decks and were docked at special docks known as car slips, with counter weighted moveable aprons with tracks which could be connected to those on the barges. The early C.P. barges were wooden with tall posts and hoglines to stiffen them and carried eight cars. The later ones were of steel and carried ten cars. All of the C.N. tugs were steel, I believe. The C.P. tugs often pushed two barges; the C.N., one.

The second largest C.N. tug in service, *NO.6*, ran on the lake from 1948 until 1973 *NO.6* moved the last barge of freight cars on the lake, the C.P. having given up the previous year. There were several smaller tugs with numbers in the C.N. service, including *NO.5*. They must have been christened by mathematicians, for only they could love a boat with a number!

The first Canadian Pacific boat on the lake, built to be a tug and nothing else, was the SS *Castlegar*, constructed of wood in the shipyard at Okanagan Landing in 1911. Next came the SS *Naramata(2)* in 1913, steel hulled and 90 feet long...The SS *Kelowna(3)*, launched in 1920, was the last of the three coal-fired steam tugs of the C.P.R.

The MV *Okanagan(3)* was in service from 1947 to 1972. She was definitely different. One hundred and ten feet long with a beam of 23 feet, and a draught of over 12 feet, her diesel engine developed 800 h.p.and she was equipped with the latest in ship to shore radio and radar...

The tugs operated day and night, and the crew lived aboard. Over the many years that the tugs ran on the lakes handling so much of the Valley's freight, there were, I believe, only two fatal accidents: a cook and a deckhand at different times fell overboard and were lost. Certainly, care had to be taken during the winter months when the barge decks would ice up.

"Queens" of the Lake

The "Queens," big white sternwheelers, beautiful, friendly and comfortable, transported on Okanagan Lake before the railways came to Penticton and Kelowna, before the highways connected us to anywhere and everywhere, before telephone and telegraph, radio and television brought us news of the world every hour, every day. These magnificent lake boats brought us our clothes, most foods, our tools, our reading, and visitors. Hundreds of Okanagan Valley men went off to war on those vessels, and those who returned came home the same way. Everything imaginable was carried by them, including horses and cattle, large steam boilers, cow hides and gold bricks. The passenger accommodation was luxurious.

One really did not know the early Okanagan unless he or she had travelled on "The Boat." There are few people living today [1989] who came in on the *Aberdeen*, but there are some, including myself, who first came down the Valley on the *Okanagan*, and later enjoyed trips on the *Sicamous*.

The crews lived on board and had a long working day with much rush at the docks,

Some Statistics of the "Queens"

SS *Aberdeen*: length 146 ft.; beam 29 ft.; gross tonnage 554; speed 12 mph; staterooms 10; saloons 3; built at Okanagan Landing; launched 1893; reign as Queen of the Lake 1893 to 1907; years in service 1893 to 1913.

SS *Okanagan*: length 193 ft.; beam 32 ft.; gross tonnage 1,079; draught 5 ft.; speed 15 mph; passenger capacity 250; staterooms 32; saloons 4; built at Okanagan Landing; launched 1907; reign as Queen of the Lake 1907 to 1914; years of service 1907 to 1930s.

SS *Sicamous*: length 200 ft.; beam 40 ft.; gross tonnage 1,786; draught 5.5 ft.; speed 20 mph; passenger capacity 310; staterooms 37; saloons 4, plus dining saloon; built at Port Arthur, Ontario, assembled and finished at Okanagan Landing; launched 1914; reign as Queen of the Lake 1914 to 1935; years of service 1914 to late 1930s.

Cutting ice on Okanagan Lake so that the SS Aberdeen *might reach the government wharf at Penticton. The winter of 1892–93 was extremely cold. Vernon Museum*

handling freight, express, mail and coal for boilers (wood for the first few years of the *Aberdeen*). During the boom days of the mines, as many as forty teams of four to six horses took freight from Penticton to the south and west, from the sternwheelers docking there.

There were some notable passengers aboard those great white boats, some of whom were the Governor-General, the Duke of Connaught on the SS *Okanagan* (who was greeted by a salute, sounded by exploding sticks of dynamite at the "old mine"); and Edward, Prince of Wales, who arrived in 1919 on the SS *Sicamous*, which caused a considerable stir in the south valley...

While the tugs and barges plodded their useful and somewhat mysterious ways, the three "Queens of the Lake," the SS *Aberdeen*, SS *Okanagan* and SS *Sicamous* lent visible sign that we were connected with the outside world. There were about thirty-two stops along the shore, where the boats put in regularly, or on signal. We find life changing at a fast rate in these last years of the 20th Century, but the change from Capt. Shorts' 22 foot rowboat to

SS Sicamous *in its glory, cruising across Okanagan Lake.*

the 200 foot *Sicamous* in thirty years was equally as great.

The *Aberdeen* and *Okanagan* were dismantled when their years of service were over. The *Sicamous* is permanently beached at Penticton and currently undergoing complete renovation.[10]

(*OHS*, 1992)

For oldtimers who have lived most or all of their lives in the Okanagan or Shuswap the mention of trains or boats evokes happy memories of a time less hurried, more gracious and more accommodating than now. Train schedules, for example, on both CPR and CNR[11] lines made it possible to leave the Valley in late afternoon or early evening, dine on the train and retire to one's berth at leisure. In the middle of the night the Okanagan sleeping car and day coach would be attached to the train passing west on the mainline, either at Sicamous or Kamloops depending on whether one was travelling by CPR or CNR. If the shunting of the cars woke the passenger he was soon lulled to sleep by the rhythmic clickety-clack of the steel wheels passing over the rail joints. Trains arrived in Vancouver about nine o'clock in the morning, in time to see to the business that had brought one to the city. The return trip too could be made at night. The Kettle Valley Railway offered a schedule between Penticton and Vancouver that was just as convenient. On this run it was laughingly said that the train travelled by night so the passengers could not see the alarming course of the track through the Coquihalla Pass.

Travel by lake boat was even more peaceful and comfortable than by train. All was dazzling white paint inside and out. Dinner was served midships on white table cloths furnished with substantial CPR tableware and polished silver. Staterooms were available for those who were ill or required a quiet place to rest or work. Aboard one met one's neighbours on their way to some business or professional appointment or to a visit with friends in another lakeside community. Young people might be travelling to or from boarding school. Some passengers were tourists who had chosen this way to see our beautiful province. Scenic round trips could be planned because sternwheelers operated on the Arrow, Slocan and Kootenay Lakes and railways furnished links.

Why the decline in train travel and the virtual cessation of boat travel? Probably more than all else because of the improvement in automobiles, trucks and roads. People could get from one place to another more quickly and conveniently, at times of their own choosing. Portal to portal pickup and delivery made trucking an attractive alternative to rail travel. But while trains and boats were in their heyday perhaps the image which speaks most eloquently of their importance to Okanagan society is that of the knot of people gathered at the station or at the wharf to witness the arrival and departure of one of these harbingers of the world beyond.

14
Growing Population

Influx of Settlers

The completion of the Canadian Pacific Railway in 1885 enabled people from eastern Canada to reach BC more easily as well as making it possible for those who came by sea to make their way into the Interior of the province. The construction of the Shuswap and Okanagan Railway, which branched off from the mainline of the CPR at Sicamous, stimulated population growth in the Okanagan just as a decade later the construction of the Great Northern line into the Similkameen Valley fostered development there. Table 1, in which federal constituency populations are shown, demonstrates the rapid change taking place. In the decade between 1891

Kelowna's business district in 1905.
BCARS F-03657

Table 1

Population	1901	1891	1881	1871
Canada	5,371,315	4,833,239	4,324,810	3,689,257
British Columbia	178,657	98,173	49,459	36,247
1. Burrard	42,060	24,360	8,417	
2. New Westminster	23,822	17,866	7,000	
3. Vancouver	27,198	18,229	9,991	
4. Victoria	23,688	18,538	7,301	
5. Yale & Cariboo	61,889	19,180	16,750	

Table 2

Population figures for main towns

Census year	1891	1901	1911	1921	1931	1941	1951	1956
Kelowna	*	*	1,663	2,520	4,655	5,118	8,517	9,181
Estimated	–	800						
Penticton	*	*	*	*	*	*	10,548	11,894
Estimated	–	50	500	4,000	4,600	5,743		
Vernon	*	802	2,671	3,685	3,937	5,209	7,822	8,998
Estimated	700							

The asterisk indicates population of this community (as such) was not included in report of Dominion Bureau of Statistics for that year.

Table 3

Population growth in smaller centres

Districts	1921	1931	1941	1951	1956	1961
Peachland	466	318	479	614	705	641
Spallumcheen	523	1,629	1,805	1,936	1,937	2,123
Summerland	1,892	1,791	2,054	3,567	3,893	4,307
Cities						
Armstrong	983	989	977	1,126	1,197	1,288
Enderby	783	555	538	877	965	1,075
Kelowna	2,520	4,655	5,118	8,517	9,181	13,188
Vernon	3,685	3,937	5,209	7,822	8,998	10,250
Penticton	–	–	–	10,548	11,894	13,859
pre-incorp	3,979	4,640	5,777			
Villages						
Lumby	–	–	–	–	786	842
Keremeos	–	–	–	–	–	563
Oliver	–	–	–	1,000	1,147	1,774
Osoyoos	–	–	–	899	860	1,022
Princeton	–	–	–	–	2,245	2,163

These statistics indicate a trend but do not show boundary changes in cities or villages. Salmon Arm did not exist prior to the coming of the CPR in 1885. By 1893 its population was 28[2]; by the mid-1950s the population was in the neighbourhood of 3,700.[3]

and 1901 the population of Yale & Cariboo, which included the Okanagan, Shuswap and Similkameen, more than tripled.

With the influx of settlers land became more valuable and a more intensive use of this resource was initiated. Old cattle ranches were subdivided and orchard plots sold. With a considerably denser population in the countryside the demand for business and professional services increased. This led to the growth of the towns. Tables 2 and 3 illustrate this development.

The new townsfolk expected a more sophisticated lifestyle. Now matters such as water supply and sewage, which had been treated in a somewhat casual manner, had to be taken more seriously. In an article on the history of Vernon, Burt R. Campbell illustrates the sudden change that was taking place in Okanagan towns.

Burt R. Campbell first visited Vernon during the fall exhibition of 1892. In 1893 he was employed by the *Vernon News*. In later years he worked on newspapers in both Kamloops and Revelstoke. He served as a director of the Okanagan Historical Society as well as contributing to its *Reports*. He was a president of the BC Historical Association.

from **Vernon's Diamond Jubilee**[4]
by Burt R. Campbell

Before 1892, Vernon had been only a sleepy little cow-town. Tronson and Brewer had ambitiously laid out a townsite (Centreville) in 1885, but few new residents had arrived to buy town lots. The completion of the Shuswap & Okanagan Railway transformed Priests' Valley into the City of Vernon. There was a real estate boom promoted by a new and energetic townsite company and, with tri-weekly train service, there was a change in agricultural production from cattle and horse raising and grain-growing to the cultivation of fruit crops.

Largely due to the energy of G.G. Mackay, townsite boomer, and Moses Lumby, Government Agent and active promoter of the Shuswap & Okanagan Railway, steps were taken in 1892 to have Vernon incorporated...

Until incorporation, the public officials were Walter Dewdney, Government Agent from 1885 until his death on January 24, 1892, his successor, Moses Lumby, J.A. Monteith, Constable and Assessor, and Leonard Norris, Constable and Clerk. There were now, however, to be civic officials...

The laying out of the townsite of Vernon was the work of the Okanagan Land and Development Company. This company was founded in 1890 with G.G. Mackay of Vancouver as president and manager, and J.A. Mara, F.S. Barnard and F.G. Vernon as members of the syndicate. In addition to putting town lots on the market, the company undertook to build two large hotels, the Coldstream and the Kalamalka, to install a system of waterworks, and to publish a newspaper, the *Vernon News*....Mackay died on New Year's Eve, 1893, and Moses Lumby, who had also taken an active part to have the city incorporated, had died on October 22 of the same year...

The first bank in Vernon was a private bank opened by Wulffsohn and Bewicke of Vancouver in October 1892...In November, the Bank of Montreal opened in the Schubert Block...

The lack of an adequate water supply was long a drawback to home-building. In the downtown area, the ditch that drained springs to the east and northeast served as a supply. Before the installation of a water system, water was supplied by wooden flumes to wooden tanks which were placed on Barnard Avenue. Here the people could fill their buckets. The Medical Health Officer had reason to complain that a menace to health was created by animals drinking from the open tanks. Some of the people obtained their water from wells... (Sometimes tread-wheels served to raise the water; at other times hydraulic rams were employed.)

The first waterworks bylaw, No. 47, was passed on June 12, 1899. It provided for the installation of a water works system with gravity feed from BX Creek and a small reservoir at the upper end of Pine Street...It was not until 1908, however, that serious consideration

was given to the problem. While R.W. Timmins was mayor in 1908 and 1909 three important civic utilities were projected. These were the introduction of the sewer extension of the waterworks, the storage system, and the building of a new school...
(*OHS*, 1952)

Vernon was not the only town to enjoy an influx of new settlers. Boat service between Okanagan Landing and Penticton gave relatively easy access to Kelowna and other places along Okanagan Lake. Among the 1892 immigrants to Okanagan Mission were the Shetland Islanders Mr. and Mrs. Gifford Thomson with their eight small children. After a very difficult beginning the family prospered, adding more land to the original twenty acres purchased. Descendants still work portions of the original property. Dorothea, the eldest daughter in the family, was the first teacher at Ellison and later taught at Benvoulin. She married W.D. Walker and it is by her married name that she is honoured in the Kelowna school named after her.

Incorporation

When the list of local concerns proliferated, citizens realized that they required an administration closer to hand than Victoria. Incorporation became the solution. Vernon was the second town to incorporate. Already Spallumcheen had become a district municipality. Other districts and towns followed. Max H. Ruhmann has listed the incorporations up to 1937.

Municipalities[5]
by Max H. Ruhmann

District of Spallumcheen. Incorporated July 21st, 1892. Reeve, Donald Graham. Councillors: Robert Wood, John A. Cameron, Thomas N. Hayes, and Donald Matheson. Municipal Clerk, Henry Seydel.

City of Vernon. Incorporated Dec. 30th, 1892. Mayor, W.F. Cameron. Aldermen: S.C. Smith, J.A. Schubert, James Lyons, A.G. Fuller and W.J. Armstrong. City Clerk, R.J. Davies.

City of Enderby. Incorporated March 1st, 1905. Mayor, George Bell. Aldermen: Robert P. Bradley, Joseph W. Evans, Noah H. Kenny, George R. Sharpe and Edward T. Smith. City Clerk, Graham Rosoman, who still holds [in 1937] the position, and is also Police Magistrate for the City and Stipendiary Magistrate for the District.

City of Kelowna. Incorporated May 4th, 1905. Mayor, Henry William Raymer. Aldermen: Elisha Reseau Bailey, David Lloyd-Jones, Colin S. Smith, Daniel Wilber Sutherland, Simon Tackett Elliott. City Clerk, Robert Morrison.

By 1940 the District of Penticton was ready to build a "modern" combined municipal hall and library. The structure has Art Deco features and emphasizes the horizontal line rather than the vertical after Frank Lloyd Wright designs. Other buildings in this style, including private homes, can be found in the area, the most notable, perhaps, being the South Okanagan Secondary School in Oliver.
Penticton Museum

District of Summerland. Incorporated Dec. 1st, 1906. Reeve J.M. Robinson. Councillors: R.H. Agur, James Ritchie, J.R. Brown and C.J. Thomson. Municipal Clerk, J.L. Logie. The first meeting of the Municipal Council was held on Jan. 21st, 1907.

District of Coldstream. Incorporated Dec. 21st, 1906. Reeve, W.C. Ricardo. Councillors: R. Gillespie, J.L. Webster, B.C.S. Turner and John Kidston. Municipal Clerk, A.T. Kirkpatrick.

District of Penticton. Incorporated Dec. 31st, 1908. Reeve, A.H. Wade. Councillors: L.C. Barnes, Sydney Hatch, Henry Murk and John Power. Municipal Clerk, Charles Were. The first meeting of the Municipal Council was held Feb. 1st, 1909. [On May 10, 1948 Penticton was officially declared a city. Reeve Robert Lyon became Mayor Robert Lyon and his councillors became aldermen.[6]]

District of Peachland. Incorporated January 1st, 1909. Reeve, W.A. Lang. Councillors: S.F. Callender, M.N. Morrison, L.D. McCall, C.G. Elliott. Municipal Clerk, H. McDougall. The first meeting of the Municipal Council was held in the Orange Hall on Feb. 1st, 1909.

City of Armstrong. Incorporated March 26th, 1913. Mayor, James M. Wright. Aldermen: F.C. Wolfenden, T.K. Smith, A.E. Morgan, J. Leverington, H.A. Fraser. City Clerk, A.J. Fifer, who still retains the position.

(*OHS*, 1937)

Armstrong had originally been part of Spallumcheen but in 1913 it was decided to separate the business and industrial section from the farming area. The conflict between town and rural interests explains the separations which also occurred in both Penticton and Salmon Arm. Today Armstrong finds itself confined by the encircling Spallumcheen with no room for growth while, in Spallumcheen, more and more agricultural land is becoming industrialized.

Other incorporations were:

Salmon Arm municipality, incorporated May 15, 1905 with Reeve J.H. Harbell and Councillors W.J. Kew and W.W. Currie. The rural area was interested primarily in the improvement of roads, whereas townspeople wanted electrical lights and a water system. Hence on March 12, 1912 the town became the City of Salmon Arm with R.K. Scales as mayor.[7]

Glenmore, incorporated as a district municipality in 1922. Held its first council meeting on November 11. A.R. Drysdale was reeve and P.A. Lewis clerk. In 1960 the people of Glenmore voted to unite with the City of Kelowna. The municipal council of The Corporation of the District of Glenmore convened for the last time on September 19, 1960.

Craiglea, the second house built for his family of nine children by Gifford Thomson who had arrived from the Shetland Islands in 1892. The building on the left is the Okanagan Mission Store. Thomson sold the house in 1906 and it was turned into a hotel. In 1951 the house was torn down. Kelowna Museum File II-20

Oliver, incorporation as a village municipality approved by the Government of British Columbia December 19, 1945. Commissioners: R.W. Smith (chairman), D. Smithers and G.A. Stuart. Clerks: S.B. Hirtle and Harold Ball. The terms mayor and aldermen were first used in 1968.

Osoyoos, incorporated as a village municipality in 1946 with the following commissioners: W.A. Andrews (chairman), Gordon Kelly and J.C. Armstrong. Village secretary-treasurer: H.H. Hesketh. Titles changed to mayor and aldermen in 1969; to mayor and councillors in 1993.

Princeton, incorporated as a village municipality September 11, 1951. Commissioners: Isaac Plecash (chairman), Winston Pilling, George Gurr, Albert Bloom and Jim Berryman. Village clerk, treasurer and assessor: Elizabeth Smith.

Keremeos, incorporated in 1956 on the fiftieth anniversary of the moving of the town from its location on the bench to the new townsite near the Similkameen River and the Great Northern Railway station. Commissioners: Fred Kickbush (chairman), Donald C. Fry and Gordon R. Thompson. Secretary-treasurer: J.S. Sykes.

District of Lakes Country, incorporated May 1995. December 2, 1996 to December 1, 1999: Mayor Bob McCoubrey, Councillors James Baker, Robin Ermacora, Russell Husch, Leslie Kendall, Gerry Morton, Thomas Witty. Administrator and Municipal Clerk Randall Rose.

Lifestyle

In the decade before the turn of the century and the decade after 1900 the lifestyle of residents of the Okanagan changed radically. Railways made it easier to bring in heavy machinery that would make farm work less onerous, as well as building supplies and large items of furniture. Domestic water systems relieved some of the drudgery associated with household tasks. Life was indeed more comfortable. New houses were built, sawn lumber and brick replacing the log structures so common a few years earlier. The grandest homes were built by old cattle barons—Greenhow and O'Keefe in the North Okanagan and Frank Richter in Similkameen—who had acquired their vast domains when land was very cheap and who had grown rich selling beef to railway construction gangs.

In 1898 Frank Richter built Inglewood, his third home, in Keremeos. This time the carpenter was brought in from Victoria. The Richter sons hauled lumber from several mills and windows and doors came in from the coast. It was the first house for miles around in which modern nails were used. Firebricks came from Wales. A gardener was employed to landscape the grounds. Richter hospitality became proverbial.

Writing from Spallumcheen in July 1888 Michael Hagen, founder of the *Inland Sentinel*, said:

> Messrs. O'Keefe and Greenhow preserved their first location and from year to year have purchased large additions to their respective properties, and are now among the largest land owners in the inland county, while their large bands of stock roam over thousands of acres of pasture land. They cultivate grain in many fields. Upon their ranches may be seen the latest improvements in agricultural implements, steam threshers, etc. and they have also, an excellent grist mill. The residence of Mr. O'Keefe is one of the finest in the country, and is furnished regardless of expense...[8]
> (*OHS*, 1952)

Mr. Greenhow must have begun building his new home shortly after the Hagen visit. Writing of events subsequent to Mr. Hagen's visit Jane Evans tells us:[9]

Greenhow decided to build a grand new house. It was to have the elegant appurtenances of an Eastern mansion. No expense was to be spared. Unfortunately, however, in 1889, Thomas Greenhow died...It is believed he had a stroke. He was not yet fifty years old. Mrs. Greenhow finished the house; it was completed in 1894 for the enormous sum of $23,000 and had 21 rooms.

Mrs. Greenhow, in the pioneer tradition stayed on and worked the ranch herself with the help of a

Vernon Lodge in winter. This magnificent house was built by Elizabeth Greenhow, the widow of Thomas Greenhow, at a cost of $24,000, for her daughter Mary Victoria and son-in-law and ranch foreman Sam O'Neal. In the name of progress the house has been replaced by the present Vernon Lodge Hotel.
Vernon Museum 1146

foreman, Sam O'Neal. O'Neal was later to marry Mary Victoria Greenhow, and her mother built them a fine house on the outskirts of Vernon. This house, now [1977] known as Vernon Lodge, was also magnificent, and cost $24,000.
(*OHS*, 1977)

The Greenhow/O'Neal building is gone, having been replaced by a motor hotel which makes more economical use of the property. However, the O'Keefe mansion with its surrounding building has been preserved and is now a museum, owned and managed by the City of Vernon. The O'Keefe Ranch is a major tourist attraction in the North Okanagan.

Among the first settlers persuaded by Lord and Lady Aberdeen to take up land in the Coldstream were William and Catherine Middleton. The Middletons arrived in 1892. In his biography of his grandparents R.M. Middleton makes some interesting comments regarding their houses.

*Invercraig, the home overlooking Kalamalka Lake, that was built by the Honourable Coutts Marjoribanks for his wife after their marriage in Scotland in 1910. Marjoribanks was the brother of Lady Aberdeen and an early manager of the Coldstream Ranch. After standing empty for some years the property was acquired by Adolphus Browne in the early 1940s. A system of pumping irrigation water from Kalamalka Lake made the planting of an orchard possible. In March 1957 the main house burned to the ground. Today the land has become a residential subdivision.
Browne family*

To serve as their first house the Middletons bought the old (probably the second) Hudson's Bay trading post in Vernon...Wheels and logs were somehow placed under the trading post and it was pulled with several teams of horses two miles up hill to its new site...

In 1906 the Middletons began to build a new house of brick just in front of their first home. At the base of Middleton Mountain it looked over the BX as well as up the valley towards the Coldstream. In its construction, conveniences and other features it was not untypical of other houses built in or near Vernon around the turn of the century. The early and fairly difficult periods of the Okanagan's history had been completed and now the pioneers could build houses of reasonable comfort. The Middleton house was Victorian in style, two and a half storeys high. It had a full basement and a lower and upper verandah on two of its walls (removed in the 1940s). A mason, Bill Inkster, spent a summer laying the foundations which were almost three feet thick. They were cut from stones collected nearby and the mortar was made by Johnny McClennan from a small limestone quarry in the hillside behind the house. The bricks, which were twice the usual size for some reason, were made at the Brickyard Hill about half way between Midmar, as the Middleton estate was called, and the centre of Vernon. The house had twelve rooms in all including a central hall with an open staircase and a fireplace whose oak and tile facing was presumably imported from the east. The kitchen, presided over by a Chinese cook, was in the basement and the food was passed to the dining room above by a dumb waiter—a well-engineered contrivance of weighted pulleys which slid up and down on its tracks. The house was lit by an electric generator—a fairly recent innovation in the Okanagan in those days. Lombardy poplars, elms and maple trees were planted around the house and over time helped to soften its vertical lines. Pine trees were also planted on one side of the driveway which curved up the hillside from the main road about three hundred yards away.[10]

(*OHS*, 1986)

LaVonne Byron in an essay entitled "The Better Halves" discusses the work and lifestyle of women in the Vernon area between the first settlements and 1920. She describes aspects of the "more genteel" lifestyle that marked town life at the turn of the century:

The common need for entertainment and company created a variety of social functions... The great favorites were the dances and balls. They were widely attended and carried out with a good deal of pomp. Attendance at the Hospital and Bachelor's Balls required formal dress, and new gowns were sometimes ordered from London or New York.

At the Opera House there were recitals with elocutionists and soloists brought in. Travelling shows made use of local talent and the San Francisco Opera Company made visits to Vernon. The Ladies Aid Society secured lecturers. Musical evenings were organized in private homes...

The established practice of visiting newcomers and presenting calling cards was important to inter-community communication in the pre-telephone days. The visiting lady left the newcomer with three calling cards, one with her own name engraved on it, and two with her husband's. She informed the newcomers of the day of the month that she would be "at home" to receive visitors and on that day an elaborate tea would await any of the ladies who could attend. Each woman took her turn and so company and friendship was provided for all.[11]

(*OHS*, 1981)

Performers at a Red Cross Fete held July 1, 1919 at the home of W.D. Walker in Okanagan Mission. Mrs. Walker (Dorothea) was the eldest daughter of Gifford R. Thomson and a pioneer school teacher. BCARS NA-41470

While entertaining at home remained a popular custom, during this new era public spaces were becoming increasingly available. Once a school was built it might be used for other community purposes. Churches and fraternal orders built halls. And very often when a merchant built a new store he left the large space on the floor above his business area open for dances, meetings and other gatherings.

With these spaces available, city bands could practise. Concerts could be rehearsed. In 1895 residents of Kelowna put on a minstrel show. By 1908 Kelowna thespians were able to present Gilbert and Sullivan's "H.M.S. Pinafore." We read that the performance "received great commendation both at home and in Penticton and Vernon, to which neighbouring towns it was taken...The performance was given in aid of the hospital."[12] Sometimes professional performers visited the Valley and were able to perform in some public auditorium. Pauline Johnson, for example, presented a recital at Enderby in 1906.[13]

Outdoor Sports

As settled communities replace the old solitary ranches team games became possible—cricket, bowling, croquet, tennis, baseball, lacrosse and polo. Westwold (Grande Prairie) became famous for its polo. E.E. Hewer writes:

Polo had its beginning in 1889 when Hamilton Gibb organized a club here. In 1899 Grande Prairie sent its first team to Kamloops and was defeated by a score of 2 to 1. Players

Natives racing in cottonwood dugouts at the Enderby bridge. The flour mill can be seen in the background. Vernon Museum 1753

Polo at Kelowna. Kelowna Museum

on the team were Walter Homfray, George Harding, Jack Kane and Frank Gordon. This sport won Grande Prairie much renown throughout the entire province. The Roper Cup was held by them for many years.[14]

(*OHS*, 1950)

In summer regattas, which included swimming races, boat races and diving competitions were popular. The Kelowna Regatta grew out of the annual Fall Fair which began in 1885. By August 1906 the regatta was an independent activity occupying a whole day and by 1910 it was a two-day event. In 1909 and 1910 J.M. Robinson arranged a successful regatta at Naramata which was attended by the premier of the province, Sir Richard McBride.[15] Okanagan Landing had its regatta too.

Horses, required for transportation, drayage and farm cultivation among other forms of work, played an important role in recreation as well. Hunts, paper chases and gymkhanas were organized. Dorothea Walker tells us that Kelowna had some fine riders, none better than Billy Barlee, "who was known for the fine saddle horses which he bred."[16]

Spawning salmon fish trap at Shuswap Lake. Vernon Museum

Fishing and hunting remained popular with all classes, with some modifications. Constance G. Cumine tells of her father, Sidney Cosens, formerly a merchant at Camp McKinney, buying an eight-room house on twenty-four acres near Kelowna.[17]

On this property was a two-acre pond which attracted the wild ducks and afforded an opportunity for shooting parties. My father and his friends used to go on shoots for ducks. Grouse hunting was also a popular sport. In those days there were no pheasants in the valley so my father imported some beautiful Chinese pheasants and successfully raised some broods. After they were released to the wild there was a moratorium put on shooting them for three years; they quickly multiplied and spread from the North Okanagan to the South.

(*OHS*, 1988)

Unfortunately the use of parathion in orchard sprays almost wiped out the bird population. The spray proved to be hard on the men engaged in spraying and was discontinued. In recent years there appears to have been a gradual increase in the pheasant population.

The Tea Party. Present are Edna and Hazel Jacques (who married, respectively, Wm. Geebbie and Ted Dickson) and Luta Pound (the dark-haired child) who became Mrs. Guy Bagnall. The fourth child is not identified.
Vernon Museum 813

Telegrams, Telephones and Newspapers
Telephones

The first private telephone line in the interior of B.C. was completed in 1891, connecting the residences of Alfred Postill and Thos. Wood, on the Vernon Mission road. It was a little over five miles in length, costing the owners $55 per mile and built on their own property, east of Duck Lake.[18]

At a somewhat later date Kaleden had a private telephone system enjoyed by the Prestons and their associated families, the Dunns and Mackenzies. Fred King describes the system:

Long before Kaleden residents received telephone service, the Preston family homes scattered all over the community were connected to each other with a barbed wire telephone system. A hand crank instrument in each home, a little insulation under each staple holding the barb wire strand chosen to carry the signal, an over-the-road connection where necessary, and the Preston ingenuity brought about the wonder and the envy of the community—their very own Preston Barbed Wire Telephone System.[19]
(*OHS*, 1986)

In 1905 the Dominion Government installed a telephone connection from Kamloops to Penticton via Merritt, Princeton, Hedley and Keremeos using trees to hold the lines. By July 1907 trees had been replaced by poles and the line extended to Vernon.[20] Drugstores were the sites of early telephones and exchanges in Hedley, Vernon and Kelowna. In Peachland the post office was the first telephone exchange as well as the receiver and sender of telegrams on the government system.

The Okanagan Telephone Company was incorporated by an Act of Parliament dated April 25, 1907...The files of the Company give very little information regarding the operation before 1907, but it is known that telephone exchanges at Vernon, Armstrong and Enderby were being operated for some time prior to that year. In 1910 the Company extended its system to Salmon Arm...
Early in 1912 the Company purchased the Lake Shore Telephone Company Limited with exchanges at Peachland, Summerland and Penticton.[21]
(*OHS* 1954)

M.J. Conroy, who was superintendent of the company, gives us the history of acquisitions and technological improvements in his article "History of the Okanagan Telephone." For example, the Naramata exchange was replaced with local-exchange service from Penticton. From 1919 on, Lumby became part of the Vernon exchange. In 1951 the company bought out Solar Telephones Limited of Revelstoke. Automatic dialing equipment was installed in the late 1940s and early 1950. H.R. Denison writes:

> Peachland, Summerland and Penticton also had local systems, and the 1909 Directory shows the Valley exchanges to have the following number of subscribers: Vernon 175, Kelowna 115, Summerland 77, Penticton 40 and Peachland 14.
>
> In 1909 Armstrong had a small local system with J.M. Wright as agent. Enderby and Lumby were connected to the Vernon exchange for long distance calls. J. Mowat was the Enderby agent and E.L. Morand the agent at Lumby.
>
> (*OHS*, 1954)

The career of Joe Biollo illustrates the changes in telephone technology and business organization that occurred within one lifetime.[22] In 1915 Joe's father was killed in a railway accident in Penticton, leaving his widow with seven small children of whom Joe, at eight years, was the second-eldest. At age nine Joe became choreboy for "Ma" Sheridan who owned a boarding house, two rooming houses and a store near the railway yards. Joe remembers "Ma" Sheridan as "a very good businesswoman and also a kind woman who helped many less fortunate people in the community."

In 1927 Syd Barton, manager of the telephone company, offered Joe a job handling repairs in the Penticton area provided that within the next two weeks he learned to drive a Model T Ford truck and to climb telephone poles. Later in life Joe would claim, laughingly, to have climbed every telephone pole between Penticton and Kelowna. About 1930 Joe worked with Cliff Greyell when the Penticton system was being converted from magneto to common battery. In January 1943 Joe joined the Royal Canadian Army Signal Corps in which he served for three years.

David MacDonald tells us:

> The Okanagan Telephone Company installed one of the first large automatic dialing systems in the Summerland exchange in 1949. During his years with the Signal Corps Joe had learned how to install and service automatic dialing equipment, so he was promoted to Manager in Summerland. His area included Peachland and later Westbank...
>
> In 1959 Joe was transferred to Revelstoke as Manager. This was an extremely busy time for that exchange, because the Mica Dam was under construction and later the Rogers Pass Highway was opened.
>
> (*OHS*, 1990)

Joe and his wife Sine retired to Penticton in 1968.

Telegraphs

Percy Clement records that when Kelowna people objected to the lack of privacy when using the telephone mounted in H.E. Wallis's drugstore the government moved the office to E.E. Millie's watch-repair shop. There telegraph instruments were installed too, because Mr. Millie was a competent operator.[23]

In the *Fifty-first Report* Tilman E. Nahm relates his experiences during the twenty-six years he worked for the Canadian National Telegraphs.[24] He began as a messenger boy in 1948 at the age of sixteen, earning $35 a month for 54-hour work weeks, and became an operator. Speaking of the importance of telegrams even in the late 1940s he says:

> It must be remembered that during this time, the late 1940s, the telegram was an important communications link in the lives of many people and businesses. This was in the days of open wire landline transmission, prior to development of microwave. Satellite transmission was just an idea in the mind of forward thinking futurists. Long distance telephone rates were relatively expensive compared to today and often the quality of long distance voice transmission left much to be desired. Telegraph rates were reasonable and, as many homes had no telephones, the telegram delivered by hand provided a service that filled a need.
>
> (*OHS*, 1987)

Newspapers

The principal newspapers of the Okanagan originated in the 1890s. Burt R. Campbell, who worked for the *Vernon News* in 1892 and later worked for papers in Revelstoke and Kamloops, has written several articles on early newspapers. Below are excerpts.

The Inland Sentinel[25]

by Burt R. Campbell

Founded at Emory Bar, about five miles below Yale, the *Inland Sentinel* made its first appearance May 29, 1880, and was then the only newspaper published in BC east of New Westminster...There was, however, no post office at Emory and on and after October 20, 1880, the paper was published at Yale.

As railway construction proceeded, the publisher foresaw better possibilities for his paper and moved to Kamloops where, on July 31, 1884, *The Inland Sentinel* made its bow to central BC. Being seven years in advance of the first Okanagan newspaper, it was but natural that the *Sentinel* should become the chronicler of news of that district...

Michael Hagen, the founder and first editor of the *Sentinel*, was a fine type of man, as honest and straightforward as they make them...

Looking over early files of *The Inland Sentinel*, there are to be found many items pertaining to the Okanagan. [For example, the death of John Carmichael Haynes warrants a paragraph July 14, 1888.]...

October 18, 1890—"The telephone line (between Sicamous and Enderby) being constructed under the superintendence of Mr. Hayman will be completed in three weeks."...

A concert was held in Lambly Bros.' warehouse at Enderby on November 27, 1890, for the purpose of raising funds for the purchase of an organ for the Presbyterian Church. The attendance was estimated at 280...It would appear that the highlights of the concert were the song "McGinty" by W.H. Barrett followed by "Widow Machree" and the rendition on the piano by Miss Chickluna of "Convent Bells."...

November 28, 1891—A news item from Vernon said: "As mentioned last week, Hon. F.G. Vernon and Mr. G.G. Mackay arrived by special train and next day proceeded to make an inventory of the Coldstream Ranch and property before handing it over to Lord Aberdeen's agents..."

There are many other items relating to the Okanagan Valley which appeared in the *Sentinel*...It should be borne in mind too that during the period from 1880 to 1891 Enderby was the most important place and centre in the Okanagan Valley. It was the head of steamboat navigation on the Spallumcheen River and later the headquarters of the railway construction contractors during the building of the S.&O. Railway.

(*OHS*, 1943)

Mr. Campbell gives a short account of all the newspapers published in our area up to 1948. Some scarcely managed to get off the ground but others are with us today. Below are excerpts:

THE VERNON NEWS—Pioneer paper of the Okanagan Valley, founded by Angus K. Stuart & W.J. Harber May 14, 1891...a year later sold to George G. Henderson and Ainsley Megraw...John A. McKelvie, former head clerk at W.R. Megraw's general store, was another to join the paper, succeeding Mr. Megraw as editor...Mr. McKelvie who developed into one of the best editorial writers that BC has known ...died in 1924. 1925 W.S. Harris arrived in Vernon, publisher and editor until his death in 1943 when paper was taken over by Frank R. Harris, a son.

OKANAGAN MINING REVIEW—Okanagan Falls in August 1893. Publishers were Henderson, Megraw and Robert Mathison ...

FAIRVIEW AND MIDWAY ADVANCE—at Fairview 1894–1902.

SIMILKAMEEN STAR—published March 31, 1900 at Princeton with James Anderson as manager. A number of owners and managers including Col. R.T. Lowery of Kootenay-

The Similkameen Star *printing plant in Princeton in 1934. When Dave Taylor, the owner-editor, left on a war assignment during World War II, Rev. John Goodfellow assumed the responsibility of getting the paper out.*
BCARS B-08973

Boundary fame. Sold to Dave Taylor April 1919...During the temporary absence of Mr. Taylor in the early 1940s, Rev. J.C. Goodfellow acted as editor.

ARMSTRONG ADVERTISER—established May 1902 by Ed. V. Chambers. Numerous owners. Sold to John E. Jamieson August 1927. Associated with him was his son James E. Jamieson.

OKANAGAN HERALD—meant to be a Liberal alternative to Conservative *Vernon News*. Few if any issues printed.

THE EDENOGRAPH—introduced in Enderby May 1904 by H.M. Walker. Incorporated with *Enderby Progress* in 1906 and published until September 1907.

KELOWNA COURIER—published first July 26, 1904 as *Kelowna Clarion and Okanagan Advocate*. First owner, R.H. Spedding; first editor, W.J. Clement. Sold October 1905 to George C. Rose. From 1947 published semi-weekly.

HEDLEY GAZETTE—founded by Ainsley Megraw in 1905. Suspended publication August 16, 1917. Plant purchased by R.J. McDougall of Penticton and incorporated with the plants of the *Penticton Herald* and *Similkameen Star*.

ARMSTRONG ADVANCE—1905. Sold to *Advertiser* in 1906.

THE OKANAGAN—1905-1909. John Kennedy and J.J. Langstaff successive editors. Supported Liberal Party.

PENTICTON HERALD—"had its beginning as the *Penticton Press* in 1906, with W.J. Clement as owner. He sold to a company formed by Shatford Bros. in 1910. The first managing editor was H.M. Blake...For a long period—about a quarter of a century—the paper prospered under the management and editorship of R.J. McDougall who took over in October 1914...He made it one of the leading weekly newspapers in Canada." In 1940 G.J. Rowland leased the paper and bought it in 1946.

SALMON ARM OBSERVER—founded in October 1907 by Fraser Bros. George W. Armstrong took over February 1909 to August 1921. Several owners before paper was bought by Frank Marshall, formerly with the New Westminster *Columbian*, in September 1944.

WALKER'S WEEKLY—(Enderby) March 5, 1908 with H.M. Walker as publisher until his retirement in 1930s. J.D. Tucker owner in 1918.

KEREMEOS TRUMPET—March 1908-December 1909.

SUMMERLAND REVIEW—August 1908. J.M. Robinson had controlling interest. Ralph E. White took over management July 1911 and became shareholder. When White left to go to *Kamloops Sentinel*, R.J. McDougall bought *Review* and ran it as independent paper until October 1929.

ORCHARD CITY RECORD—1908-1920 published by Leathley Bros. Name changed to *Kelowna Record*.

PENTICTON STANDARD—1921, published less than one year.

THE WRANGLER—published briefly in Similkameen.

OLIVER ECHO—August 25, 1937 under ownership of Herbert Berryman. July 12, 1939 name changed to *Oliver Chronicle and Osoyoos Observer*.

SUMMERLAND REVIEW (No.2)—John R. Armstrong and George R.B. Fudge, returned soldiers, started the new paper in June 1946.

OSOYOOS TIMES—Published from January 28, 1947 by Stan Stodola.

THE VALLEY SPOTLIGHT—began publication September 1948 in Princeton by Miss A. Gaustin.[26]

(*OHS*, 1948)

Although the entry of BC into confederation made important changes to Okanagan life, even greater changes came with the building of the railways and the establishment of boat service on the lakes. The huge cattle ranches were subdivided, irrigation systems were created and fruit growing became the major industry. But more of that in a later chapter.

With the increase in population, town life became more sophisticated. However, it would be a mistake to believe that everyone partook of the new conveniences and comforts. There seem always to have been people ready to carve farms out of the bush or forest and endure most of the difficulties faced by the first Europeans who entered this country. Grace and Harry Worth, both city people, after marrying in 1901 left England for BC where they took up land in Trinity Valley. Mrs. Worth's acerbic comment was: "From then on there were more flies than ointment."[27]

Grace Worth on the Trinity Valley ranch that she and her husband Harry carved out of the bush during the first decade of the century. What a contrast to urban life in England! Vernon Museum 1212

15

Tree Fruits, Ground Crops, Vines and Agro-industries

The First Orchards

In the autumn of 1886 Charles Ora Card, a son-in-law of Mormon leader Brigham Young, spent several weeks travelling through the Boundary Country and the Okanagan. He and his two companions were looking for land on which a community of Mormons might settle. Card was disappointed to find that almost all the arable land was owned by the great "cattle kings," with the result that the young men turned their attention to southern Alberta where land was available and where Cardston became the centre of a Mormon settlement.

However, the portion of Card's journal relating to the Okanagan Valley, a copy of which was presented to the *Osoyoos Times* by Brigham Y. Card, a grandson of Charles Ora Card, tells us something of the Valley in the mid-1880s. For example on October 2 the party reached Osoyoos where, in the absence of J.C. Haynes, they were attended to by the deputy customs officer. Card says, "Here we ate delicious peaches."

Near Okanagan Falls on October 5 Card writes, "Mr. Keagan made us a present of some very nice peaches and 3 apples raised on his farm." Two days later the young men were at the Mission where Card writes,

Young orchards in Coldstream, 1890s. Vernon Museum 5029

"We saw apple trees laden with fruit here and most excellent land, but monopolized by but few which is the general complaint with British Columbia."

Where had these fruit trees come from? The first fruit trees planted in the Okanagan appear to have been those planted by Hiram F. "Okanogan" Smith in 1857 on his tract of land beside Osoyoos Lake about one mile south of the International Boundary.[1] Smith, who had been a packer for the Hudson's Bay Company, carried his first trees into the Valley from Hope. It seems likely that the trees originated in the Hudson's Bay Company nursery which operated from the

167

1840s at Fort Langley. (The first apple trees in the Northwest were grown on the Hudson's Bay Company farm at Fort Vancouver from seeds brought from England by Captain Aemelius Simpson in 1826.) Smith found a ready market for his apples among the gold miners and cattlemen pushing north, especially as he was able to offer his customers dried fruit.

In 1862 the Oblate fathers planted apples at their Mission near present-day Kelowna. Some authorities say their seedling trees came from St. Mary's Mission in the Fraser Valley. D.V. Fisher of the Dominion Research Station at Summerland, in his article "History of Fruit Growing in the B.C. Interior,"[2] describes apple trees on the Indian Reserve at Inkameep which in 1978 he believed to be about one hundred years old and probably the oldest fruit trees in the Okanagan north of the 49th Parallel.

In the Similkameen Francis X. Richter planted three orchards, the first about 1880 consisting of one acre of apple trees on the "R" Ranch. The young trees came from Wm. Clarkson's Nursery at New Westminster. In 1886 Richter planted two acres, which included a planting of Italian prunes, at his Lower Ranch. This second orchard was irrigated. The prunes were dried and sold well. The third orchard was planted in 1897 at Inglewood Ranch and consisted of thirty-five acres. Layritz Nursery in Victoria supplied the trees. In 1906 Richter won twenty-three prizes at the annual Provincial Exhibition in New Westminster for his apples, pears, peaches and plums.[3] About 1869 Tom Ellis planted apple trees on his Penticton ranch. In the late 1880s John Thomson had a "well-kept orchard" in Pleasant Valley near Armstrong.

Early orchardists in the Okanagan (from the list of Dr. D.V. Fisher)

1875–76: Kelowna (George Whelan and Alfred Postill).
1890: Salmon Arm (P.M. Parsons).
1890: Vernon (Luc Girouard).
1892: Kelowna (George C. Rose, 40 acres).
1892: Summerland (Mr. Gartrell and Messrs. Barkley, Garnett and Dunston in the Garnett Valley).
1892: Coldstream Ranch, Vernon (Lord Aberdeen, 200 acres).
1892: Kelowna, Guisachan Ranch (Lord Aberdeen).
1900: Armstrong and Enderby.
1900: Okanagan Falls.
1901: Peachland (J.M. Robinson).
1901: Kelowna (Bankhead) (T.W. Stirling and Pridham Orchards).

1902: Rutland Flats.
1902: Kamloops (Canadian Real Properties).
1903: Westbank (D.E. Gellatly).
1904: Oyama (Mr. Irvine).
1905: Naramata (J.M. Robinson).
1905: Penticton (J.H. Latimer).
1905: Osoyoos (Leslie Hill).
1908: Walhachin (C.P. Barnes).
1909: Winfield and Okanagan Centre (Okanagan Land Company, Rainbow Ranch Company, and Duck Lake Fruitlands Company).
1910: Kaleden (Kaleden Estates Company Ltd.).
1913: Belgo [Kelowna].

from History of Fruit Growing in the B.C. Interior[4]

by D.V. Fisher, Ph.D, P. Ag., F.A.S.H.S.

The late 1890s and early 1900s were boom days in the fruit belt of the Southern Interior. Some of the promotional efforts in selling orchard land to overseas buyers were highly questionable and the cause of great distress to many improperly informed, inexperienced purchasers encouraged by pie-in-the-sky prospectuses of land agents. Nevertheless there also were substantial, dedicated and well-financed enterprises which tended to put the industry initially on a sound footing. Thus Lord Aberdeen (Coldstream Ranch, Vernon and Guisachan Ranch, Kelowna), T.W. Stirling and Mr. Pridham in Kelowna and the Okanagan Land Co., Rainbow Ranch Co. and Duck Lake Fruitlands Co. in Winfield–Okanagan Centre, to name a few, were important pioneers in laying the basis of the present fruit industry.

The next big boost in fruit plantings came from the opening of new areas to returned soldiers after World

Land improving. Moving rocks with a stoneboat. Notice the wooden irrigation flume between the young cherry tree and the horse. There seem to be ground crops in the foreground, perhaps tomatoes. Vernon Museum 3355

Orchard lands near Salmon Arm, c. 1912. Photo by Rex Lingford Pat McGuire Cameron

War I. These plantings were financed under the Soldier Settlement Act and resulted, in particular, in extensive developments in the early 1920s, especially in the Oliver–Osoyoos area.

Great hardships were endured by the pioneer orchardists because of totally inadequate irrigation systems, recurrent winter freezes, the planting of numerous and unsuited varieties, minor element deficiencies, the invasion of codling moth which became epidemic by 1925, and above all, by repeated failures to establish a sound marketing system backed by unified grower support...

Great changes in the economics, philosophy and practice of fruit growing have occurred since the early 1900s. Land then could be bought for several hundred dollars per acre and with the wide tree spacings of 30 x 30 and 40 x 40 feet, interplanting of row crops was common to provide income for the first ten or fifteen years before trees came into bearing. Most fruit growers also carried some livestock since farming was looked upon as a means of subsistence and a way of life. Equipment was minimal; horses provided the horse-power for orchard operations and fruit hauling and packing often was done in the orchard.

The important advances of modern science did not start to impinge upon fruit growing until around 1930. Starting about this time, fruit farming gradually developed into a business, as labour-saving devices and increased knowledge and technology provided new solutions to old problems. Twenty-five cents per hour labour is now [1978] worth five dollars per hour. Machinery and chemicals have replaced hand labour. Barring unexpected winter freezes, the grower, by following the recommendations of federal research and provincial extension authorities, can exercise almost full control over all orchard problems and cultural operations. There is adequate irrigation which is applied by permanent-set sprinkler systems; effective spray materials and machinery are available to control almost all insects and diseases; chemicals have replaced hoes to eliminate weeds; chemical materials are available to thin apples and pears; tractor-drawn mowers not only cut grass between trees, but also chop up prunings which previously were laboriously hand gathered and burned. Minor element sprays eliminate soil nutrient deficiencies. Stop-drop sprays applied prior to harvest prevent the frightful losses from windfalls once experienced by growers.

High density plantings of two hundred trees per acre have replaced the old twenty-seven and forty-eight trees per acre plantings. [By 1997 the number of trees per acre could run to well over one thousand in some cases.] Apple trees planted densely on dwarfing roots reach full bearing in seven to ten years and have the potential of producing one to two thousand bushels per acre as opposed to having to wait twenty years for full production of usually less than one thousand bushels per acre in the original orchards.

Apples and other fruits once picked in wooden bushel boxes are now hauled from the orchard in twenty-five bushel bins and transported quickly to modern, sophisticated packing houses...

A 750,000 box apple crop in 1913 had increased to 2.5 million boxes in 1925 and 4 million boxes by 1935. [In 1978 production reached between 7.5 million and 9 million boxes.] ...By 1926 the growers, realizing the perishable nature and rapidly growing volume of their products and in order to free themselves from ruthless speculation, sought legislation under which the entire production could be controlled and marketed in an orderly fashion...

After the Marketing Act was finally in effect, the B.C.F.G.A. [B.C. Fruit Growers Association] proceeded to establish central selling. As a result, in 1939, the B.C. Tree Fruits Ltd. organization came into being as the sole marketing agency for the fresh fruit crop of the B.C. Interior area. Later, the B.C.F.G.A. organized Sun-Rype Products Ltd. to handle processed products...pie fillers, juice concentrates and solid pack fruits.

Being geographically isolated from major continental and world markets, the industry has found it essential to maintain high standards of fruit grading and quality...For this reason, costly and sophisticated cold and controlled atmosphere storage plants have been erected throughout the fruit growing area. The Kelowna Growers Exchange erected the first cold storage in 1925 followed shortly by the Vernon Fruit Union, Penticton Co-op, Summerland Co-op and others...Presently [1978] the industry has about a 1,700,000 bushel capacity in C.A. storage and a 6,500,000 bushel capacity in regular cold storage. The development of the cold storage program has been essential to regulating marketing and selling the crop on world markets for eleven months of the year...

(*OHS*, 1978)

Dr. D.V. Fisher, the author of the article above, arrived in 1933 fresh from studies at the University of British Columbia to take up a position at the Dominion Experimental Station at Summerland. He was to become head of pomology and between 1971 and 1974 he was superintendent of the station. Dr. Fisher retired in 1975. We are indebted to him for a number of lucid and informed articles about Okanagan agriculture which appear in our *Reports*, among them a history of the Summerland Research Station.[5]

Summerland Research Station

The Summerland Research Station commenced operations in 1914 on land acquired from the Department of Indian Affairs. R.H. Helmer, a successful farmer, was its first superintendent. Through the years the station has supported farmers engaged in animal husbandry, horticulture and the growing of tree fruits. Remedies for soil deficiencies have been discovered, for viruses such as little cherry and for orchard pests like codling moth. Improved methods of applying irrigation water, of storing fruit in cold storage or in controlled atmosphere, of spraying to hold fruit on the tree until it can be harvested are among the discoveries that have saved Okanagan orchardists millions of dollars. New fruit varieties have been developed and methods of manufacturing products from Okanagan fruits have been perfected.

Irrigation and Land Development

Some of the early orchardists were able to plant lands they had pre-empted or acquired individually. However, most orchard development resulted when land speculators bought out the estates of the early cattlemen and subdivided these into ten-, twenty-, forty- or even, occasionally, one hundred-acre lots. G.G. McKay, who arranged the sale of both the Guisachan Ranch near Kelowna and the Coldstream Ranch near Vernon to the Earl of Aberdeen, was an early promoter of the fruit industry. The Coldstream Ranch began planting fruit trees

in 1891 and by 1908 there were two hundred acres of bearing trees. Some of the acreage was held by the Coldstream Estates Company and some sold off to settlers, most of whom came from Britain.

Among those developing orchard lands were T.W. Stirling and J.L. Pridham who formed the Kelowna Land and Orchard Company in 1904, buying out the Lequime interests. The Okanagan Land Company, the Rainbow Ranch Company and Duck Lake Fruitlands Company subdivided land and laid on irrigation in Winfield and Okanagan Centre. The Belgo district near Kelowna was developed by the Land and Agriculture Company of Canada, which was owned by wealthy Belgians led by Arthur De Jardin of Winnipeg. Later De Jardin extended the holdings to include the L & A Ranch north of Swan Lake, land he purchased from the Greenhow and O'Keefe estates. The Belgian Orchard Syndicate that developed the BX district to the northeast of Vernon was an off-shoot of the L & A Ranch interests.

J.M. Robinson developed Peachland, Summerland and Naramata, selling mainly to Canadians from the prairie. Farther south the Ellis lands were bought by the Shatford brothers, who came to the Okanagan from Nova Scotia and were always known by their initials, W.T. and L.W. becoming managing directors of the Southern Okanagan Land Company with B.A. serving as general orchard foreman. A fourth brother, S.A., remained in the North Okanagan.

When Premier John Oliver in 1918 was looking for land that might be prepared for the settlement of soldiers returning from World War I his government decided to purchase 22,000 acres from the Shatfords, a property extending from McIntyre Bluff south to the International Boundary, and to put in an irrigation system. The administrative centre of the South Okanagan Lands Project was named Oliver in honour of the premier who had brought it into being. But by 1927, when water delivery reached the border, many returned men had found niches elsewhere in the economy. Thus land was opened to others, although not on such advantageous terms as those given veterans.

A decade earlier however, on the eastern shore of Lake Osoyoos, a syndicate headed by George Fraser had purchased and subdivided the property that Leslie Hill had bought from Tom Ellis. D.P. Fraser describes the irrigation system that carried water to the subdivision's thirsty desert soil:

> In 1920 the irrigation system was installed. Its heart was a single-cylinder gasoline engine of 10-inch bore, located on the lakeshore near the present East Osoyoos Irrigation pumphouse. This engine, with 6-foot flywheels on either side, powered a belt-driven centrifugal pump. The water was pumped through a 12-inch woodstave pipe up to an

elevation of 50 feet. Here it went into a big square wooden box. From this tank wooden flumes carried the precious water north to present Highway 3, and south to the lot now fronted by Brookvale campsite. The spring run-off from Haynes Creek was used for early irrigation, a wooden flume bringing this water to the distribution box...

As soon as the spring flow from Haynes Creek diminished, the pumping plant had to be started up. This required two men to stand on the spokes of the flywheels to generate sufficient compression for the engine to fire. Once started, it went bang, bang, bang, all summer at about 15 second intervals. The ear became accustomed to the regular bangs, and it was said you never heard it till it stopped.[6]

(*OHS*, 1986)

Osoyoos c. 1930. Irrigation furrows with cucumbers planted on the ridges between. The hot caps protected the plants from late frosts.
Willi Tenning collection

Domestic water supply. Osoyoos in the 1930s.
Willi Tenning collection

In 1871 the first water right for irrigation purposes in the Okanagan had been issued on Coldstream Creek to Charles A. Vernon. Once Lord Aberdeen became owner of the Coldstream Ranch and intended planting orchards, he acquired the services of F.H. Latimer to design a system whereby water would be taken from Aberdeen Lake high in the mountains to the southeast. The Grey Canal was the principal artery and remained in service until 1970. Ann M. Davies in her article "The Grey Canal"[7] outlines the history of the Vernon Irrigation District (VID) which is owned by the people who use its water and run by their trustees, who oversee all 88.72 miles of canals, ditches and pipes with dams and syphons. Successive managers of the Coldstream Ranch have played an important part in the management of the VID. These include F.E.R. Wollaston, Tom Hill and C.D. Osborn.[8]

Irrigation systems created by adequately capitalized companies were designed by professional engineers. In Oliver, across the road from the Village Hall is a plaque which was dedicated May 11, 1950 and bears this inscription:

To commemorate our pioneer engineers, among them F.H. Latimer,
especially for his work in the major irrigation and townsite development 1905–1940
from Penticton to Osoyoos.

Erected by the Association of Professional Engineers of B.C.
and the Engineering Institute of Canada, Central B.C. Branch.

Frank Herbert Latimer, who was born in Kincardine, Ontario, May 23, 1860,[9] arrived in Vernon in 1891. There he designed an irrigation system for the Coldstream Estate Company. During his ten years of professional service in the North Okanagan, the Coldstream system was extended west to serve Okanagan Landing and north to the Swan Lake area. Between 1901 and 1905 he designed the irrigation systems in Peachland, Summerland and Naramata and laid out the townsites. In the period 1905–1942, Latimer worked for the South Okanagan Land Company and for Penticton. Between 1919 and 1924 he was in charge of the construction and management of the South Okanagan Lands Project (Oliver and Osoyoos).

Latimer probably more than anyone was responsible for the great change made in the Okanagan landscape as cattle ranching gave way to fruit growing and the main irrigation ditches along the hillsides "divided the desert from the sown," in high summer all tawny above the great flume and lush green below. In addition to his professional work Latimer found time to participate in community affairs such as his church, musical activities, the Masonic order and the Penticton School Board. He died February 10, 1948.

Not all developers could afford to put in properly engineered irrigation systems. When unirrigated land could be acquired for from $10 to $40 an acre and sold, once water had been supplied to it, for from $150 to $350 an acre[10] it was tempting to some developers to treat the promotion of the fruit lands as a "get-rich-quick" scheme. Such businessmen intended to finance the improvement of irrigation installations out of new sales. When a depression in the real-estate market about 1912 slowed investment, the original buyers sometimes

Building the Big Ditch, South
Okanagan Lands Project. Many
of the workers were
World War I veterans.
Oliver & District Heritage Soc.
OLP982.226.10.b.

The ditch north of
Oliver in operation.
Oliver & District Heritage Soc.
OLP982.78.12

Constructing the great syphon
which carried the irrigation
water across the Okanagan
River. When the workers went
back to their camps at night
Carleton MacNaughton and his
teenage friends at Oliver rode
their bicycles through
the syphon.
Oliver & District Heritage Soc.
OLP982.79.2

Young apricot orchard near Oliver with ground crops planted between the rows. Oliver & District Heritage Soc. OLP983.313.11

found themselves with totally inadequate water systems and a company which could not afford to maintain or improve their dams, ditches and flumes. So serious was the situation that the government was forced to intervene and pass legislation to protect the growers. Water was too important to be regarded as a merely private concern.[11]

Even carefully established and well-run systems could be in trouble. In "The Story of Irrigation–Lifeblood of the Okanagan Valley's Economy,"[12] Arthur W. Gray presents a comprehensive history of Okanagan and Similkameen irrigation systems and their struggle to gain assistance from both the Provincial and Federal Governments:

> With the expansion of the number of irrigated areas a logical outcome was the setting up of an association to discuss mutual problems and to speak for the irrigationists as a whole. Attempts at organization were made in 1920...Harry Everard was secretary and active officers in those days were George Heggie from Vernon, C.E. Barnes and E.M. Carruthers from Kelowna. In the depression days of the thirties the districts ran into financial difficulties, and the A.B.C.I.D. became the voice of the irrigationists in seeking some form of relief from debts owed to the provincial government...The entry of the federal government into the rehabilitation field with the enactment of the Prairie Farm Rehabilitation Act caused officials of the B.C. association to press Ottawa for extension of its terms to west of the Rockies...The first steps in this direction were taken as measures to establish veterans on the land after W.W. II, with the projects at Westbank and Cawston, which proved the thin end of the wedge...
>
> Gradually the federal government, by successive moves, reached the stage of recognizing reclamation as a national matter, and not a local problem alone, and legislation known as the Agricultural Rehabilitation and Development Act was passed by the Diefenbaker government, and federal aid to irrigation, as one of the methods of rehabilitation, became possible in any province that stood in need of this aid.
>
> In these latter days [1968] we have entered what might be called the "ARDA" period. Federal funds having become available for the rehabilitation of existing systems, as well as

Sometimes the problem was too much water. Penticton Main Street flooded in 1942. Penticton Museum 1-019b

the establishment of new ones, many districts today are modernizing their systems with this federal aid...

From the days of the miner's primitive ditch and flume of the 1860s, to the modern underground, pressurized systems, and universal use of sprinkling systems, irrigation has come a long way in a period of 100 years. For this thanks should go in no small measure to engineers and officials with foresight and imagination, and especially to a group of individuals who gave more of their time and energy than they could spare, and for small recompense, to serve as trustees of the many irrigation districts and associations.

(*OHS*, 1968)

George Heggie, who was born in 1870 in Northern Ireland of Scottish parents, arrived in Enderby in February 1895. He managed the Stepney Ranch until the death of Sir Arthur Stepney in 1910. He was then invited to manage the Land and Agricultural Company of Canada, a position which he held for thirty-two years. He was also manager for many years of the two hundred-acre Belgian Orchard Syndicate. From 1930 to 1932 he served as MLA for the North Okanagan, a position he used to further his irrigation concerns.[13] Photo: Vernon Museum

Edward Maurice Carruthers was born in 1873 in Inverness, Scotland. At the age of sixteen he immigrated to Canada with George C. Rose. They arrived in the Okanagan where "Ted" Carruthers spent several years working as a ranch hand. In 1910 he was sent to London, England to open a sales office on behalf of several Kelowna orchard companies. In 1914 he returned to manage the Belgo orchards for the Land and Agriculture Company of Canada. Ted Carruthers was also active in the real estate and insurance business in Kelowna.[14]

Fruit Growers

Where did the first commercial fruit growers come from? Many came from the British Isles. In fact it was a policy of the Aberdeens to favour immigrants from Scotland and England over Canadians. Lady Aberdeen in her October 30, 1894 entry in her *Journal* says:

Mr. Jamieson has a plan whereby we could probably soon get rid of all our available land by selling it by a system which would only require the price to be paid in 21 years, thus instituting meanwhile a sort of tenantry. But the idea does not smile on us, for all the troubles of tenants would come too, more particularly as Mr. Kelly thinks that many of the Vernon people would take up lots under these terms. They would never be able to pay, and it would be rather difficult for the Governor General to turn them out.

First homes of the Towgood family and of Robert Allison at Oyama in 1907. BCARS B-01994

William and Catherine Middleton were among the very first to succumb to the Aberdeen enthusiasm. They arrived in 1892 with the intention of establishing a dairy herd on the Coldstream Ranch and also taking up one of the Coldstream surveyed orchard plots. Others followed, many of them people of means bringing household servants and ranch hands with them. They built fine new houses amid the newly planted fruit trees and set about establishing a society as much like the one they had left as possible.

Dr. Margaret Ormsby in her *Coldstream Nulli Secundus* presents a picture of one Coldstream settler:[15]

Mrs. Kidston [Anna Euphemia], daughter of Richard Cunliffe, a Glasgow shipowner and a Clydebank shipbuilder, had reached Vernon in 1904, where she awaited the birth of her younger son and the building of her new home on the lakeshore adjacent to Coldstream Creek Road. A cook, a nurse, and a gardener accompanied her. "Miktow" was a large residence, roomy enough for a big family, and it was soon surrounded by grounds which included a tennis court and, at the lake a short distance from shore, a boathouse.

No wonder Lady Aberdeen could say with satisfaction, "But we ought to get in time a really high-class little community here." (October 30, 1894)

The Coldstream for many years remained a class-conscious society. The upper class enjoyed their big houses, entertaining friends to tea, dinner and house dances. Their children went to private schools, whereas the children of their employees went to the public school. A country club was established on Kalamalka Lake which excluded those in business in Vernon. However, as time passed the class divisions began to blur. Education, industry and native ability became more the measure of a man or a woman. By the time World War II was over, incomes from the old country which had subsidized the lifestyle of so many settlers were no longer available. Canadian military re-establishment credits tended to put all those who served in our armed forces on the same footing financially.

Following the example of Lord Aberdeen, other land developers looked to the British Isles for buyers. Hence rural society in the early decades of the century took on a decidedly English flavour. Not that all could afford the fine houses of the Coldstream nor depend on regular remittances from "home." Even some of those whose families in England might be considered gentry had to work very hard to establish themselves in the new country. David Dendy tells us that his grandfather, who was listed as "gentleman" in the British Who's Who, had to take a job as a ditch walker (or water bailiff) while his young orchard grew to the point where he could harvest a crop.[16]

Ploughing irrigation furrows in peach orchard at Summerland c. 1921. The woman handling the plow is Mrs. Enid Temple who came from England to marry Donald Temple in 1920 and settle in Summerland. Elvira (Temple) MacDonald

While the dominant culture in the valley prior to World War I was English or English-Scottish, there were enclaves of other settlers. We have already mentioned the prairie people who settled on the lands developed by J.M. Robinson through his Peachland Townsite Company (1898) and the Summerland Development Company (1903) of which Sir Thomas Shaughnessy was president. Robinson had Naramata laid out in orchard lots in 1907.

Well-to-do Belgians settled in the Belgo district near Kelowna and in the BX district near Vernon. There were many German settlers who, disillusioned with economic prospects in Europe after World War I, came to Canada and took up orcharding near the main towns and on land not taken up by veterans in the South Okanagan Lands Project. Settlers continued to trickle in from south of the 49th Parallel. The Black Mountain community north-east of Kelowna was predominately American. Japanese immigrants, like Denbei Kobayashi

Sawing ice on Swan Lake for cold storage. Later, making ice to refrigerate boxcar shipments of fruit and vegetables was an industry in the valley until the railways began to build cars refrigerated mechanically.
Vernon Museum 1526

who arrived in the North Okanagan in 1907, worked for the CPR and for growers already established. (The Coldstream Ranch paid members of their Japanese crew $1.40 for a ten-hour day.) Through thrift and hard work the Japanese acquired land on which they grew ground crops and later orchards.[17] Unlike Japanese Canadians who lived on or near the coast, settlers in the North Okanagan were not displaced during World War II. There were Chinese in the North Okanagan but they tended to grow market gardens on leased land and did not aspire to become orchardists.

After World War II there was an influx of European immigrants. But even before that there were such groups as the Hungarians that Elizabeth Minns writes about in her article "The Hungarian Presence."[18] Mrs. Minns's parents, Margaret and Joseph Renji, came with other Hungarians to Canada in the early 1920s to escape the European turmoil which was the aftermath of World War I. One day soon after she arrived in Canada, Elizabeth in typical teenage fashion was rebelling over her changed way of life. She remembers, "My mother took me in hand and told me I would one day go down on my knees and thank God for having guided me to Canada. Prophetic words indeed." After spending several disappointing years farming on the prairies the Renjis in 1928 found their way to the Okanagan, to Kelowna where George Casorso employed them along with other Hungarians. In 1930 Joseph Renji moved his family to Oliver where he was employed by Apex Orchards to look after irrigation. In Oliver the family was able to acquire ten acres of its own. Life was far from easy but they prevailed and were joined by fellow countrymen. By 1987 there were two hundred families of Hungarian origin in the Oliver and Osoyoos area, among them the Eisenhuts and the Endrenys.

Another group who were to become fruit growers were the Portuguese who began to arrive in the South Okanagan in 1952 to work as agricultural labourers. By the late 1980s almost half the orchard land in the Oliver and Osoyoos area was owned by Portuguese, much of the capital cost for which was earned working for the Aluminum Company of Canada (ALCAN) in Kitimat. Paul M. Koroscil documents this immigration in "The Portuguese in the South Okanagan":

> Most of the original immigrants who came to the Oliver and Osoyoos area in the 1950s, and those who settled permanently in the 1960s were able to adapt to the new orchard environment and they were able to eventually become successful owners of orchards. The reasons for their success can be attributed to economic circumstances in the area and the strength of the Portuguese family unit.[19]
>
> (*OHS*, 1987)

The most recent ethnic addition to the South Okanagan community is the Sikhs who began to arrive in the 1980s. By working in family units they have been able to acquire and farm growing tracts of orchard land.

Becoming an orchardist has never been an easy process whether the family was facing the difficulties of pioneer living conditions or the trials of buying into a modern highly capitalized industry. Adam Cumine, a veteran of World War I, decided to become a fruit farmer at Osoyoos soon after 1927 when the irrigation water of the South Okanagan Lands Project reached the border community. Below are excerpts from a talk he gave entitled "From Sagebrush to Fruit Trees in Osoyoos":[20]

> The area that I settled in was a barren waste of sagebrush and greasewood. For the first sixteen years there was no electricity in Osoyoos. We used coal oil lamps, the old sad irons and, for fuel, wood from the mountains. During summer we used water from the canal for domestic purposes. Many a time there would be a dead animal in it which the Ditch Rider would have to remove. On one occasion I had to rescue a deer by lassoing him, and after so saving him, he charged me. Another time I pulled out three live sheep from the canal and they promptly jumped right back in again. Until we got a well dug I hauled water from the lake with a stoneboat and barrel. In time we started cutting and storing ice for refrigeration. In those days the ice on the lake could be from 18 to 24 inches thick.
>
> Alongside of the land which I had purchased was an old construction camp known as

Camp 10. I looked over all the buildings and found one that did not leak and decided to move into this shack while I did some work on my new homestead. I ordered some fuming lumber and built an irrigation system on the place. Towards fall I was getting short of money, so I decided to take in the harvest on the prairie. I was not in a position to buy my complete fare, so I rode the rods most of the way. The crop around Calgary was still green, so with several other gentlemen of the road, we caught a fast freight to Lethbridge. In a few days the crops there were ready to cut...This was a big operation powered by a Case steam engine. I asked for the job as spike pitcher which paid top wages. We ate breakfast in the dark and with three meals and two lunches in between we worked till dusk. We slept in a travelling caboose in two tiered bunks with all our clothes on. The air in that caboose by midnight was terrific. We worked our way northward, threshing for farmers along the route and finally, late in the fall, we had to stop for snow. I returned to Osoyoos with $700.00 and moved into the shed in Camp 10.

The next job was to build a house, as I was going to get married in the spring. I decided on a very small house as I needed money to start farming. This noble structure, which was 12 feet x 12 feet, held a bed, a couple of apple boxes for chairs and a stand in one corner for a gasoline pressure stove. There was also room for my future wife's trunk, and a goodly supply of nails driven into the walls for hanging clothes.

The next job was to plow up four acres of land for the coming crop. My knowledge of this type of farming was nil. How to plant cantaloupe or what they looked like, I hadn't the slightest idea. Nevertheless, I planted 4 acres of cantaloupe and much to my surprise they came up beautifully...

Because the mice had been eating some of the cantaloupe plants, my wife spent her honeymoon transplanting cantaloupe. Well, we had a wonderful crop of melons; we packed out 1,000 40-pound crates. On my visit to the packing house it seemed to me they were packing the culls and throwing out the good ones. The net result of my work was $400.00.

We decided to go up the valley and find work...In Kelowna my wife got a job sorting fruit and I went to work at the Black Mountain dam. We returned in the late fall with $800.00.

When we got home I built a small greenhouse and decided to grow tomatoes...I was told that unless I had them in early the results would be disappointing; yet, if I planted before the snow was gone off Mt. Kobau we could have frost. I decided to take a chance and put out 3,000 plants and they appeared to be doing well. Some nine days later the weather turned cold and there was every indication of frost. I harnessed up the old black horse, hitched him to the little plow and went up and down the rows of tomatoes and plowed a light layer of soil over the plants. We had three nights of heavy frost. On the fourth day I started to uncover the plants. After two days on my hands and knees I was back in business. That year we were the first on the open market and made some $1,200.00...

That spring we had also planted 1,300 young fruit trees. The following winter was extremely cold and by the following spring we had lost them all excepting some 65 or so trees. That was a severe blow.

Our little farm was an oasis in the desert so we had a good crop of rattlesnakes. A portion of the place was in hay and I was compelled to wear gum boots. Several people were bitten but all survived...

Eventually the orchards in the valley began to bear fruit and ground cropping faded out. The years of depression finally receded and semi-prosperity came to the valley.
(*OHS*, 1983)

There was one group of settlers who were not enticed into fruit farming, the French Canadians of Lumby. They found lumbering and the hospitality industry more to their taste. As Okanagan society developed descendants of the Lumby pioneers, like those of other ethnic groups, often found their way into the professions.

Growing Concerns

Fruit Growing

Fruit growing was fraught with difficulties from its outset. For example, many of the trees in the Coldstream had been so poorly planted that replanting was necessary. Sometimes trees were put into unsuitable ground. At Guisachan, where the water table was high, apple trees did not thrive. As one old resident said, "They had wet feet." A somewhat similar circumstance existed in Salmon Arm. Ernest Doe writes:[21]

> In 1890 an order for fruit trees was placed with a salesman for the L.L. May and Co., St. Paul, Minnesota. The trees arrived the next spring from Walla Walla, Washington. The honour of planting the first apple tree, a Duchess Oldenburg, in the district, goes to C.B. Harris and J.D. McGuire...most of the trees in the order were planted in the valley. The settlers did not favour the higher bench lands, believing that irrigation was essential. Eventually they discovered that apple trees would not thrive in the bottom lands and died out.
>
> (*OHS*, 1950)

Picking ladders manufactured by Kenyon and Killick, Penticton. A ladder was measured by its steps: e.g., a 16-foot ladder had 16 steps. The tall ladders were needed for picking the big trees that were grown at the time. They were brutes to move and position next to the fruit.
Penticton Museum 3-047

It is ironical that fruit trees could be and have been successfully grown on the benchland of Salmon Arm without irrigation. One family who has successfully fruit farmed without irrigation for over sixty years is the Peterson family. Edward Peterson arrived in Salmon Arm about 1920. By 1930 he had an orchard on twenty-four acres on which he and his wife raised their five sons, Hubert, Elmer, Hjalmar, Floyd and Alf. Gradually the family holdings grew to a maximum of 150 acres.

The Petersons shipped through the Salmon Arm

Picking ladders in use. Apples are being put into regular apple boxes. In the foreground is an irrigation flume.
Penticton Museum 2-037

Farmers Exchange which had been established in 1907 or 1908 and did not close its doors until about 1958. At the height of its prosperity the exchange had a membership of between two hundred and three hundred, but during the severe winter of 1949–50 so many fruit trees were killed that many orchardists were driven out of the industry and the exchange was unable to recover as a viable operation.

There were other orchardists in the area who used irrigation and there were private shippers such as Turner and Sons. Other fruits once grown were cherries, raspberries and strawberries. Today Salmon Arm apples are packed and shipped by the Okanagan North Growers Co-op at their Winfield plant.

Winter temperatures proved a limiting factor as those who bought "fruit lands" in Kettle Valley, Westwold and Hullcar were to learn to their sorrow. In 1906 Richard Thomas Skelton arrived from England. He bought 186 acres at Hullcar and planted about forty acres of orchard which he watered from a complex flume system which he constructed. His daughter-in-law Verna Skelton reported that at the time of her wedding in 1938 only two or three dozen trees remained. Armstrong winters were simply too cold for fruit growing.

The significance of winter kill in the fruit-growing areas is the subject of a manuscript by Ralph R. Krueger and N. Garth Maguire, *The Urbanization of the Fruitlands of the Okanagan Valley*.[22] They say:

> The length of time that fruit trees remain in production is important to fruit growers. When a tree has to be replaced, not only is capital expended, but there is also a crop 'loss' until the young tree is in full production. This is most serious in the case of apples (except dwarfs) which take from 5 to 10 years to start bearing and do not reach peak production until the tree approaches 20 years of age.
> (*OHS*, 1985)

Low winter temperatures which damage fruit trees are by no means a rarity. However, there are other climatic conditions which affect production. Late spring frosts can damage blossoms; cold rainy weather may interfere with the pollenization by bees; hail; rain in cherry season; cool summers that depress the sugar content in peaches; strong wind storms that shake fruit off the branches. Advice from the Summerland Research Station has mitigated damage from the above and programs such as hail insurance have helped but still the farmer is at the mercy of the elements, a circumstance that makes fruit production a worrisome occupation, especially for those growers who work on too slim a margin or whose orchard practices are inferior.

Marketing

Grievous as climatic conditions were proving, the problem which dominated grower thinking was that of marketing their fruit. W. Gordon Wight, who was president of B.C. Tree Fruits from 1957 to 1965, presented a report entitled "Twenty-five Years of Central Selling: 1939–1964" to the 75th Annual Convention of the British Columbia Fruit Growers Association. Excerpts follow:

Our basic advantages are that as a producing area we have the potential for growing economically many varieties of fruit of the finest quality...

Our basic disadvantage has stemmed from our ability to produce more fruit than the easily accessible markets could absorb and the resulting additional costs of transportation and packing that our products have had to bear in competing against other areas...

In the late 1930s we had 37 selling agents among the shipping organizations... In 1939 B.C. Tree Fruits was designated as the sole selling agency for the domestic crop as the result of an overwhelming vote by the growers for Central Selling...With Central Selling in effect we entered the war period and in 1943 the Wartime Prices and Trade Board was established, with ceiling prices and import by permit only, into Canada...The domestic market being protected and buoyant, our sales in Eastern Canada jumped during this period from a few hundred thousand boxes to almost two million in heavy crop years...

Effective in 1947 the Wartime Prices and Trade Board disappeared, but was replaced immediately with the Austerity Program covering the late forties, which restricted imports even more rigidly than previously...The 1940s were the most prosperous years of the Industry's history and BCFGA deservedly received full credit for their contribution in these first formative years...

Trucking empties. The apple boxes are nested in threes. How many boxes is the man with the hand-truck moving? Penticton Museum

The winter damage of 1949–50 set the Industry back for many years in more ways than just the loss of trees and production. Costs rose during the 1950s throughout the Industry and with the loss in production, overhead costs were further exaggerated...During these difficult years the concept of Central Selling and the operation of all parts of the Industry, including BCFGA, were questioned by many growers. It was a period of unrest and disappointment which culminated in the Royal Commission Report of 1958 by Dean E.D. MacPhee...

The development and operation of this Industry and of Central Selling has depended upon people. Growers, delegates, committee members, elected officials, shippers, government workers and BCFGA staff have all made their contribution. However, special mention should go to three men whose influence has been greatest. Firstly, Mr. A.K. Loyd, who in 1939 was the man who brought together the conflicting groups to launch Central Selling, and, as the first President and Manager of B.C. Tree Fruits, developed it as an organization. Secondly, Mr. A.R. Garrish, whose wise counsel over many years has influenced basic policy, especially in the area of grower participation and control of Industry policy. Thirdly, Mr. R.P. Walrod who, in addition to his contribution through the development of Sun-Rype, has built up loyal and efficient staffs in both grower companies who are the envy of all other producer groups, and our main asset in meeting the problems ahead.[23]

(*OHS*, 1985)

An orchard near Winfield. Spring, a time of beauty and promise.
Vernon Museum

Twenty-five years after Gordon Wight presented the report quoted above, the BCFGA commissioned David Dendy and Kathleen M. Kyle to write a history of the organization. This interesting and informative book was published in 1990 under the title *A Fruitful Century: The British Columbia Fruit Growers' Association 1889–1989*. There David Dendy summarizes the findings of the 816-page document that Dean E.D. MacPhee presented to the government as the Report of the Royal Commission.[24]

• [Dean MacPhee] gave good marks to the management of both B.C. Tree Fruits and B.C. Fruit Processors...
• He found that the greatest part of the hostility to B.C. Tree Fruits was actually misplaced.
• He recommended consolidation and amalgamation to provide a single packing co-operative in each of the four major regions.
• The grower had to take a greater responsibility for the marketability of his fruit, rather than, as had often been the case, simply churning out fruit of uncertain quality and then making the selling agency the scapegoat when returns were unsatisfactory.

Arthur K. Loyd had emigrated from England in 1910 and had settled in the ill-fated Walhachin. After serving in the Royal Canadian Artillery during World War I he took up residence in Kelowna where he worked as a pruner for the L & A Company. Gradually he acquired an orchard of his own. Loyd rose to prominence during the "Cent a pound or on the ground" campaign of 1933 and was elected president of the BCFGA in 1935. Under his guidance the industry moved to one-desk marketing through B.C. Tree Fruits Ltd. in 1939. He was the first chairman of the board, president and general manager of that operation. In 1940 he stepped down as president of the BCFGA in order to devote himself entirely to the sales agency.

In 1946 he was made a member of the Order of the British Empire by King George VI in recognition of his services in the field of agriculture. He continued to serve the industry until 1955.

Changing Technology

In the early years of commercial production the fruit industry was labour-intensive. Apples were packed right

Arthur Garrish, in addition to operating sixteen acres planted to apples, prunes, peaches and apricots in the Oliver area and participating in his packing house co-operative, served as president of the BCFGA from 1951 to 1965. During his presidency it was settled that the BCFGA and its subsidiary organizations would be grower-controlled rather than controlled by paid officials. Recalling the winning of this battle, Garrish is reported to have said, "All that was left was to cope with the vagaries of the weather, the vagaries of the market, the bitchy-mindedness of the growers, and to keep the damn show running." [25]

The packing floor at the Vernon Fruit Union c. 1940. Each apple is wrapped in tissue paper. The nailer on the left is putting lids on the packed boxes.
Vernon Museum 812

in the orchard until growers could afford to build small packing houses on their property. Then came the co-operative packing houses and those belonging to independent shippers, where the apples and other fruits were drawn by belts along the sorting tables and delivered to packing benches. Bench packing employed the principle of the division of labour. There were dumpers, sorters, packers, pressmen, labellers and the most colourful of all, boxmakers.

Orchardist Clement Battye's long experience in the fruit industry began when as a lad of sixteen in 1916 he began making boxes in Kaleden. In "The Lowly Apple Box" Mr. Battye describes the nailer's bench and the motions necessary to create a box from the bundled components known as "shook." He writes:

> Every time the twenty-five boxes had been made a new supply of shook had to be placed in position, the wires cut and the whole process repeated. The work of getting supplies into position, cutting wires, replenishing the nail supply, making boxes, stacking boxes and trucking them away, was completed at the speed of from fifty to ninety boxes per hour, depending on the skill of the boxmaker. The writer once made four hundred boxes in four hours. There were probably eight or ten boxmakers in the Okanagan who could make a hundred per hour for a short period. [26]

Cedric Boyer, in his article "Thirty-three Years in the Fruit Industry," [27] describes the various containers manufactured to accommodate fruits and vegetables—pear boxes, peach lugs, "suitcases" for prunes, celery crates and "coffins," veneer tin-tops for cherries and grape baskets, etc. Then as pine wood became more scarce and more expensive, cardboard and cell-pack boxes were introduced.

With the introduction of the great 25-box bins into the orchards, hauling the apples out to the road by hand or stoneboat became impossible. One began to see the packing-house truck towing a fork-lift on its mission to pick up some grower's fruit. Growers began to replace ladders for picking and pruning with giraffes or girettes. All this change in technology eliminated much of the bull-work in the industry and reduced money paid out in wages but at the same time increased the capital outlay in both fruit production and packing, thus making it more difficult for young growers to become established. Escalating land prices due to urbanization also increased the capital investment in an orchard. During difficult times many young growers were forced to give

up, losing even what they had invested.

Aware of the pressures urbanization was putting on BC lands the provincial government in March 1973 brought in the Land Commission Act, Bill 42, which froze agricultural lands and initiated the examination of all lands in the province with a view to determining what use was in the public interest.[28] While the initial freeze of all agricultural land was met with vociferous resistance from some growers, it became clear that if the fruit industry was to survive the land reserve must be large enough to support the infrastructure of packing and shipping facilities and the marketing organization.

There was one development which had gradually taken place, the use of vehicles driven by internal combustion engines. Trucks began to replace horses and wagons. Soon automobile owners were demanding new roads and improved roads. This revolution in transportation was destined to affect not only the physical handling of Okanagan fruit, but also to challenge the co-operative marketing strategies. Finally, with the opening of the Hope–Princeton Highway in 1949 and the Rogers Pass in 1962 it was no longer possible to control the shipment of fruit out of the Okanagan to Vancouver over the first and to Alberta through the second. The day of the peddlers or "fruitleggers" had come. This fact was to have a profound effect on central selling. No longer could the disposal of fruit from Okanagan orchards be controlled.

*Main Street of Summerland looking east c. 1921. In the foreground is Donald Temple's democrat. Cars were driven on the left-hand side of the road until January 1, 1923.
Elvira (Temple) MacDonald*

Arthur Garrish was one of the first to realize what changes were occurring. His analysis "The Orderly Marketing System" concludes:

> I think the industry took a lot of credit for something that was possibly largely due to a combination of geography and history...I hope that my message is not entirely negative, but having extolled the virtues of the Orderly Marketing System built up by the fruit industry in British Columbia to many groups over the years, maybe it is time to get up and admit that the system is not here anymore.[29]
> (*OHS*, 1986)

In *A Fruitful Century* Kathleen Kyle chronicles the main issues faced by the BCFGA from 1978 through 1989. For example, in 1984 the Provincial Government extended Farm Income Insurance to non-BCFGA members, a policy which resulted in some growers dropping their BCFGA memberships. In the "Afterword" of the book several past presidents of the BCFGA—Allan Claridge, Charles Bernhardt, Richard Bullock, George Fraser and Gerald Geen—present their views as to the role of the BCFGA in years to come. All acknowledge the need for the organization as the voice for the fruit growers, especially in view of the increasing pressures on the industry.

When the Okanagan Similkameen Growers built their packing house in Oliver in the 1970s the plant was state-of-the-art. Instead of the apples being rolled about they were floated, thus avoiding bruising. *Sandra Smith*

Ground Crops

The soils in various parts of the Okanagan–Similkameen and Shuswap Valleys have always been suitable for field crops, but to find markets has been a problem. In 1893 Alfred Postill called a meeting at the Benvoulin school, near Kelowna, to discuss what could be done to sell the produce. It was decided to send a committee of four men—Howard Dell, Mark Howard, John Casorso and R.S. Hall—to Sandon in the Kootenay, where hard-rock mining was booming, to investigate the possibility of selling produce there. The committee constructed a warehouse near the CPR tracks in Sandon and left R.S. Hall in charge. The others returned to the Okanagan and prepared to send fruit, vegetables and hay to their new depot, thus establishing the first example of co-operative marketing in the Okanagan. In 1896 the Kelowna Shippers' Union was incorporated.[30] The next year D.E. Gellatly shipped the first carload of potatoes from his farm on the west side of Okanagan Lake to the Kootenay.[31]

During the same period men like Frank Richter in the Similkameen Valley and John Casorso of Okanagan Mission found a market in the Boundary Country and as far east as the Kootenay. Hogs and cattle were driven to market and slaughtered when a buyer was found, but the produce of the fields had to be delivered by pack horse and wagon. Leslie Hill of Osoyoos shipped his fruit and vegetables to the mining country via the Great Northern from Oroville at the south end of Osoyoos Lake.

After the turn of the century however, as mining activity diminished new markets had to be found. Casorso, blessed not only with fertile acres but with seven able and energetic sons, sent two of his sons, Charlie and Tony, to investigate the marketing possibilities in communities along the CPR tracks from Kamloops to Saskatoon. As a result Casorso decided to try the prairie market. Victor Casorso, in his book *The Casorso Story*, writes:

> When the first load of produce was ready for shipment to the Prairies, Charlie went with it, riding in the train's caboose to its destination. It sold without problems and many more carloads followed. If only a part of the produce was sold in a town and the market appeared to be saturated, the boxcar was moved elsewhere along the tracks until the fragile cargo was disposed of.[32]

So successful was this energetic marketing that more acres were brought into production to meet the demand.

The Casorso onion field near Kelowna which yielded 30 tons to the acre. The Roman Catholic Church is in the background. *Kelowna Museum*

John Casorso became known as the "Okanagan Onion King" and his onions reached as far as the Montreal market.

Victor Casorso tells an amusing story about a renegade wholesaler in Montreal who claimed that the onions shipped to him had arrived in such poor condition that they had to be dumped. Knowing that the onions had left the Okanagan in excellent condition, John sent Charlie east to pose as a prospective buyer. There in the warehouse of the dishonest wholesaler he was shown his father's entire shipment which was highly recommended to him. Charlie returned home with the payment for the onions in his pocket.[33]

In 1908 W.A. Cuthbert, the youngest son of a prominent Scottish shipping family, arrived in Armstrong and invested in five acres of bottom land at $500 an acre and twelve acres at $400 an acre. He paid the $7,300, which was a large sum in those days, in cash. This land he rented out to Chinese growers for as much as $60 an acre. From 1910 Mr. Cuthbert made his permanent home in Armstrong where he became a shipper, his firm being known as Fairfield Ranch. In 1923 Fairfield Ranch amalgamated with E. Poole and Associated Growers to form Armstrong Packers.[34]

The crop grown most successfully by both Chinese and some white farmers was celery, which had been introduced by E.R. Burnett soon after the turn of the century. So suitable were the growing conditions that Armstrong was to become the "Celery Capital of Canada." In his article "Farms and Enterprises in the North Okanagan," R.R. Heal tells us:

> Celery entails more work and more gardening skill than most crops since rust develops if there is excessive moisture on the leaves. It can be grown successfully if it has a rich soil and sub-irrigation. These conditions prevail on Armstrong's bottom lands. The rich muck land used is just south of the watershed divide and because the drop to Okanagan Lake from this point is low, the run-off is slow and much water travels just below the surface of the land through the "flats."
>
> The first Chinese gardeners came to Armstrong in 1906 or 1907. There were 400 in the district by 1914. To a large extent they operated on the bottom lands and grew the celery, lettuce and potatoes produced there...[35]
> (*OHS*, 1952)

Much of the vegetable gardening on the rich bottom land around Armstrong was done by Chinese gardeners. They were meticulous workers. ASMAS #3802

W.A. Cuthbert found an early market for Armstrong celery and lettuce supplying CPR dining cars and hotels as far east as Calgary. R.R. Heal goes on to tell us:

In World War I, when root vegetables of all kinds and, especially, potatoes were urgently needed to supply the troops, celery production slumped. After the war, however, there was increased production. About 100 acres, or one third of the bottom land cultivated by the Chinese was devoted to celery production, and approximately 1000 tons of celery were shipped annually. About 50 percent of this was shipped in straight carlots...Since 1932, Kelowna has competed successfully in the celery trade. Armstrong's acreage consequently, has gradually decreased until now [1952] only 50 or 60 acres are being grown annually.

*A fond farewell: The Chins leaving Armstrong to retire in Vancouver.
Photo by J. Jamieson
Armstrong Museum*

Two of the first Chinese to enter the labour-intensive business of growing celery were Jong Hughey and Louie Chin. Neils O. Kristensen, in his 1985 prize-winning essay,[36] names other Chinese growers: Lee Back Bongs and Wong Chog. The Chinese rented land and thus became producers. Wong Chog also shipped produce.

On the Grandview Flats northwest of Armstrong farmers grew vegetables, interestingly, without irrigation. However, as time went on and the area became a Seventh Day Adventist settlement the principal crop became potatoes. In the 1950s vegetable production throughout the Okanagan began to decrease. Irrigation projects in the prairie provinces enabled farmers there to grow vegetables and thus supply markets beyond the Rockies more economically than could BC shippers. Dolph Browne who bought Armstrong Packers in 1955 found that he had to close down the operation in 1958, thus virtually ending vegetable growing and shipping in Armstrong.

Efforts were made to emulate the organization of the fruit growers. Representatives from Kamloops, Armstrong and the Okanagan, including Oliver and Osoyoos, sat on the BC Interior Vegetable Marketing Board. Overproduction was a constant worry. So often those dreaded "stop pick" orders left good tomatoes or cucumbers rotting in the field.

One rather unusual field crop grown in the South Okanagan and Similkameen between 1935 and 1965 was the zucca melon, a giant bottle gourd (*Lagenaria siceraria*). These melons grew to four feet in length and up to 120 pounds and had the "virtue" of being tasteless, odourless and colourless. Hence their use in making candied peel for baking from the rind and a filler for jam from the flesh. These great plants, which were very hard on the soil, went out of production so completely that when the grist mill at Keremeos wanted to grow zucca melons in its heritage garden the staff had to search the continent for seeds. Finally a grower

*Louie Chin was one of the first Chinese farmers to enter the business of growing celery in Armstong.
Armstrong Museum*

A field of zucca melons at Osoyoos. Oliver & District Heritage Soc. OLP 488.60.1

Pea Growers Ltd. processed and marketed legumes for the Armstrong Spallumcheen area between 1937 and the mid-1990s. ASMAS #5214

who had the seeds was found in Sandwich, Illinois.

Tobacco was another crop tried. Helen Payne gives an account of the tobacco industry in Kelowna, describing the labour-intensive growing and curing procedures required.[37] In the 1890s Louis Holman and John Collins promoted the growing of cigar tobacco in the Okanagan Mission area. The product was more than satisfactory and a good-quality cigar was manufactured in Kelowna. However, when mining slowed down in the Kootenay and Slocan the principal market was gone. After World War I tobacco suitable for pipe smoking and cigarettes was grown but growers found it impossible to compete with Ontario and Quebec farmers who were much closer to big markets. Growers in the Similkameen and South Okanagan alike were disappointed. Only a few of the drying barns with their distinctive ventilators along the roof ridge now remain to remind us of a past era.

Pioneer farmers were not unacquainted with fruitless labour whether the cause was the vagaries of the weather or the difficulties of finding a lucrative market. Christopher Tickell tells us about some painful agricultural experiences in the Cawston area. During World War I, a Mr. Orser arrived in Cawston and set up a cannery, paying growers $8 a ton for their tomatoes. (Growers bought their field boxes from Orser.) Ownership of the cannery passed finally to the growers themselves who pledged $10 a share to the enterprise. Tickell recalls:

> About the year 1927 we experienced one of the finest years for growing tomatoes because the growing conditions were as near perfect as possible. The whole large crop was harvested and delivered to the cannery in excellent condition.
>
> Then the blow fell. We were told we would not get any money for our crop, not a cent. To add insult to injury, the $8.00 still outstanding on the shares was called in to help pay whatever it was that had to be paid...The directors sold the tomatoes to the New Westminster firm at no set price. It virtually amounted to making a present of 120 acres of tomatoes to the New Westminster firm...
>
> Shortly after the war the Department of Agriculture at Ottawa sent men around advising farmers to grow mangel seed which, owing to the war, was expected to be in demand in Europe...Fifteen of us each planted one acre...We were instructed to ship the seeds to the United Seed Growers in Penticton. There was a very good crop of seeds. After two years had

Harvesting tobacco near Kelowna, 1890s. The process of growing and curing this crop was labour-intensive.
Kelowna Museum

passed, we got a notice to pick up our seeds or they would be dumped. The seeds were dumped. The growers got nothing.

About a year later, a man arrived in Cawston promoting tobacco growing. He said he would buy all we could grow. About 20 acres were planted. A wonderful crop was grown and harvested, then placed in a drying barn. Two years later the tobacco was taken out of the barn and burned. No one got any money out of this.[38]

(*OHS*, 1975)

Grapes

Bernard Lequime tells us that Father Pandosy wrote to Father D'Herbomez in October 1859 expressing his intention of bringing grape vines into the Mission.[39] We do not know if this was done as Bernard Lequime writes that he never saw any trace of the vines. Later plantings were more successful as the following excerpt from an article by Dr. D.V. Fisher shows. The reader should keep in mind that Dr. Fisher is writing in 1981.

History of Grape Growing in the Southern Interior[40]
by D.V. Fisher

...The first record we have of a serious grape planting was that of W.J. Wilcox in Salmon Arm, who in 1907 planted about 3/4 of an acre to Campbell Early, Concord, Niagara, White Diamond and Delaware. This planting was gradually expanded to include Clinton, Thompson Seedless, Black Hamburg and Agawam. Because Salmon Arm is an unirrigated area and the vines matured early, grapes on the Wilcox place survived the various freezes reasonably well, and part of the planting still exists on the Don Raven farm. The grapes from the Wilcox planting were all packed in 6-quart wooden baskets and sold for fresh fruit purposes locally and as far away as the prairies.

According to Mr. F.E. Atkinson, a semi-commercial planting of grapes was made in Penticton in 1912 by Mr. Jim Creighton...

The pioneer commercial grape grower in the Okanagan was Mr. J.W. Hughes, who in 1926 acquired land in the Okanagan Mission and the Black Mountain areas. The Black Mountain project did not prove successful, but the one in Okanagan Mission gradually expanded until Hughes had around 300 acres in production. The Hughes plantings were dispersed between 1944 and 1949 to his foremen Dan Powell, Frank Schmidt and Martin Dulik. In the same period his Great West Vineyard was sold in pieces to George Nemeth, Tor Tovilla, W. Bata and Roy Francis. In the late 1940s and early 50s, small additional acreages were planted in the Okanagan Mission area, and in Westbank which brought the total acreage up to around 400.

About 1957, because of an increased demand for grapes by existing and new wineries, a new era in grape growing started. The emphasis at this time was upon planting of improved varieties of vinifera and vinifera hybrids to produce wines of superior quality to those formerly manufactured from grapes of the labrusca type. Accordingly, expansion of grape acreage which has taken place up to the present time [1981], when about 3200 acres are in production, has been largely in hybrid varieties.

The history of grape growing in B.C. is closely tied in with the development of wineries... Under the Liquor Control Board B.C. wineries are required to use British Columbia grapes when available, and when their needs exceed the supply, they are allowed to supplement their crush by purchase of American grapes. All these wineries operate under contracts with their growers...

Grape Variety Evaluation

The first grape variety test was planted at the Summerland Research Station by the late Dr. R.C. Palmer in 1928. This planting consisted of old standbys...By importing wine varieties from all over the world, including France, Italy, Hungary, and Madeira Islands, California, etc. the variety collection had risen to close to 150 by 1936...

When it became apparent around 1957 that a new era in grape culture was about to be initiated, the Summerland Research Station again went into a variety testing program, this time selectively choosing only varieties which had shown promise in northern areas of the North American continent, and which appeared to be capable of ripening under the heat units characteristic of the B.C. Interior…

The Rittich Brothers

The Rittich brothers, Virgil J. and Dr. Eugene A., did important variety testing work in the Ellison district near Kelowna, where they established their vineyard about 1931. The Rittiches were immigrants from Hungary and had had extensive experience in grape growing and wine making in their home country. They brought with them some 40 varieties. The Rittiches were concerned primarily with grapes for making high quality European-type wines...

It is a quirk of fate that the one successful variety of their Hungarian collection, the so-called Hungarian Riesling, did not appear in their favored list of 10. This variety is now considered to be the best high quality white European wine grape now grown in the Okanagan. It has been widely planted and wineries pay a premium for it. It is sufficiently hardy and early maturing to be grown successfully in most grape areas of the Okanagan/Similkameen Valleys. Dr. Rittich first planted this and other varieties on the Renyi property in Oliver in 1930. Mr. Mike Barzal of Osoyoos obtained cuttings of Hungarian Riesling from Renji and in time passed cuttings on to M. Keri, who gave cuttings to Mr. J.W. Detterbeak. Mr. Detterbeak made the first sizeable planting in Oliver in 1938 and later expanded it to about 3 acres...

J.W. Hughes

Any account of grape variety testing in the Okanagan would be incomplete without mention of the very important role played by Mr. Hughes in this matter. In his search for better varieties...he introduced a number of the hybrids from the Geneva Station in New York...Of these he favoured Bath and told me around 1962 that this was the best grape that had ever been grown in the Okanagan Valley. His prediction certainly came close to being true, for this variety is the second most widely planted, being acceptable for both fresh and wine purposes. It is also the most productive of the varieties we grow.

Cultural Practices

Originally, grapes were grown on the Kniffen 2-arm system and then on variations of cordon systems...Further modifications of training methods will be based upon the use of mechanized harvesting equipment such as was used in Oliver this past season. The Upright Harvester, which is similar to some other harvesters and costs about $35,000, straddles the rows and beats the fruit from the vines...This machine, which is adaptable only for wine or juice grapes, harvests 15 acres of grapes in 10 hours and, at half the cost, does the same work as hand picking by 30 men.

Irrigation, originally carried out by furrows or hand-moved sprinkler pipe has been largely replaced by overhead sprinklers on aluminum pipe placed on top of the posts supporting the grape wire trellis.

Birds, the greatest menace to profitable culture of many of the European hybrid grapes, are now successfully controlled by means of the Av-Alarm synthetic bird warning cry, combined with acetylene or propane exploders...

(*OHS*, 1981)

Free Trade and Estate Wineries

The Canada–United States Free Trade Agreement of 1988 affected profoundly the grape-growing and wine-making industry of the Okanagan. Although the upheaval was at first extremely upsetting the end result, according to John Schreiner in his book *The British Columbia Wine Companion,*[41] was a marked improvement in the quality of the wine produced.

Until 1988 domestic wines had been protected not only by tariffs on imported wines but also by the pricing and listing policies in the government liquor stores. The result was that wineries were satisfied to produce a mediocre product. In the late 1980s governments agreed to the elimination of these protective policies.

To ease the transition the federal and provincial governments set up a $28,000,000 adjustment fund to be paid to growers who uprooted their inferior vines and, if they wished, replanted with premium European varieties such as Johannisberger Riesling, Verdelet, Pinot Blanc, Gewurztraminer and Chardonnay. According to Schreiner, in 1988, 110 of 200 growers pulled out 1,335 hectares of vines...By 1995, 300 hectares of new plantings were in place. Not all commercial wineries objected to the new development. Mission Hill Winery, for example, welcomed the change and showed its faith in the industry by contracting for the grapes in 20 percent of Valley vineyards. In the change, bulk wines had suffered but premium wines had gained.

In the fall of 1989 the BC government passed legislation which enabled small vineyards to establish farm-gate wineries, at first called cottage wineries and later estate wineries, a designation suggested by Harry McWatters of Sumac Ridge Winery.

Production allowed in each estate winery was at first 30,000 gallons (about 180,000 bottles), but later this was increased to 40,000 gallons which did not include wine sold outside the province. Growers must own twenty acres of vineyards and produce their wine primarily from their own grapes. No sugar or water could be added. Some of the first estate wineries were Gehringer Brothers, Grey Monk and Sumac Ridge.

Commercial wineries were allowed to improve their bulk wines with the addition of sugar or imported wine as long as the bottling was done in BC. In return the commercial wineries agreed to give six-year contracts to the remaining vineyards. In 1990 Nick Clark of Mission Hill Wines began an eighteen-month stint as chief executive officer of the newly formed Vintners Quality Alliance, a program to identify and market top-quality BC wines.

An interesting note with regard to the wine industry is the production of ice-wines, made from grapes in which early frosts have caused the juice to crystalize to some degree. These wines were first made in Germany. By the 1980s there was a commercial production in Ontario. It was 1994 before there was extensive production in the Okanagan.

Agro-industries

Among the early attempts to process foods before marketing them we might count Francis X. Richter's drying prunes to give them a longer shelf life before selling them to miners or other settlers. But by far the most needed process was the milling of flour. Towards the end of the nineteenth century the simple grist mills such as those to be found in Keremeos (Barrington Price), Okanagan Mission (Frederick Brent) and on the Coldstream and

Armstrong Flour Mill c. 1940.
ASMAS #5210

O'Keefe Ranches were beginning to give way to more sophisticated plants.

In 1887 a very up-to-date roller mill was built in Enderby. The original owners could not make their mill pay and were forced to sell to R.P. Rithet, who paid creditors fifty cents on the dollar. Because Rithet was willing to pay farmers little more than the cost of producing the wheat, the farmers banded together under the leadership of Donald Graham to form in 1895 Okanagan Flour Mills Ltd., the first co-operative flour mill in BC. The mill operated successfully for just over ten years, at which time shareholders were informed that the mill was carrying too many uncollectible debts to remain solvent.[42] However, there was one very interesting transaction which occurred while the mill was in business. Frederick H. Barnes tells us: "The first shipment of Canadian flour to the Orient, shipped from a BC port, was manufactured at Enderby. It consisted of forty sacks marked 'J3, Kobi, Japan,' and was shipped on the 28th January, 1904."[43]

Milling was important also in Armstrong. In the fall of 1927 Charles Hoover purchased a flour mill and elevator which had stood idle at Armstrong for about twenty years. Hoover modernized the machinery, named the business Armstrong Inland Flour Mills and began to mill a good-quality white flour. He continued to manufacture Hoover's Whole Wheat Flour and porridges. In 1935 the mill began making alfalfa meal from hay and in 1936 puffed wheat, the latter shot from a gun which could be heard all over town. During the 1930s unemployed men who called at the mill were given small bags of flour and porridge.

In 1946 Charles Hoover sold the business to Buckerfields. The new firm retained the former employees including Everett Gamble who, by the time he retired in 1978, had given forty-eight years' service to the mill.[44] During World War I an evaporator had been built and vegetables were dried for use in military kitchens.

The Spallumcheen was good dairy country and two important dairy industries were established in Armstrong. The first was the North Okanagan Creamery Association (NOCA). Beryl Wamboldt tells us that in the 1920s a large herd would consist of about twenty-five milk cows. When farmers first formed a co-operative they ran into difficulties until they entered into an agreement with Pat Burns and Company to have that company finance and manage their affairs. On July 1, 1925 the new association consisting of 385 shippers went into business under the management of Everard T. Clarke, a former Burns employee.[45]

Everard Truman Clarke was twenty-four years old when he arrived in the North Okanagan and undertook the organization of the Okanagan Valley Creamery. By 1927 he had begun editing and publishing *The Cream Collector*, a periodical which was to appear monthly for the next forty years. Always in the forefront of developments in the dairy industry he encouraged artificial insemination, rural electrification and improved corn for silage. His work in NOCA brought him national and international recognition and responsibilities. A United Nations assignment in India led to his involvement in supporting two orphanages there. He also found time to serve the interests of his home community, on the Vernon City Council and on the committee that developed the Silver Star ski hill. For twenty-five years he was a director of the Okanagan Telephone Company.[46] Photo: Vernon Museum

On September 3, 1927 fire destroyed the NOCA creamery in Armstrong. Instead of rebuilding in Armstrong the directors decided to move their headquarters to Vernon. Mary H.E. Blackburn writes:

> The Vernon City Council lost no time in giving Pat Burns and Co. large facilities and concessions to centre the creamery business at Vernon and, as no such inducements or co-operation was forth-coming from the Armstrong City Council, the creamery was located in Vernon and Armstrong dairymen had to ship to Vernon or Salmon Arm or go out of business. Armstrong lost one of its most vital industries.[47]
> (*OHS*, 1983)

During NOCA's first years, buttermakers Walter Patten, Ernie Skelly and Bill Cameron made NOCA butter

INTERIOR PROVINCIAL EXHIBITION
ARMSTRONG, B.C.
SATURDAY, SEPTEMBER 9, 1989

famous. The company prospered and was able to buy out the Burns interest, expand south to Kelowna and Penticton and buy up smaller creameries until by 1976 it was the second-largest dairy in BC. In the spring of 1982 NOCA was bought out by the Fraser Valley Milk Producers Co-operative Association, better known as Dairyland. A $6,000,000 plant was built in Armstrong. In April 1996 the Okanagan administration was moved to Armstrong and the Vernon offices closed.

The second dairy industry to be born in Armstrong was cheese making which began after the arrival of Charles Busby, an experienced cheesemaker. In 1939 the Armstrong Cheese Co-operative Association was incorporated.[48] In 1941 Joe Mullen was hired as cheesemaker. In spite of a severe shortage of capital the enterprise progressed. By 1943 the co-operative was the second-largest producer of cheese in Canada. Other dairy products were added to the items manufactured and sold.

The mixed farming and fruit-growing economy fostered community-centred activities such as fall fairs where horticultural, home arts and animal husbandry exhibits competed for ribbons and small cash prizes. As improved automobiles and better roads eroded community cohesiveness many fairs were discontinued. However, Rock Creek Fair is still an annual event and the Armstrong Fair has become the Interior Provincial Exhibition, a great affair as this 1989 picture shows.
ASMAS #5208

However, by the mid-1950s the Armstrong Cheese Co-operative Association was facing new difficulties. Mrs. Blackburn believes two factors caused the board of directors to lose control of its costs: first the plant became unionized in 1953 and, second, at the request of the board of directors the BC Milk Board consented to control the fluid-milk production which meant that the price to the producer was established by the BC Milk Board, not the association. In 1958, 1959 and 1960 the association ran at a loss. Joe Mullen resigned as manager when the board would not take his advice to retrench rather than expand. In July 1961 the BC Central Credit Union called the overdraft and the plant had to close. Dairymen lost thousands of dollars.

Mary Blackburn finishes her article "Armstrong Cheese Co-operative Association"[49] with this note:

> The buildings of Armstrong Cheese Co-operative were purchased by Dutch Dairies of Kamloops. The new owners continued to make Armstrong Cheese and had the foresight to register the trade name "Armstrong Cheese" in every province in Canada...The business has since been sold to Dairyland together with the registered trade name "Armstrong Cheese" and it is still possible to purchase this excellent cheese in western Canada.

Armstrong Cheese is now made at Dairyland's Abbotsford plant. A development which had a profound effect on the lives of dairy farmers was the rural electrification which took place from 1947 under the BC Power Corporation. Not only were rural homes better lit and furnished with labour-saving equipment, but milking parlours were possible (Ernie Skyrme of Grindrod had the first in the BC Interior). Milk and cream could be kept refrigerated without the tedious work of cutting and saving ice during the winter, and pastures could be irrigated. Beryl Wamboldt writes: "Dairymen found more irrigated pastures produced better grazing, healthier animals and greater milk production which in turn brought higher monthly milk cheques. Along with green pastures control, came more grass silage and green chop feed."[50] (*OHS*, 1986)

Fruit and vegetable canning was another industry that flourished from the early years of this century. In 1909 Dominion Canners opened a plant in Peachland with Ed Todd as manager and H.O. Weatherill as assistant. So successful was this venture that the company took an option on a Kelowna plant and H.O. Weatherill was sent back to the Okanagan to supervise the enterprise. According to H.P. Weatherill the principal pack was tomatoes, ketchup, a few other vegetables and apples.[51]

In 1928 Thomas Bulman, who operated a fruit dehydrator in Ellison, decided to expand his business by building a cannery and dehydrator in Vernon. H.O. Weatherill was employed to manage the operation and stayed with the company until his retirement at the age of seventy-five. The plant, which from the beginning had been organized as a public company, survived the Depression and prospered during World War II. Mr. Weatherill served not only Bulman's but the industry as a whole, always seeking improvements within the plant and encouraging public awareness of good nutrition.

Sheep drive in 1952 along Shuswap River at Weir's Bluff (Mara Lake Road). At that time sheep being driven between the wintering pens at the home ranch and the high mountain pastures had the right of way on the highway. (Photo by Donovan Clemson.)
Clemson Family

During the canning season his wife Grace was always on the cannery floor as forelady with the responsibility of training and supervising the large force of female workers.

What led to the decline of the company? D.N. Weatherill, who spent many years in the employ of the company his father had done so much to develop, sees a number of reasons for the decline of canning in the Valley. For one thing it became difficult to get enough product when stoop labour became scarce. The bulk of the tomatoes were ripe for harvesting after students returned to school and those adults available for agricultural work preferred picking tree fruits. During the final years of operation it became cheaper to make ketchup from puree imported from Portugal than to use local tomatoes. The severe winters of 1949-50 and 1954-55 wiped out the peaches, apricots and apples needed for canning the following summer. Marketing patterns thus disrupted proved difficult to re-establish. Companies like Safeway with its vertical integration in which Safeway stores stocked their shelves with tomato and berry products canned in Safeway canneries on the prairie were tough competition. Frozen foods began to replace canned fruit and vegetables.[52] A disastrous fire about 1968 destroyed the Bulman plant.

Unfortunately H.P. Weatherill's article about his father is the only substantial treatment of cannery history printed in the *Reports of the Okanagan Historical Society*. However, information about the canneries of the Okanagan, Similkameen, Salmon Arm, Kamloops and Kootenay is being collected by Denise Nahirney, museum co-ordinator at the BC Orchard Industry Museum in Kelowna. Mrs. Nahirney believes the Peachland Jam Factory, which opened in 1888, to be the first canning operation in the Okanagan. During World War II and into the 1950s there were about forty active canneries in the Valley. By 1997 there were none.[53]

The manufacture of fruit juices in the Okanagan Valley has a happier history. On May 8, 1946 BC Fruit Processors Ltd., a subsidiary of BC Tree Fruits, was incorporated. The intention was to turn cull apples and low-grade apples into a marketable product. The new company soon absorbed small operations such as Louis Deighton's plant which he had operated since 1937 with the support of the Oliver Co-op. BC Fruit Processors produced a range of items, the most successful being various fruit juices and pie fillings. In 1959 the name of the company was changed to Sun-Rype Products Ltd. As the standard of fruit grown improved, raw product for processing decreased. However, Sun-Rype has been so successful with its juice production and its readiness to adopt new methods of packaging that in 1996 another company, Clearly Canadian, made an aggressive but unsuccessful attempt to take over Sun-Rype. BCFGA directors advised growers to reject the buy-out bid,[54] which they did.

One man closely associated with Sun-Rype through the years was Ian Greenwood, who served as general manager 1964–1982. From 1970 to 1982 this post was combined with the general managership of BC Tree Fruits. Mr. Greenwood had grown up in the Kootenays but had spent many of his student summers working in Okanagan orchards and later at the Summerland Research Station. After graduating from the University of British Columbia with a major in food science, Ian Greenwood spent 1949–1952 working in Bulman's laboratory developing new product lines. This was followed by six months in 1952 with Armstrong Cheese. Then in 1952 he went to work in the laboratory of Sun-Rype's predecessor. Thus, before assuming administrative duties, he had a very broad experience with the scientific aspect of Okanagan agro-industries.

Another person who had played a big role in the processing of Okanagan fruit and was no doubt an inspiration to Ian Greenwood was F.E. "Ted" Atkinson. Ted Atkinson grew up in Penticton, graduated from Oregon State University with a BSc in food technology and from 1929 worked as research officer for the Canadian Department of Agriculture in Summerland until his retirement in 1965. During his thirty-six years at the Summerland station he attracted national and international recognition and among other honours he was named the first honorary life member of the Canadian Institute of Food Technologists. During his busy life he found time to serve nine years as alderman in Summerland and eight years as mayor. In 1962 he founded Summerland Sweets Ltd. whose candies, syrups and jams can be found in specialty shops throughout western Canada. This family business continues to prosper.

In his article "In the Beginning" Dr. Atkinson writes about some of the early projects he worked on in the Summerland labs. The experiments in making brandy and fruit liqueurs, undertaken seriously and with the best of intentions, did not bring him acclaim. He writes:

> When the project started, Bill Hunter (Director of the Station) had asked me if I could design a still to which I replied, "Sure." I said that I had bought a 20-gallon copper kettle and outlined to him how I would proceed. He said, "Well, okay, we'll put the kettle in the back of the Chev, and take it to Leckie's Hardware in Kelowna and see Mr. Burnett, the tin-smith."...In the end we had a still which had cost $135.00, but Mr. Hunter had not received permission from Ottawa to buy a still! I paid for it with money from dehydrated fruit. This later got me into very hot water![55]
> (*OHS*, 1979)

The brandy business was given up and less contentious projects undertaken.

16
Military Matters

Early Military Organizations

Early in April [1902], Cecil Nicholson and Wm. Brent, who had served in the South African war, returned home. It was a day of much rejoicing and the two were given a rousing welcome. Unfortunately, two others who also served in the war, H.C. Stillingfleet and Ed. Hayward, did not arrive at the same time, but came separately several weeks later. Another young man, by the name of Begg, also from Kelowna, was killed in battle in South

Vernon contingent of Boer War veterans. Vernon Museum 297

Africa. All of these men had joined the Strathcona Horse, a mounted regiment completely equipped by Lord Strathcona. Bernard Avenue was gaily decorated and a huge arch, covered with evergreens, flags and bunting, had been erected a short distance from the CPR dock. They were each handed a two-foot long key to the town, made by Wm. McQueen, local blacksmith. On behalf of the citizens, D.W. Sutherland made the presentation, at the same time welcoming the two men home. Then, Cecil and Billy were hoisted into a buggy, with Archie McDonald and John Brown, the two biggest men present, at the shafts. Everyone who could put a hand to the vehicle and away they went, through the arch and up Bernard Avenue, while everyone cheered. It was an event long remembered by those present.
(*OHS*, 1960)

Certainly the event was still a vivid memory for J. Percy Clement when he wrote his article "Early Days in Kelowna"[1] many years later. There were Boer War veterans who had enlisted from other Okanagan and Shuswap centres too, but arrived in the Okanagan after the conflict and later played important roles in Valley development. They had enlisted elsewhere. For example, Jack Kermode had enlisted in Brandon, Manitoba; A.S. Hatfield in New Brunswick. Richard Guy Pearse Bagnall joined the Militia Medical Staff Corps in Ireland and served with the British army in South Africa. Veterans were numerous enough to warrant a reunion in the Valley in 1957.

Interest in military organization in the Okanagan did not begin with the Boer War. Colonel D.F.B. Kinloch tells us that the first mention of a unit of militia in the Valley may be found in the issue of the *Vernon News* dated June 9, 1898.[2] However, this first attempt to organize a unit was abortive and Vernon had to wait until 1908 before the Okanagan Mounted Rifles came into being. Five independent companies of Rocky Mountain Rangers were officially recognized July 1, 1898, Kamloops being one and the others in Revelstoke and the Kootenay. The history of this regiment appears to be continuous from that time although the Kootenay companies were soon to withdraw because of the difficulty of travelling to joint camps.

Terence B. Upton writes:

Captain J.R. Vicars commanded the Kamloops Company from 1899, and the Regiment from February 1912 till his retirement in 1925. An independent infantry company organized at Armstrong on June 1, 1908 was absorbed into the...Regiment as of March 1, 1912... [On September 3, 1912 the regimental headquarters was moved to Kamloops and two new companies added, a second in Kamloops and a re-established company in Revelstoke.]

The war clouds were now beginning to gather in Europe and the effects were clearly to be seen, even in British Columbia. In November 1913, a new company was formed at Kelowna. During 1914 the Regiment was increased to eight companies with a company at Salmon Arm (16 Mar 14), one at Vernon (15 Sep 14) and one at Penticton (15 Dec 14).[3]

It is difficult to understand from a late-twentieth-century perspective just how people in the nineteenth century felt about war and military service. They had not suffered the disillusionment of two world wars and could still believe that war was glorious. Most settlers had had military experience themselves or had close relatives who had. Vernon, for example, from its earliest days had become the home of men with military backgrounds such as Colonel Houghton and the Vernon brothers. Subsequent settlers were often men who had served in what Byron Farwell called *Queen Victoria's Little Wars*.[4] John Creighton, who could subdue the bar-room crowd at the Victoria Hotel with his flute playing, was a veteran of the Crimean War and the Indian Mutiny.[5] J.A. McKelvie, better known for his journalism and interest in politics, was a veteran of the North West Rebellion, another of the Queen's little wars. Such men found military values attractive: the discipline and order, the ceremonial parades, the codified manners and the emphasis on tradition. But beyond this taste for the military there were the fears that lay only slightly below the surface in the minds of the late-nineteenth-century establishment and which Terence B. Upton expressed in his article.

> During the last decade of the nineteenth century the scattered Whites of British Columbia's interior were much concerned that they were greatly outnumbered by Indians. In the mining districts of the Kootenays there was always threat of labour troubles, and there was an inadequate law enforcement force. In case of war with the United States—not such a remote eventuality in those days—there was literally nothing to prevent almost immediate disruption of the vital rail link of the C.P.R. Therefore, in response to repeated representations from residents of British Columbia's interior, the government authorized the formation of five independent rifle companies, with effect July 1, 1898...These independent companies were authorized to be named Rocky Mountain Rangers with effect January 1, 1900, but they were still independent companies...The pay was negligible...The officers financed many of the Company's endeavours from their own pockets...The men worked hard and played hard. The companies as much resembled exclusive men's clubs as groups of soldiers, and as long as the companies had enthusiastic officers and non-commissioned officers they did not lack for strength...

Finally, in 1908, "B" Squadron Okanagan Mounted Rifles came into being in Vernon through the efforts of Messrs. E. Copley Thompson, Price Ellison, and J.A. McKelvie. Officers and instructors were usually veterans of the South Africa War. Colonel Kinloch writes:

> Major H.A. Perry, D.C.M., a veteran of the South African War, was appointed to command. Other officers of the Squadron were: Captain H.A. Holland, Lieutenants R.S. Mutrie, M.V. Allen, E.J. Sunderland, R.O.G. Bennett and C.C. McRae...Authority was granted in 1910 to form a Regiment of Cavalry to be known as the 30th B.C. Horse. Since Major Perry had died during the year, command of the unit was given to Lt. Col. C.L. Bott. Colonel Bott was a veteran of the South African War and an officer of considerable experience...Regimental headquarters was in Vernon with Major H.A. Holland as Second-in-Command, Capt. the Hon. C.D. Finch, Adjutant, Capt. J.T. Mutrie, Quartermaster. Later Major Clarke formed "D" Squadron, taking in Penticton, Kelowna, and as far north as Winfield.
> Camp that year [1910] was held in the Exhibition Grounds just north of Vernon. Next year camp was at Kamloops, and from then on until 1914 on Mission Hill, Vernon. This was to become the site of many Militia camps and of a large Training Centre for Canadian troops in the two World Wars.[6]

G.P. Bagnall, who served as medical staff sergeant, tells an amusing story in connection with the 1911 camp held at Kamloops. "B" Squadron had ridden the seventy miles from Vernon to Kamloops and spent ten days in training. On the return journey the squadron stopped at Westwold. Mr. Bagnall writes:

> Returning to Vernon, the troops bivouacked for the night at Grande Prairie, now known

as Westwold, where they were ordered to off-saddle and place their mounts in a corral. As the horses were released inside the corral, they lined up in sections of fours, in true military formation, with Major M.V. Allen's horse in the lead, and smartly trotted around inside the corral. The riderless and tired mounts continued their performance, circling the corral for about twenty minutes, while the troops scrambled up the corral rails to cheer their mounts.[7]

World War I

In 1913 the 30th and 31st Regiments of the British Columbia Horse had attended a camp which opened June 2 on the rising ground south of Vernon near the Jubilee Hospital. The complement of seven hundred officers and men included soldiers from at least ten other companies or regiments.[8] The camp was recommended for its comforts—showers, telephones and a dry canteen. Art Langdeau tells us, "The camp remained as a summer camp throughout the war...and a tented facility."[9]

The "Whizzbangs"[10]

At the outbreak of war in August, 1914, the [Okanagan] Regiment under Col. Bott was mobilized and brought up to War establishment. It took only a matter of 10 days to recruit up to strength...The Regiment carried out intensive training; also furnishing guards for the enemy alien internment camp which had been established at Vernon.

During this period details had been worked out for turning the Regiment into an overseas unit, with the result that when the Commanding Officer [Colonel Bott] received a wire on November 6th offering him command of the 2nd Canadian Mounted Rifles, he was able to wire Ottawa a complete slate of officers. The new unit was to be formed by amalgamating the 30th B.C. Horse with the Victoria Independent Squadron...

After many months of training and waiting the Regiment received orders on June 1, 1915, to proceed overseas...On arrival in France the 2nd C.M.R.'s became part of the 2nd Canadian Division, but in December of the same year, the C.M.R. Brigade was converted into infantry and tranferred to the Third Division. As infantry, the 2nd C.M.R.'s fought through until the end of the war...

The 2nd C.M.R.'s returned to Canada in 1919 under command of Lt. Col. George Chalmers Johnston, D.S.O., M.C., who was given the unit when Lt. Col. Bott relinquished command in October, 1916. Demobilization took place immediately.

(*OHS*, 1948)

The battle colours of the regiment were deposited in the sanctuary of All Saints Anglican Church, Vernon, there to be destroyed when a fire consumed the building on September 8, 1931. Only a few fragments were rescued and these rest in All Saints Memorial Chapel. New colours were dedicated and placed in the sanctuary of the new building by Rev. Charles E. Reeve on April 24, 1955 in the presence of some fifty original enlistees who had come from various locations in BC for the ceremony. Mabel Johnson, who has recorded the history of the battle colours of the Canadian Mounted Rifles[11]—or "Whizzbangs," to use their World War I nickname—describes the colours: "The battle silks have a purple background on which 10 battle honours are emblazoned in green and gold."

The Rocky Mountain Rangers

The Regiment was placed on Active Service on August 10, 1914, for local protective duties. This meant the placement of guard detachments on the main railroad bridges of the C.P.R....

On January 6th, 1916, Lt. Col. Vicars was ordered to commence recruiting for the 172nd Battalion, which eventually sailed for England on October 25th, 1916...From England the 172nd Battalion was broken up to provide reinforcements for the Canadian Corps in the field...The Regimental Colours hang in St. Paul's Cathedral Church in Kamloops.[12]

(*OHS*, 1962)

Depleted Manpower

Readers will have noted from the above how quickly men answered the call to arms. Within a week or ten days regiments would meet the requirements of war establishment. We find an example of this patriotic zeal in the following:

> When the First World War broke out the Coldstream Municipality was drained of its manpower. It is recorded in the minutes of the council's meeting of December 4, 1914, that "In closing the meeting Reeve Giles pointed out that this must be the last meeting of the year since a quorum could no longer be obtained, Councillors Grieve, Homer-Dixon, and Cunliffe having joined regiments for active service."[13]
> (*OHS*, 1951)

Such a loss of manpower was bound to affect civilian life. T.E. Jessett wrote an amusing article about his service in what remained in Vernon of the 30th BC Horse:

> Shortly after war broke out in August 1914, the regiment was called into active service... Left behind in Vernon was a headquarters recruiting group. When an internment Camp for enemy aliens was established on Mara Avenue, the regiment was re-established with four skeleton squadrons...
> Every day the guard marched along Mara Avenue, past our house, led by the small regimental band...The 30th B.C. Horse had difficulty maintaining the necessary strength. Many older men enlisted because of the hard times, and young boys joined the band. Because I could type and take a little shorthand, I was accepted as a trooper on December 5, 1916, while only fourteen years of age. A month later I was in the Orderly Room at the internment camp under Captain Carl Grossman, the adjutant.[14]
> (*OHS*, 1979)

The Duke of Connaught reviewing the troops at Camp Vernon in 1916. Vernon Museum 914

William Ruhmann, who lived in Vernon during the war years, had many memories similar to those of Tom Jessett. However, his support of the war effort took the form of service as an agricultural worker. In his article "Soldiers of the Soil" Ruhmann writes:

Lining up for dinner at Camp
Vernon c. 1916.
Vernon Museum 22

The war was seriously depleting the work force of the Okanagan. More than 22 per cent of the manpower had enlisted...Charlie White and I, just out of the sixth grade, got a job on the Dr. Reimer twenty-acre orchard located three miles north of town on the Swan Lake Road. It had been leased by Tom Kyte. Since navy beans were in demand for overseas shipment, Kyte had planted several acres in rows between the orchard trees. Our job was to pull the weeds. After finishing the weeding I worked also as chore boy. The Kytes boarded me. This ended my daily six-mile walk. I split the firewood, carried the water from the spring for Mrs. Kyte, hilled about a half-acre of potatoes and helped prepare the packing house for the apple harvest.[15]

(*OHS*, 1983)

William Ruhmann also had a clear recollection of the internment camp comprising ten acres at the intersection of 27th Street (Mara Avenue) and 43rd Avenue and surrounded by barbed wire. Here men, women and children lived in tents. The men worked on road projects such as the Monashee Road between Lumby and the Arrow Lakes.[16]

In subsequent years William Ruhmann took on even more demanding jobs. The contribution of schoolboys was appreciated and recognized for the author says:

On March 4, 1918, the formation of a national organization was announced. It was to be called Soldiers of the Soil. This was a plan to bring boys thirteen to eighteen years of age into a work force to assist farmers...Of the 1,671 British Columbia boys who took part in the Soldiers of the Soil program 200 were from the Okanagan Valley and twenty-six from the Vernon area.

(*OHS*, 1983)

World War II

The BC Dragoons[17]

In 1920 when the Canadian Militia was reorganized the Okanagan Regiment once again became a mounted unit, the BC Dragoons (formerly called the First British Columbia Mounted Rifles). Colonel Kinloch writes:

On re-organization the Regiment had headquarters at Vernon, with "A" Squadron at Vernon, "B" Squadron at Kelowna, and "C" Squadron at Penticton...In July 1940, Lt. Col. Oswell received orders to form the 5th Canadian Motor Cycle Regiment. In doing this, he used a slate of officers from the B.C. Dragoons...The 5th C.M.C.R., after recruiting up to strength, moved to Victoria, where it trained as a Motorcycle unit for a few months, when it was again re-organized becoming the 9th Armoured Regiment (British Columbia Dragoons)...

Arriving in the Mediterranean Theatre without heavy equipment, the 5th Division was unable to commit its armour until the spring of 1944...The Regiment fought with the Canadian Corps, part of the 8th Army, up Italy to the Valley of the Po. Early in the spring of 1945, the 1st Canadian Corps moved from Italy to Marseilles and from there by road to the Northwest Europe Theatre...On the return of the Active Regiment to this Province a welcome home ceremony was held in Kelowna, at which time Lt. Col. Angle, D.S.O., E.D., a resident of Okanagan Mission, was given the Freedom of the City.

With respect to the reserve regiment, the 9th (Reserve) Armoured Regiment (BCD) under the command of Lt. Col. C.W. Husband, ED, its role was one of home defence, most of its members being either too old or too young for active service. The squadron commander was Major H.R. Denison, who like Colonel Husband, had served in the 2nd CMR and had begun his military career with the Okanagan Mounted Rifles. Colonel Kinloch finishes his article with:

At the time the Active unit was demobilized, the Reserve was commanded by Major A.H. Grant, M.C. of Naramata and Penticton, Col. Husband having retired...Col. Angle relinquished command on August 31st, 1947, and the Regiment was taken over by your author [Lt. Col. D.F.B. Kinloch], who served with the 9th Armoured Regiment, having commanded a Squadron in Italy until wounded at Rimini in October 1944. At present [1948], Regimental Headquarters is at Vernon, with Squadrons at Vernon, Kelowna and Penticton.
(OHS, 1948)

The Rocky Mountain Rangers[18]

The years 1920 to 1939 were lean years for the Militia. Appropriations were meagre and public interest at a low ebb. Only determination of its officers and men kept the units alive. The Rocky Mountain Rangers owed much to the unfailing interest of Lt. Col. J.R. Vicars till his retirement and to Lt. Col. J.E. Wood who took over the command in 1931.

On August 26th, 1939, details of the Regiment were again called to Active Service for local protection duties. Detachments were sent to Red Pass Junction, Cisco, Lytton, and Prince George to guard the railway bridges...The guard duties were gradually taken over by the Royal Canadian Mounted Police.

On June 21st, 1940, the battalion was ordered to mobilize to full wartime establishment. The strength was then eight officers and eighty-one other ranks. A month later unit strength was up to 25 officers and 565 other ranks, and camps were located at Kamloops, Salmon Arm and Revelstoke.

On October 2, 1939 the battalion was moved to New Westminster for some four months of intensive training after which it was posted to Prince Rupert and later to various Vancouver Island communities.

Drafts of Active Service personnel were taken for overseas reinforcements and their places taken by N.R.M.A. men [conscripts]...In April the news was broken that the battalion was to proceed overseas as an entity, but all personnel were to be "Active." Many of the N.R.M.A. personnel volunteered to change to Active status...Much bitterness and bad feeling was generated between "Active Service" and "Home Defence" personnel during this transition period...

The battalion sailed from Halifax on May 24, arriving on June 2 at Wathgill Tent Camp near Leyburn in Yorkshire. It soon became clear that the 13th Canadian Infantry Brigade, and the Rangers with it, were to be broken up as reinforcements for units then fighting in France. Upton finishes his history thus:

In November 1944 the final blow fell. The Rocky Mountain Rangers moved from its last

WAR MEMORIAL
PENTICTON, B.C.

The war memorial at Penticton. During World War II the cannon was melted down as scrap.
Penticton Museum #074

camp at Helmsley, near York, to Aldershot and ceased to exist. Members of the Regiment fought in nearly every theatre of war, and many achieved distinction. However, no battle honours were awarded reinforcement battalions as they were after the 1914–18 War, so that members of the 1939–44 battalion must be content in the knowledge of a job well done. The foundation for that job of work was well laid during the lean years of the Non-permanent Active Militia.

(*OHS*, 1962)

from **Salute to the Pacific Coast Militia Rangers**[19]
by Ivan E. Phillips

Even before the Japanese attack on the American Fleet at Pearl Harbor, December 1941, there was apparent in British Columbia an ever increasing disquiet and an awareness of a potential threat to the security of the province...So it was not at all surprising that, when the storm broke, those who were charged with the responsibility for defence were inundated with letters and calls seeking guidance and leadership...

Actually, plans were already in the embryo stage for raising and recruiting...a force...which followed closely the purpose and scope of the Home Guard in Britain...On February 25, 1942 the first public announcement was made...The new Corps was to be an auxiliary of the Canadian Armed Forces, and was created for the purpose of defence...Recruits from all walks of life literally besieged the recruiting centres. Looking back, it seems incredible that in the first four months 10,000 men had been sworn in as Rangers [in BC]...At West Coast Headquarters a Staff Officer was selected to work under the direction of the Chief Commanding Officer...It was understood that enlistment should not affect a volunteer's civilian occupation. Conversely this condition would be waived in the event of enemy action.

During the summer months realistic operational exercises were held. Staged in thickly wooded areas and under conditions such as the Rangers may well have had to encounter, valuable experience was acquired. Travelling instructors, selected from Active Army ranks were thus able to teach Rangers in the field. Night operations too were not overlooked...Throughout the province groups of these determined, dedicated men met in schools, halls and even private houses to continue their training under their own instructors.

(*OHS*, 1975)

The recruits had enlisted without any expectation of pay. However, by 1943 the government recognized the need for some financial support for out-of-pocket expenses for travel, hall rental, instructional materials, etc. As time progressed and Canada's commitments to Britain and its own active forces were being met, supplies for the militia were more forthcoming, but "scrounging" and "improvising" tended to remain the operative words.

J.C. Wilcox writes in a good-natured self-deprecatory tone of his personal experience in the 87th Summerland Company PCMR:[20] "My greatest pleasure was working with the Communications group. Our instructor (M.R. McLarty) had headed up such a group in World War I and was an expert. We learned the Morse Code, hand and arm signals and how to communicate by use of lights. We helped McLarty to string wires to strategic points pretty well all over the district." McLarty himself told Ivan Phillips, "All my signallers were [good scroungers]. For I recall that lots of our wire was of the kind used for baling. This was scrounged from the packing houses. We must have put up hundreds of miles of wire, much of it in almost inaccessible places." At the pre-stand-down dinner held at the Legion Hall, Summerland on October 12, 1945 Capt. George Baldwin of PCMR Headquarters praised Captain MacDonald and his men for a job well done. Of the signallers he said: "They were given nothing and yet had the best equipment in the province."

Ivan Phillips finishes his article with the following:

The story of the Rangers as told would be incomplete were no mention made of the District P.C.M.R. Official Stand Down. This was held in Kelowna. Close to 700 of the Rangers attended and there were representatives from Revelstoke, Chase, Kamloops, Salmon Arm, Vernon, Westbank, Kelowna, Peachland, Summerland, Penticton, Kaleden, Oliver and Osoyoos. They were reviewed by Major General F.F. Worthington, C.B. M.C. M.M., who was the General Officer in Command of Pacific Command.

In his address to the Rangers, the Major-General said, "When I took over Pacific Command, I had hardly heard of the Rangers. I made it my business, by personal contact, to find out what the P.C.M.R. were. I found you masters of woodcraft and scouting. You have your own communication system, which was of a very mysterious character and of your own fabrication, the like of which no man has seen before—but it worked.

"I found you had rendered valuable assistance to the army, by acting as guides, to the R.C.A.F. in searching for lost fliers and downed planes, and also that you had assisted the Royal Canadian Navy...

"The Rangers are well known throughout British Columbia...I have under my command many good men, but none better than you."[21]

(OHS, 1976)

from **The Canadian Battle Drill Training Centre Coldstream Ranch**[22]
by Col. David F.B. Kinloch

At the [Coldstream] Ranch near Vernon, in the summer of 1942, was established Canada's first and only Battle Drill School. It was set up to train officers and NCO's in the rigours of modern warfare, under realistic battle conditions so that they could return to their various units and introduce the new Battle Drill concept.

Battle Drill was the reduction of military tactics to bare essentials which were taught to a platoon as a team. Battle Drill Training...was more comprehensive. It comprised special physical training, fieldcraft, battle drill proper, battle discipline and "battle inoculation." Battle inoculation called for simulation of actual battle conditions and involved the use of live ammunition fired over the soldiers' heads and simulated mortar fire and shelling by the use of "thunder flashes" and buried electrically-fired explosives. Complete fitness was imperative for this type of training. The purpose was to teach soldiers how to behave under fire and also to develop the kind of mental and physical toughness necessary to cope with the ruthless brutality of the enemy...

On May 1st, 1942 "A31 Canadian Battle Drill Training Centre" was placed on Active Service, with Lt. Col. J.F. Scott, E.D. in Command. The first location of the Centre was Courtenay, B.C...Although the location at Courtenay appeared excellent for training, a problem arose with fire hazard which would inhibit the use of live ammunition. In the meantime someone on the staff discovered the Coldstream Ranch which contained excellent training areas. Mr. Tom Hill, the Ranch manager, agreed to allow training to be carried on throughout the 11,000 acres, including use of the pastures, fields and timber without remuneration to the Ranch. The School built a log village for street fighting, constructed a full scale obstacle course and blasted a trench in the rock on the hillside where sections would experience overhead fire from all platoon weapons...

In October 1942, A31 Training Centre was upgraded and became "S10 Canadian Battle Drill School," and as such it continued to operate until October 1943, at which time it was disbanded on the formation of "S17 Canadian School of Infantry," with headquarters in Vernon Camp. From then on Battle Drill became one of the Training Wings under direct command of S17 and once again was renamed, becoming "S17 No.2 Battle Wing." The first Commander of the new School was Brigadier Milton F. Gregg V.C. The Wing remained at

Coldstream Ranch and carried on the same type of training...S17 School of Infantry remained in operation until the summer of 1945...In all a total of 1,902 men received Battle Drill training...

There is no question that the School fulfilled its aims and objects and that the type of training given was of great value to the Canadian Infantry units as well as to the candidates who survived the courses, although they might not have thought so at the time. Certainly those who eventually faced actual battle did so with a considerably increased chance of survival, thanks to the excellent training they received at Coldstream Ranch.

(*OHS*, 1983)

A few excerpts from the War Diary of A31 Canadian Battle Drill Training Centre:[23]

21-07-42 Weather Hot. Arrived in Vernon. What a hell-hole after Courtenay. Not one bit of shade on the camp ground and the students will have to travel miles in order to get suitable training areas, which we had on our doorstep at Courtenay.

22-07-42...All being bitten to death by mosquitoes. Feel sorry for the students of the next course if this heat keeps up.

24-07-42 Weather Extremely Hot. Getting straightened around. The trouble is, we will have to do it all over again within a month when our permanent camp is ready.

4-08-42 First casualty at Vernon, Lieut. R.F. Mackay of Pictou Highlanders shot in heel. Weather—Hot.

25-09-42 Lt. Jukes hurt by Thunderflash. Apparently...defective as it exploded in his hand blowing the tip off his index finger.

10-10-42 Weather—Very cold in morning and some of the category men are feeling it. The M.O. parade gets longer each day. Living in tents without a stove is hard to take even in the best of conditions.

21-10-42 Meeting of all O.C.s with General Pearkes...One hundred percent co-operation from General Pearkes, who, we feel, appreciates the value of our school.

24-12-42 Half day in camp. The residents of this area have been exceptionally generous with their invitations for Christmas dinner and most of the students and staff have been asked out to private homes.

4-01-43...This is the coldest day yet, almost zero...Training as per syllabus under difficulties. Four of the students with frozen feet. We are short of equipment for this kind of weather.

16-01-43 Ten Below this morning and we're having a hell of a time trying to keep warm. Why we ever left the Coast area no one knows. We knew what we were up against before we left Courtenay. How we can carry on under present conditions remains to be seen. Hot as hell in summer with rattlesnakes and below zero in winter without rum and trying to live in tents. One little stove to each marquee.

17-02-43 Had our first wedding. Lt. P. Hertzberg married Miss B. Corner. Lt. Hertzberg wanted the wedding at the camp so we turned over the Officers' Ante-Room. Officers' wives were in attendance and we all had a very pleasant time...Weather—fine and warm.

8-03-43 Major General G.R. Pearkes V.C., D.S.O., M.C., Brig. Hodson, Brig. Colquhoun M.C. and Major Firminger spent the day with us...We have a real friend in Gen. Pearkes. Before he arrived here we were crying in the wilderness...

8-08-43 Beautiful Sunday. Col. J.K. Howard of the U.S. Army arrived to spend a week with us. He appears to be a grand chap.

10-08-43 Col. Howard and Yank Levy out with school. They are very high in their praise. Levy says our school is the best run in Canada. That's nothing—the Governor General and Princess Alice think we're grand. Wish some of the powers that be would think us grand enough to give us buildings. Over a year now living in tents.

(*OHS*, 1983)

Commando Bay

Just ten miles north of Naramata lies a secluded cove which until World War II was known as Dunrobin's Bay, named after its first pre-emptor, L. Race Dunrobin. Between May 1944 and September of that year the cove was the location of a Special Operations Executive (SOE) training camp and thereafter was known as Commando Bay.

The SOE trained agents to perform or teach others how to perform sabotage, subversion and guerrilla warfare behind the enemy lines. Though civilian, the SOE worked closely with the military command in the theatre of operation. In Europe this British organization employed a number of Canadians who were national or the descendants of nationals of the targeted countries. Europeans could not be used in the Asian and Pacific theatre for the obvious reason that they would be too noticeable. However, as the mainland and islands of southeast Asia had many citizens of Chinese ancestry, it was decided to appeal to members of Canada's ethnic Chinese population to serve in this dangerous work. Those approached had already volunteered for regular military service.

Francis Woodley "Mike" Kendall, an extraordinary Canadian who had spent years as a mining engineer in China and who had already, although a civilian, given aid to the allied war effort, interviewed twenty-five young men who had been vetted by the Canadian military intelligence and the RCMP. Of these he selected twelve for the first group to be trained.[24]

Access to the Commando Bay camp was by a boat leased from Hugh Leir of Penticton. Everyone lived in tents. The day started with an early morning swim, even in May! Then a full day of lessons and exercises. Army instructor Sgt. Andrew Wylie McClure taught "demolition": how to blow up things—boats, railway tracks, communication equipment; Sgt. Jack K. Clayton taught unarmed combat or silent killing and gave instruction in small arms; Maj. Hugh John Legg gave wireless instruction to three or four men while the sergeants instructed the rest in aspects of guerrilla warfare. Among the items taught by Kendall was how to move about the country at night in silence and unseen. As only four of the twelve men could speak Chinese the others had to be taught at least the basics.

Debra Faraguna's article "Commando Bay" includes material based on an interview that Maj. J.V.H. Wilson of Paradise Ranch had with Major Legg in Scotland in May 1975. (The camp had picked up their mail at Paradise Ranch, their nearest neighbour.) The following quotation gives some idea of life at the camp:

> The four month training period was highlighted by a visit from Major General George Pearkes (G.O.C. Western Command), who was invited by Major Legg to spend a week-end at the camp in late July. The General accepted the invitation but was unaware of the informality of the camp until Major Legg met him in Penticton. Legg states:
>
> "When the time came, I went down to Penticton and met the General and walking to the boat to go to the camp, there was I in a pair of shorts and a rather dirty pullover and General Pearkes complete with red tabs, and I said to him that I was afraid that he was in for a bit of a shock with our camp because there was no rank, no uniforms, everybody ate together, and everybody acted as equals of each other.
>
> The General, however, entered wholeheartedly into the spirit of the camp; by the time he arrived at the bay he was dressed in a pair of old trousers and a sweater. He joined in the same routine as the rest of the men."[25]

In September the "Oblivion" group, as they were called, left Canada for Australia where they took training in parachute jumping, use of small boats and other matters relevant to their missions. Four of the group were dropped into the interior of Borneo where with the help of Native tribes they induced the Japanese occupiers to retreat to the coast. Four of these special soldiers won the Military Medal.

On September 17, 1988 two houseboats conveyed veterans and representatives of federal, provincial and municipal governments as well as a few special guests to the cove where the Oblivion group had taken its initial training. There a brass plaque was unveiled honouring the unit. Major Victor Wilson, while president of the Okanagan Historical Society, had been instrumental in having the bay declared a heritage site. (It is now within Okanagan Mountain Park.) Douglas Jung, one of the original volunteers and twice elected Member of Parliament for Vancouver Centre, had organized the reunion. By 1988 both Mr. and Mrs. Kendall were dead—Mike, who had picked fruit in the Okanagan as a lad and had thought the locale appropriate to SOE purposes, and Betty, Chinese, an agent in her own right and the only woman at the 1944 camp. The notes to Angeline Waterman's article "Commando Bay Reunion"[26] include a chronology of the granting of the franchise to

Chinese Canadians, a matter of importance to these men who had twice volunteered to serve a land that had withheld from them the full rights of citizenship. Omitted from the chronology is the fact that Chinese Canadian veterans of each world war were granted the right to vote by the BC Legislature in 1945.[27]

Other Services

The focus in this chapter has been on service in the Canadian army, especially as the Okanagan had been the location of a great deal of army training. However, young men and young women left their Okanagan homes to serve in the navy, in the air force and in the merchant navy, the last as dangerous as any wartime activity but one not fully recognized by the government until relatively recently. There are the rather extraordinary individual stories such as that of the Native historian and archivist Glen Douglas, who had blood ties with both the Penticton and Similkameen Indian Bands. Glen crossed the border and enlisted as a paratrooper in the United States forces, serving in World War II, in Korea and in Vietnam. Some like Anthony Walsh, a veteran of World War I, joined the Legion War Services, where they did distinguished work in support of the regular army units.

When World War II broke out and before the Royal Canadian Air Force had its training scheme and equipment in place there were a number of young men who left Canada to join the Royal Air Force in England. There they participated in the Battle of Britain. Younger brothers and sisters joined the RCAF and were prepared to serve Bomber Command, a section where flight-crew casualties were about 50 per cent.

The late Harry Reginald Sheardown of Osoyoos, who logged 2,229 hours of wartime flying, 1,530 of them operational, piloting such planes as Sunderlands and Catalinas, grew up in Armstrong. He attributed the high percentage of Armstrong young men who qualified as aircrew trainees to the thorough education they received in the Armstrong High School, especially in the classes of Tom Aldworth, Art Linfield and John Murray.

Shortly before he died on March 28, 1989 Harry Sheardown completed a booklet entitled *1939–1945 Air Crew from Armstrong High School*. In her introduction to the work Florence Whitmore writes in part:

> ...[Harry] came back [to Armstrong] many times to visit family and friends. On one such visit he stopped, as he had so many times before, to look at the Armstrong Cenotaph...On this particular day, certain questions began to intrigue Harry...In what way had these men served? In what theatres of war had they seen duty? In what capacity? In short, what contribution had been made to the R.C.A.F. by men from one small town in British Columbia during that global conflict?
>
> After his retirement from active business, and even though his health was precarious, Harry commenced his own search for answers to these questions that had haunted him for so long.
>
> Harry travelled many miles to interview veterans or their relatives, made numerous phone calls, wrote dozens of letters. Enquiries were sent off to R.C.A.F. Headquarters, to Airforce historians, even to R.A.F. Headquarters in London, England...

Harry Sheardown's booklet is exquisite in its precise detail concerning the training, the missions and the fate of the thirty-three airmen he writes about. Interspersed between the biographical sketches are vignettes of a flier's personal reaction to the world in which he found himself, a young man who had never owned a car suddenly sitting at the controls of a plane with a one hundred-foot wing span, for example. This study must mean a great deal to the veterans who came home and to the families and friends of those who did not. Yet the work reaches beyond the particular. It becomes a microcosm in which we find the experience of all those young men who trained under the British Commonwealth Air Training Plan, especially those who in the first flower of their manhood faced death in a cause that concerned the welfare of us all. During the war Canada lost 17,100 aircrew killed in action. Thirteen of them were from Armstrong.

17

Communications: Roads, Runways, Radio and TV

Highways up to the Mid-twenties

By 1909 came the first motor driven vehicles and the gradual disappearance of the horse drawn buggies, democrats and wagons. One of the first motor cars to be put in use commercially was the red McLaughlin two-seater, with folding top. It was owned by William Scott, the mail carrier from Vernon to Kelowna. It first appeared in the month of June but he had to go back to horses in the winter as there was no snow clearance on the roads in those days. The next cars to be seen on the roads were the "Model T" Fords. Gradually there were fewer and fewer horses and more and more cars and trucks.

Early motorists try out the new road beneath the overhanging rock at Vaseux Lake.
Vernon Museum 3237

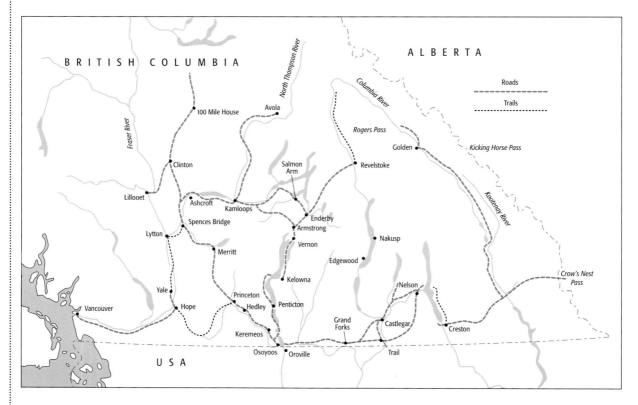

The transition from horses to motor power resulted in more and more pressure being brought on the government to improve the existing main roads.[1]
(*OHS*, 1963)

George M. Watt, the author of the above, constructed the road from Okanagan Centre to Glenmore, supervised the installation of Okanagan Centre's irrigation system and in 1912 joined the Provincial Department of Public Works. In his article "Transportation by Road and Trail in the Okanagan Valley" Watt outlines the development of transportation in the Thompson and Okanagan Valleys from fur-brigade days on.

The first roads in the pre-McLaughlin era were little more than widening of trails that had served men on

horseback. Between 1872 and 1876, for example, a road was "built" between Savona's Ferry and Okanagan Mission to a specification of seven to ten feet in width. George Watt tells us that Phillip Parke accepted a contract for $23,000 to construct the forty miles of road from O'Keefe to the Mission, contract to include the building of six bridges, one of them over Mission Creek. This road allowed passengers and freight that had travelled the Cariboo Road up the Fraser and Thompson Rivers to continue into the Okanagan. However in 1885, when the Canadian Pacific Railway was pushed through the Fraser Canyon, construction destroyed sections of the old Cariboo Road, thus disrupting the highway connection

Highway 97 along Wood Lake in the early days.
Vernon Museum 1355

which had served for twenty years between the Interior of the province and the coast. From 1885 until 1926, forty-one years, the only commercial route other than the Hope Trail from the Okanagan to the lower mainland was the railway. Hence the object of road building in the Okanagan tended to be to connect communities to this new and important link with the outside world.

R.G. Harvey tells us that in 1886 "a seven- to ten-foot-wide wagon road was rushed through from Spences Bridge to Princeton, and on to Osoyoos and Penticton, but almost all of it had to be rebuilt within the next ten to twenty years; it was primarily just a widening of existing trails."[2] This would give residents of the Similkameen and South Okanagan access to the new railway. As mining developed it was necessary to improve the standard of the road. The mining era stimulated not only the improvement of Similkameen roads but also was responsible for the government constructing a road from Fairview up past Camp McKinney into the Boundary Country and on to the towns of Rock Creek, Midway and Greenwood. This was the road on which Hester White had her stage ride described earlier.

George Watt writes of Phillip Parke's road between Vernon and Kelowna:

> The wagon road built by Phillip Parke carried the horse travel for a number of years with very little betterment of any kind. Some of the timbering had to be renewed, as also the bridges. It was a long hard climb from Vernon up over the Commonage Mountain, and down to the shore of Long [Kalamalka] Lake where the horses were driven or rode into the lake for a drink; then a lesser climb up onto the flat above Wood Lake, and the long descent to the shore of Duck Lake...
> (*OHS*, 1963)

A relocation of the road to above Long Lake, surveyed by J.P. Burnyeat in the fall of 1912, enabled motorists to avoid the four-mile climb out of Vernon "over Commonage Mountain." Kelowna for its part improved its road north towards Vernon with six and a half miles of macadam.

As the population increased so did the demand for more and better roads. The dust and washboard resulting from increased use of the roads and increased speed were an impetus for experiments with hardtop. In spite of the fact that almost half the provincial budget went to public works and the fact that increased population meant more tax revenue, the Highway Department was always short of enough money to accomplish the tasks expected of it. To overcome the shortfall the government was very happy to take advantage of the resources offered by private businessmen. James E. Jamieson tells us, "Levin W. Patten built the road from his mills on Deep Creek [in Spallumcheen] to what is now John Fowler's Corner and on into Lansdowne, this being the road used by the first stages from Kamloops to Lansdowne." [3]

A leisurely ride on a dirt road along Mara Lake, 1936. Enderby Museum #03

In 1883 a special act of the Legislature enabled G.B. Wright to build a road from Shuswap Lake to Revelstoke for which Wright was to be granted sixty thousand acres and the right to charge tolls for five years. The road was completed in 1884 but much of it was impassable by 1891.[4] In the south end of the Valley the first road between Penticton and Hedley was begun by the owners of the Nickel Plate Mine. Once the subdivision of the cattle ranges into orchard lands began it was the responsibility of the developer to put in roads which eventually became public.

Maintenance was another problem. Often landowners worked off taxes by working on their community's roads. Denis Marshall treats this matter of "statute labour" in some detail in his book *Salmon Arm's Historic Routes*.[5] No doubt, from earliest times a good many local problems were solved by volunteer effort.

Advertisement in *The Salmon Arm Observer* May 13, 1915

STOP! LOOK! LISTEN! AND GIVE A HAND
On Monday next, a number of farmers and others have very generously undertaken to give free, gratis, a day's services for the purpose of reducing the grade of the hill on the Homely Road opposite the residence of F.W. Clingan, and several teams will be available for the use of the willing workers. A hearty invitation is extended to all who have the interest of the City and public generally at heart and who can arrange to help out a movement which is certainly a step in the right direction.
   Mr. John Johnson, who is the instigator of the movement, will be in charge.[6]

"Mud, mud, mud" was too often the problem, something that Harley Hatfield remembers with a sense of humour:

> I recall, somewhere about 1930, coming to a mudhole where a long light steel wire rope (cable) was stretched on the ground beside the road. A car or truck was waiting at the far end and the driver shouted to you to hook on and signal when ready. With this pull to boost you through you then put the cable back and waited in your turn to help the next vehicle going your way...[In those days] a wise motorist carried a shovel, axe and length of stout rope, and, a really fussy one en route to a dance, a pair of rubber boots.[7]
> (*OHS*, 1985)

An interesting section of R.G. Harvey's book *The Coast Connection* deals with the efforts of Thomas Taylor, MLA for Revelstoke and chief commissioner of lands and works in the McBride administration between 1908 and 1915, to build a road between Hope and Princeton as part of the first Trans-Canada Highway.[8] This route was the choice of the Canadian Good Roads Association, a precursor of the Canadian Automobile Association. The project was interrupted by World War I. In the post-war period when the Federal Government was handing out reconstruction monies the Fraser Canyon route was insisted upon. However Taylor's penetrations from both west and east into the Hope–Princeton area remained for later road builders to extend. The completion of the Trans-Canada Highway in 1926 enabled people in the Okanagan for the first time in forty-one years to drive an all-Canadian route to Vancouver.

Road work in 1920. Four-horse grader on Mable Lake road east of Enderby.
Enderby Museum #1232

The Kelowna Crossing

For almost forty years, between 1901 and 1940, Len Hayman was ferryman on the vessels which carried men, horses and cars across Okanagan Lake at Kelowna. Fortunately his memories of that crossing were recorded.

The Kelowna crossing. Barge filled with horses towed by SS Clovelly. *Kelowna Museum File 13-237*

from **The Kelowna-Westbank Ferry**[9]

by L.A. Hayman

L.A. Hayman skippered the SS Clovelly, *which hauled passengers, horses, cars and even loads of lumber across Okanagan Lake. Kelowna Museum*

The first effort to maintain a ferry across Okanagan Lake at Kelowna was made by Eneas and David McDougall in 1885...The two brothers built a scow 10 or 12 feet wide by 16 feet long, three planks high, decked on top, posts and rails on side and loose rails at the ends for loading horses, and caulked with rags, gunny sacks, etc. The motive power was man or woman, or both. At one end a plank was removed and the rowers sat with their legs dangling down the hole with pine sweeps for oars, the thole pins on the edge of the scow. The scow carried three heavy horses or five pack horses...Eneas lived some four miles from the ferry on the west side, and it was he who ran the ferry.

At first the Kelowna–Westbank ferry was not remarkable for the efficiency of the service rendered the public. A stranger arriving on the west shore of the lake would first have to find the trail to Eneas McDougall's house and after a journey of four miles he would find sometimes that the ferryman was off on a hunting trip. He would then be forced to swim his horse across the lake. This was done by two men with a row-boat, one rowed and the other held the rope attached to the horse.

From 1901 to 1906 I had considerable to do with this scow's various successes and failures. Sometimes a wind would spring up and the scow begin to fill up in which case you had to slip the end rails and let the horses loose. The scow would begin to sink and the horses take to the water and probably swim back to the place you started from while I sat on the hand rails and let her drift until she fetched up somewhere. I would then have to bail her out and tighten up the caulking...When the wind dropped I would have to get her back to the starting point, round up the horses, reload them and start over again...

I must have crossed quite a few people before 1904...

After Price Ellison was elected MLA in 1905, tenders were called for the ferry. H.B.D. Lysons and I tendered for a launch and scow. Lysons got the contract and built a motor boat the *Skookum* (also known as the *Tut Tut*), 30 feet long with a Turscott one-cylinder engine of about seven H.P. The scow was 40 by 16 by 4 feet. The subsidy was $1000 per annum and the specifications required the ferry to make a round trip, weather permitting, twice daily, except Sundays and commence operations on April 1, 1906. The schedule of fares to be 25 cents for a passenger and $1 for a horse... [In February 1907 Hayman bought out Lysons.]

That fall I had a steam boat built in Vancouver by DeFoe and named her the *Clovelly*...This boat not only ran as the ferry to Westbank but also ran two trips a week to Bear Creek, besides hauling lumber and feed to ranches up and down the lake and fruit to Kelowna...

About 1921 cars were becoming numerous and horses scarce. I had a scow built to carry eight cars. We usually towed along side, but in rough weather we towed astern. In 1924 on a dark night in the fall we were shipwrecked. The wind was blowing fresh from the south-

west, a direct head wind, when we left Kelowna. We had six cars and nineteen passengers on board. When we were near Westbank Landing a strong north gale hit us without warning. The scow swung around and we were headed straight for the rocks. The engine was turned on full steam astern, but the wind was too strong for us. I cast off the scow and tried to save the boat but she went onto the rocks. She bumped over the rocks twice and then stuck fast. The scow struck the rocks but got clear and was carried down the lake by the wind. On board the boat there was something of a panic among the passengers. The waves were coming over the stern and over the life boat. The acetylene gas line was broken and the passengers were being gassed. However, we managed to get the life boat lowered although we could not use the davits as they were on the weather side. We got the life boat over the stern, belayed lines fore and aft and got the passengers ashore after first threatening to throw some of them overboard if they did not shut up and behave properly. I then telephoned to Albert Raymer at Kelowna and had him bring over my gas boat. We went for the scow and brought her in and we succeeded in landing every passenger and car safely on the wharf at Westbank just one hour and thirty minutes later than schedule time. But the cars could not be moved off the wharf for the fallen trees.

The next day I set men to work to bail out the *Aricia* and we patched her up sufficiently to have her taken to the shipyard at Okanagan Landing for repairs.

(*OHS*, 1943)

Barge of automobiles towed by SS Aricia. *Kelowna Museum 13-235*

MV Lloyd-Jones, *one of the last of the Kelowna ferries. Kelowna Museum 13-10,512*

The Okanagan Lake Bridge built in 1958 to replace ferry service. The bridge is 2,400 feet long. Rock causeways at both ends lead to the central span which floats on pontoons. A lift span near the Kelowna end allows tugs and barges to pass. The bridge cost $10 million. Kelowna Museum #26-4743

In 1927 the provincial government recognized the Kelowna–Westbank ferry as part of the highway system and accepted responsibility for its upkeep. That year the provincial government built the motor ship *Kelowna–Westbank* that could carry fifteen cars. By 1937 the government was running twenty-two ferries a day. In 1939 the government launched the thirty-car MV *Pendozi*, the first steel ferry on the run.

Ferry traffic grew until it became clear that a bridge was necessary. That need was met in 1958 when a floating pontoon bridge built at a cost of $10,000,000 replaced the ferry. Traffic continued to escalate. On a summer day in 1962, 3,740 vehicles crossed. Five years later this figure had become 9,100 and by 1981 the day's count was 26,400.

More About Highways

Just when the Department of Highways was beginning to mechanize its procedures the Great Depression struck. Money was in short supply and what there was went to funding relief camps. In 1931 Premier T.D. Pattullo established work camps where unemployed men, whether married or single, could live and work for $2 a day minus $.85 for board. However, the administration of these camps and their cost proved to be beyond the provincial capability.

In June 1933 the BC camps came under the administration of the Department of National Defence, the portfolio for which was held by the Honourable Grote Stirling, MP for the Okanagan. The national scheme had been recommended to Prime Minister R.B. Bennett by General A.G.L. McNaughton. Single men were to receive army-issue clothes and boots, live in barrack-like huts, eat army rations and work for an allowance of twenty cents a day. Camps were established where there were Public Works projects such as the building of airports or roads. There were four camps on the Hope–Princeton and others throughout the Okanagan and Similkameen. Although the men were adequately dressed and fed there was little satisfaction in the work they were meant to accomplish with only wheel barrows, picks and shovels. It was a period of great under-achievement and general dissatisfaction. Even when a camp was placed near a community there was little contact between the young men and the community. Often there was resentment in the general population where people sometimes had to manage their families with resources even more meagre than those allotted to the camps.

Only the outbreak of World War II put an end to the Depression in Canada. Almost overnight the unemployed young men were in the army and potential heroes in the eyes of the general public. On the Hope–Princeton the interned Japanese Canadians were put to work with picks and shovels in an effort to extend the roads begun by Thomas Taylor during World War I.

The post-war period was one of energy, confidence and high expectation for the future. No department of government benefitted more from this mood than the Ministry of Public Works. Highways were the infrastructure which would lead to economic development. Highway 97 was double-laned and hardtopped. The process of redesigning, rerouting and creating four-lane roads has been going on ever since. Contracts on the Hope–Princeton were let in 1946 and the highway was opened in 1949. Between 1949 and 1967 crews reconstructed the Southern Trans-Provincial right to the Alberta border, beginning with the Anarchist Mountain crossing where the 1893 road with its eighteen switchbacks was replaced with a highway requiring only three switchbacks. The Rock Creek Canyon bridge was opened in 1951.

Roads feeding into the Okanagan were improved and hard-surfaced. Beyond the Okanagan the Rogers Pass Highway was built and opened July 30, 1962. This highway along with the Hope–Princeton was to change forever the marketing of Valley fruit, the tourist industry and the value of Okanagan real estate. In July 1965 the new Richter Pass Highway, which carried traffic directly from Keremeos to Osoyoos, was opened while "Flying Phil" Gaglardi was still in charge of BC roads. (He was to leave the Ministry of Highways in 1967.)

The Coquihalla Highway, which R.G. Harvey terms the "ultimate coast connection," was opened with great fanfare May 22, 1986. By September 1987 this highway had been extended to Kamloops, thus completing Phase II of the construction. Of even more interest to the Okanagan was the opening of the connector between Merritt and Peachland, Phase III, in October 1990. Travel time from Kelowna to Vancouver had been reduced to four hours!

Air Travel

People of the Okanagan appear to have shared with people elsewhere the early twentieth-century ambition to be airborne, for we have a picture of a balloon ready to take off from the grounds of the Armstrong Fair in 1908. In 1914 powered flight reached the Valley. On July 1 William A. Stark of Vancouver flew a biplane at the Armstrong Fair. A few weeks later, on August 13, 1914, Weldon Cooke flew another biplane at the Kelowna Regatta. Both planes had to be crated and shipped to and from the Valley for they were not capable of cross-country flight.[10]

Young men who grew up in the Valley were not going to be left out of this fascinating adventure. C. Renfrew in his article "The First Aeroplanes to Fly in Kelowna" tells us:

Hot air balloon at the Armstrong fairgrounds July 1, 1908. ASMAS #3715

> In 1914 Ralph Bulman, George Silke, and Stanley Silke built a biplane glider at the Bulman Ranch at Ellison. This would be known now as a "hang glider." No wheels, the pilot hangs feet down, runs like h— down a slope and does the best he can if he gets airborne.
>
> Ralph Bulman unfortunately did get airborne and managed to crash land, with some personal injuries but without losing his life as might well have happened.
>
> (OHS, 1979)

At the 1919 Kelowna Regatta a Captain Trimm flew a Curtiss biplane model JN-4 into Kelowna from Vancouver. He earned a fair sum of money flying passengers off the polo field, occasionally treating them to a loop-the-loop. C. Renfrew tells about other barnstormers, flying schools and adventurers who visited the Kelowna area in those early days. Finding a suitable airport site was challenging. At one time Renfrew and Jim Browne were the only fliers to use the Ellison site on a regular basis. Few guessed that a modern airport would be established on that site and be ready for its official opening August 11, 1960. Mayor Dick Parkinson had obtained Canadian Pacific Airlines president Grant McConachie's assurance that he would schedule flights into the Kelowna airport if the city could persuade the federal government to extend and pave the runway.

The year 1919 saw another pioneering flight which included the Okanagan in its plan. On August 7, Captain Ernest C. Hoy, a native of Dauphin, Manitoba and a veteran of the Royal Flying Corps in World War I, flew a Curtiss Jenny from the coast, stopped at Vernon, then continued over the Rockies to Calgary, thus becoming the first pilot to take a plane over the Rocky Mountains of North America. The City of Vernon had agreed to pay a fee of $1,000 for the flier's attendance at its Peace Day Celebration on August 4 and 5. In 1960 while visiting Vernon Captain Hoy admitted, "If this offer had not been made it is quite possible the flight across the Rockies with the machines we had at that time would not have materialized."[11]

But to return to the pioneer days of powered flight in the Okanagan, C. Renfrew tells us:

> In 1928 to 1931 Radium Flying Service, John Blakeley, proprietor, and Lowell Dunsmore, pilot, operated a D-H Gipsy Moth at Rutland training student pilots, but as Rutland was not officially licenced made their base in Vernon on the field now occupied by the Army. Local students trained were: Anthony Pooley, Jok Mar, C. Renfrew. Vernon students at the time were: Harold Thorlakson, George Jaques, Eldon Seymour, Jim Duddle and others.

The first Vernon airfield consisted of 130 acres south of the town on Mission Hill. "The licence was applied for on February 10, 1930 and granted by the Department of Air Transport when two runways, each 300 feet wide and over 2,000 feet long, were graded, boundary markers placed, wind socks and landing circle installed and pole hazards painted."[12]

So pleased were the citizens of Vernon with their airport that they staged a great air show on September 30 and October 1 and 2 in 1931. "On that occasion, Vernon was the aviation centre of BC…Over 6,000 people witnessed this colourful event."[13] The next year the air show was repeated. Doug Kermode, a teenager at the time, talked the committee into letting him be night watchman on each occasion. The Saturday night of the 1932 show was to test the mettle of both Doug and his fellow watchman, Frank Pearson. About 5 a.m. a gale-force wind blew up, "the most violent wind in the memory of many old timers." Only the quick and decisive action of the young men saved the local and visiting planes from thousands of dollars of damage. A call to the National Hotel resulted in the arrival of many of the pilots, some still in their pyjamas. All, including Vernon residents and visitors, struggled to get the planes turned tail to the wind and fastened down. Kermode remembers:

> The only thank-you I received for my efforts at the airport came from Pat Reid, Canadian aviation pioneer and then pilot of the Imperial Oil Puss Moth. He sidled up to me prior to leaving that Sunday afternoon, and in his thick Scottish brogue asked if I would like to "Havvee a rride." So for a wonderful half an hour, I was his guest in the immaculate Puss Moth.
>
> Neither Frank nor I can recall getting paid in those days for our night watchman duties. It was an opportunity to be around the pilots and planes; just to whiff the scent of freshly painted "aircraft dope" was enough for two young airplane buffs.
> (*OHS*, 1993)

Kermode was not the only teenager to fall under the spell of this wonderful new mode of travel. In 1933 Eldon Seymour and Jim Duddle, aged seventeen and eighteen, planned the construction of their plane CF-AOM *The City of Vernon*.[14] Included in their team were Ernie Buffam, a former aircraft welder, and Jack Taylor, a retired bachelor who agreed to put up the necessary money. Ultimately the costs were to be divided four ways. Plans for the Corbin Senior Ace were purchased and the body was built. A Salmson engine was bought but some painful lessons were learned before it could be installed. After a final push, working forty-eight hours around the clock, the installation of the engine was completed in the early hours of the morning. Duddle writes:

> All it needed was oil and gasoline to determine how well the work had been done. As Eldon and Jim had daytime jobs this had to wait until noon hour. Gas and oil had been delivered to the Vernon airport in

The City of Vernon *was built by Eldon Seymour and Jim Duddle in 1933–1935. Because the Vernon Airport was absorbed by the Vernon Army Camp in 1941 and because of difficulties in finding storage facilities, the plane was sold in the 1950s "for a very small sum." In 1996 E. Seymour believed the plane was still being flown as a vintage plane by its American owner.*
Vernon Museum

the meantime. At noon the tanks were filled and it was time to start the engine by swinging the propeller. It was a great thrill when the motor fired on the first pull, and settled down to a nice smooth purr...CF-AOM was alive and eager to test her wings.
(*OHS*, 1969)

As there was no one in the Vernon area qualified to test fly the plane the young men applied to Lowell Dunsmore, then working in Drumheller, Alberta. Lowell consented to undertake the job and arrived June 1, 1935. Duddle writes: "It was his intention to taxi the plane at various speeds to get the feel of it but it was not necessary. He simply taxied onto the field and opened the throttle. The take-off was smooth and the climb rapid."

After Dunsmore had returned to Drumheller the young men could not resist the temptation to take their plane up for the occasional flip. Soon after a trip which lasted over three hours and reached an elevation of eleven thousand feet, the Department of Transport insisted that there was to be no more flying without a licence. As Eldon and Jim did not have sufficient money for each of them to train as pilots it was decided that Jim would go. On May 9, 1936 Jim set out with Len Waagen for Edmonton in *The City of Vernon*. On June 10, having acquired the coveted licence, Jim started home alone following the route east in reverse, Edmonton, Calgary, Fernie, Cranbrook, Grand Forks, Vernon. Duddle writes:

Some strong headwinds were encountered, otherwise all went well and Vernon was reached on the 12th of June. The plane had flown the Rockies—no doubt the first time for a totally home-built airplane. Probably this record has not been duplicated since.

On October 9, 1936 Jim and Eldon took the *City of Vernon* to Vancouver thus completing flights over all the mountain ranges from the Prairies to the Pacific.

The City of Vernon was flown during the period from 1935 to the end of 1941, and became familiar to thousands of people in Alberta and British Columbia. It was engaged in various air searches, photography missions, forest cruises...

The team who built the City of Vernon *were (from left to right): Ernie Buffam, a former aircraft welder; Jack Taylor, who lent the money to purchase materials; James Duddle (18 years); Eldon Seymour (17 years).*
Vernon Museum

At the end of 1941 all private flying ceased, for the Army Camp at Vernon expanded onto the airport site, and it was necessary to find new quarters. It was difficult to find storage for an airplane, even when dismantled, so in the ensuing years it was moved from here to there until an offer from Spokane was made to buy it. It was sold for a very small sum in the 1950s.
(*OHS*, 1969)

Eldon Seymour in about 1995 added a note: "We now understand that the aircraft is in possession of two engineers from the Boeing Company of Seattle and is being reconstructed as an antique aircraft."

In his article "Penticton Airport—Fiftieth Anniversary"[15] T.C. Hammell tells us that with the initiation of scheduled transcontinental air transportation in the late 1930s the Department of Transport believed it necessary to establish airports along the routes taken. Hence between 1935 and 1940 airports were constructed or were being constructed in Princeton, Oliver, Rock Creek, Midway and Grand Forks.

In Penticton there was difficulty in finding a suitable site. Finally in 1938 an agreement was reached with the Department of Indian Affairs and the Penticton Indian Band to lease thirty-eight acres. In 1940 the airport property was extended to the north and construction was underway. On May 2, 1941 the first plane landed on the runway. Mr. Hammell's carefully documented article details the development of the Penticton airport, illustrating the growing sophistication of such installations. Gone forever were the days when spreading a strip of gravel and erecting a few wind socks sufficed. According to Anne Richard the federal government spent in the neighbourhood of $1,000,000 on the development of the Penticton Airport, a considerable sum at the time.

In Vernon, after its first airport was absorbed by the military camp, it was not until June 15, 1946 that the city council was authorized to purchase land near Okanagan Landing and develop an airport with a landing strip three thousand feet long. Some citizens were bitterly disappointed that the council did not seize the opportunity to create a port on the L & A property north of Swan Lake. The Kelowna Airport, which was

Planes at the Penticton Airport.
Penticton Museum 4-079A

Penticton was the original home of Okanagan Helicopters Ltd. Here is one of their helicopters.
Penticton Museum 4-079B

officially opened August 11, 1960, served the needs of Vernon and North Okanagan air passengers from that date.

Once airports were established with their auxiliary services other businesses came into being—short-haul scheduled flights, charter services, flying schools. An interesting company formed in Penticton about 1945 was Okanagan Air Service, later to be known as Okanagan Helicopters. The company moved to Rutland where it decided to sell off its fixed-wing operation and concentrate on helicopters at a Vancouver location.

The Air Crash

The Okanagan has not been without its air accidents in spite of the navigational aids installed in the various airports. The most serious of these was the crash of CP Air's Flight 4, from Vancouver to the Okanagan and Kootenay, on the northeast side of Okanagan Mountain at an elevation of about 4,500 feet on December 22, 1950 at 1:45 p.m. To this day no one understands the cause of the crash.[16] Why was the plane flying at tree-top level as it turned in its approach to the Penticton Airport? The pilot was killed immediately and the copilot died of injuries in spite of the care administered by the stewardess, Lorna Franco, and a passenger, Ora Blackmer, who was a trained nurse. None of the passengers was seriously injured.

More than twenty years later Dorothy (Butler) Furness wrote of her experience on this flight which was to return her home to Summerland for the holidays.[17]

As we descended now we could clearly see the tree tops being snipped off by the impact of our plane ploughing through the forest—like a giant lawnmower. The trees were below us, above us, beside us—as we made the desperate struggle to recover altitude...Suddenly upwards swung the big plane and we appeared to be climbing to avoid crashing into the mountain directly in front of us. Only the Hand of Fate could save us now as we tumbled around inside the fuselage, and caught fleeting glimpses of the landscape twisting below us.
(OHS, 1976)

When the plane came to rest and the door was opened the passengers found that they had to flounder through waste-deep snow to escape a possible explosion and fire, an eventuality that did not occur due to the snow and the fact that the fuel tanks were not punctured. In spite of the desperate situation there was enough collective wisdom in the group to preserve them against the cold and any foolhardy behaviour. Mrs. Furness continues:

It was time to begin to seriously think about keeping ourselves warm and alive. The stewardess was busy looking at the emergency instructions when I arrived in the plane for a rest. Three bonfires, built in the shape of a triangle, were a signal of distress, and she was making plans for the survivors to go quickly, before darkness settled in upon us from every corner of the forest, and prepare this signal. Branches were ripped off the fir trees and the word "DOC" was formed on a clearing so perchance, if a plane sighted us, this would warn the pilot of our need for medical help.

The first ground party to reach the crash site was led by Victor Wilson, owner of Paradise Ranch and a man familiar with the mountain since boyhood. Dr. Jack Stapleton, a Penticton surgeon who carried Demerol and morphine in his pack, was in the group that struggled up the pathless mountain through deep snow. The rescue party found survivors standing around small, inadequate fires in thin suits, nylons and street shoes... "Stapleton served the injured copilot until his death at 1:35 a.m. on December 24." [18]
To go back to the Furness account:

A little while later the weary doctor came over and said, "It's all over." The stewardess cried a little as the bodies of her two fellow workers were lashed onto sleds for their final journey home.

Small groups were being formed to start the journey out to civilization...With heavy woollen socks pulled over our shoes, we began to shuffle out in the darkness. There was no feeling of fear as we edged our way along the top borderline of the canyon...The patron and matron of our group [an elderly couple Mr. and Mrs. Lipsack of Cowichan Lake, who had kept up the morale of the survivors through their own example of courage and the coffee they had kept brewing since the crash] found the going rugged, and the rescue team decided they needed help, though far be it for them to ask for extra consideration. However, two boughs were chopped from a nearby tree, and the branches stripped off. They were slung over the shoulders of two rescuers and these two brave elderly passengers gratefully placed their arms over the boughs and were thus supported and their chances of slipping off the cliff were lessened.
(OHS, 1976)

Radio

Radio was introduced in the Okanagan as an amateur activity. George Howard Dunn arrived in Kelowna in 1908. On June 23 of that year he was appointed city clerk, an office which he held for fifty-one years and for which service he was duly honoured. However, Mr. Dunn's close attention to his civic responsibilities did not prevent him from pursuing his avocation of radio broadcasting. Although he was sending and receiving from 1912 on, Dunn was not assigned his call of VE5BW until February 26, 1924. [19]

In 1914 James William Bromley-Browne (known about town as Jim Browne), another English immigrant, arrived in Kelowna with his wife Tryphena. Browne had already had an adventurous life which included service in the Boer War while he was still underage. During this military service he developed an arthritic heart, a problem which troubled him throughout his life. It was during one of his periods of being bed-ridden that James Browne discovered radio. Tryphena had bought her husband "one of those music boxes." She told John Shinnick:

> The one thing he heard that really got him thinking again was a report from the far north. The government was trying to find a young Provincial Policeman patrolling the interior on horseback...My husband was struck by radio's wonderful ability to reach across the mountains like that to touch people's lives. That started his interest in radio.[20]

Shinnick continues:

> In 1928, the Kelowna Amateur Radio Club was founded. Joining George Dunn in this endeavour were other Englishmen, such as Bobby Johnson, an engineer with A.J. Jones Boatworks, who became the club's radio engineer; Harry Blackborough, the City of Kelowna's electrical engineer, the club's first technical adviser; and, of course, James William Bromley-Browne in charge of the entertainment programming. To convert to amateur radio broadcasting, Dunn's transmitter had to be converted from morse key operation to voice. The government granted the club a licence under the call letters 10-AY, restricting the group to non-commercial broadcasting. With a walloping 50 watts of power, they broadcast a relatively ambitious schedule of programs...

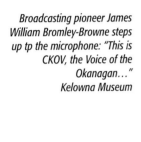

Broadcasting pioneer James William Bromley-Browne steps up tp the microphone: "This is CKOV, the Voice of the Okanagan..."
Kelowna Museum

> Across North America, radio was beginning to catch on. Newspapers folded in cities that had once supported a dozen dailies. The depression was beginning to make itself felt in every corner of society. Radio offered an inexpensive diversion...Through radio, listeners sensed that others were enduring the same hardships as themselves. Radio made people feel less isolated, less alone...Even in those early days radio was starting to prove its worth as an instrument of civic change and improvement.
>
> "Jim was having so much fun," Mrs. Browne remembers, "that he finally asked George to go in with him and start a business, get a commercial radio licence. George thought that it was a crazy idea. He had his job with the City, he said, and he wasn't interested. So Jim went on his own and applied for the licence."
>
> ...Browne received his commercial broadcasting licence in the spring of 1931 on condition that 10-AY disband. The Amateur Radio Club readily agreed to this condition for the token sum of $1.00, paving the way for the Okanagan's first commercial radio station.
>
> On November 4th, 1931, at 2:30 p.m., amateur radio station 10-AY ceased to exist. James William Bromley-Browne flicked the switch, turned on his microphone and said:
>
> "This is CKOV, the Voice of the Okanagan."...

Shinnick follows the development of the radio station including the technological changes through the years. Jim Browne Jr. became involved in the station but was more interested in the equipment carrying the signal than in planning programs. He picked up information wherever he could and became expert. Once when Jim Jr. was away on a ranch near Princeton indulging another interest, horseback riding, there was a breakdown. Shinnick writes:

> J.W.B. sent word to Jim via a bus driver who knew the owner of the ranch in Princeton. Jim jumped on his horse and rode all night across the mountains, arriving at the westside

landing at dawn in time for the first ferry. He rode out to the CKOV transmitter, walked in the door, took one look at the problem, replaced a transformer, then went home to sleep. The station was back on the air.

World War II was to effect changes in CKOV as it did in other Canadian businesses and institutions. For one thing, women found a place in broadcasting as men left to serve in the armed forces. Eileen Bowman was CKOV's first female announcer. Marion Lee was another to join the staff in those years.

Actually CKOV's unique wartime service to the Okanagan began even before Canada was committed to the conflict. Shinnick writes:

> When England entered the war on September 3rd, 1939, the Trans-Canada Network of the Canadian Broadcasting Corporation withheld the news while Prime Minister Mackenzie King and his cabinet decided whether or not Canada should enter the war. With Jim Browne Jr. broadcasting from the transmitter, J.W.B. Browne and Jack Bews monitored their U.S. news sources at the studio downtown, conveying the story to Okanagan listeners as it unfolded. The Valley, as a result, was one of the few regions in Canada to hear the story that night.
>
> "I don't know how Ottawa found out that we had carried the news of England entering the war," Jack Bews remembers. "But they found out nonetheless. The next day we got a wire telling us to cease and desist or lose our licence. They rapped our knuckles on that one."
>
> (OHS, 1981)

During the war Okanagan listeners remained glued to their radios not only to pick up local news but also to hear the latest news relayed from the Canadian Broadcasting Corporation, which in turn repeated British Broadcasting Corporation programs. J.B. Priestley's descriptions of life in wartime Britain kept Okanagan listeners in touch with the realities of war. Matthew Halton's vivid reporting of the allied drive north through Italy, accompanied with the sounds of battle captured on his tape-recorder, helped them understand what young friends and relatives were enduring.

In 1948, J.W.B. Browne established radio station CKOK in Penticton. In 1950 he sold out to Maurice Finnerty and Grev Rowland, the latter selling his share a year later to Roy Chapman. In Vernon Major Charles Pitt opened CJIB. Charles Pitt and his wife Helen will long be remembered for their contributions to the cultural life of Vernon. Mrs. Pitt was generous in her support of young artists. Bernard Webber cherishes a particular memory of Mr. Pitt. During a federal election in the late 1940s, Charles Pitt invited Webber into his office. The reader must remember that Mr. Pitt was not a member of the Co-operative Commonwealth Federation party.

"I notice, Mr. Webber, that the CCF, as yet, has contracted very little radio time for advertising during the election. The other parties are picking up most of the available spots."

"I know," replied Webber. "But the CCF has bought all the time that we can afford." In those days some politicians were reluctant to spend money they did not have on their campaigns.

"Well," said Mr. Pitt, "I think that you should be able to put your ideas before the public. I believe that that is part of the democratic process. I'll tell you what I shall do. You buy...(and he outlined a very modest program of spots, five-minute slots, etc.) And I'll give you...(and he listed a generous allotment of free radio time)."

When radio stations were established in Vernon and Penticton news reporting became more localized. Station personnel often engaged in projects important to their communities. For example Jim Browne Jr., who succeeded to the management of CKOV after his father's death in 1954, played a decisive role in obtaining an airport for Kelowna.[21]

As time went on changes in technology, changes in taste and style, and community development all influenced radio. When television arrived on the scene in the 1950s it offered a major threat but radio survived, finding its own niche in a more complex community. By the end of 1996 there were radio stations in Keremeos, Princeton, Osoyoos, Summerland, Salmon Arm, two in Vernon, three in Penticton and six in Kelowna.[22]

Television

"The challenge in local television is to be accountable to the people who allow you into their homes every night but to do the job in such a way that you look as good as the big guys with the big budgets"—the philosophy of Mike Roberts who since the summer of 1973 has served CHBC-TV in Kelowna.

from **A History of Television in the Okanagan**[23]

by Mike Roberts

The Beginning

A commercial television station in the Okanagan was the dream of the owners of Radio Stations CKOK in Penticton, CKOV in Kelowna and CJIB in Vernon. Each investigated the feasibility of operating a station in their own community, but resolved to combine forces to create one station, centrally located in Kelowna, to serve all areas. The site chosen for the offices was Alex Smith's Garage on Leon Avenue and that's where our offices are today.

In May 1957, Roy Chapman, then co-owner of CKOK Radio in Penticton, was appointed General Manager of CHBC. He retained Tom Wyatt as Chief Engineer. Actually Wyatt had already completed the job of assessing transmitter sites two years earlier. Working for R.C.A. Victor of Montreal, Wyatt had climbed all the mountains surrounding the Okanagan Valley and placed transmitters on top of them. He then drove through the various communities to see how well the signal could be received...

Dick Sharpe came to television from *The Penticton Herald*, where he had been for 18 years and held the position of General Manager. He took up his post as Sales Manager at CHBC. He became President and General Manager after Roy Chapman's death in 1976. Dick retired in 1985 and died in the fall of 1986. Russ Richardson was a member of the original 12. He came from CKOK to become CHBC's News Editor, Program Director and Film Editor. Norm Williams joined in July of 1957 as Continuity Editor, Promotion and Production Manager.

Back in 1957 the price tag for putting together a TV station was a quarter of a million dollars. The operating licence was granted by the governing body at the time, the CBC, not the Board of Broadcast Governors or the CRTC but the CBC.

A Unique Television Station

Although Vernon, Kelowna and Penticton were the original communities to receive the CHBC signal, other communities quickly erected relay transmitters, often with the help of CHBC technicians. Today [1990] 27 transmitters carry CHBC to 55 communities...

What made CHBC so unique was that in order to link the three major communities of the Okanagan together, CHBC had to utilize three transmitters to broadcast over three separate channels in Vernon, Kelowna and Penticton. The master transmitter atop Blue Grouse Mountain broadcast on Channel 2 to Kelowna and beamed the signal via microwave to a mountain-top transmitter near Penticton to broadcast on Channel 13 and similarly to Vernon to broadcast on Channel 7. Prior to CHBC going on the air the only television received in the valley was a reflector-type cable service in Penticton and Kelowna. An aerial picked up a signal from Spokane and it was distributed to a few homes in both communities.

If you wanted to watch television in 1957, you had to watch CHBC.

A CHBC First—July 19, 1958

It was in July of 1958 that CHBC undertook its first mobile live telecast. The occasion was the opening of the Kelowna Floating Bridge and Her Royal Highness, Princess Margaret, was going to do the honours. The fact that CHBC didn't own a mobile telecast facility didn't stop the intrepid 13. Chief Engineer Tom Wyatt moved studio, control room and transmitter to a vantage point 100 yards from the bridge. An immense task given the heavy tube-type equipment of the day...

Russ Richardson, the program director, confirmed that this historic telecast would commence at 11:30 a.m. and continue until the ceremonies were completed. Viewers from Salmon Arm to Penticton joined the ten thousand people in City Park who saw Princess Margaret cut the ribbon and open "The Bridge that couldn't be built," the "Most unique bridge in the Commonwealth." Sales manager Dick Sharpe estimated that 95% of the population of the Okanagan saw the telecast. In 1958 that amounted to 95,000 viewers.

Live Programming

A year to the day later the official opening of Kelowna's first enclosed shopping mall, Shops Capri, was telecast. These live broadcasts and others done from Penticton and Vernon necessitated the bending of a number of broadcasting rules. CHBC simply bypassed its main Kelowna control room and set up a micro-wave link at the location of the live telecast. Then by reversing the transmitters Penticton or Vernon became the base transmitter. What put an end to this technological innovation was colour telecasting. A better signal was necessary for colour than could be attained with the micro-wave units they'd been using.

Although live remote broadcasts got all the attention, the early days were famous for the live programming that originated in CHBC studios. "The Lions' Locker Room," a nightly visit with the B.C.Lions, who held their training camp in Kelowna from 1954 to 1958 was very popular. Moe Young was the Sports Director of the time. Now I don't remember Y.A. Tittle ever playing for the B.C. Lions but he appears on the set in one of the publicity photos. Did you catch that shot of Herb Capozzi talking with CHBC's Doug McIlraith? The studio for that show was actually the top of the City Park grandstand. Tom Wyatt, the master technician, also acted as the Movie-Tone-News style cameraman.

"Okanagan Farm and Garden" with Mike Oswell and, later, Bob Wilson of the B.C. Department of Agriculture was another popular live weekly program. Add to these programs "Pete Stoltz and his Music Pals" sponsored by Mc and Mc Hardware Stores; Don Eccleston and the "3 Rs Educational Program"; of course "The News" from 6:30 to 6:40 Monday through Friday with Russ Richardson; "Weather" from 6:40 to 6:45 with Shell Weatherman and Station General Manager Roy Chapman; "Ten Minutes of Sports;" "Bank of Knowledge"; "Meet the People," a half hour every Thursday night with Roy Chapman. But no show was more successful than "Romper Room" with Miss Betty. Six thousand children and their mothers attended four personal appearances of Miss Betty at sponsors' premises.

CHBC was on the air from 4:30 a.m. to 11:15 p.m. Monday through Saturday and from 1:30 p.m. to 11:15 p.m. Sunday.

CHBC Goes Colour

A major milestone was passed when CHBC began to broadcast some programs in colour. Supplements appeared in all the valley papers to announce that CHBC was going colour September 1st, 1966.

By 1967 staff at CHBC had grown from the original 12 to 33 and the station was getting ready to make a major leap forward. The new brick face was just a year away; colour cameras were moving into our studios so that local productions would be seen in colour; and video tape was on the horizon. Prior to video tape the only way a program could be recorded was to do it all on film, quite an expensive undertaking, or to kinescope the video as it was shot. This was done by major networks but not by stations the size of CHBC.

Micro-wave and Satellites

It's interesting to remember in this day and age of live programming from virtually anywhere in the world that it wasn't always so. Today we turn on the set and watch a live newscast from Toronto thanks to satellite transmission. Before satellites, programs were beamed via micro-wave links but the national micro-wave link wasn't completed until 1958. That meant that programs had to be shipped to CHBC on film. Hockey games arrived a week late and the National News a day late. The CBC had special high speed planes that had one job—carry the film of "The National News" with Earl Cameron across the country as quickly as possible. Local stations would pick up the film at the airport and load it onto their own projectors. Somehow it didn't seem too great an imposition in those days but you wouldn't stand for it now...
(*OHS*, 1990)

Ah, the impatience in that last line! Twentieth-century technology has made the men and women—and even children—of the Okanagan, Similkameen and Shuswap citizens of the world, participants in the concerns of nations be it environmental degradation, public health issues, economic problems or war and peace. On July 20, 1969 many of us felt that we shared a walk on the moon. Today the mass graves of the latest war lie open before us in our livingrooms. If a businessman cares to conduct his far-flung business from his home on an Okanagan mountainside e-mail, fax and cheap long-distance telephone make that possible. Should his physical presence be required, Vancouver is only a few hours away by car and less than an hour by plane and beyond that he can be anywhere in the world within hours.

But communication is a two-way street. Technology has opened up the Valley to others. People of the wider world are arriving in ever greater numbers, changing communities, escalating land values, challenging the water supply, urbanizing the countryside—a process quite unsettling to those already established there. Unfortunately, technological advance does not guarantee the Valley and its residents the time or the wisdom to consider, digest, evaluate and act upon the information and changes that are descending upon them.

Afterword

In the previous sections of this book the reader can trace the development of physical and cultural links within the valleys of the Okanagan, Similkameen and Shuswap. Similarly links with the world beyond our immediate region have been forged. We have become participants in a global economy and in global cultural exchanges. Although our soil has not been ravished by war, two world wars have changed us. Life in the Okanagan before World War I and World War II was not the same as it was after these events.

Looking back, the Great Depression of the interwar years seems not so much an event as a hiatus in our growth and development. During the 1930s residents of the Okanagan, Shuswap and Similkameen Valleys, especially orchardists looking for markets for their fruit, were very much aware of the general breakdown in the Canadian economy. Those who lived near railway tracks saw the young men riding atop the boxcars in what was usually a vain search for jobs. Each town on the line had its "jungle" where the unemployed camped, cooking over open fires what food they had been able to scrounge. However, life in our valleys was good compared with that in many places. Fruit and vegetables could be grown in back yards or obtained very reasonably from friends or relatives on farms. Hunting and fishing supplemented the meat supply. Simple pleasures were at hand—hiking, swimming, fishing, picnicking, skating, sleighing, baseball, hockey.

Many were the examples of individual generosity even towards strangers during those difficult years. Some managed to extend their charity to considerable numbers. Lyda M. Bell tells us that men who called at the Hoover flour mill in Armstrong were given "small bags of flour and porridge to cook over their campfires." Bob Hayman writes that Mar Jok, owner of Kelowna's Golden Pheasant Cafe, locked his front door when his regular customers were finished, "then opened up the back door to the hungry line-up and everybody was fed"—free.

World War II from its beginning in 1939 fundamentally affected our society. Many young men enlisted in the forces, and women too. Other women remained at home but took on responsible jobs which were left vacant when male incumbents enlisted in the military services.

Nor did things return to "normal" once the war was over. Re-establishment credits tended to place all veterans on an even footing. Hence class and ethnic lines became blurred. The comradeship established in shared combat carried over into civilian life, a condition fostered by the Canadian Legion Branches active in most communities. Bill Whitehead in his article "Armstrong Royal Canadian Legion Branch #35"[1] gives us a very good picture of the role such branches played. Starting out after World War I as clubs for returned men, their efforts to support fellow veterans and their families in adversity soon extended into charitable activities on behalf of all the needy in their areas. The Legion hall furnished not just a clubroom but also a hall for community use.

In the post-war era we became a more cosmopolitan and sophisticated people, learning to enjoy our cultural diversity. Increased affluence enables us to train our young people to achieve world standards in sports and in the arts. The foundation laid by people like Eva Cleland and F.T. Marriage produced cultural organizations such as the Okanagan Symphony and the Community Music Schools which prepared young people for national and international careers. Professional painters and potters became well known.

In 1945 Vernon skiers revived their pre-war ski club and installed a rope tow on Birnie Ridge, the third such tow in BC. That was the beginning of the development throughout the area of first-class ski facilities. Golf courses too have proliferated. Today more people can participate in sports activities, furnishing themselves with the equipment necessary to achieve international standards of performance. The improved facilities have also proved a boost to the burgeoning tourist industry.

The greatest change, however, in this post-war Okanagan is the population growth and urbanization which continue to alter our towns and countryside, put pressures on our agricultural land reserve, cause land values to increase and create unexpected problems with regard to delivering services. Common sense and good intentions are no longer sufficient qualifications for service on councils and boards where budgets run to millions of dollars. Those serving their communities must be informed on a number of matters. Murray Roed and his Kelowna Geology Committee warn of one area of concern when they write:

> Urban and regional planners are beginning to respond to some concerns regarding storm water management, hazard land evaluation, and flooding, but a suitable and detailed terrain and hydrologic data base for evaluation of these is lacking in the Okanagan.[2]

The sad experience of some who lost houses during the winter of 1996–97 alerts us all to the point being made by Roed.

The need for more sophisticated knowledge with regard to business practice becomes increasingly apparent. Those entering into contracts either on behalf of themselves or of some public group must not be casual about property lines, easements, clear-cutting, water sources or pollution. The old hand-shake society is gone forever.

We get an idea of the change that has taken place when we read the final paragraph of W. P. Lofts' article "A Short History of the Okanagan Regional Library 1936–1984." Mr. Lofts writes:[3]

> The Okanagan Regional Library enters its fiftieth anniversary year looking back on a half century of solid achievement. In 1936, the library served 26,000 people with an annual budget of $11,125. In 1985, 212,136 people received library service from an annual budget of $3,000,000.

Krueger and Maguire in 1984 pointed out the speed with which population density is developing.[4] In the decade between 1971 and 1981 the population of the North Okanagan grew by 60 percent and that of Central Okanagan by 70 percent. In 1941 the populations of the three major Okanagan cities had been fairly even: Penticton had 5,777; Vernon 5,209; Kelowna 5,118.[5] Today the population of each has increased, but Kelowna's much more so.

Today many of the newcomers to our area have had little part in our development but they have shown an interest in our history. The heritage bus tours organized by Dorothy Zoellner and Alyce Lundy at Kelowna and by R.L. dePfyffer in Vernon are over-subscribed. New books on special topics published privately or by museums find a market and Okanagan Historical Society members furnish local papers with columns on historical topics, continuing a tradition set by writers like E.W. Aldredge of Penticton, W.A. Shilvock of Kelowna and Stuart Fleming of Vernon. Visitors to historic sites increase yearly, thanks to the volunteer efforts of people like G.D. "Paddy" Cameron, H.C.S. Collett, Primrose Upton, Len Piddocke, the Marty brothers—Joe, Arthur and Stephen—Frank Pells, Denis MacInnis, Ermie Iceton, Carleton MacNaughton, Joan and Victor Casorso and to professionals like Cuyler Page and Ken Mather.

Understanding one's history matures a community, establishing relationships which effect coherence. For a number of years Jessie Ann Gamble, school librarian in Armstrong, has paired her Grade 7 pupils with retired businessmen and farmers, the youngsters interviewing the seniors and recording their experiences. Some of these essays have appeared in *OHS Reports* and all are stored in the Armstrong Museum. What a wonderful record of a community! Those young essayists will remember all their lives that afternoon spent with an elder looking back to a time sixty or seventy years before their own births.

At a meeting called in the 1980s by the Native Indian Curriculum Project in Penticton, those attending were asked to state their interest in the project. One young man said, "I want to know where I have come from and where I am going." Does not the past and the future converge for each of us in the present, the only time in which we are free to act and make a difference to outcomes?

BIBLIOGRAPHY

Below is a list of publications consulted in addition to *Okanagan History: The Annual Reports of the Okanagan Historical Society.*

Chapter 1 • The Land
Cannings, Richard and Cannings, Sydney. *British Columbia: A Natural History*, Greystone Books, Vancouver 1996.
Nasmith, Hugh. *Late Glacial History of Surficial Deposits of the Okanagan Valley*, Bulletin No. 46, Department of Mines and Petroleum Resources, British Columbia 1962.
Roed, Murray A. and the Kelowna Geology Committee. *The Geology of the Kelowna Area*, Kelowna 1995.
Yorath, C.J. *Where Terranes Collide*, Orca Book Publishers, Victoria 1990.

Chapter 2 • The First People
Armstrong, Jeannette. *Enwhisteetkwa*. Okanagan Tribal Council, Penticton 1982.
Cail, Robert E. *Land, Man and the Law: The Disposal of Crown Lands in British Columbia 1871–1913*. UBC Press, Vancouver 1974.
Carstens, Peter. *The Queen's People: A Study of Hegemony, Coercion and Accommodation among the Okanagan of Canada*. U of T Press, Toronto 1991.
Coffey, J. et al. *Shuswap History: The First 100 Years of Contact*. Secwepemc Cultural Educational Society, Kamloops 1990.
Corner, John. *Pictographs in the Interior of British Columbia*. Wayside Press, Vernon 1968.
Fisher, Robin. *Contact and Conflict: Indian-European Relations in British Columbia 1774–1890*. UBC Press, Vancouver. 1977.
Mourning Dove, *A Salishan Autobiography*. U. of Nebraska Press, Lincoln 1990.
Ormsby, Margaret *A. Coldstream Nulli Secundus*. Vernon 1990.
Rousseau, Mike K. "Early Prehistoric Occupation of South-Central British Columbia," *BC Studies, No. 99*. Autumn 1993.
Thomson, Duane. "The Response of Okanagan Indians to European Settlement," *BC Studies, No.101*. Spring 1994.
Turnbull, Elsie G. "Recollections of Maria Houghton Brent," *British Columbia Historical News, Vol. 18*, No. 2. 1984.
Webber J. ed. and En'Owkin Centre. *Okanagan Sources*. Theytus Books, Penticton 1990.

Chapter 3 • The Fur Trade
Harris, R.C., Hatfield, H.R. *Old Pack Trails in the Proposed Cascade Wilderness*. Okanagan Similkameen Parks Society. 1980.
Harris, R.C., Hatfield, H.H., Tassie, Peter. *The Okanagan Brigade Trail in the South Okanagan*. Vernon 1989.
Holt, Roberta, Jahnke, Alfred, Tassie, Peter. *The Okanagan Brigade Trail: Central and North Okanagan*. Vernon 1986.

Chapter 4 • The Colonial Era
Akrigg, G.P.V. and Akrigg, Helen B. *British Columbia Chronicle: 1847–1871*. Vancouver 1977.
Carstens, Peter. *The Queen's People: A Study of Hegemony, Coercion and Accommodation among the Okanagan of Canada*. U of T Press. Toronto 1991.
Gordon, Archie, Fifth Marquess of Aberdeen. *A Wild Flight of Gordons*. London 1985.
MacDonald, A. David. ed. *Penticton: 75 Years to Remember*. City of Penticton. 1983.
Ormsby, Margaret A. *British Columbia: A History*. MacMillan Co. of Canada. 1958.
Ormsby, Margaret A. ed. *A Pioneer Gentlewoman in British Columbia: The Recollections of Susan Allison*. UBC Press. 1976.
Ormsby, Margaret A. "Some Irish Figures in Colonial Days," *The British Columbia Historical Quarterly*. Jan.-Apr. 1950. pp.61–82.
Webber, J. "Colonial Osoyoos," *B.C. Historical News*, Vol. 23, No. 2

Chapter 5 • Missionaries and Churches
Mercier, Mrs. Jerome. *Father Pat: A Hero of the Far West*. Edinburgh 1909. Reprinted by the Vernon News Ltd.
Pash, Rev. Joseph J. *History of the Immaculate Conception Parish in the Colville Valley*. Colville WA. 1962.
Splawn, A.J. *Ka-mi-akin: Last Hero of the Yakimas*. Yakima, WA 1958.

Chapter 6 • From Colony to Province
Elections British Columbia. *Electoral history of British Columbia 1871–1986*. Legislative Library, Victoria 1988.
Hendrickson, James E. *Journals of the Colonial Legislatures of the Colonies of Vancouver Island and British Columbia*. Vol. I–V. Provincial Archives of British Columbia. Victoria 1980.

Chapter 7 • Stage Drivers and Mail Carriers
Harmon, Daniel Wm. *Sixteen Years in the Indian Country: The Journal of Daniel Wm. Hamon, 1800–1816*. ed. W. Kaye Lamb. Macmillan. Toronto 1957.
Melvin, George H. *The Post Offices of British Columbia: 1858–1970*. Vernon 1972.
Ormsby, Margaret A. *A Pioneer Gentlewoman in British Columbia: The Recollections of Susan Allison*. UBC Press. Vancouver 1976.

Chapter 8 • Community Life
Cox, Doug. *Okanagan Roots: A Historical Look at the South Okanagan and Similkameen*. Skookum Publications, Penticton 1987.
Van Kirk, Sylvia. *"Many Tender Ties": Women in Fur-Trade Society, 1670–1870*. Winnipeg 1980.

Chapter 9 • Schools
MacDonald, A. David. *Penticton: 75 Years to Remember*. Penticton 1983.

Chapter 10 • Medical Services
Okanagan Valley Hospitals' Role and Services Review. 1995.

Chapter 12 • Hard-rock Mining
Casorso, Victor. *The Casorso Story*. Okanagan Falls 1983.
Iverson, Robert M. *Camp McKinney, Then and Now*. Oliver 1984.
Peto, Peter and Greenough, John. *Geology of the Kelowna Area*, ed. M.A. Roed. Kelowna 1995.

Chapter 13 • Boats and Trains
Aberdeen, Lady. *The Journal of Lady Aberdeen*, ed. R.M. Middleton. Victoria 1986.

Chapter 14 • A Growing Population
MacDonald, A. David. *Penticton: 75 Years to Remember*. Penticton 1983.
Marshall, Denis. *Salmon Arm's Historic Routes*. Salmon Arm 1996.
Report on the Fourth Census of Canada–1901. Government of Canada.

Chapter 15 • Tree Fruits, Ground Crops, Vines and Agro-industries
Cancela, Julie. *The Ditch*. Oliver Heritage Society. 1986.
Casorso, Victor. *The Casorso Story*. Okanagan Falls 1983.
Cosgrave, Julie. "The Importance of Being Harry," *Okanagan Business*. Sept./Oct. 1996.
Dendy, David and Kyle, Kathleen M. *A Fruitful Century*. British Columbia Fruit Growers Association. 1990.
Harvey, R.G. *The Coast Connection*. Victoria 1994.
Oliver Chronicle
Ormsby, Margaret A. *Coldstream Nulli Secundus*. Corporation of the District of Coldstream. 1990.
Osoyoos Times
Schreiner, John. *The British Columbia Wine Companion*. Orca Books. Victoria 1996.
Seattle Times

Chapter 16 • Military Matters
Farwell, Byron. *Queen Victoria's Little Wars*. London 1973.
Surtees, Ursula. *A Shadow Passes*. Published by author. 1993.
Wong, Marjorie. *The Dragon and the Maple Leaf*. London ON 1992/94.

Chapter 17 • Communication: Highways, Planes, Radio, TV

Broadcaster. November, 1996.

Harvey, R.G. *The Coast Connection*. Victoria 1994.

Marshall, Denis. *Salmon Arm's Historic Routes*. Salmon Arm 1995.

ENDNOTES

Chapter 1

1. *Fiftieth Annual Report of the Okanagan Historical Society*, 1986. pp. 164–166. Hereafter notes referring to the *Annual Reports of the Okanagan Historical Society* will be printed thus: OHS 15: 164–166. 1986.
2. *OHS 47*: 137. 1983
3. *OHS 6*: 26. 1935.
4. *The Geology of the Kelowna Area*, Murray A. Roed et al. Kelowna Geology Committee, 1995, p.13.
5. S.J. Schofield, FRSC, "The Origin of Okanagan Lake," *The Transactions of the Royal Society of Canada*, Sec. IV, 1943. pp.89–92. Reprinted in *OHS 13*: 9–13. 1949. Today the Ministry of the Environment measures lake levels by taking the mean June average, which tends to be the high for the year. Thus they have established the following figures: Wood and Kalamalka Lake, 391.76 metres; Okanagan Lake, 342.32 metres; Skaha Lake, 337.93 metres; Vaseux Lake, 327.91 metres; Osoyoos Lake, 278.14 metres. (Information from Shaun Reimer, 1997.)
6. Roed. p.19.
7. Roed. pp.146, 150–154.
8. C.J. Yorath, *Where Terranes Collide*, Orca Books, Victoria 1990. p.91.
9. bid. p.40
10. Roed. p.31.
11. C.C. Kelly, *OHS 18*: 21–23. 1954.
12. Roed. pp.149–150.
13. Rev. John Goodfellow, "The Keremeos Columns," *OHS 5*: 32–34. 1931.
14. Dorothy Hewlett Gellatly, "Basaltic Columns at Westbank," *OHS 9*: 11–14. 1941.
15. Roed. p.135.
16. Hugh Nasmith p.42.
17. *OHS 6*: 242–243. 1935.
18. George H. Morkill, "The Shuswap and Okanagan Railway Company," *OHS 6*: 115–116. 1935.
19. *OHS 50*: 11–12. 1986.
20. Max H. Ruhmann, "A Unique Faunal Area in Southern BC," *OHS 1*: 4–5. 1926.
21. Richard Cannings and Sydney Cannings, *British Columbia: A Natural History*, Greystone Books, Vancouver 1996. p.234.
22. Okanagan Similkameen Parks Society Newsletter, December 1998. Summerland. p.3.

Chapter 2

1. *OHS 50*: 171. 1986.
2. American spelling of "Okanogan" is used by writer who lives south of 49th Parallel, rather than the Canadian "Okanagan."
3. This essay, along with several quoted below, appears in *Okanagan Sources*, edited by J. Webber and En'Owkin Centre and published by Theytus Books, Penticton 1990.
4. *B.C. Studies*, No. 99, Autumn 1993. p.140.
5. *Ok. Sources*. 1990. pp.10–50.
6. Readers may be interested in the archaeological reports of G.W. Robert's Inkameep Project and of Mike K. Rousseau's Tsinstikeptum (Westbank) Project, which can be found in *OHS Reports 39* and *51* respectively.
7. Mourning Dove, *A Salishan Autobiography*, University of Nebraska Press, 1990.
8. *Ok. Sources*. pp.54–89.
9. Peter Carstens, *The Queens People*, University of Toronto Press, 1991. pp.16–17.
10. *Ok. Sources*. p.30.
11. *Ok. Sources*. p.59.
12. Conversation by telephone with Louise Gabriel.

13. *OHS 18*: 24–29. 1954.
14. *Ok. Sources*. pp.167–168.
15. *OHS 6*: 125. 1935.
16. *OHS 12*: 16–17. 1948.
17. *B.C. Historical News*, Vol. 18, No. 2. pp.21–22.
18. *Ok. Sources*. pp.34–35.
19. Robin Fisher, *Contact and Conflict*, University of British Columbia Press 1977. p.38.
20. Robert E. Cail, *Land, Man and the Law*, University of British Columbia Press 1974. p.222.
21. *Oliver Chronicle*, December 17, 1997.
22. *OHS 54*: 77–91. 1990.
23. Duane Thomson, "The Response of Okanagan Indians to European Settlement," *B.C. Studies*, Spring 1994. pp.110–111.
24. *OHS 54*: 86. 1990.
25. Fisher. pp.191–192.
26. *OHS 14*: 110–118. 1950. E.V. de Lautour was a cousin of Lord Aberdeen. After working on the Coldstream Ranch he settled for some years in the Christian Valley to the east of the Okanagan. Later he worked as a provincial fruit inspector.
27. *OHS 6*: 122–130. 1935.
28. Robert L. de Pfyffer, "Okanagan Indians Non–Registered: The Reason Why," *OHS 54*: 77–91. 1990.
29. *OHS 12*: 24–28. 1948.
30. Jeffrey Smith, "From the People: a Brief History of the Okanagan Indian Cultural Project," *OHS 47*: 66–67. 1983.

Chapter 3

1. *The Similkameen Star*, Princeton, February 4, 1937.
2. *OHS 13*: 28–37. 1949.
3. The fur-trading post established at the mouth of the Columbia River by the Lewis and Clark Expedition in 1811 was named Fort Astoria after John Jacob Astor of Boston and New York, the founder of the Pacific Fur Company. Hence those associated with the company were called "Astorians." When the War of 1812 broke out the Canadian North–West Company bought out the American interests on the Columbia and Fort Astoria was renamed Fort George.
4. *OHS 17*: 38–40. 1953.
5. *OHS 44*: 9–18. 1980.
6. *OHS 43*: 142. 1979.
7. *OHS 57*: 7. 1993.
8. Ibid. 22–31.
9. Ibid. 22–31.
10. *OHS 45*: 74–78. 1981.

Chapter 4

1. G.P.V. Akrigg and Helen B. Akrigg, *British Columbia Chronicle*, Vancouver 1977. pp.1–2.
2. *OHS 6*: 40–43. 1935.
3. *OHS 11*: 19. 1945.
4. *OHS 6*: 198–199. 1935.
5. Ibid. 195–199.
6. Ibid. 233–241.
7. Ibid. 239.
8. *OHS 57*: 30. 1993.
9. *OHS 10*: 59. 1943. The Canadian Census for 1881 lists the Haynes household thus: John C. (48 yr.), Emily (29 yr.), Fairfax (9), Valentine (5), Hester Emily (3), William (1), Irene (5 1/2), Mary (14), John (12). Fairfax was the son of Charlotte Moresby whom Haynes married in 1869 and who died in 1872. Mary and John would be the children of the Native woman Julia who had been Haynes's country wife. In January 1875 Haynes married Emily Pittendrigh. John later farmed at the Mission, where Haynes Road is named after him.

10. *OHS 18*: 144. 1954.
11 *OHS 6*: 75. 1935.
12. Anonymous, "Overland to the Cariboo," *OHS 25*: 61–71, 1961. The editor and author of this book thinks it very likely that the anonymous author was Elizabeth Aramson Schubert, wife of James Schubert. The late Margaret Hunter told the author that the article "James Armstrong Schubert: Okanagan Pioneer" (*OHS 13*: 132–134) attributed to M.E. Hunter was written by her mother, Elizabeth Aramson Schubert.
13. Ibid.
14. *OHS 14*: 129–133, 1950.
15. *OHS 15*: 43, 1951.
16. *OHS 21*: 81–62. 1956.
17. *OHS 14*: 28–34. 1950
18. A. David MacDonald, *Penticton: Years to Remember*, Penticton 1983. p.5.
19. *OHS 14*: 98–109. 1950.
20. *OHS 18*: 135–155. 1954.
21. *OHS 25*: 78–101. 1961.
22. Ibid. "Frank Richter and his first wife, Lucy Richter, had five sons: Karl (Charlie) 1869–1949; William 1872–1921; Joseph 1874–1971; Edward b.1876; and Hans (John) 1878–1961. All were born in Lower Similkameen at the 'R' Ranch and they became almost as well known throughout the country as their father…Frank Richter and his second wife, the former Miss Florence Elizabeth Loudon of Loomis, Washington, whom he married in 1894, had five daughters: Florence Elizabeth (Mrs. A. Pendleton); Frieda Marie (Mrs. Norman Shaw); Frances; Helen (Mrs. H. Clark); Kathleen (Mrs. P. Durnan); and one son, Francis Xavier Richter."
23. *OHS 6*: 177–184. 1935.
24. Margaret Ormsby, "Captain Houghton's Exploratory Trip, 1864," *OHS 13*: 38–44. 1949.
25. *British Columbia Historical Quarterly*, Jan.–Apr., 1950. pp.61–82.
26. Margaret A. Ormsby, *British Columbia: A History*, Vancouver 1958. p.240.
27. Peter Carstens, *The Queen's People*, Toronto 1991. p.70.
28. *OHS 58*: 41–45. 1994.
29. *OHS 17*: 87–91. 1953.
30. *OHS 6*: 300–302. 1935
31. *OHS 23*: 104–105. 1959.
32. *OHS 6*: 27. 1935.

Chapter 5
1. Georgina Maisonville, "Reverend Father Pierre Richard, O.M.I., 1829–1907," *OHS 13*: 83–89. 1949.
2. *OHS 6*: 57–60. 1935.
3. *OHS 48*: 79. 1984.
4. Ibid. 79–83. 1984.
5. *OHS 2*: 12–16. 1927.
6. *OHS 26*: 141–145. 1962.
7. *OHS 13*: 83–89. 1949.
8. *OHS 25*: 76–77. 1961.
9. *OHS 6*: 28–37. 1935. This article was written originally in 1927.
10. *OHS 13*: 109–116. 1949.
11. *OHS 28*: 55. 1964.
12. Ibid. 37.
13. *OHS 12*: 78–79. 1948.
14. *OHS 18*: 153–154. 1954.
15. *OHS 23*: 97. 1969.
16. *OHS 44*: 112–120. 1980.
17. *OHS 15*: 55. 1951.
18. *OHS 6*: 76–80. 1935. The article was first published in 1929 in the *Third Report*.
19. *OHS 28*: 98–103. 1964.

20. T.B. Beames, A. Waterman, "The Reverend and Mrs. W.S. Beames," *OHS 50*: 133. 1986.
21. *OHS 23*: 13–18. 1959.
22. Mrs. Jerome Mercier, *Father Pat: A Hero of the Far West*, Edinburgh 1909. Reprinted by Vernon News Ltd. pp.40–41.
23. James E. Jamieson, "Spallumcheen Masonry Through Seventy-five Years," *OHS 27*: 36–45. 1963.
24. Kathleen A. Aikens, "The Peachland Story," *OHS 37*: 73–79. 1973.
25. *OHS 46*: 55–67. 1982.
26. *OHS 13*: 169–171. 1949.
27. *OHS 49*: 94–98. 1985.

Chapter 6
1. James E. Hendrickson, ed., *Journals of the Colonial Legislatures of the Colonies of Vancouver Island and British Columbia 1851–1871*, Provincial Archives of British Columbia, Victoria. 1980. Vol. IV, pp.245, 327.
2. Ibid. Vol. V, pp.3, 107, 267.
3. Stuart J. Martin, "Vernon's Street Names," *OHS 13*: 157. 1949.
4. *OHS 15*: 41–43. 1951. The account of how two men chose the first member for Yale constituency was written in 1925 by the late B.R. Atkins. Mr. Atkins was a partner of Burt R. Campbell in newspaper work in Revelstoke in 1897–98, and in 1899 served as private secretary to Premier C.A. Semlin. Later he was customs officer for many years at Revelstoke, and when he retired from this office, in the early 1920s, contributed historical articles to the *Vancouver Daily World*, the *Vancouver Daily Province* and *The Tranquillian*, the forerunner of the anti-tuberculosis magazine *Your Health*. He died in November 1941.
5. Kathleen Stuart Dewdney, "The Hon. Edgar Dewdney, C.E.P.C. (1835–1916), *OHS 22*: 92. 1958. In 1879 Edgar Dewdney was appointed Indian commissioner for the North-West Territories, an office which he continued to hold after he became lieutenant-governor for the NWT from 1881 to 1888. In 1888 he became MP for Assiniboia and served on the Privy Council. When retired and returned to British Columbia he was appointed lieutenant governor for the province 1892–1897.
6. *OHS 31*: 154. 1967.
7. *OHS 51*: 140. 1987. Susan Steinke's essay "Forbes George Vernon Loses the Provincial Election of 1894," pp.139–147, reveals the change that was taking place in the electorate. With the coming of the railway settlers were pouring in, only to find the best land in the hands of the big landowners. The dissatisfaction was exacerbated when a scandal regarding the S&O Railway came to light.
8. *OHS 12*: 48–58. 1948.
9. For details concerning the local granite used in the courthouse see David G. Falconer's article "Hewers of Granite" in *OHS 41*: 59–66.1977.
10. *OHS 10*: 41. 1943.
11. *OHS 18*: 159. 1954.
12. *Electoral History of British Columbia 1871–1986*, Elections British Columbia & the Legislative Library, Victoria 1988. pp.153, 156, 517.
13. *OHS 43*: 55–57. 1979.
14. *OHS 20*: 36–40. 1956.
15. A. David MacDonald, "Kathleen Dewdney Day: August 26, 1979," *OHS 44*: 96–100. 1980.
16. *OHS 5*: 34. 1931.

Chapter 7
1. *OHS 52*: 37–40. 1988.
2. W.K. Dobson, "Canada's Okanagan," *OHS 27*: 147. 1963.
3. *OHS 52*: 37–40. 1988.
4. *OHS 6*: 252–256. 1935.
5. *OHS 19*: 108–109. 1955.
6. Ibid. 114–115.
7. *OHS 7*: 21–24. 1937.

8. Ibid. 23.
9. *OHS 13*: 141–143. 1949.
10. Daniel Wm. Harmon, *Sixteen Years in the Indian Country: The Journal of Daniel Wm. Harmon 1800-1816*, ed. W. Kaye Lamb, Macmillan, Toronto 1957. pp.151–152.
11. Ibid. pp.163–164.
12. Margaret A. Ormsby, ed., *A Pioneer Gentlewoman in British Columbia: The Recollections of Susan Allison*, UBC Press, 1976. pp.32–33.
13. *OHS 14*: 31. 1950.
14. *OHS 20*: 75. 1956.
15. George H. Melvin, *The Post Offices of British Columbia: 1858-1970*, Vernon 1972. p.88.
16. The information included in this text is but a portion of what George H. Melvin has to say about the post offices in the Okanagan and neighbouring areas in his book *The Post Offices of British Columbia: 1858-1970*. After World War II Mr. Melvin returned to Vernon where he had been stationed at one time in the army camp. He lived in Vernon until his death in 1983 at the age of 77. He had served as alderman, chaired the museum board for 25 years, was declared Good Citizen for 1970 for his many contributions to the city's activities and was a member of the Okanagan Historical Society. At the 1972 convention of the Northwest Federation of Stamp Clubs George Melvin was presented with the Distinguished Philatelist Award for his *Post Offices of British Columbia* (*Vernon News*, June 1, 1972). He had not only researched and written the book but also financed its publication and distribution.
17. *OHS 19*: 112. 1955.
18. *OHS 60*: 43–46. 1996.

Chapter 8
1. *OHS 6*: 98. 1935.
2. Hester White, "Charlotte Haynes," *OHS 16*: 37–44. 1952.
3. *OHS 6*: 258. 1935.
4. *OHS 16*: 37. 1952.
5. *OHS 13*: 116. 1949.
6. *OHS 30*: 79. 1966.
7. *OHS 6*: 47. 1935.
8. "Many tender ties." The expression originated with Sir James Douglas and is used by Sylvia Van Kirk as the title of her study of *Women in Fur-Trade Society, 1670-1870*, Winnipeg 1980.
9. Conversation with Isabel Christie MacNaughton. The remark is attributed to Lucy Richter.
10. *OHS 60*: 8–20. 1996.
11. Ibid. 8–20.
12. Mel Rothenburger, *The Wild McLeans*, Victoria 1993. pp. 111–112.
13. *OHS 14*: 141. 1950.
14. *OHS 6*: 49. 1935.
15. Ibid. 147.
16. *OHS 30*: 117. 1966.
17. *OHS 25*: 57–60.
18. *OHS 9*: 52–53. 1941.

Chapter 9
1. *OHS 46*: 38–44. 1982.
2. *OHS 23*: 47. 1959.
3. *OHS 10*: 59. 1943.
4. *OHS 14*: 106. 1950.
5. *OHS 38*: 54, 55. 1974.
6. *OHS 6*: 53–55. 1935.
7. *OHS 25*: 84–85. 1961.
8. *OHS 15*: 137–143. 1951.
9. *OHS 23*: 131. 1959.
10. *OHS 57*: 98–104. 1993.
11. *OHS 53*: 38. 1989.

12. A. David MacDonald, "Schools," *Penticton: Years to Remember*, Penticton 1983. pp.87–94. (Mr. MacDonald acknowledges the contribution of H.D. Pritchard in researching the subject of Penticton schools.)
13. *OHS 41*: 150. 1977
14. *OHS 40*: 99. 1976.
15. *OHS 53*: 104. 1989.
16. *OHS 49*: 70–78. 1985.
17. *OHS 12*: 160–165. 1948.
18. In 1982, when the Okanagan Summer School of the Arts was celebrating its Twenty-first Anniversary, Jean Webber was commissioned to write a comprehensive history of the school, which was given the title "Venture: The Story of the Okanagan Summer School of the Arts, 1960-1961." Part I of the history appears in the *Forty-sixth Report* (1982), pp.139–160, and Part *II in the Forty-seventh Report* (1983), pp.154–176.
19. *OHS 46*: 160. 1982.
20. *OHS 50*: 112–113, 1986. Bernard Webber, "Review of *My American Cousin*."

Chapter 10
1. *OHS 6*: 81–84. 1935.
2. *OHS 6*: 296. 1935.
3. *OHS 14*: 106. 1950.
4. *OHS 27*: 117. 1963.
5. *OHS 28*: 35–37. 1964.
6. *OHS 14*: 105. 1950.
7. *OHS 19*: 48. 1955.
8. *OHS 58*: 68. 1994.
9. *OHS 22*: 7, 8. 1958.
10. *OHS 36*: 104. 1972.
11. *OHS 16*: 75. 1952.
12. *OHS 51*: 13–14. 1987.
13. *OHS 6*: 296. 1935.
14. *OHS 46*: 45. 1982. During those "lost" years Florence Ann McDonald, mother of the author of this work, trained and graduated from the Vernon Jubilee Hospital. Florence later married Dolph Browne. There were others in her class, among them Madge Dickson who was to become Mrs. W. Seaton.
15. *OHS 40*: 12–15. 1976.
16. *OHS 49*: 85–88. 1985. In the early 1920s the Okanagan Health Unit was established under the authority of Dr. H.E. Young, provincial health officer. The unit served Kelowna and district with Dr. G.A. Ootmar in charge. Gradually the area of its coverage was enlarged. In 1944 the North Okanagan Health Unit came into being. Before the formation of the health units there were public health nurses in some localities. In Penticton there was a Miss Whitaker who was associated with the Red Cross. Oliver and Osoyoos were served by Miss Lucy Crafter, Victorian Order of Nurses community service.
17. *Okanagan Valley Hospitals' Role and Services Review* (Feb. 1995) .

Chapter 11
1. *OHS 14*: 121. 1950.
2. *OHS 13*: 132–134. 1949.
3. *OHS 34*: 14. 1970.
4. *OHS 48*: 117–118. 1984.
5. *OHS 55*: 18–23. 1991.
6. *OHS 30*: 130. 1966.
7. *OHS 6*: 291–297. 1935.
8. *OHS 21*: 95. 1957.
9. *OHS 30*: 130. 1966.
10. *OHS 26*: 157–158, 1962.
11. *OHS 19*: 89. 1955.
12. *OHS 34*: 165. 1970.

13. *OHS 30*: 116–122. 1966.
14. *OHS 35*: 25–26. 1971.
15. Ibid.
16. *OHS 12*: 109. 1948.
17. *OHS 34*: 159–160. 1970.
18. *OHS 59*: 6–13. 1995.
19. *OHS 20*: 82. 1956.
20. *OHS 44*: 66. 1980.
21. *OHS 49*: 51. 1985.
22. *OHS 55*: 44–49. 1991.
23. *OHS 47*: 46–50. 1983.

Chapter 12
1. *OHS 22*: 67. 1958.
2. *OHS 46*: 134. 1982
3. Robert M. Iverson, *Camp McKinney, Then and Now*, Oliver 1984. pp.2, 4.
4. *OHS 7*: 41–43. 1937.
5. *OHS 13*: 147. 1949.
6. *OHS 34*: 14. 1970.
7. Victor Casorso, *The Casorso Story*, Okanagan Falls 1983. pp.92, 93.
8. *OHS 15*: 148–149. 1951.
9. *OHS 12*: 67–88. 1948.
10. *OHS 18*: 148. 1954.
11. *OHS 48*: 84–89. 1984.
12. *OHS 50*: 54–57. 1962.
13. *OHS 48*: 88. 1984.
14. For a history of the Brenda Mines see the article by Peter Peto and John Greenough in *Geology of the Kelowna Area* by Roed et al. 1995. pp.114–118.
15. Beryl Wamboldt, "Enderby and District: from Wilderness to 1914," *OHS 33*: 37. 1969.

Chapter 13
1. Ernest Doe, "Salmon Arm More than Half a Century Ago," *OHS 14*: 66–67. 1950.
2. *OHS 6*: 114–116. 1935.
3. Lady Aberdeen, *The Journal of Lady Aberdeen*, ed. R.M. Middleton, Victoria 1986. pp.20, 21.
4. *OHS 51*: 143. 1987. The whole article: pp.139–147.
5. *OHS 25*: 84. 1961.
6. *OHS 51*: 20. 1987.
7. H.R. Hatfield, "Commercial Boats of the Okanagan," *OHS 56*: 20–33. 1992. Readers who are particularly interested in this subject are advised to consult this article as printed in the *Fifty–sixth Report*. For the sake of brevity specific information about some boats has been omitted.
8. Harley Hatfield, in a note, refers to an article in *OHS 18*: 42. 1954. He says: "Mrs. Hester White wrote a most interesting story about a trip up the lake in October of 1888. [This was the year that Judge Haynes died and Hester was eleven at the time.]...Mrs. White gave the name of the boat they were on as the *Mary Victoria Greenhow* and that of a boat which passed them as the *Penticton*. According to all other accounts of lake shipping of that year the first was out of service by 1888 and the latter not launched until 1890. The boat they travelled on must have been the *Jubilee*, the second of Shorts' steamers. It was in operation that year, wood fired like the *M.V.G.* and about the same size...Michael Hagan wrote an article for the *Victoria Colonist* describing the launching of the *Okanagan (1)* alias *Red Star (1)* on the lake and his trip on her to Penticton in July 1888. So the boat which passed Mrs. White and party was the *Okanagan (1)*.
9. *OHS 54*: 30–37. 1990.
10. *OHS 53*: 7. 1989.

11. Before World War I Mackenzie and Mann surveyed a line for the Canadian National Railway from Kamloops through Grande Prairie (Westwold), over Grandview Flats to Armstrong. However, construction did not begin until 1919. By 1925 CNR service had reached Vernon and the next year it was in Kelowna. There was some sharing of trackage with the CPR.

Chapter 14
1. Report on the Tenth Census of Canada–1961, Table 6.
2. Denis Marshall, *Salmon Arm's Historic Routes*, Salmon Arm 1996. p.6.
3. Ibid. p.11.
4. *OHS 16*: 45–58. 1952.
5. *OHS 7*: 28. 1937.
6. MacDonald, *Penticton: Years to Remember*, p.62.
7. Marshall, pp.8–9
8. *OHS 16*: 18–19. 1952.
9. *OHS 41*: 30. 1977.
10. *OHS 50*: 154–155. 1986.
11. *OHS 45*: 67. 1981.
12. *OHS 18*: 113. 1954.
13. *OHS 33*: 39. 1969.
14. *OHS 14*: 53. 1950.
15. *OHS 22*: 56. 1958.
16. *OHS 19*: 95. 1955.
17. *OHS 52*: 134. 1988.
18. *OHS 23*: 123. 1959.
19. *OHS 50*: 159–160. 1986.
20. *OHS 12*: 67–88. 1948.
21. *OHS 18*:106–108. 1954.
22. *OHS 54*: 142–154. 1990.
23. *OHS 24*: 158. 1960.
24. *OHS 51*: 7–12. 1987.
25. *OHS 10*: 54–63. 1943.
26. *OHS 12*: 140–150. 1948.
27. *OHS 23*: 82. 1959.

Chapter 15
1. *The Seattle Times*, Dec. 29, 1957.
2. *OHS 42*: 68. 1978.
3. *OHS 25*: 91–93. 1961.
4. *OHS 42*: 68–75. 1978.
5. *OHS 54*: 49–58. 1990.
6. *OHS 50*: 22. 1986.
7. *OHS 45*: 56–60. 1981.
8. *OHS 32*: 69–80. 1968.
9. *OHS 52*: 99–101. 1988.
10. Lydia Baumbrough, "Irrigation and Water Legislation in the Pioneer Years," *OHS 43*: 5–10. 1979.
11. Ibid.
12. *OHS 32*: 69–80. 1968
13. Hilda Cochrane, "George Heggie," *OHS 26*: 104–106. 1962.
14. W.R. Carruthers, "Edward Maurice Carruthers, J.P.," *OHS 32*: 63–68. 1968.
15. Margaret A. Ormsby, *Coldstream Nulli Secundus*, Corporation of the District of Coldstream, 1990. p.29.
16. David Dendy & Kathleen M. Kyle, *A Fruitful Century*, BCFGA, 1990. p.30.
17. *OHS 47*: 99–103. 1983.
18. *OHS 51*: 38–42. 1987.
19. Ibid. 43–49. 1987.
20. *OHS 47*: 131–136. 1983.
21. *OHS 14*: 73–74. 1950.

22. Ralph R. Krueger, N. Garth Maguire, *The Urbanization of Fruitlands of the Okanagan Valley*. Manuscript 1984. Findings were based on Orchard Survey for 1935–55 (Government of British Columbia); The Report of the Royal Commission on the Tree-fruit Industry of British Columbia; Geographical Bulletin, No. 20, 1963 (Author: Ralph R. Krueger).
23. *OHS 49*: 35–41. 1985.
24. David Dendy, A Fruitful Century: The British Columbia Fruit Growers' Association 1889–1989, BCFGA, Kelowna, 1990. pp.101–109. E.D. MacPhee, Dean of Commerce, UBC and sole commissioner of the Royal Commission on the Tree-fruit Industry of British Columbia, began his investigations Jan. 30, 1957. His report was delivered to the government in October 1958 and released to the public in early 1959.
25. *Oliver Chronicle*, April 3, 1996.
26. *OHS 48*: 29. 1984.
27. Ibid. 28–45.
28. In subsequent legislation, the Land Commission Amendment Act, 1977, Bill 88, and Agricultural Land Commission Act, 1980 made the commission responsible for agricultural land only.
29. *OHS 50*: 60–65. 1986.
30. *OHS 15*: 148–149. 1951.
31. *OHS 16*: 128. 1952.
32. Victor Casorso, *The Casorso Story*, Okanagan Falls 1983. p.115.
33. Casorso, p.116.
34. James E. Jamieson, "North Okanagan Nonagenarian," *OHS 37*: 65–67. 1973.
35. *OHS 16*: 123. 1952.
36. *OHS 49*: 115. 1985.
37. *OHS 46*: 29–37. 1982.
38. Kathleen S. Dewdney, "Christopher Tickell," *OHS 39*: 85–86. 1975.
39. *OHS 7*: 18. 1937.
40. *OHS 45*: 31–35. 1981.
41. John Schreiner, *The British Columbia Wine Companion*, Orca Books, Victoria 1996. p.70.
42. *OHS 44*: 20–22. 1980.
43. *OHS 6*: 205. 1935.
44. *OHS 48*: 119–121. 1984.
45. *OHS 40*: 80–84. 1976. The first NOCA directors were: C.J. Patten, Armstrong, president; R.J. Coltart, Enderby, vice-president; R.A. Copeland, Lumby; W.S. Cooke, Armstrong; Thomas Gray, Mara; and Major P.J. Locke, Lavington.
46. Beryl Wamboldt, "Everard Clarke, 1901–1990," *OHS 55*: 127–129. 1991.
47. *OHS 47*: 52. 1983.
48. First board of Armstrong Cheese Co-op. Assoc.: A.E. Sage (president), J.W. Evans, secretary-treasurer; Edgar Docksteader, A.E. Warner, E.A. Norman and H.W. Pritchard.
49. *OHS 47*: 52–56. 1983.
50. *OHS 50*: 48. 1986.
51. *OHS 57*: 136–138. 1992.
52. Telephone conversation with D.N. Weatherill, Oct.1, 1996.
53. Interview at Kelowna Oct. 10, 1996.
54. *Oliver Chronicle*, July 24, 1996.
55. *OHS 43*: 15–18. 1979.

Chapter 16
1. *OHS 24*: 117–166. 1960.
2. Lt. Col. D.F.B. Kinloch, "A History of the Okanagan Regiment," *OHS 12*: 151–159. 1948.
3. Terence B. Upton, "The Rocky Mountain Rangers," *OHS 26*: 74–86. 1962.
4. Byron Farwell, *Queen Victoria's Little Wars*, London 1973.
5. *OHS 6*: 147. 1935.
6. *OHS 12*: 152–153. 1948.
7. *OHS 20*: 91. 1956.
8. Art Langdeau, "Vernon and its Military Tradition: The Early Years, 1908–1918," *OHS 48*: 135. 1984.
9. *OHS 48*: 138. 1984.
10. *OHS 12*: 151–159. 1948
11. *OHS 19*: 142–144. 1955.
12. *OHS 26*: 74–86. 1962.
13. *OHS 15*: 82. 1951.
14. *OHS 43*: 71–72. 1979.
15. *OHS 47*: 68–76. 1983.
16. R.G. Harvey, *The Coast Connection*, Oolichan Books, 1994. p.84.
17. *OHS 12*: 156–159. 1948.
18. *OHS 26*: 80–86. 1962.
19. Ivan E. Phillips, "Salute to the Pacific Coast Militia Rangers, Part I," *OHS 39*: 147–150. 1975.
20. *OHS 48*: 160–161. 1984.
21. *OHS 40*: 78. 1976.
22. *OHS 47*: 19–22. 1983.
23. Ibid. 22–28.
24. Marjorie Wong, *The Dragon and the Maple Leaf*, Pirie Publishing, London ON. 1992/94. pp.112, 125.
25. *OHS 41*: 85–89. 1977.
26. *OHS 53*: 19–24. 1989.
27. Wong, p.151.

Chapter 17
1. George M. Watt, "Transportation by Road and Rail in the Okanagan Valley," *OHS 27*: 50–57. 1963.
2. R.G. Harvey, *The Coast Connection*, Victoria 1994. p.60.
3. *OHS 26*: 158. 1962.
4. Harvey, pp.59–60.
5. Denis Marshall, *Salmon Arm's Historic Routes*, Salmon Arm Branch of Okanagan Historical Society, 1995. p.15.
6. Marshall, p.124.
7. *OHS 49*: 167–168. 1985.
8. Harvey, pp.76–84.
9. *OHS 10*: 39–44. 1943.
10. C. Renfrew, "The First Aeroplanes to Fly in Kelowna," *OHS 43*: 64–66. 1979.
11. *OHS 25*: 131–135. 1961. In August 1969 the Vernon Flying Club staged the celebration of the 50th Anniversary of this historic flight, bringing Captain Hoy from his home in Georgia to fly the original route between Vernon and Calgary. Doug Kermode's article "Captain E.C. Hoy's 50th Anniversary Return Flight in 1969" (*OHS 59*: 56–62) captures the imagination, energy, co-operation and enthusiasm which made this event a reality. This historic re-enactment, once it was initiated by the Vernon club, received practical support from aviation companies and individual aeroplane buffs in western Canada.
12. Anne Richard, "Airfields in the Okanagan and Similkameen Valleys," *OHS 16*: 129–131. 1962.
13. Doug Kermode, "The Big Windstorm 1932," *OHS 57*: 107–109. 1993.
14. *OHS 33*: 88–92. 1969.
15. *OHS 57*: 34–45. 1993.
16. John Peter Shinnick, "Plane Down in the Okanagan," *OHS 46*: 9–19. 1982.
17. Dorothy (Butler) Furness, "A Miracle at Christmas," *OHS 40*: 84–93. 1976.
18. Shinnick, p.17.
19. J.D. Bews, "George Howard Dunn," *OHS 29*: 26–30. 1965.
20. Shinnick, "CKOV: the First Fifty Years," *OHS 45*: 36–55. 1981.

21. The Browne family have been generous supporters of the Okanagan Historical Society. In 1968 Jamie Browne, son of Jim Jr. and grandson of J.W.B. Browne, became involved full-time with CKOV, first in programming and finally in management. Under his management the station funded the annual student essay contest prizes offered by the Okanagan Historical Society. After the station was sold to Mel and Dean Cooper on Sept. 1, 1988, Jamie Browne personally undertook to meet this annual obligation in honour of his grandfather.
22. *Broadcaster*, November 1986.
23. *OHS 54*: 59–67. 1990.

Afterword
1. *OHS 58*: 25–29. 1994.
2. Murray A. Roed, *Geology of the Kelowna Area*, Kelowna 1995. p.136.
3. *OHS 51*: 66. 1987.
4. *OHS 49*: 25. 1985.
5. *OHS 49*: 18. 1985.

INDEX

A

Aberdeen (sternwheeler), 90, 150, 151, 152
Aberdeen, Lord and Lady, 79, 142, 159, 168, 175
Act of Union, 1866, 78
Adolph, Charles John Felix. *See* Pandosy, Father Charles Marie
Agricultural Rehabilitation and Development Act, 174–75
Agriculture: agro-industries, 190–94; apple introduction, 179–80; crop damage, 179, 180, 181; effect of electrification on, 192; fruit packing, 181–82; grapes, 188–90; ground crops, 184–88; irrigation systems, 169, 170–75; marketing, 131–32, 170, 180–81, 182–83, 184–85; orchards, 167–70; pressures on Agricultural Land Reserve, 225; spraying, 161, 169
Akrigg, Dr. G.P.V. and Helen, 45
Aldredge, E.W., 144–45
Allison, John Fall, 55–57
Allison Pass, 56
Allison, Susan, 56, 88, 91–92, 93, 95, 109
Allison Trail, 60
Anderson, Alexander Caufield, 40
Andrew, Dr. F.W., 109–10
Anglican Church, 69, 70, 71–74, 76
L'Anse au Sable, 38, 57, 61
apples, 13, 179–80
Armstrong, 92, 157
Armstrong Cheese Co-operative Association, 192
Ashford, Dr. H.E.D., 71
Ashnola, 35
Atkins, B.R., 78–79
Atkinson, F.E. ("Ted"), 193–94

B

Bagnall, G.P., 197–98
Baha'i religion, 75
Baptist Church, 74–75
Barnard, Francis Jones "Frank," 78, 79, 84
Barnard, Francis Stillman (Sir James), 78, 141, 155
Barnes, Frederick H., 191
Barnes, Harry D., 69, 132–37
Battye, Clement, 182
BC. See British Columbia
Begbie, Matthew Baillie, 47
Belgian Orchard Syndicate, 171
Bell, Lyda M., 116–17
Bennett, William Andrew Cecil (W.A.C.), 81–82
Bennett, William ("Bill"), 82

Bird, Jessie Ewart, 86
birds, 19, 20, 161
Blackburn, Mary H.E., 191, 192
Blanchet, Father Norman, 65
boats, commercial, 142–43, 145–52
Boer War, 195–96
Bone, Narcisse, 22–23
Boundary, Canadian-American, 39, 42–43, 45
Bowell, S.R., 120
Boyce, Dr. B. de F., 109, 127
Brent, Frederick, 61
Brent, Joseph, 61
Brent, Maria Houghton, 28–29, 34
Brent's mill, 119
brick-making, 124–25
Brigade Trail, 36–40, 60, 61
British Columbia: civil service, 82–83; as Crown colony, 47, 78; elected officials, 78–82; participation in Confederation, 77
BC Dragoons, 200–201
BC Fruit Growers Association, 170
BC Fruit Processors, 193
British Columbia Horse Regiment, 198
BC Tree Fruits, 180, 181
Bromley-Browne, James William, 218–20
Browne, Adolphus, 186
Buckerfields, 191
Buckland, Frank Morgan, 39–40, 60, 61–62, 99–100, 131–32
Buddhist religion, 75
Bulman, Thomas, 192–93
BX Ranch (Barnard Express Ranch), 84
Byron, LaVonne, 160

C

Camp McKinney, 128–31, 132
Campbell, Burt R., 52, 53, 155–56, 164–66
Campbell-Brown, Rev. Colin, 69
Campbell-Brown, Dr. Hugh, 76
Canada-United States Free Trade Agreement, 1988, 190
Canadian Battle Drill Training Centre, Coldstream Ranch, 203–204
Canadian Mounted Rifles ("Whizzbangs"), 198
Canadian National Railway, 149, 152
Canadian Pacific Airlines, 214
Canadian Pacific Railway: building of, 140–43; destruction of Cariboo Road, 208; as market for farm produce, 132; owner of Kettle Valley Railway, 144–45; passenger runs, 152; and proposed Okanagan Canal, 17; tugboats, 150
canals, 17–18
canning industry, 192
Cariboo gold rush, 46–50
Cariboo Mining, Milling and Smelting, 128–31
Cariboo Road, 59–60, 84, 87, 208

Carney, B.J. and Co., 123–124
Casorso, Giovanni ("John"), 66, 94, 131, 184, 185
Casorso, John Jr., 132, 184
Casorso, Rosa Bevi, 94
Casorso, Victor, 131, 184, 185
cattle ranches, 54–59
Cawston, Mary Ann, 93
Cawston, R.L., 93, 99, 108, 109
Cawston, Verna B., 69, 93
celery, 185–86
Central Interior Tribal Council, 35
CHBC-TV, 220–23
Cherry Creek Silver Mine, 49
Chin, Louie, 187
Chinese: market gardeners, 185–86; veterans, and right to vote, 206
Chinook language, 33
Christie, James Halbold, 34
Christien, Annie Curran, 92
Christien, Joseph, 92
churches. *See* Anglican Church; Baptist Church; Methodist Church; Presbyterian Church; Roman Catholic Church
City of Vernon (airplane), 145, 215–16
CKOK Radio, 220
CKOV Radio, 219–20
Clarke, Everard Truman, 191
Cleland, Eva, 105
Clement, J. Percy, 101
Clovelly, 211
coal mining, 139
coldstream, 57, 157
Coldstream Ranch, 30, 31–33, 58, 118, 142, 168, 170–71, 176, 203–204
Columbia River, and Great Divide, 16–17
Commando Bay, 205–206
Confederation, 77
Cooper, Rev. Canon William, 74
copper mining, 136–37, 139
Coquihalla Highway, 214
Cosens, Arthur K.W., 128–31
Cosens, Sidney, 161
Cowan, Joan N., 123–24
Cowan, Robert, 110–11
Cox, W.G., 47–50
Cumine, Adam, 177–78
Cuthbert, W.A., 185, 186

D

dairy industries, 191
Dairyland, 192
Dallas, Alexander Grant, 42
dams, 19
dances, 95, 96
Davies, Ann M., 171
Dawson, Dr. George Mercer, 13

Demers, Father Modeste, 38, 65
Dendy, David, 181
Denison, H.R., 163
dentists, 111
Deschiquette, François, 42
DeSmet, Father Peter John, 38, 65
Dewdney, Edgar, 41, 79, 82, 140
Dewdney, Kathleen Stuart, 57, 82–83, 100
Dewdney, Walter Robert Jr., 82–83
Dewdney, Walter Sr., 82, 155
Dewdney Trail, 41, 59–60, 131, 140
District of Lakes Country, 158
Dobson, D.A., 18–19
doctors, 109–11, 127
Douglas, David, 38
Douglas, James, 30, 46, 47
Doyle, Bishop W. Emmett, 65
Duck Lake Fruitlands Company, 168, 171
Duddle, Jim, 215–16

E

education: in arts, 225; for children with dis-
    abilities, 103–104; governesses, 98–99;
    Herbert Business School, 106; Okanagan
    Baptist College, 75; Okanagan Summer
    School of the Arts and Other Artistic
    Activities, 105–106; Okanagan University
    College, 106; private schools, 104–105;
    public schools, 99–104; Roman Catholic
    residential schools, 34, 66–67; Round
    Prairie School, 120; rural schools, 97–98;
    St. Michael's School for Girls, 104; Vernon
    Preparatory School, 104, 105
Ehmke, Henry Jergen, 93
Ehmke, Magdalene, 92, 93, 109
elected officials, 78–82
electricity, 136, 192
Ellis, Kathleen, 54–55
Ellis, Thomas, 54–55, 72–73, 77
Ellison, Price, 80–81, 96
Ellison, Sophia Johnson, 101
Enderby (Fortune's Landing), 156
Eneas, Jerry, 22–23
En'Owkin Centre, 35
entertainment, in pioneer days, 95–96
Evans, Olive, 11–12

F

Fairview (freighter), 147
Fairview Camp, 126–27
Fire Valley Trail, 60
First Nations: arrival of, 23–24; ceremonies,
    24–25, 28; children, of white fathers,
    94–95; contact with first Europeans,
    29–33; culture, 24–28; diseases, European,
    29; education, 34–35, 66–67; fishery, 24,
    27; food, 24–25; fur trade, 29–30, 36–44;
    kinship and marriage, 27; land access
    restrictions, 62; leadership, 28; legends
    and stories, 28–29; medicines, 26–27;
    mixed marriages, 94; reserves, 30, 48;
    shelters, 27–28; sweat lodge, 26, 28
Fisher, D.V., 168–70, 188–89
fishing, sport, 95, 161
Flewelling, Rev. E.P., 70
flood control, 19
flour mills, 61, 117–19
forest industry, 119–24; 149–50
Fort Okanagan (Okanogan), 29, 37
Fortune, Alexander Leslie, 51, 52, 53, 66, 67,
    119
Fortune, Bathia, 52, 53, 92
Fraser, Mrs. H.A., 52
Fraser River, and Great Divide, 16–17
Fraser Valley Milk Producers Co-operative
    Association, 192
fruit, 167–68, 175–78, 182, 193. *See also*
    apples; grapes
Fulton, Clarence, 101, 102
Furness, Dorothy Butler, 217–18

G

Gabriel, Louise, 25–27
Garrish, Arthur, 181, 183
Gay, George, 105
Gehringer Brothers Winery, 190
geology, 13–16
Girouard, Luc, 59, 77, 86
glaciers, in Okanagan Valley, 16
Glenmore, 157
gold mining, 46–50, 51, 86, 128–31, 132–37
Goodfellow, Rev. John Christie, 15, 50, 55–57,
    70, 71, 144
governesses, 98–99
grain, milling, 61
Grant, Capt. J.M., 41
Gray, Arthur W., 174–75
Great Depression, 213–14, 224
Great Divide, 16–17
Great Northern Railroad, 136, 143, 153
Greenhow, Thomas, 58, 59, 146, 158–59
Greenwood, Ian, 193–94
Grey Monk Winery, 190

H

Hack, Lucy, 112
Hagen, Michael, 158, 164
Hall, Robert S., 85–86, 132, 184
Hamlin, L.B., 17
Harmon, Daniel William, 88
Haskins, Frank, 75
Hatfield, Harley R., 40–41, 145–52, 210
Hayman, L.A., 80, 210–13
Haynes, Charlotte Moresby, 92
Haynes, Emily Josephine, 93
Haynes, Hester Emily, 93
Haynes, John Carmichael, 30, 48, 49–50, 54,
    65, 78, 82, 92, 93, 94, 98, 99, 109, 119–20
Haynes, John (Native son of J.C. Haynes), 94
Heal, R.R., 186
health services. *See* medical services
health units, 114
Hedley, Rev. J.W., 69, 136
Hedley Camp, 132–37
Heggie, George, 175
Helmer, R.H., 170
Herbert Business School, 106
Hewer, E.E., 160–61
Hill, James J., 144
Hoover, Charles, 117, 191, 224
Hope-Princeton Highway, 183, 210, 214
Hope Trail, 41, 208
horses, 29, 38, 48, 85, 95, 96, 161, 195–96,
    198
hospitals, 112
hotels, 155
Houghton, Capt. Charles Frederick, 29, 57–58,
    60, 78–79
houses, of cattle barons, 158–59
Hudson's Bay Brigade Trail, 36–40, 60, 61
Hudson's Bay Company: discouragement of
    settlers, 44; and establishment of US bor-
    der, 39, 42–43, 46; fruit tree growing,
    167–68; and fur trade, 36–44, 46; and
    gold, purchase from First Nations, 46; and
    James Douglas, 46; surrender of Rupert's
    Land to Government of Canada, 77; trad-
    ing posts, 37, 42–44
Hughes, J.W., 188–89
hunting, as sport, 95, 161

I

Indian Act, 34
Indian Road Trail, 60
The Inland Sentinel (newspaper), 164
Innes, Frances Stuart, 73–74
insects, of southern interior valleys, 20
Interior Salish Nation, 23
internment camps, 177, 200
Invertebrates, of southern interior valleys, 20
irrigation systems, 169, 170–75
Irwin, Rev. Henry ("Father Pat"), 70, 73–74

J

Jaffray, Rev. J.A., 67, 68–69
Jamieson, James E., 120
Jamieson, Roland A., 149
Japanese, 65, 176–77, 214
Jesuit missionaries, 65
Johnson, Pauline, 160
Jubilee (freighter), 145, 146

K

Kass, Joe, 120, 122–23
Kelowna, 156, 214, 216–17
Kelowna General Hospital, 112
Kelowna Geology Committee, 14
Keremeos: incorporation, 158; trading post (of Hudson's Bay Company), 42–43
Kermode, Doug, 215
Kettle Valley Railway, 90, 144–45, 152
Kinloch, Colonel, 197
Kruger, Chrestenza, 71–72, 93

L

Lacey, Katie, 126
lakes, and water supply, 18–19
Lambly, C.A.R., 133, 136
Lambly, Robert, 107, 108
Land, Laurie, 43
Land and Agriculture Company of Canada, 171
Lang, Arthur H., 13
Latimer, Frank Herbert, 171
Latour, E.V. de, 31–33
Leir, Hugh Charles Musgrave, 121
Lequime, Bernard, 60–61, 120, 188
Lequime, Eli, 60–61
Lequime, Marie Louise, 60–61, 91, 93, 109
library service, 225
livestock, 48, 131, 184
Lloyd-Jones, David, 115, 120, 124–25
Lord, A.R., 101–102
Loyd, Arthur K., 181
Lumby, Moses, 59, 88, 141, 155

M

McCormick, Lucy, 97–98
MacDonald, David, 103, 163
MacDonald, Dr. K.C., 80–81
McDougall, John, 94–95
McIntosh, James, 53–54
McIntyre, Peter, 51
McKay, G.G., 155, 170
McKenna-McBride Commission (1913–16), 30
McKenzie, Angus, 99, 100
Mackie, Hugh F., 104, 105
McLean, Roderick, 41, 42–43
MacPhee Royal Commission, 181
mail delivery, 84–85, 88–90
mammals, of southern interior valleys, 19
mangel seed, 187–88
Mar, Jok, 224
Mara, John Andrew, 53–54, 79, 141, 155
Marjoribanks, Coutts, 159
Marriage, R.F., 89
Mary Victoria Greenhow (freighter), 146, 147
Mather, Ken, 84–85

medical services: 107–108, 109–11, 112–14, 127
Melvin, George H., 89
Mercier, Mrs. Jerome, 73
Methodist Church, 67, 69, 136
Middleton, William, 159–60, 175
midwives, 108
military organizations 224–25, 195–206
mills: flour, 61, 117–19, 190–91; sawmills, 119–24, 149–50
mining: camps, 126–27; coal, 139; copper, 136–37, 139; gold, 46–50, 51, 86, 126–31, 132–37; molybdenum, 139; and road improvement, 208–209; silicosis, among workers, 137–38; silver, 50
Mission Hill Winery, 190
Mitchell, Margaret, 71
Moberly, Walter, 41, 140–41
molybdenum mining, 139
Monteith, J.A., 155
Morkill, George H., 18
Morris, Dr. Osborne, 110
Muir, S.A., 112–13
municipalities, incorporation dates, 156–58
music, 95, 160

N

Nahm, Tilman E., 163
Nasmith, Hugh, 16–17
Native People. *See* First Nations
newspapers, 164–66
Nez Percé Indians, 30, 31–33
Nickel Plate Mine, 86, 132–37
N'kwala, Sophie, 29
Nobili, Father, 38, 65–66
Norris, Leonard, 45–46, 47–50, 155
North Okanagan Creamery Association (NOCA), 191
North-West Company, 36
nurses, 112, 113–14

O

Oblate missionaries, 60, 64–67, 68, 98, 168
Okanagan (sternwheeler), 146–47, 150, 151, 152
Okanagan Baptist College, 75
Okanagan Canal, 17–18
Okanagan Flour Mills Ltd., 191
Okanagan Helicopters Ltd., 217
Okanagan Indian Curriculum Project, 34–35, 226
Okanagan Lake, 11–12, 142–43, 146–47, 213
Okanagan Land Company, 168, 171
Okanagan language, 23
Okanagan Mounted Rifles, "B" Squadron, 197–98
Okanagan North Growers Co-op, 180

Okanagan River, dams, 19
Okanagan Summer School of the Arts and Other Artistic Activities, 105–106
Okanagan Tribal Educational Committee, 34
Okanagan University College, 106
O'Keefe, Cornelius, 59, 158, 159
O'Keefe Ranch, 118
Oliver, 158
Ormsby, Dr. Margaret Anchoretta, 36–39, 52–53, 57–58, 92, 175–76
Ormsby, G.L., 122
Orr, Mary Gartrell, 13
Osoyoos, 158
Osoyoos Desert Society, 20
Overlanders, 51–54

P

Pacific Fur Company, 29, 36
Palmer and Miller expedition, 61–62
Pandosy, Father Charles Marie, 60, 64–66, 100, 188
Pandosy Trail, 60
Pat, Father (Rev. Henry Irwin), 70, 73–74
Patterson, Rev. John W., 67
Paynter, Edwin C., 125
Paynter, Sheila, 125
Peachland, 157
Peachland Townsite Company, 176
Pelkamulox II (Okanagan), 24
Penticton, 157, 217
Penticton (freighter), 146, 149
Peterson, Edward, 179
pharmacists, 112–13
Phillips, Ivan E., 202, 203
plants, of southern interior valleys, 19
Plecash, Dr. and Mrs. Myles, 11–12
police force, and Cariboo gold rush, 46–50
polo, 160-161
Pope, Judith N., 17–18
population, 153–55, 225
post office, 84–85, 88–90
Postill, Alfred, 132, 162, 184
Postill, Edward, 93
Postill, Mary Dickenson, 93–94
Postill & Patton mill, 119, 120
Presbyterian Church, 67–69, 70, 127
Price's mill, 119
Pridham, J.L., 168
Princeton (Vermilion Forks), 158
Pritchard, H.D., 101
private schools, 104–105
public schools, 99–104

Q

Quesnellia, 15

R

radio, 218–20

Railroad, The (land strip between Wood and Kalamalka Lakes), 14, 18

railways: Canadian National Railway, 149, 152; Canadian Pacific Railway, 140–43, 144–45, 152, 208; Great Northern Railroad, 143–44, 153; Kettle Valley Railway, 144–45, 152; Shuswap and Okanagan Railway, 90, 141–42, 153, 155; Victoria and Eastern Railway, 136; and lifestyle, 158; and mail, 89–90; and mining industry, 136–37

Rainbow Ranch Company, 168, 171

Red River carts, 51

religion. *See* Anglican Church; Bah'ai religion; Baptist Church; Buddhist religion; Methodist Church; Presbyterian Church; Roman Catholic Church; Sikh religion

Renfrew, C., 214, 215

Richard, Father Pierre, 64, 65, 66

Richter, Charlie, 94, 95

Richter, Francis S., 81

Richter, Francis (Frank) Xavier, 57, 94, 95, 158, 168, 184

Richter, Joe, 116, 131

Richter Pass Highway, 214

Rittich, Dr. Eugene A., 189

Rittich, Virgil J., 189

roads: Cariboo Road, 59–60, 84, 208; construction work camps, during Great Depression, 213–14; Coquihalla Highway, 214; Hope-Princeton Highway, 183, 210, 214; Richter Pass Highway, 214; Rogers Pass Highway, 183, 214; and stagecoach rides, 86–88. *See also* trails

Robinson, John Moore, 74–75

Rocky Mountain Rangers, 198, 201–202, 203

rodeos, 96

Roderick, Matt, 129–31

Roed, Murray A., 15

Rogers Pass Highway, 183, 214

Roman Catholic Church, 34, 38, 64–67. *See also* L'Anse au Sable; Pandosy, Father Charles Marie

Rosoman, Graham, 110–11

Ross, Alexander, 29, 36

Rothenburger, Mel, 94

Round Prairie School, 120

Royal Air Force (England), 206

Royal Canadian Air Force, 206

Ruhmann, Max H., 19

Ruhmann, William, 199–200

Rural schools, 97–98

S

S&O Railway. *See* Shuswap and Okanagan Railway

salmon, in Okanagan River, 19

Salmon Arm, 157

Salvation Army, 76

sawmills, 119–24

Schofield, S.J., 13–14

schools. *See* education

Schubert, Catherine, 51, 92

Schubert, James Armstrong, 51, 52–53, 115–16

Scott, Douglas, 75

Scott, Rev. William, 67–69

Scudder, Dr. Geoff, 20

settlers: American, 176; Belgian, 176; Chinese, 177; discouraged by Hudson's Bay Company, 44; English, 175; French Canadian, 178; German, 176; Hungarian, 177; Japanese, 176–77; Overlanders, 51–54; population growth, 153–55; Portuguese, 177; Scottish, 175, 176; Sikhs, 177

Seventh Day Adventists, 76

Seymour, Eldon, 215–216

Shatford brothers, 171

Sheardown, Harry Reginald, 206

Sheridan, "Ma," 163

Shinnick, John, 219–20

Shorts, Capt. T.D., 18, 86, 146

Shuswap and Okanagan Railway, 90, 141–42, 153, 155

Shuswap Falls, legend of, 28–29

Shuswap Lake, commercial boats, 148–49

Shuswap Nation, 23

Sicamous (sternwheeler), 90, 150, 151, 152

Sikh religion, 75

silicosis, among miners, 137–38

Sillitoe, Rt. Rev. Acton Windeyer, Bishop of New Westminster, 71, 72–73

Similkameen (Keremeos) trading post (of Hudson's Bay Company), 42–43

sink-holes, 13

Sismey, Eric, 121, 122

Skaha Lake, commercial boats, 147–48

Sky Line Trail, 60

slides, Okanagan Lake, 11–12

Smith, Hiram F. ("Okanagan Smith"), 88, 167

Social Credit Party, 82

Society for the Revival of Indian Arts and Crafts, 34

South Okanagan Lands Project, 171

Sovreign, Rt. Rev. A.H., 73–74

Spallumcheen, 156

sports, 95, 160–61, 225

St. Michael's School for Girls, 104

stagecoaches, 84–88, 134–35

Steinke, Susan, 80, 142

sternwheelers, 150–52

Stevenson, Thomas, 96

Stirling, Grote, 81

Stirling, T.W., 168

storytelling, 95

Strathcona Horse Regiment, 195–96

Stuart, David, 29, 36

Stuart, John, 36

Sumac Ridge Winery, 190

Summerland, 157

Summerland Development Company, 176

Summerland Research Station, 170, 190, 194

Sun-Rype Products Ltd., 193

Surel, Brother, 64

T

Taillis D'Epinettes, 38

technology: agriculture, 116–17; communications, 218–23; fruit industry, 169–70, 181–83; mining, 126–27, 135–36

telegraph, 163

telephones, 136, 162–63

television, 220–23

Thompson, David, 88

Thomson, Gifford R., 157, 160

threshing machines, 116–17

Tickell, Christopher, 187–88

tobacco, 187, 188

tomatoes, 187–88

trails: Dewdney, 41, 59–60, 131, 140; Fire Valley, 60; Hope, 41, 208; Hudson's Bay Brigade, 36–40, 60; Indian Road (Allison Trail), 60; Pandosy, 60; Sky Line, 60. *See also* roads

transportation methods: air travel, 214–18; automobiles, 207; commercial boats, 142–43, 145–50; for fruit, 182–83; horses, 29, 38, 48, 85; railways, 17, 89–90, 132, 136–37, 140–45; stagecoaches, 84–88; trucks, 183; wagons, 51, 61–62

transportation routes: canals, 14, 18; ferries, 210–13; lakes, 145–52; roads, 59–60, 84, 86–88, 183, 208–10, 213–14; trails, 36–40, 41, 59–60, 131, 140, 208

Treaty of Washington, 45

Trutch, Joseph W., 17

tugboats, 149–50

U

Upton, Primrose, 66

Upton, Terence B., 196–97

urbanization, and population growth, 225

V

Vancouver Island, as Crown colony, 46, 78

Vernon (Priest's Valley, Centreville), 155–56, 215, 216

Vernon, Charles A., 57, 58, 171

Vernon, Forbes George, 57, 58, 79, 80, 142, 155

Vernon Jubilee Hospital, 112, 113
Vernon Preparatory School, 104, 105
Victoria and Eastern Railway, 136
volcanoes, in Okanagan Valley, 15

W
Walker, Dorothy, 160
Walker, W.D., 160
Walsh, Anthony, 34
water supply, 18–19, 155–56, 158, 170–75
Watt, George M., 207–208, 209
Weatherill, H.O., 192–93
wetlands, habitat destruction, 19
Whitaker, Grace, 109
White, Hester Emily Haynes, 25, 87, 94, 131
White, Dr. R.B., 109, 127
Whitmore, Florence, 206
Wight, W. Gordon, 180
Wilcox, J.C., 202
wineries, 189, 190
Witcher, Herman, 107, 108
women: childbirth, 109; as governesses,
    98–99; medical skills of, 95, 112–14;
    Native, as wives of white men, 94; Native,
    skills of, 25–27; as supporters of the arts,
    105; as teachers, 99, 103, 156; upper class,
    160; as wives of church officials, 67–69,
    73–74; as wives of pioneers, 51–54, 91–94
Wood, Thomas, 58, 59, 162

Y
Yorath, C.J., 15
Young, Annie Ellen, 92
Young, Benjamin Franklin, 85, 92
Young, W.C., 65

Z
Zosel Dam, 19
zucca melons, 186–87